How To Do A Leveraged Buyout

for yourself, your corporation or your client

3rd Edition

by

J. Terrence Greve

Business Publications, Inc.

San Diego, California

Business Publications, Inc.
San Diego, California

"This publication is designed to provide accurate and authoritative information in regard to the subject matter covered. It is sold with the understanding that the publisher is not engaged in rendering legal, accounting, or other professional service. If legal advice or other expert assistance is required, the services of a competent professional person should be sought."

— *From a Declaration of Principles jointly adopted by a Committee of the American Bar Association and a Committee of Publishers.*

ISBN 0-9610808-7-6

(Certain portions of this book were previously published as "How To Do A Leveraged Buyout or Acquisition" — 1st and 2nd Editions.)

Printed in the United States of America

DEDICATION

This book is dedicated to God, who gives us the wisdom and strength to accomplish any worthy task. And to my family (Shirley, Scott and Darren), whose encouragement and support made it easier.

ACKNOWLEDGEMENTS

Behind any successful book are those many individuals whose contributions and critiques make it easier for the author and better for the readers. *How To Do A Leveraged Buyout* was no exception. The author would like to express his sincere appreciation to the following individuals for their insights and and contributions: Nicholas Wallner, whose dealmaking techniques are the very heart and soul of this book; Maurice Pfursich and Mike Podolny for their insights on M&A intermediaries; Robert Smiley and Neil Wassner for their contribution on structuring ESOP LBO's; Bertram K. Massing, Myron Lieberman and Darrel Rice for their contributions and critique on legal issues; and Glen M. Desmond for his help on the subject of valuations.

In addition, the author wishes to express his gratitude to the following firms for their contribution of Appendix materials: Winstead, McGuire, Sechrest & Minick; Ervin Cohen & Jessup; Wallner & Co.; Citicorp Venture Capital; and Deloitte, Haskins & Sells.

MEET THE AUTHOR...

J. Terrence Greve is the Managing Partner of Greve Investment Co., a private investment firm specializing in the acquisition of middle market companies in the U.S. These acquisitions are usually structured as leveraged buyouts in which key operating managers participate in the ownership of the company. Since 1981, Mr. Greve has participated as a principal in 15 leveraged buyout transactions with aggregate sales in excess of $1 billion.

Mr. Greve is involved in all aspects of the leveraged buyout process, including pre-acquisition evaluations, structuring and financing the transaction. In addition, he is a director of several portfolio companies and plays an active role in the post-acquisition monitoring of investments.

Mr. Greve is a well-known speaker and author on the subject of mergers, acquisitions, and leveraged buyouts. He is the past publisher of *The Journal of Buyouts & Acquisitions* and has written numerous articles on the subject of mergers and acquisitions. His educational background includes a B.S. in Chemistry from the University of Cincinnati, an M.S. in Chemistry from the University of Minnesota, and a Masters in Business Administration from the University of California at Los Angeles.

Mr. Greve resides in La Jolla, California, with his wife, Shirley, and sons, Scott and Darren.

TABLE OF CONTENTS

PREFACE

WHY THIS BOOK WAS WRITTEN (AGAIN!)

In 1981 the first edition of *How To Do A Leveraged Buyout* was published. Although it was subsequently updated for changes in the tax code in 1984, I felt strongly that most of what I knew on the subject was contained in the pages of the book. At that time, a pledge was also made to myself (and my family) that it "was both the first and last book I would ever write!"

So why yet another edition — the 3rd — of *How To Do A Leveraged Buyout*? There are several reasons. First, in the years that have passed since the previous editions were published, my involvement in several more leveraged buyouts convinced me of how much I *didn't* know at the time the book was originally written. Secondly, while the earlier editions provided good insights on the leveraged buyout process, they needed further embellishment on how to effectively orchestrate all the steps that must be taken to reach the closing table. And, in looking back, I must confess that the material was biased in its presentation from an outside investor's perspective rather than that of incumbent managers. Finally, there have some new innovations in how leveraged buyouts are financed along with changes in the marketplace — and tax laws — that affect how deals are structured.

It was quite apparent that a new revised and expanded edition of *How To Do A Leveraged Buyout* was needed to address these "shortcomings" and changes in the marketplace. The 3rd Edition is the latest attempt to share with you my own personal insights on leveraged buyout techniques. I believe this book has some valuable, new information whether you have read prior editions or not. It contains a total of 15 chapters compared to 10 in the previous editions. The new chapters are:

Chapter 1: The Leveraged Buyout Process
An overview of the LBO process and the respective roles of the major participants.

Chapter 3: Who Are The Sellers?
A more in-depth analysis of who the typical sellers are and what makes them tick.

Chapter 7: Orchestrating the Deal
A detailed blueprint of how to keep everything on track and put the deal together.

Chapter 8: For Managers Only
A chapter written strictly for "insiders" and how they can improve their position in the buyout.

Chapter 15: After the Closing — Managing the Buyout
Proven techniques for making sure that the deal works after you own it.

In addition, 7 of the original 10 chapters have been substantially revised or expanded to reflect my own personal experiences and issues that weren't covered in the 2nd Edition. In effect, the book has been almost completely rewritten to incorporate the latest developments in the field.

WHO THIS BOOK IS WRITTEN FOR

Like the previous editions, the 3rd Edition of *How To Do A Leveraged Buyout* is written primarily for the following individuals:

- **Entrepreneurs or investors** who wish to buy a controlling interest in a company, but either lack the necessary financial resources or wish to minimize their financial commitments.
- **Incumbent managers** who may have the opportunity to buy the company they now operate, but have limited capital.
- **Business owners** who want to expand via acquisitions, but do not wish to deplete their company's capital resources in the process.

Although the book is written from a buyer's perspective, its contents can be equally valuable to other parties that are major participants in mergers and acquisitions. These include:

- **Sellers** (owners or privately held companies or executives responsible for divestiture decisions) who want an intimate look at the leveraged buyout process from the "other side" of the table.
- **Professional Advisors** such as lawyers, accountants, or intermediaries who must advise clients on either side of the leveraged buyout transaction.
- **Institutional Lenders and Investors** who need further insights on the chemistry of putting together a leveraged deal.

HOW THIS BOOK IS ORGANIZED

In writing this book, my major objective was to provide a practical step-by-step blueprint on how to put together a leveraged buyout. Its contents are based upon my own personal experience in 15 deals, as well as countless discussions with others involved in numerous leveraged acquisitions. The book is organized into three major sections or "phases" that roughly parallel the stages of the leveraged buyout process.

Phase I: Searching and Screening (Chapters 1-6). Since most buyers must start at the beginning and first find a company to buy, these chapters deal with the sometimes frustrating task of finding viable acquisition candidates. It provides practical tips on how to access key sources of deals and get them to cooperate. More important, you'll learn how not to waste your most precious resource — time — by filtering out those deals that don't make sense and the sellers who aren't for real.

Chapters which were included in the 1st and 2nd Editions were substantially revised to address the delicate issue of how and when to discuss price. They also clarify the critical question of when to negotiate with the seller and tie the qualification process to other essential steps in making the deal.

Phase II: Orchestrating the Deal (Chapters 7-12). Once a viable leveraged buyout candidate is identified, the buyer must do a number of things to keep the deal alive and move inexorably toward the closing. These include preliminary due diligence, getting financing commitments and negotiating with the seller and incumbent managers. Many of these steps must be taken simultaneously, making the task of satisfying all the players a real challenge.

The chapters included in Phase II will tell you how to put all the pieces together. Chapter 7 (Orchestrating the Deal) deals with the issue from an outside buyer's perspective, while Chapter 8 (For Managers Only) views it through the eyes of incumbent managers. Of all the new material included in the 3rd Edition, I believe this to be the most important. It gives you a very clear blueprint of exactly what to do and when to do it. The remaining chapters in Phase II provide detailed instructions on how to evaluate, structure, and finance the deal.

Phase III: Negotiating and Closing the Deal (Chapters 13-15). The final three chapters deal in much greater depth with major issues related to negotiations and post-acquisition operations. Particular emphasis is given to the role of professional advisors. You will not only learn how to select the most qualified advisors, but also how to control the legal, accounting, and other fees that, if not watched carefully, can quickly get out of hand. This section also contains a thorough discussion of the impact of the 1986 Tax Reform Act and gives you specific suggestions on how to structure deals under the new law. Finally, a completely new chapter has been added on how to operate and monitor the progress of the highly leveraged company. The specific steps outlined will help you anticipate problems, maximize cash flow, and, ultimately, generate a more attractive return on investment.

Needless to say, I believe that the 3rd Edition of *How To Do A Leveraged Buyout* really does contain within its pages everything I know about this fascinating topic. But if the business continues to evolve as rapidly in the years ahead as it has in the past. . .would you believe — a 4th Edition?

J. Terrence Greve
La Jolla, California

A BLUEPRINT FOR THE LEVERAGED BUYOUT PROCESS

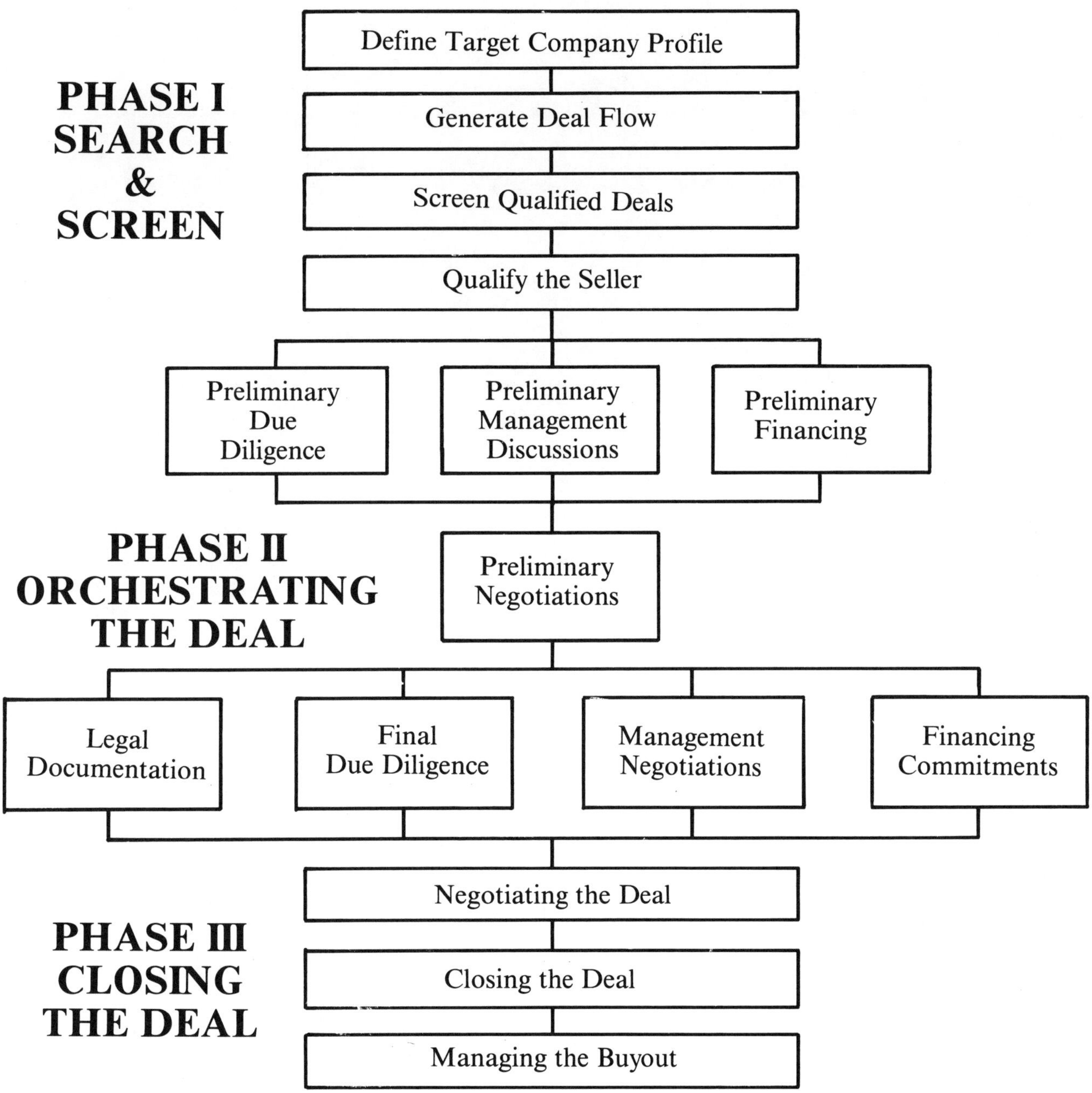

PHASE I
SEARCH & SCREEN
(Chapters 1-6)

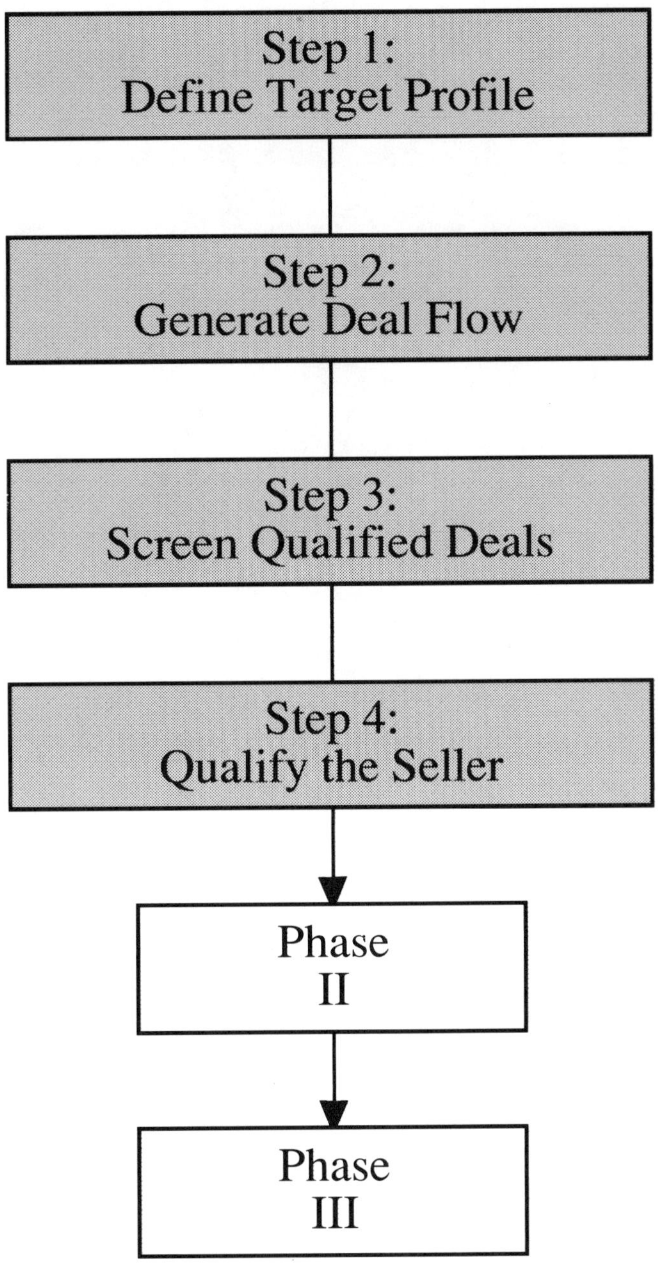

1

THE LEVERAGED BUYOUT PROCESS

In recent years the leveraged buyout (LBO) has emerged from obscurity to become a major factor in the transfer of corporate ownership. The rising tide of LBO transactions started slowly in the early 1970's and reached a feverish peak in the mid-1980's. Deals increased both in size and frequency, leaving both managers and investors with substantial stakes — and sometimes significant profits — in their newly owned companies.

This is not to infer that leveraged buyouts are a new phenomenon. LBO's have played a consistent role in American economic history since the turn of the century. This is particularly true with respect to the sale of slower growing, closely held companies to incumbent managers and outside investors. Until the 1970's, these transactions were financed primarily by large private capital pools controlled by wealthy families such as the Rockefellers and Whitneys. But in recent years there has been a proliferation of new financing sources that have dramatically broadened the LBO arena and generated new wealth-creating opportunities for both managers and investors.

However, much of the LBO process remains shrouded in mystery. To many managers and entrepreneurs, leveraged buyouts are deals done by the "big guys on Wall Street." While it is true that the highly publicized "blockbuster" deals engineered by sophisticated Wall Street investors represent a significant percentage of total dollar volume, it is also a fact that they account for only a small portion of total LBO transactions.

The majority of leveraged buyouts involve small to mid-size companies whose owners, for strategic or personal reasons, have decided to sell. These represent excellent opportunities for both outside investors and incumbent managers to increase their wealth. However, to capitalize on the opportunity, it is necessary to understand the vagaries of the LBO transaction and how it differs from the typical corporate acquisition. The remainder of this chapter will provide some overall perspective to the LBO process and the role of the major participants.

UNIQUE CHARACTERISTICS OF LEVERAGED BUYOUTS

A leveraged buyout is defined as "the acquisition of a business primarily with borrowed funds that are repaid from the target company's earnings and/or sale of excess assets." It differs from the typical corporate acquisition in several important respects. Before delving into the particular aspects of how to do a leveraged buyout, it is important for prospective participants to fully understand the unique characteristics of this acquisition technique.

Simultaneous Recapitalization and Change of Ownership

The typical corporate acquisition, in most cases, simply involves a transfer of ownership from the seller to the buyer. Usually, the financial make-up of the target company in the acquisition is left intact and any funds required to finance the acquisition are supplied directly by the acquiring company or borrowings from its bank(s).

The LBO differs in that, along with the transfer of ownership, there is also a complete restructuring of the target company's balance sheet. Using its assets and/or cash flow as security, lenders will advance new loans to the target company, which in turn, disburses funds to the seller. Overnight, the target company's balance sheet has been transformed from a very "clean" (debt-free) condition to a highly leveraged state.

More Parties Involved in the Transaction

This added dimension of leverage necessitates the involvement of more players. In addition to the seller, lenders and investors, who provide the bulk of the financing (and their lawyers, of course), are major participants in negotiations. And trade creditors often get very nervous when they discover the target company's balance sheet will soon turn "upside-down."

The larger number of players — and lawyers — dramatically increases the complexity of the transaction. As a result, the LBO takes longer than a typical corporate acquisition, and there is a much greater chance that something may occur which will kill the deal.

The "Buyer" is a "Partnership"

In the typical unleveraged corporate acquisition the "buyer" is easy to identify. It is the corporate entity that provides either the cash or stock to pay for the target company. With the LBO it is not quite that simple. The "buyer" consists of a collection of individuals and/or firms, each of which bring different "essential ingredients" to the deal.

Financing sources, because they often assume greater risks, will insist upon ownership participation. Another important participant in the ownership is the operating management team. For this reason, leveraged buyouts are often referred to as "management buyouts." In some cases, ownership is extended to all employees through an employee stock ownership plan (ESOP). This multiple ownership characteristic of LBO's also increases the complexity of the deal and makes it more difficult to close.

The inclusion of incumbent management in the buying group also gives rise to some unique problems that are not encountered in the standard corporate acquisition. One is the conflict of interest created by management's dual role as an "employee of the seller," on one hand, and a "partner of the buyer," on the other. Further complications arise when managers and outside investors must address the question of how the "equity pie" is divided up among them.

Rapid Growth Is Not The Goal

When a company is acquired by a large public corporation, its mandate is often to "grow as rapidly as possible." The underlying assumption is that the parent company will supply whatever capital is needed to finance the growth.

With an LBO, because the target company's balance sheet has been highly leveraged to finance the acquisition, it is very difficult to finance rapid growth.

Cash flow is primarily allocated to service existing debt and essential working capital needs.

This re-orientation of corporate priorities often is difficult for operating management to accept, particularly those who have long lived with the principle that rapid growth is essential for survival.

THE CHEMISTRY OF AN LBO TRANSACTION

These principal differences between an unleveraged corporate acquisition and a leveraged buyout provide some insight into the LBO process. But to gain a better perspective of the "chemistry" involved in putting together the leveraged buyout transaction, it is necessary to take a closer look at the *essential ingredients* of a deal and the various players that provide them.

Any corporate acquisition transaction, whether it is leveraged or unleveraged, must have the following ingredients for it to be successful: (See Exhibit 1-A.)

- Adequate capital to pay off the seller.
- Dealmaking and financing skills to complete the transaction.
- Management skills to operate the newly acquired company.

In the unleveraged corporate acquisition or merger, all of the above, except management talent within the target company, are provided by a single entity — the acquiring corporation. Funding is usually provided directly by the acquirer from its cash reserves or bank lines of credit. And one person — usually a high-level executive — takes full responsibility for the negotiations. As a result, the overall effort is highly controlled and coordinated.

The leveraged buyout is quite different. Each of the essential ingredients is provided by a different business entity, which necessitates the formation of a new partnership at the outset of every deal. Outside lenders and investors provide the necessary capital. Incumbent managers possess the essential management skills and experience to operate the company and service the new acquisition debt. And, most important, a third party is often involved to bring all of the pieces together — the LBO "sponsor."

THE ROLE OF THE SPONSOR

The sponsor is the person or firm who makes the deal happen. He is the catalyst, the quarterback who orchestrates the entire transaction. His knowledge of the dealmaking process and the of various players involved enables him to do the right thing at the right time. As the focal point of the deal, the sponsor performs most of the following functions: (1) structuring the deal, (2) arranging the necessary acquisition financing, that most often includes some of his own capital, (3) negotiating the transaction with the seller, (4) coordinating the legal and accounting activities, (5) closing the deal, and (6) monitoring the operations after the close.

Structuring and Financing the Deal

The main task of the sponsor is to devise a financial structure that is appropriate for the unique characteristics of the target company. To do so, he must call upon his knowledge of the various types of financing sources and their respective needs. He must relate this to the financial circumstances of the company and determine which lenders and investors are most appropriate.

While knowledge of financing is important, it alone is not sufficient to make the deal happen. Lenders and equity investors make decisions based upon their perception of the deal and the capabilities of the buying group, including the sponsor. Thus, the sponsor's relationship with lenders and investors and their confidence in his abilities is a key factor in getting the financing commitment. Without this combination of financing knowledge, understanding of the company operations and personal contact with key lenders and investors, the financing effort is not likely to be successful.

Negotiating the Deal

Due to the relatively large number of parties involved in a typical leveraged buyout, the sponsor must be a capable negotiator who is able to cultivate a good relationship with the seller and resolve any differences among members of the buying group. In a typical management buyout, the incumbent operating management is placed in the awkward position of negotiating with its current employer. This potential conflict of interest situation is mitigated by the presence of a sponsor who can negotiate price and terms with the seller as an objective outside investor.

Coordinating and Closing the Deal

Coordination of the legal and accounting services is another important function of the LBO sponsor. Most experienced sponsors have excellent working relationships with experienced deal-oriented attorneys. These relationships and the sponsor's experience are invaluable to other members of the buying group, especially incumbent managers, who are less familiar with the legal procedures and documentation. In larger deals, it is often necessary to utilize the services of outside accounting firms to conduct a "businessman's review" as part of the due diligence effort. The sponsor, as the coordinator of the deal, makes sure that these outside services are provided on schedule so that the transaction moves forward.

Post-Acquisition Monitoring

Finally, depending upon the particular type involved, the sponsor can play an important role in monitoring the company's operations after the buyout is completed. This function may range from taking an active part in all strategic and policy decisions to a more passive advisory role. The degree of involvement will be determined by a number of factors, including prior experience, strength of the operating management and the expectations of the other members of the buyout group.

TYPES OF SPONSORS

Occasionally, sponsorship activities are provided by incumbent managers who possess the necessary dealmaking and financing skills. In most cases, however, operating managers are not familiar with the nuances of the LBO financing process. Their expertise lies in managing the business, and they usually must depend upon outside experts to arrange the financing required to complete the buyout. Outsiders who perform sponsorship functions are classified as "principal sponsors" or "agent sponsors," depending upon what they contribute to the deal.

Principal Sponsors

The "principal sponsor" is one who will own a significant percentage of the equity in the acquired company. Typically, this player has direct control over substantial capital pools and has money at risk in the deal, either through direct investment or guaranties. As a result, the principal sponsor usually has controlling interest in the acquired company or is the spokesman for those investors who collectively represent controlling interests. He is always represented at the board level and has a major voice in policy decisions.

The degree and manner in which the principal sponsor is involved in the financing and operating activities is largely a function of his professional experience. In this regard, there are two varieties of principal sponsors. The first consists of financially oriented individuals or groups who tend to come mainly from the venture capital or investment banking communities. These groups are familiar with the dealmaking process either as a lender or investor (in the case of the venture capital background) or as an intermediary (in the case of investment bankers). They tend to be highly creative in the financial structuring of deals. In addition, they often have large captive equity and subordinated debt capital pools and are well-connected with additional financing sources.

A second type of principal sponsor is those individuals or groups with strong operating experience. In recent years, many capable executives, flush with funds from hefty "golden parachute" packages, have become more active as LBO sponsors. These groups often invest their own equity capital or personally guarantee a portion of the acquisition debt. Because of their strong operational experience, this type of sponsor takes a more active role in operations, most often at the board level and in cooperation with the operating management team. Some, however, are not reluctant to "roll-up their sleeves" and become more active in the day-to-day operations if such involvement is required. Strong operating skills allow this type of sponsor to participate in buyouts that would be considered "off-limits" to others. These include "turnaround" situations or companies lacking strong management teams.

Agent Sponsors

The agent sponsor differs from the principal sponsor in several respects. Perhaps the most notable difference is the fact that he functions more as a facilitator of the proposed transaction than an investor in the newly acquired company. Although he may receive a minority interest in the stock of the acquired company, most of the agent sponsor's compensation is derived from transaction fees which are paid only if the deal is closed. Unlike the principal sponsor, the agent sponsor usually does not have any capital or personal guaranties at risk, even if he receives a carried interest in the equity. His equity participation is granted on the basis of promotional services (putting the deal together).

Another major difference between the principal and the agent sponsor is their respective roles in the company after the acquisition. Because the agent sponsor has less of an ownership position, he is less involved in monitoring the company's operational performance. His role is usually that of an advisor rather than one who wields power and influence over management activities. Depending upon the degree of equity participation, their level of expertise and the particular needs of the company, some agent sponsors take a seat on the board of directors.

Most agent sponsors are experienced individuals who are acting in an investment banking capacity. Their position as an investment banker places them in the mainstream of deal activity and in contact with the major institutional lenders and investors. In addition to the people exposure, the qualified investment banker also has the necessary experience in corporate finance to perform the functions of the leveraged buyout sponsor.

TRENDS IN SPONSORSHIP

In the early years of the current wave of leveraged buyouts, most deals were crafted by agent sponsors. At that time there were relatively few capital pools specifically earmarked for LBO's. As a result, most deals were financed by a handful of venture capital funds and insurance companies. Investment bankers who had close working relationships with these capital sources were in an excellent position to sponsor LBO transactions without investing any of their own capital.

But, as the industry grew, a large number of equity and subordinated capital pools were formed and competition for deals intensified. In order to differentiate themselves from the competition, many financing sources marketed themselves as a "one-stop financing source" for management buyouts. Moreover, they would provide all other sponsorship functions. At the same time, incumbent managers became more educated on the LBO financing process and started making direct contact with financing sources. The result was obvious: the role of the LBO sponsor was increasingly played by principal sponsors with captive control of capital or more enlightened incumbent managers. The agent sponsor, who had only his expertise to offer, became less of a factor.

THE "LEVERAGED BUYER" DEFINED

With this brief overview of the leveraged buyout process and the major players involved, it is possible to define more explicitly the term "buyer" as it applies to LBO's.

> *"The 'buyer' in a leveraged buyout is a partnership consisting of financing sources, operating management and third parties which provide necessary capital or perform vital sponsorship functions that are essential if the deal is to close."*

Since it is the most frequently used word in this book, it is important for the reader to understand precisely what is meant by the term "buyer." Does it refer to the financing sources, operating managers, outside sponsors, or all three?

In a legal sense, the buyer is any party who ends up with an equity interest — or rights to an equity interest — in the acquired company. But from the standpoint of explaining how to do a leveraged buyout, it is necessary to singularize the "buyer" and refer to it as that individual (or firm) who is *controlling the deal.* As one might expect, this varies with each deal depending upon how it was initiated and the experience of the particular players involved.

Most leveraged buyout transactions are initiated in one of the following manners.

- Incumbent management is advised by the owner of the business that the company is for sale and they have the opportunity to buy it.
- An outside investor makes contact with the owner of the business (usually through an intermediary) regarding the acquisition of the company. Incumbent management is later contacted by the outside investor regarding their possible ownership role in the proposed buyout.

The "buyer" — at least for the sake of explaining the buyout process — is different in each of the above situations. In the first case it is assumed that management has been given a period of time within which to secure its financing commitments and close the deal. During this time, the "management entrepreneur" is clearly in control. At the point when the key financing players become interested, they too will become a part of the "buyer" and become involved in major decisions. But until that happens, the role of "buyer" is solely played by the managers.

In the second case, the outside investor is clearly in charge from the beginning. This may be a small private investor in search of a specific type of company or an institutional pool of equity capital seeking to invest in LBO's. In either case, the investor makes the initial contact regarding the deal and is referred to as "the buyer." Incumbent management, although they may later become part of the ownership group, are relatively passive players in the initial negotiations.

Key Question For Buyers

Because the term "buyer" may refer to either an incumbent manager or outside investor, it is important for the reader to ask the question: *"What kind of buyer am I?"*

If he is an incumbent manager, the entire LBO process is immensely simplified. In fact, this type of buyer could conceivably skip the first six chapters of the book because he has already identified the target company and has intimate knowledge of both the seller and the company. His major task is structuring, financing, negotiating and closing the transaction.

As "insiders," incumbent managers have an entirely different perspective of the LBO process than outside investors. These are considered in detail in Chapter 8, "For Managers Only."

On the other hand, if the buyer is an "outsider," he must start at the beginning. Because many buyers fit into this latter category, this book assumes the buyer must "start from scratch." Therefore, the term "buyer" as it is used throughout the book, especially in the first six chapters, refers to "outsiders" —investors or entrepreneurs — rather than incumbent managers.

EXHIBIT 1-A

Comparison of a Typical Acquisition and a Leveraged Buyout

Essential Ingredient	Typical Acquisition	Leveraged Buyout
Acquisition Funding	From general funds of acquiring company or its bank lines of credit.	From outside financing sources based on assets and/or cash flow of target company.
Dealmaking Skills	Provided by top operating management or staff experienced in M&A transactions.	Usually provided by outside "sponsor" or investor.
Financing Skills	Provided by chief financial officer of acquiring company.	Usually provided by outside "sponsor" or investor.
Operating Management Skills	Provided by incumbent managers of target company who become *employees* of the acquiring company.	Provided by incumbent managers who now become *owners* in the target company

2

DEFINING THE COMPANY

Before embarking on any long and difficult journey, a wise traveler will first make the necessary preparations to ensure he arrives at his final destination. He must be realistic as to his natural limitations and how they will impact reaching that destination. Above all, he must be adequately prepared with the necessary "supplies" to complete the trip.

Adequate preparation is no less important for the leveraged buyer in search of a company. He must first conduct a thorough self-examination and pinpoint his strengths, weaknesses and limitations. Only then will he be able to clearly define the types of companies which "fit." This process may take time, but in the end it will save the buyer substantial amounts of time and "dead-end" trips.

Before addressing the particulars of how to define the target company, it is instructive to examine more closely the key qualities of successful buyers. With a knowledge of these important attributes, a buyer will more likely be successful in his quest to buy a company.

CHARACTERISTICS OF SUCCESSFUL BUYERS

There are many individuals, groups and companies who purport to be buyers. The fact of the matter is, however, that many of these are not "real buyers" and, as a result, will never close a deal. A *real* buyer — one who is capable of closing a deal — has certain personal and professional characteristics which are essential to successful dealmaking. Although many of these qualities are required for success in any endeavor, the process of buying and monitoring an operating company seems to call for an extraordinary measure of these characteristics.

Desire

An obvious essential quality is a strong desire to own or control a substantial portion of a company. This strong entrepreneurial desire must be reflected in a willingness to take a reasonable risk. Many "would-be-buyers" possess the desire, but lack the intestinal fortitude to take appropriate action (and risk).

Sense of Timing

Patience and a sense of timing are other traits possessed by successful buyers. There are certain points when he must act quickly and decisively to maintain the necessary momentum. At other times, however, the best course of action is to do nothing. Successful buyers have good instincts on seizing the right moment to do the right thing.

Persistence

Perhaps the single most distinguishing characteristic of successful buyers is their persistence. There are many inevitable set-backs and disappointments on the road to buying a company. Some of these come very late in the process and can be extremely discouraging. Only the individual with a high degree of perseverance can overcome these obstacles and either salvage the deal or move on to another one.

Uses Time Effectively

Finally, the successful buyer is highly disciplined in the allocation and use of his most precious resource: time. He knows his boundaries and stays within them. Straying beyond reasonable personal, financial, and experiential limitations only serves to postpone, or perhaps entirely eliminate, the ultimate goal of closing a deal.

THE TARGET COMPANY PROFILE

Before any buyer can find a company, he must first define the kind of company he wants and is realistically able to buy. This entails the development of a "target company profile" which describes the preferred leveraged buyout candidate in terms of the following criteria:

- Industry
- Type of business (manufacturing, distribution, retailing, or service)
- Type of products
- Location constraints
- Size
- Financial characteristics

These criteria can range from very specific to quite general, depending upon the particular circumstances of the buyer. However, if too specific, they will place a severe limitation on the buyer's universe of prospective companies. On the other hand, criteria which are too general serve little or no purpose and will result in a very time-consuming, inefficient search procedure. Therefore, the buyer should endeavor to maintain a proper balance between generality and specificity in his definition of acquisition criteria.

There are two important reasons why it is absolutely essential for the buyer to prepare a detailed "target company profile." First, it will enable him to focus only on realistic investment candidates and, as a result, conduct his search in the most efficient manner. Secondly, the profile is the cornerstone of the "buyer's promotional package." This package, which consists of selected background information on the buyer, is distributed to various direct and indirect sources of potential deals. It is often a major factor in creating and enhancing the buyer's credibility in the eyes of professional intermediaries. A "buyer's package" which fails to include a clear profile does little to enhance the buyer's esteem in the eyes of either sellers or intermediaries. In fact, a poorly conceived profile will certainly reduce the number of deals to which the buyer will be exposed and substantially lower his chances of ultimately buying a company.

The "target company profile" is determined by a number of factors relating to the personal or corporate goals, financial circumstances, risk preferences, and business experience of the buyer. In addition, certain external factors (i.e., economic conditions and the outlook for specific industries) will have some impact upon the type of business to be sought. Some of these factors will conflict with each other and will require the buyer to make difficult trade-offs and compromises. For example, the buyer may want to live in a certain geographic area, but there may be very few companies in that area which can directly utilize his experience. He may choose another less familiar type of industry or business or move to another area of the country.

DETERMINANTS OF THE TARGET COMPANY PROFILE

The process of resolving these internal conflicts and developing the "target company profile" is not a simple one. It requires considerable thought and introspection. It means asking some rather difficult and provocative questions about personal or corporate strengths, weaknesses and goals. Above all, the buyer must be totally honest and realistic with himself in answering these questions. To assist the prospective buyer, some of the more important personal, financial, and business factors to consider in defining investment criteria are discussed in the following paragraphs. Although most of the comments are directed to the individual entrepreneur, the concepts apply to the corporate leveraged buyer as well.

Personal or Corporate Goals

The first, and most important, criterion for filtering out unlikely candidates is a determination of the degree to which they conform to the buyer's personal objectives. At the root of this self-analysis is the question: "Why do I want to buy a company in the first place?" Although there may be a number of answers to this important question, the most common considerations are: (1) the accumulation of wealth, (2) investment diversification, (3) the desire to gain professional and financial independence ("run my own show"), (4) to continue living in a certain geographic area, and (5) to escape the large corporate environment.

Whatever reasons the buyer has for buying a company, they will have a direct impact on the size, location, and characteristics of the business which is ultimately acquired. For example, if the buyer's primary objective is to gain independence without any outside control, the size of the company will necessarily be limited by the amount of his own financial resources plus whatever funds he can borrow to finance the acquisition without diluting ownership. If location is an important criterion, the potential universe of investment opportunities is automatically reduced. Thus, the buyer may have to relax his criteria somewhat in regard to the various industries and types of companies he will consider. Generally speaking, the more restrictive the geographic constraints, the more liberal the size and business type criteria must be if the buyer expects to see a reasonable number of acquisition candidates.

Another key question the buyer must ask himself is: "To what degree do I want to be involved in the day-to-day operations of the company?" The degree of involvement in the management function is a very important factor in defining the "target company profile," for it will determine the type and depth of management required.

Some private buyers want a company in which they are the key operating figure. The career considerations of the transaction are just as important as the investment considerations to them. Their primary objective is to increase personal wealth while managing their own company, or at least one in which they have a major stake.

Other buyers may not be interested in the day-to-day operations of the business. They see the deal primarily from an investment perspective and will be interested only in companies with a proven management team already in place. Any given deal usually represents one of several such investments, none of which require a disproportionate amount of their time.

Financial Circumstances

Financial circumstances obviously play an important role in defining realistic prospective buyouts or acquisitions. In some cases, the buyer's professional experience and credibility can offset the impact of limited financial resources. However, if he is unwilling to share equity with outside investors in the company, the size of the company will be limited by the amount of cash available to invest. Even if very high leverage is used, lenders are often reluctant to allow the financing obligations to become overly disproportionate to the buyer's net worth.

Financial resources also become an important factor in determining how the buyer conducts the search for a company. The process of buying a company usually takes six months to a year of intensive effort. An exception to this would be the management buyout, where the incumbent management does not have to find the deal. The first-time buyer without a captive deal must conduct the search properly and have adequate financial resources to support himself during the acquisition process. These resources can be in the form of savings, other liquid investments, or a continuing stream of income. If the buyer is employed on a full-time basis, it may be impossible to take the necessary time required to conduct the search and acquire the company. Because part-time efforts are usually insufficient, the buyer should be prepared to take the risk and consider any depletion in savings as part of his equity investment in the company.

Financial and employment circumstances will also directly affect the geographic criteria of the buyer. For example, a buyer restricted by limited financial resources or employed on a full-time basis will find it difficult to consider companies located two thousand miles away. A buyer in this situation must limit his universe of prospective deals to those companies located within a geographic area which is easily and economically accessible.

Risk Preferences

Another key consideration is the buyer's attitude toward risk. If he is adverse to risk, the buyer may wish to employ only conservative leverage. This, along with available equity, will determine the maximum limits of his purchase price range. To the financially conservative buyer, the obvious benefits of utilizing a high degree of leverage to finance the acquisition are not worth the increased risk of failure.

Risk preference factors should also be reflected in the overall condition of the target company. Some buyers, because of their past experience and willingness to take risks, may want to consider a turnaround or troubled business. These types of companies, in effect, usually have the leverage in place before the acquisition. Unlike his conservative brethren, the risk-oriented buyer may be attracted to these types of situations.

Business Experience Factors

When substantial new borrowings are incurred to buy a company, some or all of this money will be at risk, even if it is not in the form of equity. Before making the decision to invest, therefore, the various sources of outside financing must be assured of the return of their principal and a reasonable return on the investment. The starting point of any such analysis is the business experience and management capabilities of the buyer. A buyer with a strong track record which is directly related to the business of the proposed buyout or acquisition candidate can often offset the negative impact of limited financial resources or extraordinarily high leverage. On the other hand, a weak track record or business and managerial experience which is unrelated to the industry in which the target acquisition competes will turn the outside financing sources off in a hurry. Therefore, a buyer must be sure to define a target company profile that is reasonably consistent with his past experience.

The need for a close correlation of the buyer's prior experience to the specific business of the target company will depend upon a number of factors, including (1) the type of buyer, (2) his prior track record, and (3) the size of the deal. If the buyer is an individual investor or entrepreneur who intends to be directly involved in day-to-day management decisions, his prior experience should be directly related to that of the target company. On the other hand, if the buyer is a proven investor/operator or investment group which has successfully acquired and monitored a number of unrelated businesses, there is a lesser need for direct experience in the industry or business of the target company. Size is also a factor, since the larger transactions almost always involve the participation of the incumbent management team and thus reduce the importance of the direct operational experience of other investment principals.

In cases where direct experience is an important factor, first priority should obviously be given to the industries that are acceptable. Preferably, the buyer should restrict his universe of target companies to those industries in which he has had actual experience. Not only will he be aware of the basic business dynamics affecting supply, demand, and profitability, he will also have a broader base of personal contacts. Long-standing relationships with competitors, suppliers, and customers will significantly increase the odds of seeing more potential deals. If opportunities are limited or undesirable in a specific industry, the buyer should at least select those industries which in some way capitalize on his skills and experience. Needless to say, a buyer should avoid industries in which he has little knowledge or experience.

The next important experientially related determinant of the target company profile is the type of business. Businesses are generally classified as manufacturing, wholesale distribution, retail distribution, mining, or service. Within these major groups are numerous sub-groups which further define the business. Also within the major classifications are certain characteristics that are common to all companies so categorized. These common denominators usually result in the development or refinement of certain skills and experience which are applicable to many types of companies, even though they may operate in industries that are totally different. For example, experience in one manufacturing company may be directly applicable in another, even though the products and processes of one firm are quite different from those of the other. Similarly, the operational experience gained in one wholesaling company can be very useful in any company engaged in distribution. The prospective buyer should be aware of the importance of these basic skills and experience and consider companies where such skills can be utilized.

If the buyer is to be intimately involved in the operation, he must also give strong consideration to his own functional abilities and preferences. Every business has needs in the areas of general management, marketing and finance. Depending on the type of business, it may also require expertise in research and development, engineering, production and personnel. If the buyer has had only narrow experience in one of the functional areas, this must be considered in defining both the type of company to buy as well as the personnel it should have. For example, a buyer with a strong marketing background would be well advised to concentrate on marketing-oriented businesses and avoid those which are engaged in sophisticated manufacturing processes or are R&D intensive. He should also give priority to companies which already employ individuals whose skills compliment his own (e.g., finance and accounting.)

External Economic Factors

In addition to the personal, financial and business experience considerations of the buyer, there are external factors which will have some bearing on both the type of company and the timing of the acquisition. Such considerations include general economic conditions and forecasts as well as the impact of these conditions on specific industries. Current and projected conditions within the financial markets are other factors which should strongly influence a buyer's plans.

When economic conditions and the financial markets are uncertain, many buyers assume it is not the time to buy a company. While it is true that a sluggish economy and high interest rates may increase the business and financial risks attendant any deal, they also create increased buying opportunities which result in more attractive terms from the seller. When the price/earnings ratios of public stocks are low, there is less competition from corporate buyers. At the same time, the public companies themselves become sellers rather than buyers in order to increase their liquidity. Thus, from the standpoint of supply and demand, the worst economic times are often the best time to buy a company.

Economic and financial conditions may have a direct impact on the feasibility, and hence the desirability, of companies within a particular industry.

Companies in highly cyclical industries, (e.g., automobiles or housing) may not be realistic candidates for inclusion in the universe of potential target companies. The primary reason is the difficulty encountered in attracting the interest of financing sources. High interest rates may preclude the buyout of many companies unless a substantial amount of equity or inexpensive subordinated debt is used. This may require the buyer to (1) reduce the size range of the target company or (2) share the equity with outside investors.

As suggested by the foregoing, there are many variables and considerations that will impact the profile of a target company. Since some of these variables are conflicting, a buyer may be required to make some difficult decisions. In doing so, however, it is imperative that the buyer be both honest and realistic with himself. The buyer should be sure that these criteria are internally consistent and reflect the reality of his personal and financial circumstances as well as his professional goals.

The Target Company Profile: An Example

The objective of the intensive self-analysis described in the foregoing paragraphs is to crystallize, as clearly as possible, the description of potential companies which qualify for further consideration. The final result should be a profile that describes the ideal or acceptable target company in terms of the following: size, location, types of business(es), industry(ies), incumbent management requirements, personal investment limitations and ownership criteria. As an example of how this process of delineation and refinement works, the following hypothetical example is presented.

In this case, let us assume that the buyer, age 45, is currently employed as V.P. and General Manager of a division of a large public company. Although he is currently making a very comfortable living with an attractive salary and bonus, he has no equity participation in the company. Moreover, he has become increasingly frustrated with the imposition of corporate directives and their consequent impact on his ability to capitalize on new opportunities for his division, a manufacturer of specialty valves and controls for the chemical and petroleum industries. His primary objective, therefore, is to hold a major interest in a company that can provide a greater opportunity to create personal wealth and increased operational autonomy.

The potential buyer rose through the ranks of his current employer primarily on the engineering and manufacturing side of the business, although he did serve briefly as a marketing manager prior to being promoted to General Manager. He has made several significant contributions to the firm, most noteworthy of which has been to design and implement improved lower cost proprietary production techniques. He has accumulated in excess of $500,000 in cash and marketable securities and has approximately $150,000 in equity in his home. His living expenses are approximately $8,000 per month. He is willing to invest $300,000 of his liquid assets in an acceptable deal. In addition, it is estimated that he could generate $5,000 per month in consulting fees working about 40 percent to 50 percent of the time. Based upon this information, the target company's profile might appear as illustrated in Exhibit 2-A.

THE "BUYER'S PACKAGE"

A "buyer's package" is absolutely essential for anyone who is serious about buying a company. It paints the image of the buyer in the minds of sellers and intermediaries. The package is the primary marketing tool and generator of deal flow. Its purpose is twofold. First and foremost, it should establish and enhance the buyer's credibility in the eyes of intermediaries, referral sources and potential sellers. Secondly, it must define the buyer's criteria and thereby narrow the universe of potential target companies.

The importance of credibility in generating deal flow cannot be underestimated. Due to the large number of "tire kickers" who have little chance of closing a deal, deal sources are very skeptical of many buyers. The first impression left by a buyer often determines whether he will be perceived as a "real buyer" in the minds of the seller or intermediary. A package which is attractive and well-prepared is a key factor in creating the desired perception. A well-conceived and complete package communicates the fact that an individual is serious about this business of buying a company and has taken time to think about what he can and cannot buy. It also helps to answer the major questions in the minds of professional intermediaries, sellers and referral sources:

- "Is this buyer financially and experientially able to close the deal?"
- "Is this buyer someone to whom I want to sell my company, division or subsidiary?"
- "How will this buyer reflect on me professionally if I refer him to my clients or contacts?"

The package itself consists of any information which will accomplish its primary purpose to establish credibility and more specifically define the target company. Therefore, it is important that a well-prepared "target company profile" be included. In addition, the buyer should have a biography of himself and other key participants on the buying team. Any news releases or articles and reprints of any relevant publications should be included. Generally speaking, personal financial statements should not be included in the initial package.

Buyers who have or plan to invest in more than one company should have a professionally prepared brochure. This brochure may incorporate all the major components of the buyer's package. Such buyers usually include reprints of "tombstones" which announce previously closed deals. These are very effective in enhancing the buyer's credibility in the eyes of sellers and intermediaries. (An example of a professionally prepared brochure, complete with a "tombstone," is shown in Appendix B.) For the one-time buyer, it is usually not feasible to incur the added expense of a printed brochure. However, a professionally typed, attractively covered package should be more than sufficient to accomplish the desired result.

EXHIBIT 2-A

Target Company Profile

Criteria	Prefer	Will Consider
1. Company Size		
Purchase Price	\$5-\$15 Million	\$3-\$15 Million
Annual Sales	\$2-\$10 Million	\$10-\$20 Million
2. Company Location	Southwest Southeast	Anywhere except upper Midwest
3. Type of Business	Manufacturing Processing	Wholesale Distribution
4. Type of Products	Valves & Measurement Devices	Industrial Supplies
5. Industry(ies)	Chemical Petroleum Pulp & Paper	Any relevant to process control experience
6. Incumbent Management Requirement	Sales/Marketing Financial	—
7. Ownership Participants		
Current Owner	No	No
Incumbent Mgt.	Yes	Yes
Outside Investors	No	Yes

8. Other Criteria
Company must have proven record of consistent earnings and be in good financial condition.

3 WHO ARE THE SELLERS?

After the buyer has carefully defined his criteria, he is ready to begin the process of searching for companies that closely match his requirements. The most effective methods of conducting the search are described in Chapter 4 ("Finding the Company"). However, before considering how to locate suitable acquisition prospects, it is important for the buyer to understand just who the sellers are and what motivates them to sell.

THE UNIVERSE OF POTENTIAL SELLERS

The term "seller," as used throughout this book, refers to those individuals or business entities that control the business activities of the target company and, as a result, the decision to sell the company itself. In some cases, the power to make such decisions is under the direct control of one or two individuals, which makes the negotiating process more straightforward. In other situations the decision to sell is diffused among a larger group of individual shareholders or committee members. This makes the selling process more cumbersome and increases the risk that not all the "sellers" will agree to move forward on the proposed transaction.

The sellers with whom the leveraged buyer must ultimately deal consist of four major groups:

- Owners of privately held companies ("Private Sellers")
- Corporations seeking to divest subsidiaries or divisions ("Corporate Sellers")
- Public shareholders (including institutions) who are willing to tender their shares to private leveraged buyers ("Public Sellers")
- Institutional investors seeking to cash in on their investment ("Institutional Sellers")

Each group has its unique characteristics and motivations for selling out. And some groups are more appropriate for certain types of buyers than others. The remainder of this chapter will address the various seller groups, what motivates them to sell, and the types of buyers with which they prefer to deal. A buyer who is aware of the distinctions and preferences of the different types of sellers can save himself a great deal of time and effort in searching for prospective acquisition candidates.

PRIVATE SELLERS

By far the largest pool of sellers in the U.S. consists of the owners of privately held companies. Typically, these are entrepreneurially oriented individuals who have invested a significant amount of their capital — and their life — in the business. As both the individual and the business itself grows and matures, the owner reaches important junctures at which he must consider the sale of the business. At these critical junctures, a number of personal and business considerations arise that will dictate whether the owner should sell.

The main factor that sets the private seller apart from all others is that both his capital and career are embodied in the company. This is particularly true where the dominant shareholder is also the key operating figure. However, it can also be the case where the owner has worked very hard to bring the company to the point where his daily presence is no longer essential. In many such instances, he still has a strong emotional attachment to the business.

The primary reason why most private sellers decide that it's time to sell is to effectively separate their capital from their career. Generally speaking, his holdings in the company represent a disproportionate share of his net worth. The quickest means of liquifying and diversifying his estate is to sell the company. His emotional attachment to the business, employees, customers, etc., makes the private seller less dispassionate than a pure investor or corporate seller. The decision to sell is more than a bottom line return on investment; it also represents the final chapter of a very substantial segment of his life.

This tug-of-war between the private seller's rational financial objectives and his emotional sentiments create some unique problems that the buyer must be prepared to deal with. Foremost among them is an increased risk that the private seller will change his mind unexpectedly at any point during the process of finalizing the deal — even up to the closing date. Unless the buyer is attuned to these peculiarities and carefully qualifies the seller, he may end up without a company to buy after spending much time, effort and money.

Personal Reasons for Selling

In addition to the seller's desire to separate his capital from his career, there are several other personal reasons that might cause him to sell. These include:

Retirement. This is something all business owners must ultimately face, whether they like it or not. It is a more relevant factor in cases where the owner also plays the key operating role and desires to pursue other interests. This presents no problem if someone in the immediate familiy is prepared to take over these responsibilities. In some cases, however, the owner has no one in the family to assume control of the business and decides to sell, either to incumbent management or to outside investors.

Health Problems. Sometimes the owner of a privately held company is forced to sell because of illness. Nothing forces an owner to reevaluate his priorities as much as a serious or continuing illness. This type of introspection may lead him to conclude that he no longer has the desire or strength to continue in the business. Or, if the owner is passive, health problems may wake him up to the need to liquify his estate or pursue other leisure activities.

Divorce. Divorce is another personal trauma that often precipitates the sale of a company. In some cases, a sale is the only means of raising the money to effect a settlement. In other instances, the owner may lose interest in the business and decide to sell because of the emotional trauma associated with a divorce.

Family Pressures. Pressure resulting from intensive involvement in a growing business is another reason why some owners choose to sell. They may reassess their priorities and opt for a slower or different pace in their career. This is a particularly difficult situation for the active owner, since a part of him may want to sell while another part of him doesn't. Buyers should be aware that such owners are more susceptible to "seller's remorse."

Business Reasons for Selling

Aside from the foregoing personal reasons, there are some important *business* reasons that cause owners of private companies to sell out. The most common is that the company, in order to survive and prosper, requires more capital than the owner is willing or able to provide. In these cases, he may have several options:

- sell stock to the public,
- raise capital by means of a private placement, or
- sell the entire company to a buyer with greater financial resources.

Of the total universe of private companies, relatively few qualify for a public offering. That is because the public markets are quite fickle and selective, except in rare periods of heavy speculation. And, even if their company qualifies, some owners want no part of "going public." Many correctly rationalize that the excessive cost and headache of public ownership is too much to pay for fresh capital. Private placements may be more appealing to these owners, but these often result in substantial dilution of ownership and, in some cases, control. In general, this approach is the highest cost of capital to the owner.

In view of these disadvantages, some owners choose to sell the entire company to a financially responsible party rather than bits and pieces of it to outside investors. This approach may simultaneously satisfy the company's need for additional capital and the owner's desire to diversify his assets.

While such situations may represent excellent opportunities for well-capitalized corporate buyers who are willing to invest additional funds after the closing, they are usually not good LBO prospects. As Chapter 5 will explain, one of the important characteristics of a leveraged buyout candidate is that the company does not require substantial additional capital infusions after the closing.

Another very real, but unspoken, reason that the private owner decides it is time to cash in, is that the fortunes of the company have taken a turn for the worse. It must be assumed that no one knows the future prospects for the business better than its current owner. He may offer perfectly rational reasons for selling, but the *real* reason is that the fundamentals of the industry or business have deteriorated. Although the astute buyer should be able to flush out any negative developments in the business during his evaluation of the company, he must always live by the oft-quoted exhortation — *Caveat Emptor!*

Regardless of his reason(s) for selling, the private seller is indeed a complex individual who must be understood and dealt with for two simple reasons. First, they represent the largest number of potential LBO prospects in the total universe of sellers. Secondly, they are the only possible type of seller that many buyers —particularly those without an established track record — will be able to access.

CORPORATE DIVESTITURES

According to statistics published by W.T. Grimm & Co., for every two acquisitions reported by major public companies, there is one divestiture of a subsidiary or division. Many of these divestitures are excellent prospects for private leveraged buyers. The very qualities which often make a company unwanted by a corporate parent, (e.g., size, mundane products and slow growth) are very desirable for leveraged buyers.

Corporate sellers usually are motivated by strategic and economic reasons. Personal reasons, other than the corporate political impact on those responsible for the selling decisions, seldom enter into the selling equation. Careful evaluation of the reasons precipitating the divestiture of a subsidiary or division is necessary.

Reasons for Divesting

Restructuring Pressures. In the 1980's divestiture activity accellerated as top executives scrambled to restructure their diverse corporate empires. Initially this restructuring was largely voluntary as managers reacted to Wall Street investors who placed higher values on more strategically focused businesses. This resulted in the widespread divestiture of many subsidiaries and divisions which no longer fit the strategic mold of the parent.

But with the rapid emergence of the junk bond market, the pace of restructuring quickened. Because relatively small corporate raiders could borrow large sums of junk financing to take over previously untouchable large corporations, top managers were forced to divest on a larger scale. It no longer became a choice; it was a necessity if management wanted to maintain the independent status of the parent company.

Source of Capital. Aside from these compelling external forces, there are other sound business reasons for divesting. Growing corporations always need money to sustain growth, to service debt, to acquire other companies, or a combination of all these. Corporate managers can raise long-term debt through private placements with insurance companies or pension funds, via public debt underwritings, or they can turn to the public markets for public offerings of debt or common stock. When the private or public markets are not receptive to any kind of equity or debt offering, the only other alternative may be to sell or redeploy assets which may include product lines or operating subsidiaries and divisions.

Too Small. The size of a division or subsidiary, and especially its size in relation to its parent, is another important consideration. Corporate managers subscribe to the theory that it takes as much time to manage a small or medium-sized subsidiary or division as it does a larger one. Indeed, the smaller unit may require more time since it cannot support the quality and depth of management that a larger unit can. A small deal makes sense to a corporate owner only if it has extraordinary sales growth and earnings potential in relation to the parent company's investment.

In today's business climate, it is necessary for a division or subsidiary of a major corporation to maintain certain sales volumes to support the overhead allocated to it. This overhead consists of many expenses of which the following are only a few: financial reporting to the Securities & Exchange Commission, corporate planning, corporate specialists for OSHA, labor relations, affirmative action and EPA matters, employee benefits, retirement plans, health, medical and dental plans and the people required to administer them. It is apparent that these overhead expenses have made some larger companies less efficient than smaller privately held or autonomous businesses. In the future, therefore, more smaller divisions and subsidiaries will be spun off or liquidated because they cannot support the overhead allocated by their corporate parents.

Poor Earnings. Earnings also bear very heavily on divestment decisions. Flat or declining earnings are incompatible with the public corporation's mandate of consistent growth. The amount of earnings also has its impact on corporate decisions. A small amount of earnings in dollars simply will not get top management's attention since corporate charges to the unit often reduce these earnings to insignificant levels. A company may be a constant earner and have a reasonable pattern of growth, but the return on assets employed may be less than that earned by other businesses of the parent corporation. Another factor negatively impacting the earnings of a small unit is the need for major expenditures to upgrade products, marketing organizations or manufacturing facilities. The requirements may be above and beyond the capability or desire of the parent company of the subsidiary to generate the needed funds.

It is clear that divestitures will continue to represent a significant portion of merger and acquisition activity. Most are excellent candidates for leveraged buyouts because they possess many of the characteristics needed for leveraging: mundane products, relatively slow growth and undervalued assets. For these same reasons, many divestitures are not attractive to other corporate suitors.

Realistically, most divestiture leveraged buyout candidates are difficult to access for the typical leveraged buyer. Incumbent managers have become more sophisticated in the LBO financing process and are often able to negotiate and finance the buyout on their own. In addition, these deals are controlled by the large investment banking firms who are quite selective about which potential buyers are able to see the deal.

Needless to say, the buyer who wishes to play the divestiture game must be both experienced and sophisticated. The investment bankers who control the corporate sellers will have it no other way.

PUBLIC COMPANIES

Although increased divestiture activity has contributed substantially to the increasing number of LBO opportunities, entire public companies themselves have been frequent targets of leveraged buyout artists. Many public companies were ripe LBO candidates because of the wide disparity between their depressed stock prices and the underlying value of corporate assets.

Initially all public LBO's were "friendly transactions" with the full cooperation of incumbent management. Shareholders, who suffered through several years of a sagging stock market in the late 1970's and early 1980's, looked favorably upon the offers by leveraged buyers to take companies private at a significant premium over the prevailing market price of their stock.

As stock prices increased in the mid-1980's, "going private" transactions continued to flourish, but at much higher valuations. A major force behind this increased momentum was the ready availability of junk bond financing. This not only led to much larger deals, but also led to a proliferation of hostile leveraged buyout attempts, a concept that was considered out of the question just a few years before.

Realistically, leveraged buyouts of public companies are the exclusive domain of a few highly sophisticated and well-capitalized investment groups. The closure rate on this type of buyout is much lower because buyers are dealing with large numbers of shareholders, some of whom will surely contest any transaction. Another factor is that these deals are closely scrutinized by the SEC, resulting in heavy legal expenses.

INSTITUTIONAL SELLERS

The proliferation of leveraged transactions in the late 1970's and early 1980's has created yet another source of new LBO opportunities: recycled companies. Some companies, originally acquired five or more years ago via a leveraged buyout, have again changed hands or gone public. While many of the companies were acquired by corporate suitors seeking strategic "fits," more than a few were recycled to a new LBO investment group or exclusively to the incumbent managers.

While the recycling of companies is not a new phenomena — many companies have been sold three or four times to different leveraged buyers — it has been more prevalent in the past few years. The primary reason behind an increase in corporate recycling is the significant drop in interest rates in the mid-1980's and consequent increase in valuations of companies. The "seller's market" prompted many early LBO investors — including managers — to cash in their chips while the window was still open.

An equally important factor has been the tendency of LBO investors, such as venture capital pools, to convert their mature investments to cash after four to six years and to reinvest the capital in a new deal with greater upside potential. In fact, many institutional investors tie their original investment to the ability to either "put" their shares in the company to management or to buy management's shares at a predetermined multiple of earnings or book value. Most often, management buys out the investors and ends up owning the entire company. In some cases, however, a new investment group is brought into the deal to completely cash out the old investors and partially cash out management's interest.

While recycled leveraged buyouts may create new opportunities for new financing sources, they really don't offer much to the new entrepreneurial leveraged buyer, unless he is a pure investor. These transactions more closely resemble recapitalizations where ownership is reallocated among management and old and new investors. The common denominator in most LBO recycles is that management stays involved in the company and usually increases its ownership stake.

GENERATING DEAL FLOW

Knowing who the sellers are and what makes them tick is important. But it doesn't mean much if the buyer cannot identify those specific sellers that fit his criteria and ultimately gain access to them. Because buyers usually outnumber sellers, there is an active competition among buyers for access to the best acquisition prospects.

In the dealmaking trade, the active pursuit of uncovering acquisition prospects is often referred to as generating "deal flow." Most active — and effective — buyers pursue a number of strategies to maximize deal flow. These include establishing extensive networks of intermediary contacts who have access to sellers. For many, particularly corporate buyers with specific target criteria, it involves a direct approach to the sellers. Whatever method is employed, the top priority of every buyer is to have enough deal flow. The next chapter discusses this most important step as we now consider how to find prospective LBO candidates.

4

FINDING THE COMPANY

Of all the steps involved in buying a company, the most difficult, frustrating and time consuming is finding the right company to buy. This is especially true for the first-time buyer who frequently underestimates both the time and effort involved in obtaining access to viable buyout or acquisition candidates. Novice buyers frequently begin an active search for acquisition candidates without being fully prepared. The result is early disappointment, and often disenchantment, with the whole idea.

THE SEARCH PROCESS IS A MARKETING EFFORT

Many buyers erroneously assume there are an unlimited number of companies available for acquisition. In most cases, the exact opposite is true. The number of buyers usually far exceeds the number of good deals in the marketplace. The various sources of deals are certainly aware of this fact and, consequently, immediately seek to separate the "unqualified buyers" from the "real buyers" — those who are realistically able to close.

Thus, the obvious task for a buyer is to convince deal sources that he is a real buyer. One does not accomplish this by merely telling the world: "I'm open for business, please send deals." Rather, the process should be viewed as a well-organized marketing program in which the buyer's ability to close a deal is clearly and effectively communicated. The key to success is to present oneself in the best possible light to those who will decide if the buyer is to be exposed to various investment opportunities. If successful, the buyer's payoff will be an ever increasing flow of potential acquisition candidates.

Any successful marketing program must begin with a thorough consideration of the needs of the marketplace to which the effort is being directed. The "marketplace" in this case consists of those individuals who determine whether the buyer will get a "closer look" at any given deal.

As we will see in this chapter, there are several approaches to generating deal flow. But none is more important than developing effective working relationships with M&A intermediaries. Therefore, the first step in any successful search for leveraged buyout prospects must begin with a thorough understanding of these key players.

WORKING WITH M&A INTERMEDIARIES

The most important source of acquisition candidates for buyers, whether they are just beginning or have been at it for years, are professional intermediaries who make their living by linking up buyers and sellers in corporate merger and acquisition transactions. These individuals and firms provide a vital service to buyers by searching out those firms that are truly sale candidates. This is no small task since, at any given point in time, only a small percentage of companies are for sale.

Since M&A intermediaries dominate a majority of the seller relationships, any meaningful effort by a buyer to generate deal flow must have as its cornerstone an intensive effort to establish an effective network of these key players. To ignore them would result in a very limited selection of acquisition opportunities. Because of their importance, this chapter discusses in detail the major issues behind effective intermediary relationships.

The Intermediary Community

More than 17,000 individuals in the U.S. function as intermediaries, or middlemen, between buyers and sellers. About 95 percent of the professional intermediaries are small business opportunity brokers who focus primarily upon smaller local deals. The other 5 percent are more sophisticated and participate in larger transactions on a regional, national or even international basis.

Although the latter represent only a small proportion of the total intermediary community, they dominate merger and acquisition activity involving "middle market" companies (those with a purchase price of $5 million to $100 million). Therefore, it is important for any corporate or private buyers who seek acquisition candidates of middle market companies to understand who these major players are and how they function.

The more sophisticated M&A intermediaries can be broadly classified into three major groups: (1) large, full service investment banking firms; (2) commercial bank affiliates; and (3) smaller "independent" firms.

Investment Banking Firms. These notorious dealmakers tend to work exclusively with large corporate clients and a select group of active private buyers. In recent years, the "top bracket" investment banking houses have also taken a more active role as a principal or major source of equity financing for buyouts and acquisitions.

Most major investment banking firms have M&A departments that generate fee income solely from merger and acquisition transactions. This activity is a logical extension of their other corporate finance services such as underwriting new securities and arranging private placements of debt and equity. Intermediaries affiliated with investment banking houses are highly sophisticated and generally focus on larger transactions with purchase prices in excess of $50 million.

In recent years, this class of intermediary has increasingly utilized the so-called "investment banker's auction" as a method of brokering deals. This approach is designed to maximize the selling price for the client (the seller) by selectively exposing acquisition prospects to a relatively small number of qualified buyers. These buyers are invited to submit sealed bids, and the ultimate "winner" is then selected on the basis of price, terms and ability to perform. It should also be stated that the sealed bid approach to maximizing purchase price is not the exclusive domain of the large investment banking houses. It has also been used quite effectively by other types of intermediary firms.

Unless a buyer has an excellent track record involving larger corporate transactions, it is unlikely he will generate any meaningful deal flow from this type of professional intermediary. Possible exceptions to the tendency of full service investment banking houses to work only with larger clients are the case of regional investment banking firms. Because they focus on the corporate finance needs of smaller local companies, regional investment bankers are more inclined to work with a broader base of buyers.

Commercial Bank Affiliates. The intermediary associated with a commercial bank is a relatively new phenomenon. It is a direct consequence of the rapidly changing regulatory climate affecting financial institutions in the 1980's. The major impetus for this development is the banks' search for additional sources of revenue, necessitated by the removal of interest rate ceilings on certificates of deposit. At the same time, the Federal Government has taken a more relaxed attitude toward regulatory constraints which had previously drawn a sharper line of distinction between investment banking and commercial banking activities.

The predominant commercial banking players in the merger and acquisition arena are the large money-center banks. To a lesser extent, some regional banks have set up M&A departments. Regardless of size, the primary strength of bank-affiliated M&A intermediaries is the extensive base of customers with whom the bank has a lending or depository relationship. With these established corporate connections, it is much easier for this group of intermediaries to access companies that might be available for sale or looking to make acquisitions.

Although the banks have made a strong effort to capture some of the larger deals from traditional investment bankers, this has been a slow and difficult process. Long-standing relationships between investment bankers and their corporate clients have proven to be a formidable barrier for the banks to penetrate. As a result, banks have tended to focus their M&A activities more on middle market companies with whom there is an existing banking relationship.

Independent M&A Intermediaries. Numerically speaking, the majority of intermediaries who deal with mergers and acquisitions involving small or middle-sized companies are the so-called "independent" firms. These range from "one-man shops" to firms comprised of a dozen or more experienced professionals. These individuals may have previously decided, for personal and financial reasons, to set up their own firms. In recent years, an increasing number of retired corporate executives have also been lured into the M&A field by the prospect of large fees and occupational independence.

Independent M&A intermediaries, because of their larger numbers, handle the bulk of the transactions involving privately owned, middle market companies. Although they also maintain client relationships with the large multinational corporations, it is primarily in regard to the company's needs as a buyer. As was previously stated, the large investment banking firms usually handle the "sell side" involving the major corporations, including most divestitures.

Depending upon his level of experience, the independent intermediary may be more inclined to work with a broader spectrum of buyers. And unlike his large investment banking and commercial banking counterparts, some will work as a pure "finder" rather than an exclusive agent of either the seller or buyer. This will be discussed later in greater detail.

Services Provided

By definition, the primary function of an M&A intermediary, whether it is a large investment banking firm or a one-person operation, is to identify and qualify buyers and sellers, and ultimtely bring them together in a successful transaction. However, depending upon the size of the firm and the experience of the professionals, M&A intermediaries may also provide a number of other services that are related to the merger and acquisition process. These include:

Strategic Planning and Consulting. Some intermediaries, particularly those with corporate backgrounds, are experienced in the strategic planning process and provide such services to buyers and sellers with respect to their acquisition plans.

Valuations. An integral part of any acquisition is the valuation of the target company. In some cases, the intermediary will include a valuation of the company he is representing as part of his overall service. In other situations, the M&A intermediary will render an independent opinion of value for a company or an ESOP for which he is paid a negotiated fee.

Fairness Opinions. Closely related to the valuation is an opinion that a proposed transaction is fair to selling shareholders. Fairness opinions are often used in LBO transactions to minimize director liabilities to selling shareholders.

Financing. Some M&A intermediaries have both the expertise and essential contacts to assist in the financing of leveraged buyout transactions. If there is active involvement in the financing process, the intermediary will usually charge an additional financing fee.

In screening intermediary firms, buyers should ascertain what additional services, if any, will be required and select the firm(s) that have those designated capabilities.

Fee Arrangements

While separate fees are often charged for the foregoing ancilliary services, the intermediary's primary source of compensation is the commission, or as it is sometimes euphemistically called, the "success fee." It is paid only if and when the transaction is completed.

For many years the generally accepted standard for computing the intermediary's commission has been the so-called "Lehman formula." It prescribes a fee equal to 5 percent of the first million dollars in purchase price, 4 percent on the second, 3 percent on the third, 2 percent on the fourth and 1 percent on the purchase price in excess of $4 million.

Although the Lehman (or 5-4-3-2-1) formula is still used today by many firms, a number of variations of the formula — and even some new creative approaches to fee structure — have become more prevalent. Among the reasons cited by intermediaries who no longer use the straight Lehman formula are (1) it does not adequately compensate for smaller deals, and (2) the incentive to get the seller a higher price is diminished.

Variations on the Lehman Theme. The variations of the straight Lehman formula are based upon the above perceived shortcomings. One approach has been to increase the percentages on smaller deals (e.g., a 7-6-5-4-3 formula on deals under $5 million in purchase price). Another modification is to apply the percentages to larger increments, e.g., 5 percent of the first $2 million, 4 percent of the next $2 million, etc. Some firms have even gone so far as to use a "double Lehman," or 10-8-6-4-2 formula for smaller deals.

Some intermediaries have used novel approaches to create more incentive to generate a higher price for the seller. One such method is to use the so-called "reverse Lehman" or 1-2-3-4-5 formula. Using this approach, the higher percentages would apply to those increments of the purchase price in excess of the seller's expectations. A similar approach is to charge a smaller fee, say 2 percent, on the book value and a higher amount, say 8 percent, on any premium over book value. These fee structures strongly incentivize the intermediary to generate the highest price for the seller. Obviously, they must be custom designed to fit the requirements of any given transaction.

In very large transactions, fee arrangements between investment bankers and sellers are based upon a substantial retainer ($50,000 to $100,000) plus a smaller success fee (1 to 2 percent) because of the size of the deals. It has been well-publicized that these fees, in spite of the smaller percentages, can reach monumental proportions.

Cash Only, Please. The intermediary almost always demands to be paid in cash at closing. This may cause a problem for sellers who take back notes for a large portion of the purchase price. For smaller deals there is sometimes very little cash left for the seller after the intermediary fees are paid. In these cases the seller will often insist that the fees be paid "in kind," that is, in the same manner that the seller receives his proceeds. For this reason, intermediaries may have a natural aversion to leveraged acquisitions in which the seller finances a portion of the deal with purchase money notes.

Some intermediaries, particularly those who have been active for a while and are not in dire need of cash, may be more flexible regarding deferred fee arrangements. In fact, some may be willing to take an equity interest in the target company in lieu of their fee if it is to be paid by the buyer. Because this creates an immediate income tax liability without cash to pay it, only those intermediaries with sufficient liquidity are likely to participate in this manner.

Who Pays the Fee? To the intermediary, the question of "who pays the fee" is really not the major issue. His real concern is who will *protect* him, i.e., *guarantee* his fee will be paid if a transaction is completed. With this in mind, the buyer should consider the following with respect to the issue of "who pays the fee":

- Sellers customarily pay the fee, but there are cases where they will not. In these situations the buyer must agree to pay the fee or he won't see the deal.
- If the buyer must pay the fee, he should merely add this amount to the purchase price in his feasibility analysis. If the deal is priced too high with the fee, it shouldn't be done and the fee will not be paid. In reality, few deals are rendered infeasible because a fee must be added to the seller's asking price.
- If the company being sold has protected the fee, it is an obligation of the company, not its stockholders. At the time the stock (or the assets) of the company is sold, the assets will be depleted by the amount of the fee *unless* the stockholders have agreed to pay it. In a seller-protected situation which is to be a sale of stock, the buyer should clarify whether the company or the stockholders will pay the fee.

- All arrangements with an intermediary on fee payment should be in writing to eliminate any misunderstandings or false expectations.

Modes of Operation

Although the intermediary will maintain an inventory of both buyers and sellers, most will follow a specific pattern, or mode of operation, in how he conducts the business of bringing the two together. At the heart of how the intermediary conducts his business is who, ultimately, protects his fee. The following are some of the more common approaches used by intermediaries in conducting their business.

Exclusive Seller Representation. Because the number of buyers in the marketplace usually exceeds the number of sellers, the key to the intermediary's success is the ability to develop an inventory of qualified selling candidates over which he has control. The mechanism preferred by most intermediaries to achieve this is an exclusive arrangement requiring the payment of a fee by the seller if the company is sold. In some cases the intermediary will require a retainer from the seller which is non-refundable, but is credited toward the fee if and when the transaction closes.

An exclusive agreement with the seller assures the intermediary that he will be paid a fee if the company is sold, regardless of who it is sold to and who made the initial contact with the buyer. This is important, not only to the intermediary, but also to prospective buyers for two reasons. First, it is a strong indication that the seller is serious and the company is *really* for sale. Secondly, it means that the buyer will not have to add the payment of intermediary fees to the purchase price and financing requirements in his feasibility analysis.

Although the buyer may think, at first glance, that he is better off if the seller pays the intermediary fee, this is not necessarily the case. Seller-protected deals almost always mean the intermediary has a mandate to extract the highest possible price. As a consequence, the company is exposed to a greater number of buyers, resulting in more competition and *usually* a higher price. Thus, the buyer with a policy of considering "only deals where the seller has agreed to pay the fee" (or worst yet, "only those where the intermediary has an *exclusive* from the seller") is asking only for higher priced deals. In fact, sophisticated buyers actually prefer to see opportunities where *they*, rather than the seller, protect the fee.

In cases where the intermediary represents the seller on an exclusive basis, he has a clear fiduciary obligation to either the shareholders or the target company itself. He is obligated to represent only the seller's interests and may not collect fees from any other parties to the transaction unless it is disclosed to the seller. The buyer should be aware of these implicit legal obligations of the intermediary.

Exclusive Buyer Representation. In certain cases, M&A intermediaries will represent buyers on an exclusive basis in conducting an acquisition search. This usually occurs when a corporate acquirer is seeking a highly specific strategic acquisition and lacks the in-house resources to conduct the search. In these situations, the intermediary is almost always paid a retainer which is credited against any future success fees resulting from a completed transaction.

In the absence of a retainer, it makes little sense for either the buyer or the intermediary to work on an exclusive basis. For the buyer, it precludes him from accessing potential deals through other intermediary firms. This can significantly inhibit the search effort. To the intermediary, history has proven that exclusive buyer representation is not the best way to make money. The reason is that the scarce commodity is the seller, not the buyer. (Buyers often outnumber sellers by a factor of 10 to 1.) Therefore, the most effective intermediaries focus their attention on prospective sellers, at least with respect to exclusive relationships.

Non-Exclusive Representation of Buyers and Sellers. In many cases, the owner of a company may truly desire to sell the business, but is unwilling to sign an exclusive agreement with an M&A intermediary to represent him in the sale. He may, however, be willing to assure the intermediary in writing that a fee will be paid if the company is sold to a buyer procured by the intermediary within a prescribed time. Many M&A intermediaries would strongly argue that an unwillingness to grant exclusivity actually diminishes the seller's chances of receiving the best possible offer. Their rationale is that someone else (the seller or another intermediary) could undermine their efforts to sell the company by approaching other buyers. Because he may invest time and effort with no payoff, the intermediary will be reluctant to make a major commitment to market the company.

An even worse scenario (from the intermediary's standpoint) occurs when the seller refuses to either pay a fee or guarantee payment in writing in the event of a sale. To invest time and effort in such situations is very risky for the intermediary because, at best, there is no written guarantee that a fee will be paid and, at worst, the seller has stated categorically that no fee will be paid. In these cases, the intermediary will always seek "fee protection" from prospective buyers, usually in writing, before identifying the acquisition candidates. "Fee protection" letters state, in effect, that "the undersigned (buyer) agrees to pay the intermediary fee if the seller will not."

When the M&A intermediary has no agency relationship with either the seller or buyer, his primary emphasis is on connecting parties and moving on to the next transaction. Little, if any, effort is expended on conducting a well-planned search on behalf of a buyer or seller. In such situations, intermediaries are often preoccupied — even paranoid — about the payment of their success fees, as well they should be. In the absence of a written agreement from either the buyer or seller to pay a fee, the intermediary is often "squeezed" or, in the worst case, ends up with nothing.

Areas of Concern for Intermediaries

The astute buyer must be aware of the major concerns or fears of the professional intermediary. He should remember that there are several critical questions in the mind of the intermediary in his relationships with both buyers and sellers. Ignorance of, or indifference to, these important issues can only result in a less effective working relationship and, consequently, fewer potential acquisition candidates to evaluate.

"Will My Fee Be Paid?" The payment of a fee in the event of a completed transaction is the primary and overriding concern of the professional intermediary. An intermediary usually avoids all situations and all buyers where his ability to collect the fee is questionable. This means that they will insist upon written "protection" from either the buyer or seller. A buyer must be extremely sensitive to this reality.

Many buyers, particularly if they are inexperienced in the realities of the merger and acquisition game, have a great deal of difficulty with the "large fees" paid to intermediaries. What they fail to realize is that it takes substantial time and effort to dig out, qualify, and nurture those sellers who are true sellers. For each transaction that closes, the intermediary will have dealt with more than 100 that did not. Some of these "dead end trips" are expensive and time consuming for which there is zero compensation. Thus, when the intermediary is paid a fee that seems out of proportion to his efforts, it must be remembered that this makes up for all the times he was not paid.

It is important for all serious buyers to accept the fact that the intermediary earns his fee, even if it appears that he doesn't. The buyer must also be willing to offer "fee protection" to the intermediary if the seller will not. And he must avoid, at all costs, "chiseling" on any fees he has agreed to pay. With these policies, he will achieve his primary objective: see more potential acquisition opportunities.

"Is This Buyer Qualified?" One of the intermediary's most important functions is to select only the most qualified buyers for his client, usually the seller. This is even more important when the seller has not protected the intermediary on the fee. Such sellers are less likely to give the intermediary a second chance if he has arranged a visit by a clearly unqualified buyer. Therefore, if the intermediary is doing his job properly, he will carefully screen out those buyers who will not be able to complete the transaction. Remember, the intermediary gets most, if not all, of his payoff only when the company is sold.

To the intermediary, the "most qualified" buyers are those who (1) are willing to pay the seller's asking price (preferably in cash), (2) have a track record of prior acquisitions, (3) have a bona fide strategic reason for buying the company, and (4) have the necessary financial resources to close the deal. In addition, it is very helpful if the buyer has an annual report, brochure, or printed credentials that will favorably impress the seller. It is important to remember that the intermediary only has so many "trips to the well"; in other words he can expose only a limited number of prospective buyers to the seller. If he presents unqualified buyers, he not only wastes everyone's time, but also loses credibility with his client (usually the seller).

To avoid these problems the truly professional intermediary carefully interviews prospective buyers with detailed questions to ascertain their qualifications. These include:

- How many acquisitions have you (or your firm) closed within the last two years?
- What was your last transaction and when did it close?
- Why are you interested in this particular deal? (If the buyer is inquiring on a specific company.)
- What are your (or your firm's) financial resources? (Be prepared to send an annual report, financial statements or provide bank references.)
- How fast can you (your firm) move?

The buyer should not be intimidated or offended by such questions. By asking them the intermediary is only doing his job. In fact, if there is no attempt to qualify the buyer, it is a good sign that the intermediary is either inexperienced or incompetent. The buyer should be prepared for such questions and attempt to put his best foot forward. He should remember that, at this stage, it is a marketing game: he must sell the intermediary that he is a qualified buyer, one who can — and will — close the deal.

But what if the buyer is new, has yet to close a deal and has limited financial resources? Make no mistake about it: it's going to be a more difficult undertaking. New buyers are competing with other more experienced and well-heeled buyers. It will be tougher to get the attention of the intermediary community and gain access to sellers. But the key is to accentuate the positives. In the absence of an acquisition track record, a buyer must emphasize his operational or financial skills and how they relate to specific targets. If he lacks financial resources, strong working relationships with institutional financing sources must be developed to establish credibility.

"Is This a Leveraged Buyer?" It was previously mentioned that leveraged buyouts may cause problems for the intermediary because the seller may be asked to finance a portion of the transaction with purchase money notes. This is distasteful not only to the seller, because he gets less cash, but possibly to the intermediary, because he may be asked to take his fee "in kind" (i.e., some cash/some notes). But there is a more fundamental reason why both the seller and the intermediary look with some disdain upon LBO transactions: they are more complex and take longer to close. Because there are more parties to the transaction (third party lenders, investors and their lawyers), there is a greater chance of something going wrong.

Another problem often arises in the case of privately-owned companies whose owners resent the idea of someone "buying my business with its assets." Although somewhat irrational, it is often a very real psychological impediment to a transaction. It becomes an especially difficult issue when the seller is asked to finance the deal and subordinate his loan to outside lenders. This is less of a problem with corporate sellers who are less emotional when divesting a subsidiary.

Aside from these problems, it is a fact of life that leveraged buyers usually cannot pay as much for a quality business as an operating company which is making a strategic acquisition when both are competing for the same deal. The leveraged buyer is limited to what he can pay by the ability of the target's cash flow to service the acquisition debt. And, although the corporate buyer also has return on capital constraints, it may be able to "reach" on price because of the operational synergies of combining the two entities. The relative disadvantage of the leveraged buyer may increase with the 1986 tax reform, which reduces the after-tax value of debt financing.

Does this mean that the intermediary will not respond to the leveraged buyer? Absolutely not! In spite of the foregoing disadvantages, the leveraged buyer usually has an important advantage over the corporate buyer: he is more entrepreneurial and not entwined by massive corporate bureaucracy. As a result, he is often more motivated and able to react very quickly to opportunities. The key is how much control he has over his financing sources.

The bottom line is that the leveraged buyer must first realize his strengths and weaknesses. He must offset his limitations with the ability to move quickly with controlled sources of capital. While he may not want to flaunt his status as a leveraged buyer, he shouldn't be ashamed of it either.

"Will This Buyer Maintain Confidentiality?" In dealing with intermediaries, there are other unwritten codes of conduct which the buyer must observe if he wants to get optimum results. This first involves confidentiality of information received on a specific company. In many cases, the employees, customers, and suppliers of the company are unaware that the company is for sale. If an indiscreet buyer broadcasts to the business community that the company is for sale, word quickly gets around and directly reflects on the intermediary. Most buyers respect confidentiality while they are actively looking at the deal. After their interest in the target ceases, however, some are more inclined to breach confidences. Not only can this lack of confidentiality result in a lawsuit, but it also is the intermediary's primary concern in situations where he doesn't have an "exclusive" with the seller. When the seller's availability leaks out, the intermediary can quickly lose the deal (and the fee) to another intermediary. Such indiscriminate disregard for maintaining confidentiality will surely result in a termination of any working relationship with the intermediary and, if it continues, a bad reputation in the entire M&A community.

Confidentiality is also important with regard to any financial data submitted on the target company. To minimize the unauthorized dissemination of financial data, many intermediary firms will require the buyer to sign a legally binding "confidentiality agreement," which prohibits the buyer from disclosing the information to anyone outside of its organization. If, however, the intermediary has any reason to doubt the integrity of a buyer with regard to maintaining confidentiality, he would not provide it, in spite of the buyer's willingness to sign any "agreement." The buyer should assure the intermediary of his intention to maintain confidentiality. He should also be sensitive to these issues when performing his due diligence and respect confidentiality among employees, customers, suppliers, and competitors.

Establishing Relationships With Intermediaries

Establishing effective working relationships with M&A intermediaries is not an event, but a process. The extent of the process will depend upon the goals of the buyer (or seller). If the objective is just to buy (or sell) one company, the process will be relatively short; it will last only until the mission is accomplished. On the other hand, if the buyer is continuously active in the market, the process of establishing and maintaining intermediary relationships never ends. There is an on-going search for deals and the people that dig them out.

There are two ways to make initial contact with an M&A intermediary. One is for a buyer to approach them on the basis of his general acquisition criteria in an effort to elicit their cooperation. One must remember there are many more buyers than sellers, so the intermediary's reception to a "cold call" may not be very warm. A buyer must get his attention and differentiate himself from the hundreds of other nameless, faceless buyers with whom he is competing (at least) for the attention and interest of the intermediary). Most important, he must quickly convince the intermediary he is a "real" buyer — one who has the ability to close a deal.

An excellent source of intermediary contacts is *The Directory of Merger & Acquisition Intermediaries,* published by Business Publications, Inc. This publication lists over 300 of the nation's top M&A intermediary firms and their principal contacts. In addition, it describes their "mode of operation," fee structures, and other valuable information on each firm. These firms can be contacted by letter describing the buyer's acquisition criteria. But, for maximum effectiveness, it should be followed up with a telephone call or, preferably, a personal visit.

The problem with the above method of approaching M&A intermediaries is that everyone else does it this way. Therefore, it is very difficult to capture the intermediary's initial attention, much less have him remember specific needs a month or two in the future. There is a better way. That is for a buyer to contact an intermediary on a specific deal (a) where he (the intermediary) is representing the seller, and (b) which fits the buyer's acquisition criteria. By doing so, the buyer will immediately focus the intermediary's attention on a specific company with which he is familiar. This approach will not eliminate the necessary qualification process; a buyer must still prove himself as a qualified player. But it provides a much better opportunity to establish credibility and, at the same time, pursue a specific acquisition candidate.

Where can buyers find these acquisition candidates and the intermediaries who control them? The best source available is *The Acquisition Mart,* also published by Business Publications, Inc. It is a monthly newsletter that contains over 50 new companies for sale in each issue and the intermediaries to contact for further information. It puts buyers in direct contact with the leading active intermediaries on specific acquisition candidates. The company also publishes *The Acquisition Mart* in electronic form on a floppy disk for use on IBM compatible computers. This product (DealBase) enables buyers to conduct selective searches for acquisition candidates meeting their specific criteria. (See Appendix K for a more detailed description of these aids.)

Maintaining Momentum

Once the initial contact is made, a buyer must maintain momentum to have any chance of establishing an effective working relationship with the intermediary. If he has merely made general contact regarding criteria, this should be followed up, preferably in person, at a later date. There should be a continuous effort by the buyer to re-contact the intermediary to remind him of the active interest as well as the specific acquisition criteria. The "squeaky wheel" approach works in generating deal flow just as it does in other endeavors.

If initial contact was made regarding a specific deal, the buyer should get a commitment from the intermediary to "send a package," i.e., a more detailed description of the company along with pertinent financial information. Upon receipt of the package, it should be reviewed promptly and the intermediary should be called back. The purpose of the call may be to (a) ask for more mation, (b) arrange to move forward and take the next step, or (c) explain why there is no interest in pursuing the deal.

The worst thing a buyer can do is not respond at all. Equally damaging is the practice used by some buyers of later rejecting an acquisition proposal for reasons that were clearly known in the initial discussion with the intermediary. Both responses serve to alienate the intermediary because they show total disregard for his most valuable asset: his time. Such practices substantially diminish the chance of a buyer seeing future deals. In the end, his "investment" of time to establish the intermediary relationship will go down the drain.

Most important, the buyer should not get discouraged. He must always keep in mind that this effort is a search for the right intermediaries and, ultimately, the right deal. Like any search, there will be a blind alley here and there and some disappointments. Not all intermediaries will welcome new buyers with open arms. Some won't even respond. But buyers who persist will eventually establish relationships with a handful of intermediaries who are a vital link with that elusive goal: the right deal.

Helpful Hints

The process of establishing and maintaining effective working relationships with intermediaries does not happen overnight. It takes time, effort, and persistence. It also takes an intelligent approach and obedience to the "rules of the game." Here are some proven hints on how to make the "hunt" for an acquisition easier.

- Intermediaries earn their fees, even though it may not appear that they do. (If you doubt this, try making a living at it for a while; you may get hungry before you get rich!)
- Intermediaries are paranoid about getting "protected" on their fee. (If you were "squeezed" as much as they are, you would be too!) Ease their mind by giving "fee protection" if the seller will not.
- Remember that a "good deal" is a scarce commodity and buyers are plentiful. Therefore, don't expect the intermediary to celebrate your initial call.
- The buyer's primary task is to convince the intermediary that he is a "real" buyer, i.e., one who can and will close a transaction.
- For long-term success, honor your commitments to keep sensitive information confidential. (You will be rewarded with more deal flow.)
- Don't promote yourself as a leveraged buyer unless you have an excellent grip on your financing sources. (Intermediaries are like the rest of us: they want to keep things simple!)
- When you receive a "package" on a deal, the worst thing you can do is nothing. Even if the deal is terrible or doesn't "fit," call the intermediary and tell him why.
- The best way to increase deal flow is to close a deal. (Nothing succeeds like success!)

WORKING WITH REFERRAL SOURCES

The professional intermediary is the best source for finding a suitable company because that is his business. However, the intelligent buyer will not limit himself to this source in his pursuit of deal flow. He will also access a variety of contacts who have some influence over sellers. In the dealmaking trade, these contacts are known as referral sources. These include a wide range of professional people such as bankers, trust officers, lawyers, appraisers, management consultants and CPA firms.

Although none of these sources are in the business of bringing together a buyer and seller for a fee, they are often in close contact with both parties. Such contacts with company owners are usually based upon client relationships which result in greater respect for the opinions of the referral source. This can be of great value to the prospective buyer if the referral source will speak on his behalf to the potential seller.

There are two ways in which these referral sources can be utilized to open the door for the buyer. The first, and most effective, is for the referral source to take the initiative and contact the potential seller on behalf of the buyer. By taking this more assertive posture, the referral source is making a strong statement with respect to the buyer's integrity and ability. Another, somewhat less effective, way is to merely provide names to the buyer and allow him to use the referral source's name when initially contacting the seller.

In the case of the professional intermediary, the decision to work with a buyer is based upon the perceived ability of the buyer to perform and the probability of receiving a fee. In other words, the intermediary's major concern is "What's in it for me?" With a referral source there is the same deliberative process before a commitment is made to help a buyer. But, since he is not getting paid, at least not directly, his major concern often becomes "What do I have to lose?" The livelihood of lawyers, CPA's and other professionals is based largely upon their reputation. Accordingly, if they perceive their reputation could, in any way, be damaged by referring the buyer to their client, it will not happen.

The buyer must be conscious of this concern and seek to offset it with potential rewards. It is a good idea to let a referral source know that his services will be retained during the current or future transactions. Again, the key element is the way the buyer prepares and presents himself to these sources. If the buyer has done his homework and appears to know what he wants, his chances of getting good referrals are much greater. With this in mind, the primary referral sources and their role in helping the buyer find a deal will now be considered in greater detail.

Banks

The best starting place is a local commercial bank. The commercial loan department and the trust department of such an institution can be excellent sources of companies for sale. The commercial loan officer is often very close to the owners of companies and is aware of their future plans. As a result, he can put the buyer directly in touch with an owner who wishes to sell. He will do so, however, only if he has confidence in the buyer's abilities and believes that a transaction would not result in the loss of business by the bank. Thus, in the initial conversation with the banker, the buyer should emphasize his intent to continue utilizing the bank's services.

On some occasions, the bank may be saddled with a troubled loan and may be able to influence the owner of the company to sell to someone in whom the banker has more confidence. If the buyer has strong operational experience which has included turnaround or troubled situations in his target company profile, he may be able to persuade the bank to lend the company more money to complete the acquisition and operate the company.

Although bank trust departments may have more healthy companies, the opportunities are usually fewer in number than on the commercial side. Trust departments are good prospects because they usually lack the know-how to manage or monitor a closely held business on behalf of an estate. If bank personnel must be extensively involved in management decisions, they will usually prefer to sell.

Attorneys

Lawyers are another group of individuals who are often close to potential sellers. Clients tend to respect the opinion of their legal counsel more than any other professional. If a lawyer suggests "talking to so and so" as a potential buyer of the business, the client will usually do it. Like the banker, the lawyer must be assured that both his reputation and future business will be left intact after a deal.

CPA Firms

In recent years many major CPA firms have established separate departments to facilitate the purchase and sale of companies. Their primary objective is the retention or creation of auditing and tax accounts or possible management service consulting fees. They don't function as a classic intermediary who is paid a transaction fee, although they do get paid for services rendered to either the seller or the buyer. The "Big 8" accounting firms often maintain a national data base of potential buyers and sellers. Local accountants can also be an effective referral source.

The perception of the transaction's effect upon their business is paramount in both cases. In this regard, the buyer should be aware of a problem sometimes encountered by large CPA firms who are the auditors for the selling corporation. If the transaction involves contingent payments, seller warranties or seller notes, the CPA firm cannot represent both the seller and the buyer in an auditing capacity. As a result, the large CPA firms will normally try to avoid bringing buyers into transactions that will result in a loss of substantial auditing business with seller clients.

Financial Planners

Whether they are involved with securing key man insurance, managing the investment of company profits or providing pension plan services, financial planners or other investment consultants are quite often retained by owners of middle market companies. These professionals specialize in providing investment counseling for estate planning purposes. In most cases, an owner's most valuable asset is the stock of his company. Under appropriate conditions, a financial planner will point out the risks and disadvantages of over-concentration of wealth in a single asset, particularly if the owner is older and has no heirs to run the business.

Increased liquidity and portfolio diversification can be achieved via a sale or merger. Because the financial planner is intimately involved in the decision process, he is among the first to know of the company's availability.

Business Appraisers

The dissolution of a marriage or differences between co-owners often necessitates a professional evaluation of a business entity to determine the shares to be received by the respective parties. And since disputes of this nature frequently result in the sale of a jointly or separately owned business, evaluation firms are frequently able to identify attractive sale situations.

Manufacturer's Representatives

In lieu of employing an in-house sales force, many middle market manufacturers elect to utilize the services of commission-based salespersons to market their products. The typical manufacturer's representative serves a number of different manufacturers of the same or similar product lines. These individuals are frequently consulted by business owners who have expressed an interest in selling or otherwise terminating their involvement in their businesses. And since they deal with both buyers and sellers of products, they can provide valuable leads on available client companies, as well as companies to which a manufacturer's products are sold.

Management Consultants

Any number of one-time events may cause a business owner to retain the services of a professional consultant. Among the assignments typically handled by these experts are: the preparation of a marketing plan or advertising campaign for a new product or technology; development of a strategy for diversification; or generally to provide objective and unbiased feedback regarding a firm's operations and objectives. Occasionally, a consultant's analysis of a company and the market in which it competes leads to a recommendation that the company be sold or merged. Accordingly, management or other professional consultants can be a useful source of target companies for qualified buyers.

Networker Concerns

A critical factor in establishing effective relationships with networking sources is an appreciation of their concerns in making referrals. While the degree of concern may vary from one group to the next, the major considerations of networking sources fall into three categories: credibility, confidentiality, and compensation.

Credibility. Paramount among these issues is the credibility of the individual or firm to whom relevant information is given. If a professional feels that a referral will in any way harm a client relationship, it is highly unlikely that any referral will be made. Accordingly, would-be acquirers must convince the networking source that they possess not only the financial resources to acquire the target, but also the dealmaking and operational expertise to get the deal done and ensure a smooth post-acquisition operation. First-time dealmakers may need to collaborate with a seasoned acquisition professional in order to develop the credibility that stems from a track record of successful acquisitions.

It is equally important that potential deal sources perceive the buyer's search effort as organized and focused. A buyer who asks to look at "everything" may ultimately see no deals at all. A request to see all deals is often reflective of a mere "window shopping" expedition by an inexperienced and uncommitted buyer. At the outset, therefore, a buyer should devise specific acquisition parameters indicating the size, location, industry, union status, purchase price, product or service of desirable acquisition candidates.

Confidentiality. Publication of the fact that a business owner is seeking to sell can cause extremely harmful results. And the concerns of business owners in this regard will invariably be shared by their professional advisors. Consequently, a networking source will take all steps necessary to ensure that any potential acquirer will appreciate and observe the need for discretion. Aspiring acquirers must be prepared to execute Confidentiality Agreements and to undertake any other measures designed to avoid disclosure of the owner's decision to customers, suppliers and employees of the target company.

Compensation. Since a change in ownership of a business can result in the loss of a client, many professional advisors will not actively assist an owner-client in locating a qualified buyer. Indeed, some advisors may become major impediments to a successful transaction. Delaying the submittal of critical financial information by an accountant or a lender's refusal to allow loan assumptions, are just a couple of the ways in which recalcitrant third parties can extend or completely abort the acquisition process.

Astute acquirers are prepared to address these very real financial concerns of networking sources. Often, an assurance that the new owner will continue the professional relationship will transform an initially uncooperative professional into an active proponent of the transaction.

In some cases, it may directly benefit the referral source to bring a new buyer into the picture. For example, a lender who is nursing a bad loan will usually be more than willing to facilitate the transfer of the business to an owner with greater financial resources.

Direct and Indirect Rewards. Since most networking sources are not in the business of identifying acquisition candidates, one should not anticipate a flow of acquisition prospects immediately following an initial contact. In most cases, networking sources must be cultivated over a course of weeks or months which are marked by regular telephone conversations and written reminders.

The process and the rate of deal flow can also be substantially expedited by converting these basically passive professionals into active deal referral sources. One obvious method of incentivizing referral sources is to offer some form of direct compensation for referrals that lead to consummated transactions. Whether it is an agreed upon percentage of the sale price or a fixed amount, a so-called "finder's fee" usually provides a sufficient monetary incentive for most networking sources. This approach, however, is not always feasible. For example, taking a fee from a buyer for referring his client is not a general practice for a lawyer or accountant. Most would feel compelled to disclose such arrangements to avoid potential conflicts of interest and would be reluctant to do so.

It is also useful to point out other monetary benefits that advisors can derive from the sale of a client's business. For example, a financial planner will often generate fee income by investing the sale proceeds. Assuming they possess the requisite merger and acquisition expertise, the seller's attorney and accountant may perform the legal and tax work necessitated by the transaction. The buyer must remember, however, that the referral source will weigh any fees to be made in a transaction against those which could be earned in a continuing relationship. To the extent that referral sources can be assured of continuing compensation after a change in ownership, they will be motivated to cooperate.

Buyers must not assume that networking will in some way create a magical deal stream. However, a carefully selected and properly incentivized network of professional referral sources can increase the number of acquisition candidates that are made available within a reasonable time frame.

DIRECTLY APPROACHING POTENTIAL SELLERS

The advantage of working through professional intermediaries is that companies brought to the buyer's attention are usually "for sale." Thus, a good part of the search effort — identifying companies for sale — is performed by someone else. Working strictly through professional intermediaries, however, limits the number of potential deals that the buyer can see. This is especially true for first-time buyers who lack the requisite credibility or who are burdened by restrictive criteria. For this reason, many buyers supplement their intermediary sources by contacting referral sources and by directly approaching potential sellers.

The direct approach has been widely used for many years by larger corporations in their search for acquisition candidates. It opens up a much larger universe of potential companies. Howver, it also requires a much longer lead time to find and close a deal. This presents a major problem for the buyer who must complete a deal within a relatively short period of time.

The psychological climate between the buyer and the target company is also different when the direct method is used. Because the owner of the target company usually has not thought seriously about selling before being contacted, he is more likely to be unrealistic in regards to asking price. A great deal of time can be wasted with potential sellers who are not really sellers at all. They are merely curious to see how much someone would be willing to pay. In spite of the negative aspects of the direct approach, it should not be totally rejected by the buyer. All means at one's disposal may be needed to generate deal flow.

The key to an effective direct search program is to develop a list of potential target companies which conform to the buyer's profile. The best starting point for generating such a list is personal contacts — people known to the buyer and who are also willing to share information. Obviously, referral sources are prime candidates. In some cases, these sources are unable or unwilling to directly contact prospective sellers on the buyer's behalf. But they often disclose the names of potential sellers and, in many cases, allow the buyer to use their name in contacting the company. The buyer should also use all industry contacts such as suppliers, creditors, competitors, customers, distributors and dealers. These individuals, especially suppliers, are in the mainstream of information and are often one of the first to know if an owner is contemplating a sale.

Directories and Reference Sources

After exhausting personal contacts, the buyer can further expand his list of companies to contact by consulting various publications. Some of the more important sources include:

- The Encyclopedia of Associations
  A Trade Association list can be an excellent source of company names that are highly specific as to business or industry. This publication lists numerous trade associates and how to contact them for membership lists.
- State Business Directories
  Most states publish annual directories of manufacturing companies headquartered in the state. These directories provide detailed information on the size, ownership, products, and management of profiled companies.
- Local Business Directories
  The Chamber of Commerce for most municipalities publishes a list of all business members and a brief description of the operation and the names of owners or top management.
- The Thomas Register of American Manufacturers
  This comprehensive publication lists companies alphabetically, geographically, by SIC code and gives some indication of asset size.
- Dun & Bradstreet Million Dollar Directory
  This three-volume directory lists public and private companies with a net worth in excess of $500,000. Companies are classified alphabetically, geographically and by SIC code. Approximate annual sales and number of employees is also indicated.
- Dun & Bradstreet Reference Book
  A comprehensive listing of companies listed by state with an indication of relative financial strength.
- Standard & Poor's Register of Corporations, Directors and Executives
  This reference contains a list of public and private companies segregated geographically, alphabetically and by product line. It also contains information on officers, directors, number of employees and years in business.
- Directory of Corporate Affiliations
  An exhaustive listing of all major companies with multiple affiliations. Firms are listed by both parent and subsidiary names with names and addresses of the parent company provided. This directory is an excellent source for potential divestiture candidates.

Computer Data Bases

Most large directories are maintained on electronic databases that can be selectively accessed by buyers in accordance with their acquisition criteria. For example, a buyer may identify all companies in a given 4-digit SIC code with sales in excess of $50 million within a specific geographic region.

Both Dun & Bradstreet and Standard & Poors have large databases of public and private companies that can be accessed in this manner. Although only a small percentage of these companies may be for sale at any given time, it is a very effective way to identify highly targeted, potential acquisition candidates.

Databases of companies which are actually for sale are more difficult to find. Many intermediary firms and larger CPA firms maintain in-house databases, but these are usually limited in scope and available only to clients.

One commercially available database of companies for sale is DealBase™, also published by Business Publications, Inc. It consists of more than 500 companies for sale and is available on a floppy disk (updated bi-monthly) that can be used on IBM compatible PC's or XT's. It also allows the user to selectively search the database for companies that meet specific acquisition criteria.

Making Contact

Once a list has been compiled from various personal and published sources, the most efficient means of contacting the companies is by direct mail. The material sent should be a personal introductory letter along with the selected information from the "buyer's package." After the mailing, the buyer may want to conduct a selective telephone follow-up campaign.

Another method of directly contacting potential sellers is to place an ad in the classified section of a financial or trade publication. *The Wall Street Journal,* which emphasizes business opportunity ads on Thursday of each week, is probably the best medium for such advertising.

Regardless of how the buyer chooses to directly access potential sellers, it must be remembered that this method takes longer and is less efficient than indirect methods. In this approach the buyer is performing many of the tasks normally handled by a professional intermediary. If it is employed, the direct approach should not be used exclusively, but in conjunction with attempts to generate deal flow on an indirect basis.

DEVISING THE SEARCH STRATEGY

A buyer's initial objective is to personally contact or get a buyer's package in the hands of individuals who control, represent or know of businesses available for purchase. These individuals may be directly involved with the company as owners or high level employees, or they may be indirectly involved as professional intermediaries, advisors, consultants or bankers. Although most buyers utilize both a direct and indirect approach in contacting sources of potential deals, the emphasis and manner of the specific type of approach will depend upon a number of strategic factors related to the background and circumstances of the buyer.

Before embarking on a marketing program, the buyer is well advised to consider several factors, a few of which have been touched upon in Chapter 2. Perhaps the most important of these considerations are the time and financial resources available to the buyer for conducting the search. A buyer who is tied down to a full-time job in the West has little reason to contact deal sources in the East or Midwest unless they also have access to western deals. Time constraints usually preclude the consideration of deals located too far away. Likewise, limited financial resources may rule out deal contacts that will result in substantial travel expenses. For this buyer, the best strategic approach to the search is to contact local or regional intermediaries and companies by direct mail and to follow up these initial overtures by personal visits where feasible.

Another very important factor which dictates search strategy is the buyer's particular background. Unless the buyer has a distinguished track record in a corporate operating environment or has previously closed buyouts involving incumbent management, gaining access to corporate sellers may be extremely difficult. This difficulty stems from the fact that the larger investment banking firms usually function as intermediaries in such deals. These firms, as well as the selling corporations themselves, usually prefer to deal only with the professional or high level corporate executive buyer. If the small, less-known private buyer sees any corporate spin-offs, they are usually smaller, troubled units that the larger, more sophisticated buyers have already rejected. Similarly, deals in which public companies "go private" are usually so large and complex that only the highly sophisticated professional investment group or investor/operator can put them together.

For these reasons, the first-time investor or entrepreneurial buyer is usually restricted to the private seller as his universe of potential deals. In his efforts to find a deal, therefore, this type of buyer should emphasize those professional intermediaries which specialize in the sale of private companies. He should also utilize other indirect referral sources who are in contact with potential private sale situations as well as direct contacts to the companies themselves.

Two additional factors directly influencing the search strategy are (1) the degree to which the buyout or acquisition criteria have been defined in the target company profile and (2) the time available to the buyer to complete the acquisition. A precisely defined set of criteria and ample time to close a deal frequently result in a more specific acquisition search procedure which emphasizes direct contacts with target companies. This procedure is often utilized by the small to medium-sized corporate buyer that has a stable cash flow and wants a target company with specific features to complement its own operation. A more broadly defined set of criteria or time constraints, on the other hand, will dictate a more general acquisition search procedure. This approach emphasizes the utilization of indirect contacts to gain access to companies that are, officially or unofficially, "on the market." The general approach is more appropriate for the private buyer who has limitations on the amount of time that can be expended in pursuing a deal.

Since the process of directly approaching prospective companies is costly and time consuming, the indirect approach is the method selected by most buyers to generate prospective deals. This technique involves the use of third parties as the initial contact point between the buyer and seller. These individuals are most often professional intermediaries whose income is primarily derived from fees charged for bringing a buyer and seller together. Involved to a lesser extent in this process are the so-called referral sources — individuals who have a client relationship with the seller.

5

QUALIFYING THE COMPANY

WHEN THE DEALS START TO FLOW

The buyer, unless he is an incumbent manager of the target company, must be prepared to invest substantial time and effort in searching out potential leveraged buyout candidates. But, if the suggestions outlined in the previous chapter are followed, his investment will begin to pay off. Within a month or two, the buyer's network of contacts will grow and ultimately he will begin to see some deal flow.

A "deal" is a package of information on a company enabling buyer to determine if the acquisition opportunity is worth pursuing. It can range from a very comprehensive, professionally prepared "investment memorandum" to a set of financial statements with a brief description of the business. It all depends upon the source who exposed the deal to the buyer and their relationship to the seller.

Information Required

Although the deal package need not be extensive or elaborate, it should contain enough basic information to enable the buyer to ask intelligent questions of the deal source (usually a professional intermediary). This includes:

- A balance sheet for the latest fiscal year.
- Income statements for the last three fiscal years.
- Interim financial statements (if more than three months have passed since the fiscal year-end).
- Product literature, brochures, etc., or other material that provides some insight on the target company's basic business.

Of course, it is easier to qualify the deal if more detailed information is provided. And, in fact, most professionally prepared packages do include additional facts such as market data, analysis of competition, union contract information, etc. However, the buyer should not mistakenly believe that a real deal must be wrapped in an elaborate package. Additional facts can be gathered later in the dealmaking process. The key, at this point, is to determine if the proposed buyout candidate makes "the first cut."

Use Time Judiciously

To make the process as efficient as possible, it is extremely important for the buyer to take a disciplined approach to allocating his time. With the exception of the hard-earned capital he will ultimately invest in the buyout, time is probably the buyer's most precious resource. To waste it on deals that have little or no chance of closing is counter-productive in several respects. The most tangible effect is that it precludes the buyer from pursuing other companies that are more logical and realistic leveraged buyout candidates. But it can also have a significant negative psychological impact when, after investing a a great deal of time and effort (and sometimes money for professional fees), the buyer ends up with an empty hand.

This is not to suggest that buyers can foresee at an early stage every possible event or circumstance that will cause a deal to "blow up." There are many unpredictable occurrences that can cause even the best-appearing deals to abort. So a certain amount of wasted time and lost opportunity are an inevitable consequence of the acquisition process. The key, at this stage, is to avoid those situations that clearly are "high risk" from a time investment perspective.

HOW TO TELL IF A DEAL IS DOABLE

The initial qualification of prospective leveraged buyouts is a critical juncture in the overall process of buying a company. If it is carried out objectively and methodically, the buyer will improve his odds and shorten the time required to close the deal. His goal is to quickly eliminate those candidates, which for one reason or another, have little chance of ever closing. Or, to look at it another way, the buyer must pursue only doable deals.

The Five Marks of a Doable Deal

This can be accomplished by looking objectively at each deal package and asking the following questions:

- Does the target company generally conform to the "buyer's profile"? (As described in Chapter 2.)
- Does the company appear to have a strategically viable business?
- Is the seller really motivated to sell?
- Are the seller's price expectations "reasonable" and consistent with the anticipated financing strategy?
- Can the proposed buyout be financed?

If the answer is "yes" to the above questions, there is little doubt that the deal should be pursued. However, it may be difficult to get unequivocal "yes" answers to these questions at this stage. Most often the answer will be a tentative "maybe." On the other hand, if one or more of these questions can be answered with a certain "no," the buyer may be better off spending his time continuing the search rather than chasing a deal that, at least on the surface, does not appear to be doable.

Before doing anything, however, the buyer must make an all-out attempt to answer the above qualifying questions as completely and objectively as possible. How can this be done at such an early stage when he has limited information on the business and has yet to make direct contact with the seller? To answer this question it is necessary to take a closer look at each of the qualifying characteristics and how to assess them at this juncture.

Conformity With Buyer Criteria

The first order of business is for the buyer to determine if the deal "fits." If his criteria have been properly defined at the outset, this should not be a difficult problem. He may discover, however, that the criteria are too specific, resulting in a high rate of rejection. If this is the case, it may be necessary to relax some of the requirements, at least in the early stages of the search when there are not many deals from which to choose.

If the buyer does relax some of his criteria, he must guard against being so general that deal sources will not respond at all. And, of course, they must be realistic. No purpose is served by increasing the flow of deals that never have a chance of closing in the first place.

A buyer will quickly learn, however, that many intermediaries fail to carefully read a tendered profile and will send non-conforming deals. Where this occurs, and there is a substantial inconsistency between the criteria and the parameters of the deal, the buyer should not waste time dealing with it. Instead, the intermediary or referral source should be notified of the disparity between the deal and the criteria defined in the profile. This will serve the dual purpose of enhancing the relationship with intermediary or referral source and ensuring more qualified deals in the future.

Viability of the Business

If satisfied that the prospective company meets his personal criteria, the buyer's next consideration is the viability of the business itself. If it is acquired, the company will represent a substantial investment of the buyer's time as well as money. Therefore, the business should have a good chance of succeeding and generating a return commensurate with the risk.

Admittedly, it is difficult to answer this important question with such limited information and, perhaps, some preliminary briefing with the source of the deal. And one might correctly argue that these issues are better dealt with during the buyer's due diligence (Chapter 9). While it is true that the detailed evaluation of the target company should uncover any inherent weaknesses of the business, the buyer can save much time and trouble if major flaws are discovered earlier. If so, time that would have been wasted on due diligence can be better spent on more qualified prospects.

The key issue is the company's *strategic viability.* Is it in an industry or market where it can survive with a heavy debt load? Is it vulnerable to competition, especially from abroad, from companies with more favorable cost advantages? Does it have a "niche" of its own that offers a safe harbor from competition? These and other questions should be discussed with the source of the deal, who should know more about the company's business. The financial information submitted to the buyer should also be compared with others in the same industry.

In the effort to "weed out" the strategically questionable target companies, buyers must guard against the tendency to look for the perfect deal. The deal without any flaws may exist, but it will probably take forever to find it. The key is to avoid those fatal flaws, problems that call to question whether the business, in in the long run, can survive. This requires judgment on the part of the buyer, and it may be difficult at this early stage to make an intelligent assessment. But, at the very least, the buyer should begin to ask himself these important questions.

Seller Motivation

The issue of seller motivation will be discussed in detail in the next chapter

(Qualifying the Seller). And, although it may be difficult to determine the level of seller motivation without looking him in the eye, the buyer should ask the same questions of the deal source that he would ask the seller when and if they meet.

By identifying half-hearted sellers early in the game, buyers can save themselves a great deal of time, trouble and expense. More importantly, if the seller is truly motivated, the issue of price becomes less of a stumbling block.

Seller's Price Expectations

It is important for the buyer to establish, as early as possible, what the seller expects for his business without making it a major issue. This is particularly important to the leveraged buyer, who has some financial constraints on how much money can be borrowed. In most cases, the seller has set an "asking price" for the company that is communicated to the buyer when he receives the initial package from the source of the deal.

If price has not been established, it is not good news for the buyer. It either indicates the seller is conducting a "controlled auction," or he has not seriously thought through the key issue of selling the company — how much is it worth? This type of seller may be on a "fishing trip" to find out how much buyers are willing to pay rather than making a sincere attempt to sell the company. Experienced buyers often say the only thing worse than an "overpriced" deal is a deal without a price.

As important as price is, some buyers focus too much on what the seller wants rather than why he wants it. Ultimately, if the seller has a good reason to sell and is truly motivated to do so, the market will determine the price. Therefore, the buyer, in discussing price with the deal source (or later with the seller himself), should direct his questions at the seller's real motivations and not get drawn into arguments that "the price is too high." Such discussions are counterproductive, resulting in a polarization of attitudes between the buyer, the seller, and the intermediary; and inhibit any real dialogue.

In the final analysis, the buyer must make a judgment call on the basis of the facts available to him at the present time. If it appears that the seller is firm in his price expectations and is in no hurry to sell, the buyer must objectively assess the value of the company (see Chapter 10) and the feasibility of financing the buyout. If the premium is too high or there is a significant financing shortfall, the buyer should "pass" on the deal. On the other hand, if the seller is highly motivated and the financing gap not too wide, the buyer should take the next step to work out the differences.

Steps to Determine Financing Feasibility

As most of the money used to pay the seller will be borrowed against the assets or cash flow of the target company, it is important to determine very early if the necessary financing can be raised. For this reason, it is imperative that the buyer receives financial statements that describe the company's asset base and historical cash flows in sufficient detail. Without this information the buyer is unable to answer any of the key questions in his efforts to qualify the deal.

The systematic procedure for determining financial feasibility is described in detail in Chapter 11 ("Structuring the Deal"), but is summarized here:

- Determine the maximum amount of equity capital that can be invested by the buyer and his immediate investment group.
- Determine the difference between the estimated selling price and this amount of equity capital. The difference represents the "financing gap," the approximate amount of funds that must be raised from outside sources.
- Based upon the evaluation of the company's historical financial statements, estimate the approximate amount of senior debt that can be borrowed against the assets from a secured lender or against the cash flow from unsecured lenders.
- Determine the difference between the total "financing gap" and the amount of senior debt. This difference represents the additional capital that must be raised from either subordinated debt or equity sources.

The above exercise will indicate how much financing can be raised and the extent of any shortfall. If the gap is significant, the buyer may be better off moving on to the next deal, unless the deal source has indicated that the seller is prepared to finance some portion of the acquisition as a subordinated lender or the business is unusually attractive.

FINANCING CRITERIA

In assessing the financial feasibility of the proposed buyout, the buyer must see the deal through the eyes of the lender. The lender's perspective is described in greater detail in Chapter 12 and should be studied before seriously attempting to determine how much money can be borrowed. At this point, however, it will be helpful to the buyer in his effort to qualify the leveraged buyout candidates if he is aware of the key criteria that lenders look for in financing deals. Not all businesses are appropriate candidates for a leveraged buyout or acquisition. The burden of a substantial amount of debt is often too much for certain types of companies or industries. The leverageable company has certain unique characteristics that make it attractive to the buyer. In the preliminary evaluation of prospective deals, these characteristics, and their impact on the financeability of the company, should be considered.

Strong Balance Sheet

If significant cash proceeds are to go to the seller rather than to existing short-term lenders or trade creditors, the target company must have a relatively strong balance sheet. Its assets should consist of tangible liquid assets that are unencumbered so they can serve as collateral for the new secured lenders. If the assets are not to be secured, the new lenders and institutional investors will require unencumbered assets prior to the acquisition so that the target company's income is sufficient to service the new debt.

Limited liabilities is another characteristic of a strong balance sheet. New lenders, as a general rule, do not like to take out existing lenders. To the extent that they are required do so, there is less cash available for the seller or more cash must be invested by the buyer, both of which reduce the attractiveness of the deal to the respective parties. It is also imperative that trade credit not be out of proportion or overly "stretched" prior to the acquisition. If trade credit is excessive or "aged," there will be additional working capital requirements for the company.

Leveraged acquisitions are sometimes possible if the company is already substantially in debt. These, however, are usually special situations or workouts that may or may not involve the participation of new lenders and/or investors. Since the leverage is already in place, there is little cash available for the seller, unless the buyer commits additional equity. For the seller to take little or no cash up front, there must be a real need perceived by the seller or existing lender for the buyer's expertise or subsequent contributions to working capital. These turnaround or workout situations only make sense if there are clear solutions to the underlying problems and the buyer has sufficient expertise to implement them.

Asset-Based Companies

It will be seen in Chapters 11 and 12 that many leveraged deals are financed by asset-based lenders. To attract the interest of such lenders, the assets not only must be unencumbered, but must also constitute attractive collateral. This means that their values must be readily documented, and they can be quickly liquidated for their loan values.

The preferred assets for most secured lenders are accounts receivable with a good collection history. Ironically, while lenders like fast collecting receivables, buyers prefer high quality but slower moving receivables that can be collected faster with improved collection procedures after the deal is closed. This can be an important source of working capital for the new owner.

Inventory is not as appealing an asset to lenders because of its lower liquidity and more volatile swings in value. The particular class of inventory is also important, with raw materials and finished goods having more collateral value than work-in-process.

Fixed assets, such as machinery, equipment and real estate are more difficult to finance because of the lack of liquidity. However, lenders are more willing to advance funds on fixed assets that are general purpose in nature and have a well defined and liquid market. Companies with "hidden asset values" are particularly appealing to the leveraged buyer. Hidden asset values occur when the book value of a company is substantially below the current replacement value of its assets. This may occur when plant and equipment assets have been written off at an accelerated rate or the replacement cost of the asset has increased substantially. In such cases, most or all of the purchase price can be financed, provided it is not a substantial premium over book value.

Consistent Cash Flow

While the composition of the balance sheet will play a large part in qualifying a prospective leveraged deal, of equal importance is the company's historical earnings performance. Because of the significant amount of new leverage that will be in place after the acquisition, the earnings and cash flow from operations must be both sufficient and consistent to service the debt.

The key number that leveraged buyers — and lenders — look for is "operating cash flow." This is defined as earnings before interest and taxes (EBIT) plus any depreciation and amortization. Using this as a base cash flow, the buyer should then measure the impact of any new capital expenditures or working capital requirements on the target company's ability to generate a consistent cash stream to service the new debt.

For this reason, highly cyclical businesses are not good candidates for leveraged buyouts or acquisitions. If deals of this type are considered, the debt must be structured to allow for periodic contractions in earnings. This may be in the form of revolving credit lines which will cover advances in excess of a specified figure, or moratoriums on principal payments.

Mundane Product Lines

One of the consequences of utilizing substantial leverage in an acquisition is that most of the company's cash flow must service the debt. This means that little cash remains for working capital and research and development expenditures. For this reason, businesses that are growing very rapidly or are engaged in high technology are not good LBO candidates. Rapid growth requires large infusions of working capital for increased receivables, inventory and productive capacity. High technology products often have a high obsolescence factor, thus requiring a constant infusion of new capital for research and development. In addition, because of the high obsolescence factor, these products are often not attractive as collateral to lenders.

Both of these demands on capital are avoided or minimized when the target company has mundane product lines. Such products have a slow but steady growth rate and are not subject to rapid technological obsolescence. Concerns producing such lines are therefore able to commit most of their cash flow to service acquisition debt.

Low Capital Intensity

Another extraordinary call on capital exists in companies that require sizable regular commitments of capital equipment funds to maintain their competitive position. Leveraging is most appropriate where such expenditures are low and productive machinery and equipment have long, useful economic lives.

One factor that the buyer must be aware of is the impact of impending technological changes on the competitive position of the target company's capital equipment. If new technology makes available more productive equipment, the company's ability to compete may be impaired and there may be substantial new capital requirements to mainain the company's competitive position. These issues are usually covered during the due diligence phase, but it doesn't hurt to ask questions early.

Dominant or "Niche" Positions

Another characteristic that the leveraged buyer should be looking for in a prospective company is a dominant position in the market in which it competes. This principle is true whether the target serves a local, regional, national or international market. Since the company is exposed to the financial risk of leverage, it should have some control over its destiny in the marketplace. Companies with dominant positions in a fragmented industry or at least a second position in a concentrated industry generally have a greater degree of control. Such companies are usually price leaders or have sufficient economies of scale to remain competitive without too much erosion of profit margins.

If the company is not a market leader, it is essential that it have a protective "niche" in the market — something it does better and/or cheaper than its competition. This could be a proprietary product or process, well-established marketing or distribution channels or anything that would be both difficult and expensive for competition to replicate.

IS IT QUALIFIED?

After answering the key qualification questions, a buyer should have a preliminary indication of price, value and leverageability of the company. If the pieces of the puzzle fit, the deal has passed the test of preliminary qualification and should be taken to the next step. If they do not, no further time should be expended. And a buyer who elects to proceed further should be very cautious about how much time is invested.

The buyer should realize that the preliminary qualification step is only the first of many attempts to qualify the company as a doable deal. It should be viewed as the first of several "filters" or "screens" through which each deal must pass before the buyer arrives at the final destination: the closing.

Buyers must understand that acquiring a company is a very dynamic undertaking which is subject to sudden and unexpected changes. Today's "hot prospect" may be tomorrow's addition to the "dead deal" file. Therefore, it is imperative that the buyer continually ask the question: "What are the chances of this deal closing?"

If the buyer can now objectively say that the chances are "reasonably good" that deal will close, he is prepared to take the next important step — meeting with and qualifying the seller. If not, he should continue his quest for the "right" deal.

6

QUALIFYING THE SELLER

MOTIVATING THE SELLER TO MEET
Role of the Intermediary

PURPOSE OF THE MEETING
Establishing Personal Rapport With the Seller
Enhancing the Buyer's Credibility
Qualifying the Seller
Confirming the Viability of the Business
Confirming the Financial Feasibility of the Deal

IS IT TIME TO NEGOTIATE?

MOVE ON OR MOVE OUT?

The buyer now has identified a company that, at least on the surface, appears to warrant a further investment of his time. The company has the necessary characteristics required of a viable leveraged buyout candidate. These include the following:

- It is consistent with the buyer's criteria.
- It has the necessary business and financial attributes to generate interest among financing sources.
- There is a reasonable relationship between the seller's "asking price," the financing that can be raised, and the buyer's own financial resources.

Although he has made a great deal of progress, the buyer is by no means within grasp of his ultimate goal — a successful closing. There are additional filters through which the prospective LBO candidate must pass before the mission is accomplished. One of the most important is the next step — qualifying the seller.

Until now, the buyer has been making his assessment of prospective acquisitions on the basis of written material, historical financial data, and, perhaps, verbal discussion with a third party such as an intermediary or referral source. Unless he has made a "direct approach," which is an unusual practice in searching for LBO's, the buyer has not had any direct contact with the seller. Obviously, for any deal to move forward, there must be a personal encounter between the principals on each side of the transaction. In our journey through the LBO process, that time has come.

The buyer's initial meeting with the seller is one of the most important events in the entire dealmaking process. Obviously, it is an opportunity for the buyer to further qualify the business and the seller's reason for making it available. The meeting also marks the beginning of a relationship, the success of which will have a significant bearing on whether a deal is consummated. In almost all cases, a seller will only sell his company to someone whom he respects. It should, therefore, be one of the buyer's primary objectives to cultivate a positive relationship with the seller. This process begins when the two parties meet face-to-face for the first time.

MOTIVATING THE SELLER TO MEET

Just because the buyer decides that the time has come to take a closer look at the target company does not insure that the seller will agree to meet with him. Like any businessman, potential sellers have busy schedules and strive to make the best use of their time. Visits by and meetings with prospective buyers take time and often distract the owner and his key employees from other important tasks. And if the buyer is totally unqualified, meeting with him is a total waste of the seller's time.

For these reasons, sellers — and especially the intermediaries who represent them — are very selective about which buyers they will agree to meet. Just as the buyer attempts to screen out unqualified sellers, the same process is occuring in the other direction. Buyers must be aware of this desire of the seller to be selective and be prepared to deal with it.

Role of the Intermediary

In our discussion on how to work effectively with intermediaries (Chapter 4), it was noted that one of their primary functions is to screen out unqualified buyers. This is in his best interest as the absence of unqualified buyers improves both his chance of closing the deal and his credibility with the seller. Therefore, if the particular deal under consideration has come to the buyer through an intermediary, it is highly probable that the buyer has already proven his qualifications or he wouldn't have seen the deal in the first place. However, some intermediaries may review the buyer's qualifications more closely when a visit with the seller is requested because more is at stake.

In cases where the buyer meets resistance from the intermediary — or the seller himself — to arrange an initial meeting, the root cause is that either one or both are not totally convinced of the buyer's qualifications. Lingering in their minds are two basic unanswered questions:

- Does the buyer have the necessary financial resources to complete the transaction?
- In the absence of a successful track record of closing prior deals, how can I (the seller) be assured that the buyer has the necessary expertise to close the deal?

As discussed in earlier chapters, even inexperienced buyers can take steps to alleviate these real concerns on the part of deal sources and company owners. Ignoring them will only reduce any chances of taking the next key step — meeting the seller.

PURPOSE OF THE MEETING

Assuming he is able to arrange an initial meeting with the seller, the buyer should have five specific objectives firmly in mind:

- Establish personal rapport with the seller.
- Enhance his credibility as a qualified buyer.
- Qualify the seller as a true seller.
- Further qualify the viability of the business.
- Confirm his ability to finance the deal.

Establishing Personal Rapport With the Seller

Only rarely will the seller who is not under a great deal of pressure to sell make a deal with a buyer he doesn't like and respect. This does not mean that the parties must agree on every point involved in the transaction. A buyer and seller often have strong differences of opinion on various aspects of the target company's operations. During the early stages of the relationship, however, the buyer should make every effort to avoid conflicts with the seller. Emphasis should be placed upon building a rapport based upon mutual respect. A buyer who is on good terms with the seller will substantially improve his chances of closing the transaction.

There are several rules to follow to get the relationship with the seller off on the right foot. First, the buyer must remember the meeting is not a stage to openly boast of his past accomplishments. Certainly, he wants to increase the seller's confidence in his ability to perform. However, this can be done in a professional manner which clearly conveys these abilities without being boastful. The buyer's ego, at all times, should be subordinate to that of the seller. This is accomplished by listening rather than talking. The private seller should be given center stage to "toot his horn" about how he built this company. In the case of corporate sellers, the conversation should be focused on corporate goals and their relationship to the proposed divestiture, and how the spin-off will benefit both concerns.

The buyer should also take every opportunity to compliment the seller on the positive features of the business. This does not mean false, lavish praise when it is not deserved. People can see right through such facades. But, if the company has a nice, well-kept facility, a modern new computer installation, or courteous employees, the buyer should not be reluctant to mention these features. A sincere compliment will make the seller feel better about himself, the company, and the buyer. Remember, few sellers — especially private sellers — ever sell their company to buyers they don't like.

Many inexperienced buyers do exactly the opposite of what they should. They feel the only way to make a good impression is to tell the seller, in no uncertain terms, how smart they are. Fearing that complimenting the seller will make it more difficult to negotiate later, these buyers take the opposite approach by making derogatory comments about certain aspects of the business. This, they believe, will help to "soften up" the seller's expectations on price, when in reality, all it does is antagonize him. It is little wonder, then, that for buyers using this heavy-handed approach, the first visit is also the last.

Enhancing the Buyer's Credibility

While establishing meaningful rapport with the seller or his representatives is an important step, it means nothing if the seller is not also convinced that the buyer can perform. Of course, if the seller didn't believe this, the meeting would have never been held in the first place. But the buyer should clearly understand that one of the seller's primary objectives during the meeting is to further qualify him and his ability to close.

The question in the seller's mind is the same as before: Does this buyer have the money and the expertise to close the deal? How does the buyer handle this in the most diplomatic and effective manner? To answer these questions, it is necessary to address each of the two major issues — money and expertise — separately.

On the matter of financial resources, this concern is most easily handled by flashing a fat financial statement overflowing with liquid assets. However, not all buyers are flush with funds. But they do have excellent operating management credentials. These skills often serve as excellent "collateral" to LBO financing sources who are seeking to wed their money with outstanding operating management skills. The only missing link is a qualified target company. In such cases, the cash poor, but talented buyer can establish working relationships with LBO financing sources. The difficulty with this approach is the "chicken/egg" syndrome in establishing meaningful relationships with financing sources. Most are reluctant to talk unless there is a real deal. But, by using persistence and finesse, the buyer can develop sufficient financial reference sources to overcome this problem with the seller.

The other question — buyer expertise — is less of an issue. Obviously, if the buyer has already closed one or more transactions, he has instant credibility. Even if he has no prior track record, the buyer can overcome seller concerns by conducting himself properly. By asking the right questions and taking the proper steps at the appropriate times, the buyer looks as if he knows what he is doing. This will enhance his credibility in the seller's eyes.

Qualifying the Seller

After establishing rapport and credibility with the seller, the buyer's next task is to determine the depth of his motivation to sell the company. Since private and corporate sellers have such different characteristics, they are discussed separately as to how the buyer can best qualify their real intent.

Qualifying the Private Seller. One reality the buyer must face is that not all sellers are *real* sellers. Unfortunately, the *real* sellers don't wear labels or business suits of a certain color to mark their identity. Initially, all sellers look and even talk alike. But the intelligent buyer can — and must — subjectively evaluate the motivations of the seller to determine if he is the real thing or a charlatan.

To accomplish this, the buyer must understand, before he ever has his initial encounter, that the seller fits into one of the following categories:

- *Non-sellers* — Those who say the company is for sale, but either have no intention of doing so or have placed an unrealistically high price or conditions on the deal.
- *Nervous sellers* — Those who think they want to sell and have valid reasons for doing so, but have yet to face up to the consequences if it really happens.
- *Real sellers* — Those who have a valid reason for selling and are prepared — even eager — to accept the consequences of the deal closing.

It should be one of the buyer's primary objectives in the first meeting to determine which one of the above categories best describes his seller. He must assess, at the gut level, the specific motivations of the seller and, more important, the intensity of these motivations.

It was noted in Chapter 3 that the sale of his company by a private owner can be one of the most traumatic events in his lifetime. It is understandable, therefore, that the private seller might have some feelings of ambivalence during the process of selling the company. However, the buyer must objectively assess whether the seller's true motivations are strong enough to overcome the inevitable feelings of remorse that occur as the transaction proceeds. He must carefully review all of the personal and business reasons for selling and zero in on those most relevant for this seller. Only after he has carefully questioned — and listened to — the seller's response, will the buyer be able to make a sound judgment as to the depth of his motivation.

The buyer should first ask the seller very directly why he wants to sell. Depending upon the response, the buyer should follow up with a series of questions. The answers to which will confirm the stated purpose of the sale or raise questions as to its authenticity. For example, if the seller states that the "desire to retire" is the real reason for selling, the buyer should ask the following additional questions:

- "How do you plan to spend your time after retirement? (A vague response is a good indication that the seller hasn't given this too much thought and may change his mind as the closing approaches.)
- "What is your timetable for completing the sale? (Lack of a crystalized timetable often means the seller has yet to accept the reality of releasing the company and may yet change his mind.)

This method of selective questioning is not foolproof. Some private owners are totally convinced that they should sell and have valid reasons for doing so. They may even go through all the motions of selling — listing with an intermediary, meeting with buyers, even verbally agreeing to deal at his price. As the day approaches when the contract must be signed, intense feelings of "seller's remorse" begin to up well inside him. The reality finally hits and these would-be sellers realize that by signing they will relinquish control of the company to which their lives have been committed. What will they do with their time? Where will they go the morning after the deal closes? After contemplating this unsettling prospect, many sellers elect to cancel the deal. This is one of the inherent risks of the deal business. But it is a risk that can be controlled if the buyer proceeds with intelligence and caution in qualifying the private seller.

Qualifying the Corporate Seller. Corporate sellers, by definition, are less complex and emotional than private sellers. They are usually motivated by strategic and economic considerations rather than by a mixture of personal, family, and financial factors. The decision to sell is made on the basis of specific, current economic needs or strategic aims designed to satisfy earnings, cash flow, and operational requirements. At times, there may be factions within the company that oppose a particular sale and may even try to kill the deal. This typically occurs when a senior manager involved in the divestiture formerly managed the subsidiary targeted for sale. In some management buyout situations, there may be jealousy of the buyout group among the corporate staff. But these are, for the most part, isolated incidents and only slow the deal process down rather than kill it.

As was pointed out in Chapter 3, the dramatic increase in divestiture activity in recent years has led to more control of these deals by prominent investment banking firms. Because of the heavy interest in divestitures from many LBO investors, the investment bankers have utilized the "sealed bid auction" method to sell the company. To some extent this has made the process of interfacing with corporate sellers much more regimented and reduces the importance of personal chemistry in dealing with corporate sellers. In many cases, buyers will not be invited to bid on the company, because in the eyes of the investment banker, they are not qualified.

In spite of these changes in some of the larger divestiture transactions, the corporate seller, when accessible, is much easier to figure out. The decision to sell is made at high levels and conforms with long-range corporate strategic and financial goals. These decisions are usually tied to a specific timetable (e.g., the fiscal year-end or quarter) so that a public announcement of the sale can be made. Unlike the private seller, the corporate seller is working against a natural deadline and is thus forced to respond more quickly to inquiries concerning price, terms, and conditions.

The bottom line is that most corporate sellers are prequalified. The buyer's most difficult assignment is to gain access to this class of seller through the rather small, exclusive group of investment banking intermediaries that control this segment of the market.

Confirming the Viability of the Business

In addition to establishing a relationship with the seller and determining the depth of his commitment to selling the company, the initial visit is an opportunity to confirm the viability of the business itself. This does not require a detailed analysis of the operation. However, in his discussions with the seller, the buyer should ask pertinent questions regarding the past, present, and future operating results of the company.

These questions should be asked in a friendly, non-threatening manner within the context of the primary purpose of the meeting — getting to know each other. An excellent question to ask the private seller is: "How did your company get started in this business?" This will give the seller the opportunity to boast about accomplishments and, at the same time, provide the buyer with a much better feel for the business. Another question designed to get the seller to embellish on accomplishments is: "What have been the most significant events or decisions in the history of this company?"

To draw out the potential trouble spots of the business, the buyer might inquire: "What have been the greatest difficulties you have encountered in building this company to its present size?" Although future problems are not necessarily the same as past problems, the response may provide some insights into the company's potential. Another question which will give some indication of the needs of the business is: "How can new working capital be most effectively used in the company's operations?"

Aside from a tour of the facility and an initial look at the company's assets, the buyer will want to "inspect" the human resources. The seller's impressions of the key people will provide some clues as to the depth of management talent. In some cases it may be appropriate to have preliminary discussions with key managers as to their role in the proposed buyout, including future equity participation. However, it is best not to get too specific at this point since the buyer knows little about management's capabilities, financial resources, or motivations.

Confirming the Financial Feasibility of the Deal

In his first meeting with the seller, the buyer's final objective is to confirm his initial assumptions on how much cash can be generated from borrowings related to the target company's assets or cash flow. If the purchase is to be structured as an "unsecured" transaction (see Chapter 11), the potential borrowings will be determined primarily by cash flow criteria which are not ascertainable until the due diligence process is completed. If, on the other hand, the deal is to be structured as a "secured" transaction, this meeting is an excellent opportunity to determine the financeability of the company's asset base. The buyer should especially observe the physical assets such as real estate, machinery and equipment, as well as the firm's inventory.

The buyer should make this inspection for the purpose of answering the following questions:

- How is the inventory allocated among raw materials, work-in-process, and finished goods?
- Is there a substantial amount of old or potentially obsolete inventory?
- Is the real estate general purpose in nature?
- What is its approximate age?
- Is it located in an attractive neighborhood?
- How old is the machinery and equipment?
- Is it readily usable by other businesses (and therefore more marketable and leverageable) or is it highly specialized and single-purpose in nature?
- Are there more recent models of the equipment which are substantially more productive?
- What is the current replacement value and market value of the equipment?
- Is there a significant amount of deferred maintenance?
- Does the seller have any recent appraisals?

The answers to these and similar questions discussed in Chapter 12 will assist the buyer in estimating the amount of funds that can be borrowed against the target company's assets. These answers will also have a significant impact on the financial feasibility of the deal and the manner in which it can be structured.

Inventory often becomes the most controversial asset when valuing or financing a business. Most businesses have some slow-moving or obsolete inventory which will negatively affect value. Depending upon the particular industry, each company will have a different mix of raw material, work-in-process, and finished goods inventory. The buyer should emerge from this meeting with a much clearer idea of the value of the inventory, its allocation among the various classifications, and the consequences on loan advance rates.

Confirming the viability and his ability to finance the deal are very important steps for the buyer. If the initial visit uncovers significant problems with the business or a questionable asset base to support financing requirements, he must face the reality that this may not be a feasible transaction. Once this determination is made, it is far better to pull out and utilize his time pursuing a stronger deal than to attempt to make a weak one work.

IS IT TIME TO NEGOTIATE?

One might expect the issue of negotiations to be high on the buyer's agenda for his initial encounter with the seller. Yet, it is conspicuous by its absence on the list of objectives to be accomplished at the first meeting. This is not to suggest that negotiating an acceptable price is not important, for it certainly is the central issue in every transaction. Why, then, avoid any discussions about this most important topic?

First of all, the buyer should not avoid the issue of price if it appears to be a major stumbling block in the deal. It can be an effective means to flush out the "non-sellers," i.e., those who have set unrealistically high valuations on their companies, from real sellers. However, if the subject of price is discussed, it should be done *after* the buyer has achieved his other primary objectives, particularly in qualifying the seller as to *real* the reasons — and intensity of his motivations — for selling. After all, if an owner has a good reason for selling and is highly motivated to do so, price will be dictated by the marketplace and does not usually become a major issue.

It is also assumed that the buyer has determined some idea of the seller's expectations during the process of qualifying the feasibility of the deal. If these expectations are excessive and there is no indication of flexibility, the buyer has no business visiting with the seller in the first place. It is not a doable deal and the buyer should be spending his time elsewhere. If price has not been previously discussed, it is appropriate to bring it up at the initial meeting, but again, after the other objectives have been accomplished.

In some cases, the seller may not have yet established an asking price. This is not a healthy situation, because it means the seller has not really crystallized his thinking on how much he can reasonably expect if the company is sold. No matter how much he gets, it may not be enough. Such situations may be a sign that the seller really isn't a seller at all; more likely he's on a "fishing trip" to find out what his company is worth. In such cases, the buyer should carefully qualify the seller's real motivations.

Some inexperienced buyers make the common mistake of placing price negotiations in front of all other issues in the first meeting. They rationalize that by "softening up" the seller on price, it will be possible to extract a more favorable deal. This is counterproductive because it creates a strong adversarial relationship even before the two have a chance to get to know each other. Opening the relationship with conflict destroys any chances of building communication bridges through which they can ultimately resolve any real differences. In the end, this approach diminishes whatever chances there are of completing a transaction.

If the seller's asking price is "in the ballpark" and he appears to be genuinely motivated, serious negotiations are best left to a future date. This should be *after* the buyer has conducted his preliminary due diligence and has gotten some preliminary feedback from his financing sources. The timing and tactics of negotiations are discussed in more detail in Chapter 7 ("Orchestrating the Deal") and in Chapter 14 ("Negotiating and Closing the Deal").

MOVE ON OR MOVE OUT?

At the completion of his initial meeting with the seller, the buyer must make a very important decision — whether or not to pursue the deal. This decision should be based upon consideration of all the factors related to the feasibility of the proposed buyout. The following questions should be answered objectively:

- Based upon the information now available, does the company justify the ultimate investment of time and/or money?
- Is it feasible to finance the acquisition within the constraints of the seller's expectations, borrowing power of the target company, and the financial resources of the buyer?
- Does the seller have a valid reason to sell and is he motivated to do so?
- Does the seller have any significant hurdles (e.g., minority shareholders) that must be cleared before the sale can be consummated?
- Is the relationship between the respective parties strong enough to make a successful transaction appear likely?

If the answer to one or more of these questions is an unequivocal "no," the buyer should *move on* to the next deal. This may be easier said than done because by now the buyer may have a substantial "emotional investment" in this particular deal. He may really want the deal to happen, but that doesn't change the fact that an objective assessment of the above questions strongly indicates that it has little chance of closing. For this reason, it is important to maintain an objective perspective throughout the dealmaking process.

When the answer is "yes" — or at least "probably" — to these questions, it is time for the buyer to *move out*. This means moving into the next phase of the LBO process — orchestrating the deal.

EXHIBIT 7-A
PHASE II
ORCHESTRATING THE DEAL

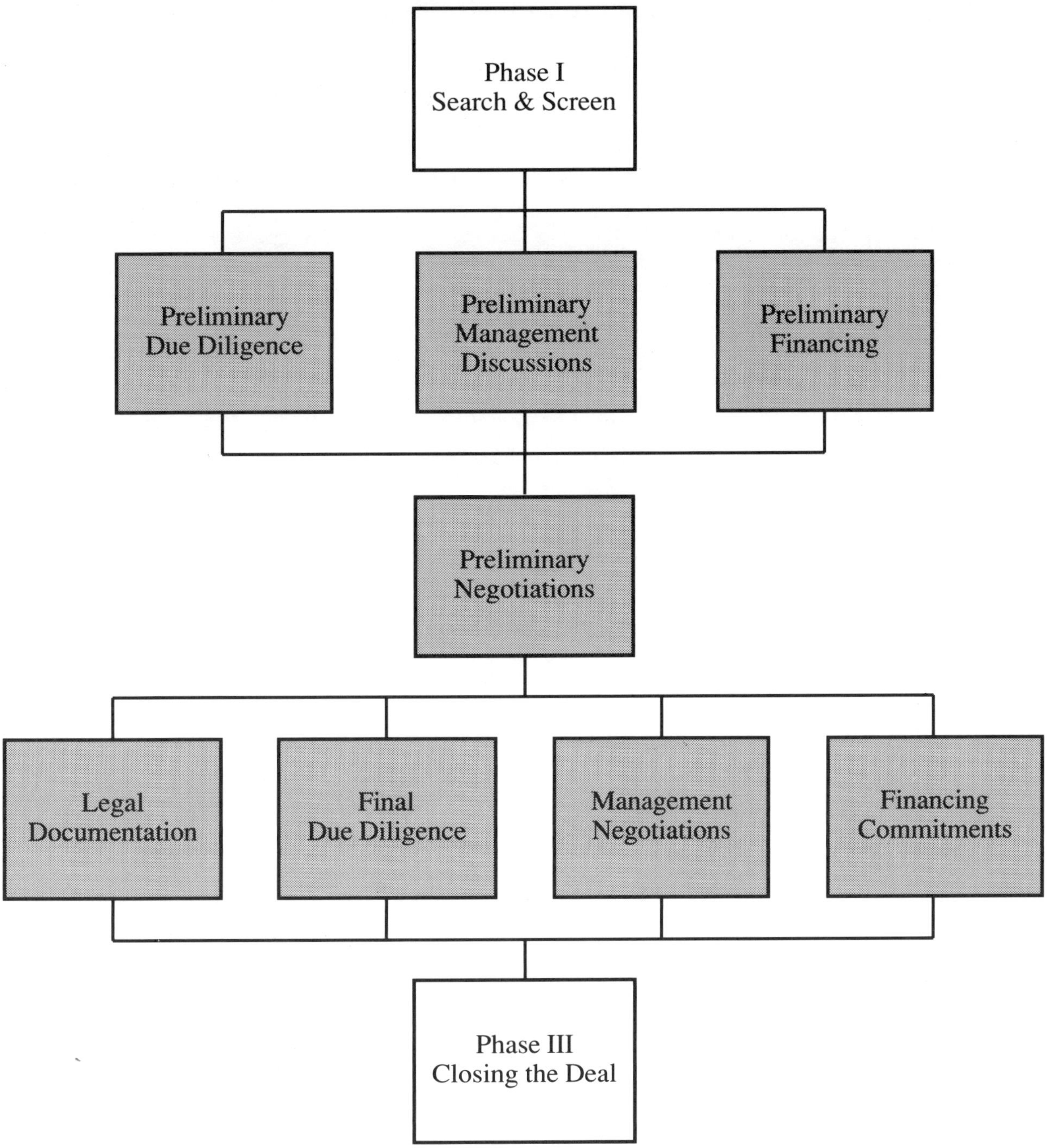

7

ORCHESTRATING THE DEAL

Even if the outcome of his first meeting with the seller is positive, it is not unusual for the buyer to experience ambivalent feelings. On one hand, there is a mild state of euphoria because, after months of searching, he has finally found a company that appears to have all (or most) of the characteristics for which he's looking. On the other hand, he may feel overwhelmed at the task lying ahead — bringing the seller to the closing table. Some buyers may even be able to relate to the dog who has been tirelessly chasing an elusive fire engine when it suddenly stops. Both might utter the question — "Now what do I do?"

There may not be much that the dog can do with the fire engine other than continue barking at it. But there are some specific steps the buyer can and must take to maintain the momentum that he has created. Momentum in a deal is that intangible attribute that can't be seen, but sure can be felt. When it slows or disappears, everyone senses it and instinctively knows that the deal will die a slow death if it isn't restored.

THE ROLE OF THE DEALMAKER

How does the buyer maintain the necessary momentum to keep the deal alive? He does it by moving out on several fronts simultaneously to insure that all the necessary hurdles between now and closing are anticipated and cleared. Any acquisition transaction involves a number of obstacles that must be overcome before the deal is finalized. In a leveraged buyout the process is even more complicated because there are so many different players with different needs and expectations. The process of bringing them all together is called "orchestrating the deal." This is where the dealmaker earns his stripes.

Perhaps the best analogy of what is about to happen is to compare the buyer's role to that of the symphony orchestra conductor. The conductor must synchronize the talents of a variety of individuals with different musical instruments to play the same or harmonious notes at an identical moment. In much the same manner, the leveraged buyer must motivate, cajole, or coerce a disparate group of people to agree upon a variety of complex economic and legal issues at the same time. It requires a unique combination of knowledge, analytical abilities, negotiating skills, salesmanship, and — last but not least — patience. Some of these are instinctive, but many can be learned by diligent study and simply going out and doing it!

A quick glance at the blueprint for Phase II of the LBO process at the beginning of this chapter provides some insight on why this segment raises new challenges for the buyer. Altogether there are eight specific steps — major procedures or events — that must take place. More significant is the fact that several of these must occur almost simultaneously. Although the symphony conductor label vividly describes his role, the buyer often feels it's more of a juggling act.

SETTING THE STAGE

Any symphony conductor (or juggler) worth his salt will always make sure that the stage is set before beginning his act. The sound system must be in working order and all the props must be in their proper place. In like manner, the knowledgeable leveraged buyer will make sure that everything is in place before beginning his orchestration act.

This starts with communicating early with the seller on what immediate steps the buyer plans to take, the approximate timetable for such action, and how the seller and him employees must cooperate. As indicated in the diagram preceeding this chapter, there are three separate steps the buyer is about to take, two of which directly affect the seller: preliminary due diligence and (perhaps) preliminary management discussions. Whether discussions are held with management at this stage will depend upon a number of variables including their influence over the seller, their perceived abilities, and their relative importance to the deal's success. The seller should be informed that the buyer (or his employees) will begin his preliminary due diligence on a specific date (the sooner the better) and that this máy involve discussions with operating management. Nothing should be said to the seller about the preliminary financing step; this is between the buyer and his lenders.

Setting the stage with the seller is important because it clearly conveys the idea that the buyer knows what he is doing. He has made a plan with a timetable, and that builds confidence with the seller. It lets him know this buyer is different from the rest of the pack who say: "Let me think things over and I'll get back to you."

PRELIMINARY INVESTIGATION

With the seller put on notice and fully cooperating, it is time for the buyer to spring into action with his preliminary investigation. This includes due diligence, financing feasibility analyses, and perhaps some initial discussions with management on their future roles. These steps are essential before the buyer can decide to proceed with the potential buyout. In the interest of saving time and maintaining the momentum, these are addressed simultaneously. However, for the purpose of understanding what happens, each is described separately.

Due Diligence

In most cases, the buyer's analysis of the target company undertaken during the qualification stage is, at best cursory. The general nature of this review stems from the fact that it is based upon limited information about the company. The next step in the process involves a detailed analysis which digs much deeper into the company's financial records, as well as overall conditions prevailing in the appropriate marketplace. The kind of analysis to be undertaken is frequently referred to as the due diligence review.

Most people tend to think of this process as a single, prolonged investigation of the target company by the buyer, his employees, and hired professionals such as lawyers, accountants, and consultants. While this may accurately depict what happens in larger corporate acquisitions, the practice is usually different for most small or medium-sized leveraged buyouts. In these transactions, the due diligence process is often divided into *two* segments — the preliminary investigation and the final analysis. The main reason for this two-step approach in leveraged buyouts is related to the financing contingency. Unlike many strategic corporate acquisitions where financing is not a major problem, it is critical to establish — as early as possible — whether the numbers make sense. If they don't, it serves no purpose to conduct a more detailed investigation of the company.

The buyer's primary objective in the preliminary stage of the due diligence effort is to quickly assemble enough factual information on the business so that he can effectively dialogue with lenders and investors. At the same time, he should conduct his own valuation analysis to determine the fairness of the seller's asking price (if it has been specified) or to establish his offering price. This should be accomplished within two or three days at the most. And, by the time he has completed this portion of the due diligence, the buyer should have sufficient knowledge and financial information to construct the following:

- An adjusted current balance sheet that reflects the true economic value of the assets as well as their estimated liquidation values.
- An adjusted historical income statement that shows the impact of any adjustments to income and expenses, including the proposed debt service.
- Proforma financial statements, including cash flow, for a ten year period.

These reports will numerically summarize the buyer's perceptions and expectations of the business at present as well as in the future. They will serve to confirm (or question) the conclusion of the preliminary analysis — that the company represents a good investment. Furthermore, they will form the foundation for the buyer's imminent discussions with potential lenders and investors.

The scope of the due diligence effort is explained more fully in Chapter 9 ("Analyzing the Company"). The reader is provided with a "road map" of how to evaluate the target company and its prospects. But, buyers need to be careful not to become too immersed in unnecessary details. It should be kept uppermost in mind that the primary goal of due diligence is to determine if the business can support the anticipated leverage and whether financing sources can be convinced of this assertion.

To focus the investigation and make the best use of his time during the visit, the buyer should leave the seller with the short form Due Diligence Checklist (Appendix D) at the time of his initial meeting. This will not only ensure that the buyer has access to the necessary information, but also is another indication to the seller that the buyer has a sound game plan.

Most sellers, if they are *real* sellers and the buyer has convinced them that he is a real buyer, will cooperate during the preliminary due diligence. There may be some reluctance to "open the books" completely to some buyers, especially if they are perceived as potential competitors. The only way to overcome this reluctance is to assure the seller that all financial information, as well as the fact that the company is for sale, will be kept strictly confidential. Obviously, many sellers are quite concerned that their competition will begin spreading negative rumors to the company's customers. For this reason, buyers should generally refrain from contacting outsiders, including customers, at this stage of the due diligence process. If all else fails, the buyer must confront the seller with the fact that he must reveal important financial information before any offer can be made. If he still refuses, he is not a *real* seller.

Financing Feasibility

Shortly after the buyer has completed his preliminary due diligence and constructed his proforma financial statements (see Chapter 11), he must take one of the most critical steps in the entire LBO process: approach potential lenders and/or investors to determine if the deal can be financed. Unless he is reasonably convinced that the money will be available when it's needed to close, there is no purpose in pursuing the transaction.

Of all the factors that contribute to the success of a leveraged buyout, none is as important as the buyer's control over the financing process. The ultimate degree of control over the financing is for the buyer to be able to write a check for the entire purchase price. In that case, it would not be a leveraged buyout and the potential returns to the buyer would substantially diminish.

But "control of the financing process" does not necessarily mean the buyer *must* have deep pockets. It does mean that he has established good working relationships with lenders and investors and fully understands their underwriting criteria and approval procedures. It also means that after the buyer describes the essential components of the deal (e.g., business description, key financial data, asset base, price, etc.), the lender will give a good preliminary indication that it can be financed. Furthermore, "control" implies that the lender will ultimately fund the money requested by the buyer. Without the ability to explain the deal to lenders or investors and some reasonable assurance that they will commit and ultimately fund the required financing, the buyer has nothing to offer the seller. His words are strictly "hot air" and, sooner or later, will be revealed as such, much to the detriment of the buyer's credibility.

How can the buyer achieve some meaningful degree of "control" over financing sources? Naturally, some prior success goes a long way toward attracting the interest and attention of lenders. That doesn't mean it is impossible for those without established track records to secure LBO financing. It just makes it more difficult. It starts with developing *personal* working relationships with lending and investment officers who have the *authority* — or necessary *influence* — to make the investment decision. This is not always easy to do, but it must be done. And these relationships should be established long before the buyer actually needs the preliminary commitment. What this means is that the buyer has had prior conversations with the lender(s) regarding the target company before he conducts his preliminary due diligence activities. This usually occurs during the process of qualifying the deal or at least before the buyer meets the seller for the first time.

Knowledge of the lender's underwriting criteria and loan approval process are other key factors that dictate how well the buyer controls the financing process. What collateral preferences and cash flow coverage ratios are used in determining how much will be advanced? Who makes the ultimate decision and how long does it take? Are appraisals needed? When? These are just a sampling of the kind of questions that buyers should be able to answer. These issues are fully explained in Chapter 12 ("Financing the Transaction"), but are mentioned here to provide buyers with some idea of the preparations that are necessary.

The best procedure for the buyer to follow is to visit with the lender after the preliminary due diligence effort and go over the entire deal, including cash flow projections. It is not necessary at this point to have a complete financing package. Remember, the mission is not to get a firm commitment, but an answer to the following question: "If the information presented is accurate, what is the probability that this financing request will be approved?" Buyers must be careful to make the lender or investor aware of all relevant factors that may affect his decision. Nothing is worse than having a lender discover something much further down the road and state that, "You didn't tell me about this!" It all gets back to the buyer knowing the deal *and* his financing sources.

Management Discussions

In every conceivable case, most discussions held during the preliminary due diligence are with key executives responsible for running the business. If this is the seller himself, the buyer must address the issue of who will run the business after the deal closes. In some cases operating management may own a minority share of the company, but wish to continue in a management capacity under a new owner. Most frequently, the key managers hold no shares in the company.

One of the advantages of leveraged buyouts — and a key factor in attracting lender and outside investor interest — is the continuing role of proven incumbent managers in the business. This continuing involvement implies some degree of equity participation in the new company that acquires the business of the target. Therefore, it is not unusual for the managers to bring up the issue of their ownership role during the due diligence investigation. How the buyer responds will depend upon a number of factors. In some cases the seller will expressly forbid buyers to discuss the issue at this point in the process. In other cases, managers have a strong influence over the seller and to whom the company is sold, in which case, the issue must be addressed head-on.

As a general rule, any discussions with managers at this stage should be conceptual rather than specific. A proper response might be as follows: "Basically, I believe in incentivizing key managers with the opportunity of equity participation. But it is premature to get too specific on the issue until we have made further progress on the deal itself." To be any more specific would be inappropriate. There are just too many unknowns. For example:

- What are the true capabilities of the managers?
- Will their personalities and management styles be compatible with the buyer's?
- Are they the type of individuals that the buyer wants as partners?

In fact, one of the buyer's objectives is to assess management's abilities and how he would relate to them as future partners. The company's operating performance is the best indication of management's abilities, although it sometimes can be deceiving. The owner may have meddled in the operation or not have given management adequate financial support to carry out their plan. The buyer should consider these factors in his due diligence and assessment of management. If, in his mind, they are not qualified, he may want to reconsider the whole deal, because this will make it more difficult to finance and monitor, not to mention, the increased risk.

Buyers should also be aware of possible hidden agendas of incumbent managers. This includes the possibility that the managers themselves may be trying to buy the company. This issue should be raised with the seller during the initial visit so that the buyer is walking into the deal with his eyes wide open. Another situation that may arise is where managers favor one buyer (or investment group) over another. Reasons may range anywhere from promises of larger equity stakes, more autonomy, future options to buy out the investors to personal preferences. This is more prevalent in cases where managers have a strong influence over the seller/owner, either by virtue of their unique abilities or loyalties from the owner. Either way, buyers must be prepared to deal with such situations. These issues will be discussed in greater detail and from a manager's perspective in the next chapter.

PRELIMINARY NEGOTIATIONS

After completing his preliminary due diligence and determining the feasibility of financing the transaction, the buyer should have a firm grip on the deal. He is now in a position to negotiate the major issues, or "deal points," with the seller. If he has conducted himself properly up to this point, the buyer will have avoided any major negotiating sessions. Until now, he hasn't had sufficient information to know his limits and whether he could finance the purchase price. In fact, the main reason the buyer should refrain from negotiating until he has *all* the facts is to avoid changing the deal. Nothing is more psychologically damaging to a deal than agreeing to something and later changing it. It is also important for the buyer to select the time at which serious negotiations take place. By doing so, he improves the chances that the setting will be proper and the moods of the parties will be favorable.

The primary purpose of the preliminary negotiations is for the buyer and the seller to come to a basic understanding on the key deal points. These include: price, terms, contingencies, and timetable. Usually, if the buyer and seller can agree on these key issues, the deal stands a reasonably good chance of coming together.

There are two ways to approach the seller on the key deal points. One is to call a meeting with the seller to verbally present and discuss the offer. Another is to present the offer in writing and suggest a meeting to further discuss the proposal. Both approaches work and each has advantages and disadvantages. The particular technique utilized will depend upon the type of seller involved and the personal preference of the buyer. A discussion of preliminary negotiation strategies and tactics is contained in Chapter 14 ("Negotiating and Closing the Deal").

If all goes well, the preliminary negotiating session ends with a "handshake" between buyer and seller. This represents a milestone for the buyer in his quest to buy the company. Not that major obstacles and pitfalls don't lie ahead; they most certainly do. But the most difficult portion of the trip is behind him.

NAILING DOWN THE DETAILS

In spite of his achievements, the buyer has little time to rest on his laurels. Much remains to be done before victory can be claimed. And if it seemed like too many things were happening at once prior to the negotiations, that was nothing compared to the weeks that lie ahead. During this period, the buyer, his advisors, and lenders will be working on four separate fronts to keep the deal alive. Orchestrating the deal now takes on increasing complexity — and expense — as the buyer moves slowly but surely toward the closing. Here is a brief description of what has to happen.

Legal Documentation

The first order of business is to begin the process of preparing the legal documents that reflect the respective obligations of each of the parties to the transaction. This is more commonly referred to as the "Acquisition Agreement" or "Agreement of Sale."

Until now, most of the communications between buyer and seller have been direct, with a relatively minor role played by their lawyers. In fact, the preliminary negotiating sessions should have been conducted, if at all possible, without the presence of counsel for either side. But now it is time for the lawyers to assume a larger role. This begins with drafting the acquisition documents.

Experienced buyers *always* have their lawyer prepare the original draft of the Acquisition Agreement. Although this may result in higher legal expenses, there are definite psychological advantages and, more importantly, the buyer retains control of the tempo of the deal. The basic deal points should be relayed to the attorney, who, if he is qualified, will discuss other issues that should be included in the contract. It should be emphasized that the buyer must select legal counsel who has demonstrable experience in prior acquisitions, preferably leveraged buyouts. Improper choice of counsel can be a serious impediment to his chance of closing the transaction.

If the buyer's lawyer does his job properly, the seller's lawyer will have a first draft of the Acquisition Agreement to review within a week to ten days. The agreement will reflect the basic understanding between the buyer and seller and not contain an abundance of conditions which disproportionately favor the buyer and penalize the seller. Nothing will turn off the seller's counsel faster than an "unfair" contract.

The initial draft of the acquisition documents will set the stage for another inevitable round of negotiations between the buyer and seller, this time with a full complement of attorneys on each side. But that is still a few weeks off. In the meantime, there is lots of action on the other fronts.

Final Due Diligence

While the lawyers are ironing out the legal issues, the buyer must complete his due diligence of the target company. Remember that the preliminary due diligence was relatively quick (two or three days) and highly focused in order to enable the buyer to confirm the feasibility of financing the transaction. Because of the abbreviated time of this effort, many important — but, hopefully not critical — questions remained unanswered. Now is the time to find the answers.

The depth of this additional probe into the company's operations will depend upon a lot of factors, including the size of the transaction, complexity of the business and the condition of the company's books and records. A good practical guide for this phase of the buyer's due diligence is Appendix F, an outline of the Businessman's Review process used by *Deloitte Haskins & Sells.* In some cases, the buyer may wish to retain an accounting firm to perform a Businessman's Review of the target company. While this report is limited in scope as compared to an audit, it will flag major problem areas, particularly in the company's accounting procedures.

The buyer himself should conduct further investigations into the company's competitive position in the marketplace, including a more intensive analysis of the competition and a selective evaluation of key customers. The primary emphasis should be on finding the "Achilles heel" that may have been overlooked thus far. The buyer will be presented with a difficult dilemma if a "problem" is uncovered at this stage.

Since he has invested substantial time and emotional effort into reaching this point, there is a strong tendency for the buyer to be less than objective in the evaluation of the deal. However, one must not lose sight of the fact that the decision to do the deal is first and foremost an investment decision. And, if some major problems are overlooked in the evaluation, at best, additional capital contributions may be necessary and, at worst, the company may not survive. Therefore, it is imperative that the buyer remain totally objective while conducting his detailed analysis.

In attempting to be objective, however, a buyer must be careful not to be overly pessimistic. Inexperienced buyers now may begin to experience feelings of "buyer's remorse" and may begin to look at the dark side of a business, finding many reasons not to buy it. With such an attitude it is unlikely that any deal will ever be made. The buyer's attitude should be one of open-mindedness and objectivity. While he should be willing and able to walk away from the deal if some irreversible negative trends or unsolvable problems are detected, it must be recognized that most businesses have weaknesses. In many cases, however, problems confronting a business are relatively minor and do not adversely affect long-term viability. The task, therefore, is to differentiate between minor problems and "deal busters."

Management Negotiations

By this time the transaction has reached the serious stage and management may be growing increasingly anxious about where it stands with the potential new owner of the business it is running. If the buyer is strictly an investor who intends to remain relatively passive in the business and is depending heavily on management to make it work, he should also be thinking about how to incentivize the key managers. This includes some form of equity participation in the new company.

The degree of equity participation will depend upon a number of factors, including the following:

- Management's experience and proven capabilities.
- Management's relative importance to the overall success of the company.
- Management's unique skills or attributes and the difficulty of finding acceptable replacements.
- The magnitude of management's financial investment in the proposed buyout.

In general, management participation ranges from 5 percent to 50 percent, depending upon the unique circumstances of the deal. In most cases, incumbent managers end up owning between 15 percent and 25 percent of the target company. Lenders and investors typically like to see management with both a significant (in terms of their net worth) commitment to the deal and an ownership position.

In cases where managers have little or no capital to contribute or have less than impeccable credentials, the buyer may want to defer any equity participation until the management has proven itself to the new ownership. One effective means of dealing with this while still incentivizing managers is to allow managers a specific share of the equity (say 10 percent to 15 percent) which is to be vested over a five year period. If, for some reason, it doesn't work out, management's stock can be repurchased by the buyer at a specified pricing formula.

In some cases the seller will have strong loyalties to management and insist, in his negotiations with the buyer, that managers get a "fair deal." This could mean a minimum equity participation or guaranteed compensation package, or both. If this is the case, the buyer will have to assess the reasonableness of such conditions as well as the financial and operational impact on the transaction.

Financing Commitments

The final, but certainly not the least important, task of the buyer is securing the financing commitment from the lenders and investors that he promised (or implied that he had) to the seller. This should not be a major problem if the buyer knows his lenders and has factually presented the relevant information on the company.

At the same time the buyer is completing his due diligence, the lenders (and investors) are conducting their own evaluations to confirm the data they were given. If the lenders are "asset-based lenders," this will include an audit of accounts receivable and inventory records as well as liquidation appraisals of fixed assets. If venture capital sources are involved, there will be more intensive checking of management and a thorough evaluation of the business. These should be fairly routine confirmations if the buyer has accurately analyzed the facts of the deal and related them to the lender. The more closely the buyer has worked with his financing sources, the more they will trust him and accept his information without any major second guessing.

Knowledge of the lender's approval processes and timetables is very important. It is necessary to know who is ultimately responsible for approving the financing request and when they can be expected to do it, because this must be dovetailed with the legal documentation and further discussions with the seller.

Needless to say, if the buyer cannot get the lenders and investors to produce firm commitments to advance the necessary financing, the deal is in deep trouble! Unless the seller is highly motivated to do the deal with this particular buyer for other reasons, it will be extremely difficult for the buyer to renegotiate either the price or terms of the deal. This only serves to re-emphasize the importance of the buyer's relationship with his lenders and control over the financing process.

This concludes our global perspective of what the buyer must do to orchestrate the deal. It should be clear that the process requires simultaneous control over several interrelated steps. It's not easy, but can be done with adequate preparation, attention to detail and a strong motivation to see it through.

8 FOR MANAGERS ONLY

The previous chapters have been directed toward buyers who are entrepreneurs or investors. Because these "outsiders" usually have no prior knowledge of or contact with the ultimate target company, they must sift through many unqualified deals and sellers to find the few that make sense. In the process, they may travel up a few blind alleys (hopefully not too far) before discovering that the deal can't be done. This can be an extremely frustrating experience for the "outside" buyer.

In some situations the buyer — the person or group that *controls* the acquisition transaction — is not an "outsider." It is the incumbent managers, those key executives who are responsible for running the business. These "insiders" do not experience many of the same obstacles and frustrations as do outside buyers. They must view the LBO process from a different perspective. In some respects, incumbent managers have some major advantages over outside players. But they also have unique problems that must be resolved. This chapter focuses on some of these important issues and how managers can effectively deal with them.

MANAGEMENT POSTURING

Before addressing specific actions which managers can take, it is helpful to take a closer look at their relative posture in the LBO milieu and the factors influencing it. This will enable both managers and outside investors to accurately assess their relative strengths in any given transaction.

As a decision to sell the company is made by its owner, management typically begins positioning itself to optimize its own interests in the eventual outcome. The first concern may be for the security of their positions. The uncertainty of working for a new owner typically creates some anxiety for any employee, and top managers are no exception. But even if the management team is confident in its abilities, another strong emotion may start to take hold: the desire to control their own destiny and get rich in the process! Managers may reason, correctly or incorrectly, that their abilities are critical in the eyes of any buyer. And, if a leveraged buyout appears to be a feasible alternative, they may believe that any particular outside buyer (investor) needs the management more than the managers need them.

Thus begins the process whereby managers maneuver for control over their own destiny. One must assume that incumbent managers, when they sense the possibility of a leveraged buyout, will begin to focus their attention on achieving the following objectives:

- Maintain their position as the key operating people in the company.
- Structure a deal which gives them as much control or influence as possible.
- Maximize their ownership of the company.

While not all managers would approach the situation in this manner, it is reasonable to assume that most would. These are perfectly normal human motivations. Management's ultimate success will depend upon a number of factors that will determine how much control or influence the managers have over the situation.

WHO'S IN CONTROL?

First, let's review the possible scenarios where the three main participants in a leveraged buyout — the seller, outside investors (entrepreneurial buyers and/or institutional financing sources), and managers (inside buyers) — come together. These were briefly explained in Chapter 1.

- The owner prefers, for a variety of reasons, to sell the company and give incumbent management the "first shot" at the deal.
- The owner makes the company available to all qualified buyers, but gives management no preferential treatment.
- The owner excludes the possibility of selling the company directly to management and refuses to negotiate with them as a buyer.

In each case the company is clearly for sale, but management's negotiating posture is dramatically different. The key question all potential buyers — both "insiders" and "outsiders" — must ask themselves is: what degree of control does the incumbent management have over the owner/seller? Or looking at it from a different perspective: how much loyalty and sentimental preference does the owner/seller have toward his managers? The answer to these questions will dictate how management, outside buyers, and financing sources will proceed.

When Management Is In Control

In the first case management is clearly in control of the deal. This situation usually arises out of strong feelings of loyalty by the seller to his key managers. They may have worked for him (or the parent company) for a number of years and been a major factor behind the success of the firm. Or the owner may want to minimize any disruption among employees and customers caused by a transfer of ownership. The best way to satisfy any of these sentiments is to quietly sell the company to management.

In some situations, this can be costly to the seller. His strong preference to sell to management may preclude him from exposing the company to other potential buyers who may be willing and able to pay a substantially higher price. This is especially true if the company is of sufficient size and engaged in a business that can attract strategic corporate acquirers. Most often, this type of buyer is able to justify a higher purchase price than managers with the financial constraints of leverage.

Although the situation where there are strong loyalty ties between the owner and his management is more prevalent with private sellers, it can also occur with corporate sellers. In those situations, there may be close personal ties between senior executives in the parent company, who made the decision to divest, and operating managers in the subsidiary or division. There are limits, however, to how much favoritism can be shown to incumbent corporate managers. Top executives have a fiduciary responsibility to shareholders to maximize the value of the company's assets, and independent directors are increasingly sensitive to this issue. These factors, plus the fact that top managers look good when they are able to extract a higher price, have led to a more frequent use of "controlled auctions" supervised by the parent company's investment banker. If the parent company attracts other corporate buyers, this places incumbent management of the target company in a much weaker position to ultimately end up owning a share of the business.

Not withstanding these issues, management has a great deal of influence in situations where they have strong loyalty ties with the seller. The seller usually gives management much more time to raise the financing and is much more forgiving if deadlines are missed. Some even are willing to accept a lower price to accommodate management. Outside buyers must be sensitive to the reality of management's influence and control when strong loyalty ties exist.

When Management Is Just Another Buyer

This situation typically arises when the seller's sole objective is to maximize his net proceeds from the sale. Although he may have a long-standing relationship with his top managers, the seller will not allow it to stand in the way of getting his price. By opening the sale up to all qualified buyers, the seller stands a better chance of stimulating competition among them and, consequently, of getting a higher price.

To this type of seller, management is just another buyer. He has no problem with their making a bid for the company, but will not give them any preferential treatment. In fact, in this situation, the seller typically considers management as a buyer as an afterthought, or only after being approached by management. However, with the rising popularity of leveraged management buyouts and the proliferation of LBO financing sources, both private and corporate sellers are giving more serious consideration to management as a bona fide buyer. This is particularly true of corporate divestitures, where many of the subsidiaries and divisions being divested lack the necessary attributes to attract other corporate suitors. For legal reasons, as previously discussed, top managers of many corporate parent companies submit all divestitures to a competitive bidding process as a matter of policy. Managers are most often invited to submit a bid.

Just because management does not have an inside track, or "lock," on the deal does not mean they have no influence. That depends upon a number of other factors, including the quality of the business and the relative importance of management to its success. These will be discussed shortly.

When Management Is Excluded As A Buyer

In certain cases, the seller may refuse to negotiate with management as a potential buyer. Although this is rare, it can occur when the owner has either a bad relationship with management or no confidence in their ability to finance the transaction. In some instances, especially in corporate divestitures, the decision to sell is often precipitated by a lack of confidence in management's operational abilities. While such sellers are willing to talk to these managers as potential buyers, they will adamantly refuse to finance any portion of the acquisition with purchase money notes (see Chapter 12). The only exceptions might be where the note is well secured or guaranteed or the seller has no better alternative.

Some private sellers are reluctant to negotiate with any buyer who plans to include management as an equity participant at the front end of the deal. These individuals usually have excluded management from ownership in the past and are fearful of possible repercussions if the deal with the more generous buyer does not materialize. The rationale is that once the managers' expectation levels are raised there will be resentments toward the current owner if a transaction is not completed.

When the seller specifically excludes managers, it is very clear that the latter have no influence whatsoever over the selection of the buyer. Clearly, the managers are viewed as just another, albeit intangible, asset of the target company. The outside buyer must make his deal directly with the seller and include the management later, if such action is warranted.

Owner/Operator Situations

The foregoing scenarios all assumed that the seller, whether it was a private individual or corporation, was not actively involved in the day-to-day management of the company. This was the role of incumbent managers, who in most cases, own little or no equity in the target company. Most leveraged buyouts have this particular set-up, where there is a continuity of operating managers who now also share in the ownership of the company after the closing.

In some deals, particularly the smaller transactions, the seller is also the key operating figure. If the buyer is an entrepreneur who merely replaces the seller as the key operator, management participation is not an issue. The buyer becomes the new manager. However, if the seller plans to remain active in a management role after the closing, it raises some interesting issues for the outside buyer (or financing sources). If this seller is cashed out completely, is it reasonable to expect him to have his heart in the operation? Presumably, he is a much richer individual and, more importantly, is now an employee rather than an owner. These factors may lead to a lower level of motivation and performance. To avoid this problem, most investors and lenders will insist that the seller maintain an equity interest in the target company. This partial "cash out," in theory, offers the seller the best of two worlds — substantial dollars in his pocket *and* a continuing interest in "his" company.

OTHER FACTORS THAT DETERMINE MANAGEMENT INFLUENCE

In addition to the previously discussed considerations, there are other factors that will have a direct bearing on how much influence incumbent managers have over the ultimate sale of the target company. Some of these are related to the characteristics of the company while others stem from the skills and abilities of the managers themselves.

Quality of the Target Company and Its Management

The nature of the target company's business and its past performance will have a direct impact on whether a leveraged buyout is the most probable transaction *and* what influence management may have over the ultimate buyer. It was pointed out in Chapter 5 that ideal leveraged buyout prospects have certain financial characteristics that make them attractive from a financing standpoint. Ironically, some of the characteristics that add to their appeal as LBO candidates, such as slow growth, mundane product lines, etc., make them less appealing to public corporate buyers. The latter are more preoccupied with growth potential and are less concerned than LBO investors with cash flow constraints. Thus, if the company does not conform to the general criteria outlined in Chapter 5, it may be "too good" for a leveraged buyout. Either the seller wants a premium price because of its growth prospects or the LBO cannot be financed due to the company's working capital requirements. In these situations, the most likely buyer is another corporation and management has little choice but to remain an employee.

At the other end of the spectrum, if the company has a very poor operating history, lenders and investors will have little confidence in either the business, management, or both. This type of company is very difficult to finance. If a deal is done, the seller often must participate as a subordinated lender and outside investors usually have demonstrable operating experience.

Management's influence and control in such circumstances is less than it would be if the company has a sound operating history. But the ultimate degree of influence will depend upon the real source of the operating problems. If the company is engaged in a dying business, the seller may perceive a sale to management as the only viable alternative to liquidation. In these cases, the management is in a relatively strong position, but perhaps should think twice before plunging into ownership of a business with bleak prospects. On the other hand, if management has done a poor job, the seller will often attempt to involve an outside investment group with proven experience in turnaround management and management will have little control over the process.

From management's perspective, the best possible scenario is if the company meets all the criteria for a leveraged buyout and management has done an excellent job of running the business. This will increase the attractiveness of the deal to outside investors and give the management a greater selection of potential partners.

CAN MANAGEMENT SPONSOR ITS OWN DEAL?

The degree of influence and control held by incumbent managers will have a dramatic impact on the role they play in the buyout process. It will also determine how much equity they end up owning in the new company that is formed to acquire the business. In effect, the managers' influence and control will determine who acts as the "sponsor" in the deal.

Can management act as its own sponsor? The answer is a qualified "yes." In addition to influence and control, it depends upon a number of other factors including their dealmaking instincts, knowledge of financing, negotiating skills, and the amount of time that can be sacrificed from operating responsibilities.

Review of Sponsorship Functions

For management to determine what role it should play in sponsorship activities, it is necessary to review just what the LBO sponsor does. Remember that the sponsor is the catalyst who brings together all the necessary components of the deal to make it happen. He is the orchestrator whose activities were described in Chapter 7 from the perspective of an "outsider." When management "orchestrates the deal," it does so from an "insider's" perspective, but basically performs the same functions.

Structuring and Financing the Deal. Based upon his knowledge of the company and its finances, the top manager must meet with potential lenders and investors and obtain the financing commitments needed to complete the transaction. This requires not only some knowledge of the LBO financing process, but the ability to negotiate the best possible deal with alternative financing sources. If the manager knows how the alternative financial structures relate to his business, he can seek out those financing sources that would result in minimum dilution of his equity.

Negotiating the Deal. In addition to lenders and investors, the management sponsor must negotiate the purchase of the company from his current employer. This may present some problems for a manager, since the person on the opposite side of the negotiating table is his boss! The manager must be sensitive as to how and when to negotiate the deal if he wants to do it alone.

Coordinating and Closing the Transaction. The orchestration process doesn't end when the price has been negotiated and the financing is in place. Many details remain that have to be handled. And, invariably, there are unpleasant "surprises" that threaten to blow the deal. These must be quickly resolved and the sponsor is the "designated hitter."

There are obvious advantages to managers taking a more active role in the sponsorship function if they have the necessary influence and control. The most significant is the freedom to negotiate with various financing sources in order to maximize their equity interests. Another is more direct control over what is happening.

On the other hand, there are also some clear disadvantages. One is the inordinant amount of time that managers are required to spend away from the operations. This can sometimes impact performance and possibly threaten the financing plan or dilute management's equity share. Another is the risk that management, because of its lack of experience in this area, will do the wrong thing at the wrong time and blow the deal.

Regardless of their influence, aptitudes, and preferences, it is impossible for managers to escape some involvement in the LBO transaction process. Lots of things must happen and managers are, by virtue of their position, in the eye of the hurricane. Nevertheless, they have the choice of whether or not they want to be the quarterback. It could be to their advantage to select outside investors who have the proven ability to perform the major sponsorship functions. Selecting outside sponsors may result in little, if any, dilution of their equity and it will enable them to focus their energies on what they do best — running the business.

A BLUEPRINT FOR MANAGERS

Most professional managers are experts when it comes to managing their businesses, but are at a total loss when an opportunity presents itself to buy the company they run. This is not surprising, since most managers have no training or experience in the complexities of mergers, acquisitions, and working with outside financing sources in pin-striped suits. In many cases, they have never concerned themselves with financing the business. If capital was needed, they merely called the "bank," the treasury of the parent company or the owner of the private company.

The prospect of putting together a complex leveraged buyout transaction can be very intimidating to the uninformed and unwary manager. Unless they are prepared for what is about to happen, they may lose whatever influence they have over the deal. To give incumbent managers a better idea of what to do and when to do it, the following paragraphs provide a step-by-step description of the major steps that management must take to facilitate a leveraged buyout. It is assumed that they have the desire, aptitude, and time to carry out these activities. Although these suggestions are directed mainly toward managers working for larger divestiture candidates, they are equally relevant for those working for private owners. Where there is a clear difference between the two situations, it will be pointed out.

Establish That the Company is for Sale

Obviously, before incumbent management can make a move to buy the company, it must *really* be for sale. The surest sign a business is on the selling block is when its owner takes some overt action that gives a clear signal of his (its) intentions. For example, a large public company may announce a major restructuring program that includes divesting certain subsidiaries. Or the owner may have retained the services of an investment banker to sell the company.

In our discussion on *Who's In Control,* it was assumed the owner had already sent a clear signal that the company was on the market. This, however, is not always the case. In some instances, the seller sends subtle signals indicating the company *may* be for sale under certain circumstances or at the right price.

A good example is when a corporate subsidiary is not meeting the return on investment (ROI) hurdles imposed by top managers of its parent company. Very often the General Manager is asked to submit a plan of all the alternatives that could resolve or eliminate the problem, including possible divestiture or liquidation. In the case of a privately held company, the owner may drop hints that he wants to diversify his assets or spend his time and energy on other pursuits. In both cases, the owner has not made a clear statement that he *is* a seller, but has said that he *may be* a seller.

In this situation, management should, at the appropriate time, diplomatically confirm the owner's real intentions and the strength of his motivation to sell. If management is convinced the owner has a good reason for selling and is motivated to do so, it is time to take the next step.

Planting the Seed

Any time a key manager approaches his employer regarding the possibility of buying the company, he must realize that the relationship between the two will never be the same. That doesn't mean it will be better or worse, but it definitely will change. Management will be perceived in a whole new light with a slightly different agenda than the owner may have assumed in the past. Depending upon the seller's mentality and how the subject is broached, management's stature may improve or diminish.

For this reason, managers who aspire to buy the company must carefully select the time, place, and manner in which they initially express their interest to the seller. The objective is to "plant the seed" in the seller's mind that management is an interested buyer without arousing any apprehension regarding their continuing loyalty to the owner. How and when mangement plants the seed will depend upon the unique circumstances surrounding each deal. But it should be done in a relatively low key manner at a time when it is relevant to bring up the subject.

If the owner has already "announced" that the company is for sale, there is less of a problem in using a more direct approach. However, from management's standpoint, if this has already happened, they may have lost the inherent advantage of being an "insider." The seller has already committed to expose the company to a broader marketplace. By waiting too long to make their move, management has lost some control over the process. Assuming they have some influence over the seller, the most propitious time for management to plant the seed is *before* the seller has sent a signal to the world that he is a seller. This enables management to make their move before anyone else can.

Some managers are reluctant to approach their bosses to express an interest in buying the company. They are fearful that such an action might be interpreted as a sign of disloyalty. While this sometimes happens, the seller's reaction mostly depends on how well management conveys their interest. The best approach is to view the situation as a "problem" for the seller. He wants to sell — for whatever reason. The management should see themselves as a "solution" to the problem. They are potential buyers who also happen to be the managers of the company. While this does raise some interesting new dimensions to the buyer/seller relationship, most sellers are comfortable with this situation. Therefore, managers should not be reluctant to bring up the subject, but it should be done diplomatically and at an appropriate time.

Get Key Commitments from the Seller

If and when the seller responds that he would be receptive to a management buyout proposal, management has some important decisions to make. Should they negotiate the price now? Should they bring in outside help? Should they make any promises to the seller? Tough questions. Important questions. To get the right answers, management must do some serious soul-searching regarding its influence and control, aptitude for performing most sponsorship functions, and its available time.

In general, it is a mistake to begin serious negotiations with the seller at this stage. The seller may have a general idea of what price he wants, but may not yet be prepared to negotiate. This is fine. But management should attempt to determine the seller's "ballpark" price expectation. And, if the seller responds with a high number, management should not gasp and fall off their chairs. This is not the time to negotiate. It is the time to get cooperation and commitments from the seller to pursue the buyout. Specifically, management should attempt to obtain the following commitments:

- The seller's approval to share the company's financial information with prospective lenders and investors.
- A reasonable period of time (60 to 90 days) to meet with potential financing sources, after which both sides will negotiate the price and terms.
- The seller's approval for management to spend some of their time away from the business working on the buyout effort.

If the seller is unwilling to make these commitments, management must question his real desire to sell the company to management, if at all. And they should reassess their own perception of their influence over the seller.

Negotiate the Financing Commitments

With the seller's blessing, management is now in a position to "shop" for financing. Armed with the knowledge in Chapters 11 and 12 along with the financial status of the company, managers can intelligently approach lenders and investors. Since they may not have a great deal of time for this, management must carefully select potential financing sources that seem most appropriate for their deal. An excellent tool to help narrow down the field is *The Directory of Financing Sources.* (See Appendix K)

Management should view this initial phase of the financing process as an interview of potential sources to determine the following:

- Their degree of interest in the deal.
- The procedure and timetable for approval.
- Their "chemistry" with the people representing the lender or investor.
- What happens next and who's responsible.

At the conclusion of these discussions, management should be able to assess their ability to work with certain lenders or investors. They should also set a definite date for a response from the financing sources and a preliminary indication of how much each is willing to commit.

The most difficult aspect of this effort is the mezzanine and equity financing, because these sources always insist on a share of the ownership. So the question is not only, "how much money will you lend or invest?", but also, "how much equity do we have to give up?" The latter is a more difficult question to answer at this time as the investor has not done any due diligence, or "crunched the numbers," to determine his required equity split. But the managers should definitely raise the issue in the initial discussions and ask to be provided with some idea of how much equity the investor will require. If management does not deal with this issue up front, it will be unable to evaluate its risk capital sources and will be in a weaker negotiating posture as the deal progresses.

This is not to suggest that the equity split is the most important issue. The investor's ability to move quickly, give a firm commitment, *and* fund the deal on schedule may well be worth giving up a little equity. Therefore, the management should also focus on the investor's track record and timetable. It also is a good idea to check references of other deals they have closed.

Within a prescribed time, the financing sources that were "interviewed" should give a preliminary indication of how much they are willing to lend or invest. This will not be a binding commitment, but should be sufficient to enable the management to negotiate with the seller. Of course, the ability of the lender to respond in a timely manner will be improved if the management is well prepared with financial projections for the initial meetings.

Management may have difficulty finding the time to meet personally with all of its initial financing prospects. This can be alleviated by some preliminary telephone screening. But it is important to meet in person before making any final decisions as to which lenders to choose. Financing, above all, is a *people* business!

Negotiate With the Seller

The management is now in a position to engage in serious negotiations with the seller — and vice versa. They should have a reasonable handle on how much money, including their own investment, can be raised. This enables them to put realistic limits on how much can be paid to the seller.

Management may decide to include one or more of the financing sources in these negotiating sessions. This would most likely be the equity or mezzanine source, since these are most pivotal to the financing process. Inclusion of the key financing source in the negotiations can serve two important purposes. First, it dramatically increases management's credibility in the eyes of the seller. The actual presence of the risk capital source will largely eliminate the seller's primary question regarding a sale to management — "Can they finance the deal?" Another advantage of including a "financial partner" is psychological. If the going gets tough in negotiations, the outsider can be the "bad guy." Management is not placed in a position of taking an adversarial position against the individual for whom they still work. Rather than sitting across the negotiating table, they remain on the sidelines in a secondary role.

Closing the Deal

Upon the conclusion of negotations, if they are successful, the management (and outside investors, if they are present) should insist upon a "lock-up" on the deal for a reasonable period of time. This commits the seller to allow the management an option or exclusive rights to buy the company for a specific period of time. During this period, the management must firm up its financing commitments and close the deal. This can be accomplished with a "letter of intent" (see Appendix C) or a simple option agreement. Obviously, it will be necessary to involve legal counsel at this point in the deal.

At the same time, legal counsel for each side will be working on a definitive agreement. More negotiations lie ahead as minor details, such as representations and warranties, etc., rise to the surface. Again, the lead equity investor can play an important role in spearheading these sometimes difficult final negotiations. Throughout the entire negotiating process, management should attempt to maintain a healthy relationship with the seller. After all, if the deal blows up, they may still need a job!

KEY ISSUES IN MANAGEMENT BUYOUTS

The foregoing "blueprint" should give incumbent managers a realistic perspective of what steps they must take and when to take them. During the process there are some particularly important issues, some of which have already been touched upon, that warrant further discussion.

Corporate Politicking

During the "seed planting" stage, managers may be tempted to engage in some form of corporate politicking to enhance their influence and control of the deal. This is more prevalent in corporate divestitures where politics are accepted as a way of life. It may take the form of seeking the support of some top executives, who, in management's opinion can help their cause. Using such tactics can be risky, because management may be unaware of the complex interpersonal dynamics in the corporate hierarchy. What they believe to be a "strong internal sponsor" can turn out to be a political adversary of the individual who really makes the decisions.

Management's best policy is to play the game honestly and straight forwardly with *all* parties engaged in corporate decision making. There are no prescriptions on how to deal with this issue other than approaching the buyout from the perspective of its added value to the parent company as well as its satisfaction of their own objectives.

Conflicts of Interest

Management cannot avoid the fact that, when it declares an interest in buying the company it runs, there is a conflict of interest with the owner. On one hand, management is still an employee and, as a result, has a legal and moral responsibility to the owner to represent his best interests. On the other hand, they are seeking to buy the company at the best possible price. While this is not an insurmountable problem, it should be recognized by both sides and dealt with in an effective manner.

One way of diffusing this issue in negotations was already discussed — interposing a third party "sponsor," who can deal with the owner on a more objective, less emotional basis. However, if management insists upon playing the primary role in negotiations, it should recognize the risks of alienating the owner to the point of losing both the deal and their jobs. Furthermore, regardless of their role in negotiations, management should *never* use proprietary financial information on the operation exclusively for its own purposes to the detriment of the seller. Nor should the operations be manipulated to improve its negotiating posture. Such actions are patently dishonest and, in addition, may dampen the interest of the financing sources.

The seller, if it is a large corporation, usually handles the conflict problem by appointing an individual or task force to handle the divestiture process. Any discussion with such individuals should, of course, be open and honest. In the end, honesty is always the best policy.

As the negotiations proceed, there is often an increasing polarization between management and the seller or its responsible individuals. This is normal as both managers and the seller begin to accept the reality that the umbilical cord will be cut shortly. In spite of this, management should attempt to maintain the relationship with its current employer on a high plane and attempt to view the process from the perspective of "solving a problem" for the seller.

Negotiating With Investors

While this subject has already been discussed, there is more to say. In particular, management is often confused on how many sources to approach and how and when to nail down the equity sharing agreement.

In general, management is better off, at least initially, seeking out several equity sources as *potential* investors. While many of the sources would disagree with this approach (sometimes referred to as "shot-gunning" the deal), it is management's only means of determining the market for their deal. It is the only way to determine how much equity they will be able to keep.

Once the investors have been initially approached and *before* negotiations with the seller begin, management should select one lead equity or mezzanine financing source and get a commitment regarding the financing amount, structure, terms, *and* equity required *in writing*. Because the final purchase price may not have been determined, the investor may be unable to commit to a specific equity split. But they should be able to give a range that relates back to the estimated purchase price range.

On the issue of how the equity pie is divided, management must realize that investors have certain return on investment targets to meet or they won't do the deal. Based upon their projections, lenders and investors will determine how much equity they need to achieve these targeted returns on their expected investment. Although there may be some differences from one investor to the next, they should not be the overriding factor in management's selection of a financial partner.

A more critical issue for management may be to evaluate more closely the people they are dealing with in the particular lending concern or investment firm. Do they have the authority or influence over major decisions? Are they responsive to critical questions? These are extremely important considerations because during the LBO process there will arise many opportunities for the investor to "change the deal" or lose control within his own organization. Therefore, management must subjectively assess whether the investor will honor the original commitments, assuming there have been no material changes in the facts upon which they were based.

Exit Strategy

A related matter concerns the compatibility between management and outside investors *after* the deal has closed. Both will have to "live" with the other for some period of time and probably encounter some difficult challenges in the years ahead. Therefore, it is imperative that management carefully evaluate whether its goals are consistent with those of the investor(s) *before* any long-term commitments are made by either side.

Of course, the obvious goal of both managers and investors is to make money by reducing debt and increasing cash flow. Beyond that, however, the needs and expectations of the two groups may be quite different. One area of potential conflict relates to "exit strategy" or the method by which both managers and outside investors will ultimately cash in on their respective holdings in the company. There are basically three different ways that investors and managers can convert their ownership in the company into cash or more liquid securities. Each has different implications for management.

Sale or Merger. The most obvious route to liquifying the investment is the same one that started it in the first place — sell (or merge) the company. If management has done its job properly, the company should reduce a significant portion of the acquisition debt over a five year period. At the same time, if operating earnings (before interest) show slow but steady growth, the company could be an attractive acquisition target for another private or corporate buyer. A sale could result in both managers and investors receiving substantial cash or, if the acquirer is a public company, stock.

While this is a common exit strategy, it sometimes conflicts with management's long-term goals. Quite often the reason managers are attracted to the concept of a buyout is to escape the corporate bureaucracy. This independence is lost if the company is acquired by a larger suitor. In some ways, they are right back where they started, working for someone else rather than themselves. Of course, if their profit from the sale is substantial enough, it may be much easier to "adjust" to this new working environment.

Management Buyout. In cases where managers value their independence more highly than the possible benefits of a sale, they may buy out investor interests themselves. This can be accomplished by refinancing the company and redeeming the shares of outsiders. The implicit assumption is that the company's operating performance and financial condition would permit a recapitalization with capital sources that would not dilute management's equity in the company.

Many equity investors are so concerned about recycling their investment that they assure themselves of an exit route. Typically this is an option to "put," or sell, their ownership to management at a specific price formula within a particular time period. Or they may have the dual option ("put" and "call") to either sell to management or buy management's shares. The pricing formula is usually a multiple of cash flow, book value, or a combination of both.

Initial Public Offering (IPO). In some cases, it is possible for the company to sell stock to the public and thus create a market where both managers and investors can subsequently sell their shares. This is more prevalent in high technology and rapidly growing markets than the mature industries that are more typical of LBO's. However, when the company shows above average growth prospects *and* the market conditions are good, IPO's are a viable route to liquidity. In recent years there have been numerous examples of public companies that have "gone private" via an LBO only to reappear as a public company a few years later. And several divestitures have also had successful IPO's. The most notable was the Gibson Greeting Card deal engineered by William Simon in the early 1980's.

Although the IPO may create substantial "paper profits," it is not easy for managers and investors to convert their holdings to cash immediately. Under SEC rules, they are limited to how much stock can be sold into the market over a period of time. And, even if such restrictions do not apply, the sale of substantial blocks of stock by management or other "insiders" will have a negative effect on the market for the company's shares. Therefore, if the IPO is the primary route to liquification, managers and investors must be prepared to be patient.

Regardless of which "exit route" is chosen, it should be clear that this matter must be discussed early between managers and their outside investors. If there appears to be some basic conflict as to certain objectives and how to achieve them, management may be better off finding some new investors.

9

ANALYZING THE COMPANY

THE PURPOSE OF DUE DILIGENCE

FINANCIAL STATEMENTS: AN OVERVIEW
- Limitations of Audited Statements

ANALYSIS OF THE BALANCE SHEET
- Cash or Cash Equivalents
- Accounts Receivable
- Inventory
- Machinery and Equipment
- Real Estate
- Prepaid Expenses
- Goodwill
- Accounts Payable
- Notes Payable
- Accrued Liabilities
- Long-Term Debt
- Deferred Taxes
- Unrecorded Liabilities
- Equity

ANALYSIS OF THE INCOME STATEMENT
- Factors Influencing Sales
- Cost of Sales
- Selling Expenses
- General and Administrative Expenses
- Interest Expense

9

KEY FINANCIAL RATIOS

Current Ratio
Quick Ratio
Average Collection Period (ACP) Ratio
Inventory Turnover
Debt Ratio
Return on Sales
Debt Coverage Ratio
Purchases to Trade Payables (PTTP) Ratio

THE PURPOSE OF DUE DILIGENCE

Before the buyer makes any financial commitment to go forward with the transaction, he must complete his analysis of the company's finances and operations. The role of the due diligence process in the overall leveraged buyout process was briefly explained in Chapter 7 (Orchestrating the Deal).

To recap, the due diligence effort in a leveraged buyout should be divided into two segments: preliminary and final. In each case the basic objective is the same. That is to confirm the original assumption that the company is a viable LBO prospect and can be financed. Beyond this, however, there were some major differences between the preliminary and final due diligence in terms of both scope and intensity.

In the preliminary stage, the buyer was under some time constraints to quickly get the information he needed. He had to dig for the essential facts, but didn't have the luxury of time to dig too deeply. In addition to his basic objective of determining viability and financial feasibility, the information gathered would form the basis of a valuation analysis and subsequent negotiations with the seller.

The final phase of due diligence is more detailed and comprehensive. More time is available to the buyer, or his professional advisors, not only to confirm the original assumptions, but also to look for hidden skeletons in the closet. This effort may even include a "Businessman's Review" performed by an outside accounting firm. The timing of this more in-depth (and expensive) analysis of the target company is *after* the buyer has completed his preliminary negotiations with the seller and confirmation of the financing from his sources.

In conducting his due diligence, especially in the preliminary phase, the buyer must be sensitive to the fact that customers, competition and some employees may not be aware of the pending sale. The extent of this knowledge should be discussed with the seller so that discretion may be exercised.

FINANCIAL STATEMENTS: AN OVERVIEW

The cornerstone of any due diligence effort is the financial information of the company being investigated. Before discussing financial statements in detail, however, a few comments about their preparation and limitations are in order.

The buyer, of course, always prefers the historical financial statements of the target company be audited by an independent certified public accountant. (In many cases, lenders require it.) Unless a sale of the business is anticipated or he is required by lenders to do so, however, the owner of a small, closely held company will rarely incur the additional expense of generating audited statements.

Audited statements are always available if the target company is publicly held. Where the target is a subsidiary of a public company, the audit is prepared for the parent's entire operation. Depending upon its relative size, the subsidiary's financial data may not be material when compared to the total operation of the parent. In such cases, key financial adjustments which are very significant to the buyer (e.g., inventory reserves) may not be material to the parent company's consolidated statement and will not alter the auditor's "opinion letter." Thus, buyers should not take comfort from a "clean" opinion of the parent company's financial statement alone. They must look closely at the materiality of any adjustments to the target company itself. In addition, the accounting systems of some selling parents will not be organized in a manner which will render an accurate statement of the financial condition of the company being sold. This problem frequently attends the spin-off of product lines of divisions with shared production facilities or sales forces.

When the financial statements of the company to be purchased are not certified, the buyer assumes a greater risk that the financial information upon which he is basing a decision may not be accurate or reliable. Usually, the seller will not want to incur the additional expense of an audit of past results just because the buyer wants it, and the buyer does not want to spend money to complete an audit of a company he doesn't yet, and may never, own. In such circumstances, the buyer may want to employ a CPA firm to conduct what is known as a "Businessman's Review." In this procedure, the accountant does not perform a complete analysis of the company, and hence does not offer a certified opinion. This abbreviated review tests specific accounts and verifies that information which is most crucial to the analysis of the business. (An outline of some of the questions asked in the businessman's review is set forth in Appendix F.)

Limitations of Audited Statements

Even if complete, audited financial statements with a "clean" (unqualified) opinion from a well-known accounting firm are available, it is important for the buyer to recognize their limitations. For example, even if the opinion states that "the foregoing financial statements fairly represent the financial position of Company XYZ as of December 31, 1987," the accountant bases this opinion on the "conformity of results with Generally Accepted Accounting Principles (GAAP)." These principles are mainly concerned with the consistency with which the selected accounting methods are applied from year to year, not with the economic reality of the results. This emphasis leads to certain deficiencies in representing financial data in a form which is meaningful to the buyer. Some of the more important of these deficiencies are:

- Most assets are reported at cost. In highly inflationary periods, such as the 1970's, this significantly understates asset values.
- Some assets and liabilities are omitted entirely. Examples of excluded assets are patents, licenses, trademarks, copyrights, mailing lists, contracts, and goodwill. Liabilities that are often omitted include lease obligations, compensation or union contracts, and pending litigation claims.
- Inventory accounting methods may distort asset values and operating results. The choice of First In, First Out (FIFO) vs. Last In, First Out (LIFO) accounting methods may have a significant impact on both the balance sheet and income statement.

It is not intended here to suggest that certified statements prepared in accordance with GAAP are not useful. However, the buyer must be aware that they are limited, look beyond these basic financial data and, if necessary, make appropriate adjustments.

ANALYSIS OF THE BALANCE SHEET

The logical starting point for the due diligence process is the target's balance sheet. An exacting review of the nature and mix of assets and liabilities will provide a floor or foundation for valuing the company. It will also serve to refine previous assumptions made in connection with the structuring and financing of the proposed acquisition.

Cash or Cash Equivalents

In private transactions, the company may have significant cash balances which will impact the personal tax considerations of the owner/seller. Rather than take this cash as dividends and incur ordinary income tax liabilities, it used to be more advantageous for the seller to adjust the purchase price and pay the lower capital gains tax rate. With the enactment of the 1986 Tax Reform Act, ordinary income tax rates are the same as those for capital gains and personal tax rates are lower than corporate rates. As a result, many owners may be converting to sub-chapter S corporations and extracting all excess cash from the company.

In the case of corporate divestitures, cash in subsidiaries is usually funnelled back to the parent through intercompany accounts. However, the buyer may stipulate a minimum cash balance for working capital purposes if the transaction is structured as a purchase of stock. Cash balances are also possible in cases where public companies "go private" utilizing the cash merger technique. (See Chapter 12.)

Where cash is an asset of the company to be purchased, this reflects favorably in the financing process. Although the purchase price is usually adjusted to reflect it, a cash balance improves the liquidity of the balance sheet and increases the down payment that can be made to the seller.

The buyer must verify that the cash is freely usable for any purpose of the company. If any part of it must be held as compensating balances for bank loans, this fact should be noted and reflected in the cash flow plan. If the company has foreign operations, it is important to determine whether the cash is in the form of U.S. dollars or some other currency. The latter funds may be subject to restrictions or changes in value.

Marketable securities are usually not included in the assets of a company to be sold. If they are, the buyer must ascertain their true market value, assuming they are to be immediately liquidated. A determination of any restrictions on transfer is also in order.

Accounts Receivable

Accounts receivable are a key asset. If any borrowings are to be made against the company's assets to finance the acquisition, receivables are the prime collateral. They can be quickly turned into cash to provide working capital to support company operations. Therefore, they must be evaluated very carefully.

First of all, receivables generated in the normal course of business (trade receivables) and other receivables which may have a longer term (e.g., loans to shareholders) must be differentiated. It is imperative that the seller provide a current aging of accounts receivable. With this aging, the rate at which receivables are being collected can be determined. This must be compared to the normal terms which the company offers on its trade credit as well as the credit policies of the industry.

If there is a significant amount of past due trade receivables, the reasons must be determined. It could just be a poor collection effort, which can be easily remedied by tighter procedures. On the other hand, the problem could stem from conditions attached to the sale or to unsound credit policies, either of which may result in uncollectible accounts.

The buyer must determine the approximate amount of uncollectible accounts receivable and, if it is substantially larger than the company's allowance for bad debts, make the appropriate adjustment to the value of accounts receivable carried on the balance sheet. He should also note if there are any conditional sales or liberal return provisions. These will negatively impact how the lender views the accounts receivable assets as collateral.

Inventory

In a manufacturing, wholesaling or retailing business, inventory is one of the primary assets and must be studied closely. Unfortunately, inventory is the most difficult asset to evaluate and is the most suspect as to its value on the balance sheet. As will be seen in Chapter 12, inventory is often the pivotal asset in the financing decision because of the wide disparity of classifications and lender preferences.

The starting point in an analysis of inventory is a detailed list which, preferably, has classified inventory by product line, age and type (i.e., raw materials, work-in-process, finished goods). The seller should be queried on the procedures and frequency of taking physical inventory counts and the method whereby this is reconciled to the perpetual inventory records. Next, the inventory should be physically inspected and evaluated as to its usability, marketability and fungibility. Some determination must be made as to the amount of obsolete or slow-moving inventory. The simplest way of measuring this is to compare the company's inventory turnover ratio to (1) its ratio for previous years and (2) the turnover ratio of other companies in the same industry. For this purpose, the *Almanac of Industrial and Financial Ratios* (published annually by Prentice-Hall) is an excellent source.

If the products manufactured or distributed have recently been improved or redesigned, there will no doubt be some "dead" parts or finished goods inventory. The seller should be questioned on the procedures and frequency of revaluing inventories to the lower of cost or market and the establishment of adequate reserves. The reserves and write-downs for the last two or three years should be scrutinized.

If the company is engaged in manufacturing, the cost system and its impact on inventory must also be analyzed. Standard cost systems of large corporations often burden inventory with excessive overhead, resulting in bloated book values of inventory. The frequency of updating the standard cost system should be ascertained. Likewise, a determination should be made on the reasonableness of the burden factor on inventory values.

The method by which inventory is accounted for can have a dramatic impact on its balance sheet value and reported net income. This is especially true where material costs have rapidly escalated due to inflation. Where inventory is accounted for on a First In, First Out (FIFO) basis, the balance sheet more accurately reflects the true value of inventories while income is overstated. If the Last In, First Out (LIFO) method is employed, and there is a substantial amount of product purchased at "old" prices, inventory values may be understated on the balance sheet. From a financing standpoint, this could have a favorable impact if the effect of LIFO accounting on inventory values can be documented. In such cases, the lender may raise his loan advance rates to reflect the increased economic value of the inventory.

Other considerations in the evalution of inventory are (1) irrevocable purchase commitments, (2) stock held on consignment or consigned to others for sale, and (3) if the company is involved in long-term contracts, the adequacy of accounting methods and their impact on inventory values.

The ultimate objective in the evaluation of inventory is to determine if any significant adjustments to purported values are in order. The job is made easier if the target company has recently been audited and given an unqualified opinion with respect to the inventory. In the absence of an audit, or if the buyer is unfamiliar with the particular business, this is an area which may require the services of an outside consultant or accountant.

Machinery and Equipment

Machinery and equipment assets are often understated on the books because of the combined effects of inflation (which results in higher replacement costs) and the establishment of depreciation reserves for accounting purposes. Thus, it is not unusual to have assets costing $500,000 five years ago on the books at $100,000, but with a real economic value of $700,000. (This is a good example of the "hidden asset values" discussed in Chapter 5.)

The buyer's task is to determine the real economic value of these assets and make the appropriate adjustments to the balance sheet. This process is greatly simplified if there has been a recent appraisal of these assets by a qualified independent appraiser. It should be understood that an appraisal of fixed assets is different from an appraisal of the entire company as a "going business." A fixed asset appraisal is based upon the estimated values of the assets if sold in a liquidation process. This usually means the amounts which could be generated in an auctioneer's sale. This figure is used by the asset-based lender in determining the maximum amount which can be borrowed against this class of assets.

The main focus of the buyer's attention should be on the degree of technological obsolescence of the equipment and the resulting impact on future capital spending requirements. After reviewing a detailed list of equipment which includes model, serial number, date of purchase, purchase price, accumulated depreciation and current book value, the equipment should be physically inspected. This inspection should be more thorough than a cursory look taken during the initial visit to the target's facilities. The relative proportion of manual, semi-automated and fully-automated operations should also be observed. A high degree of manual labor associated with the equipment may be a sign of impending obsolescence.

After the inspection, representatives or distributors of the equipment's manufacturers should be contacted and questioned about the market value of the equipment and productivity in relation to more recently developed models. At the same time, future equipment and its impact on the value of existing models can be determined. If there are some substantial innovations ahead, the company's assets may be over-valued on the books. Moreover, the buyer may be required to invest in new machinery and equipment after the company is purchased in order to remain competitive.

Another key aspect of the equipment is its marketability to other users. Such will usually depend upon whether the assets are general purpose in nature or highly specific to the processes of the target company. If the latter case is true, the assets will obviously be more difficult to sell or finance.

Real Estate

Real estate assets are much like machinery and equipment in that they are often understated on the books and have appreciated in value. Because of the more rapid appreciation in land values and the fact that improvements have a much slower rate of technological and functional obsolescence than equipment, there is often greater "hidden asset value" in the real estate. This is especially true with corporate sellers, where the hidden value of real estate assets is often dwarfed by the magnitude of the target's other assets. Until recently, this type of seller did not pay too much attention to understated real estate values. However, as corporate America has become more "asset-conscious," corporate officers responsible for divestitures have looked more closely at underlying real estate values and reflect them in the asking price.

Plants, warehouses, and office facilities should be physically inspected and evaluated as to their adequacy to support future needs. If the facilities are leased, with the primary assets consisting of leasehold improvements, all leases must be carefully reviewed. A write-off of these assets may be required if the company is forced to move or terminates the lease. The impact on capital requirements for plant modernization and additional leasehold improvements should also be noted and incorporated into the cash flow plan to be developed later.

As with machinery and equipment, the collateral value of real estate to the lender is directly proportional to the degree to which the facilities will service general purpose operations. A large, single-purpose facility will be more difficult to sell or finance to generate acquisition debt or future working capital requirements.

Prepaid Expenses

These assets, which consist of items such as insurance premiums, license fees and taxes, are usually not significant. However, they should be reviewed to ensure they are not overstated. This is also a good way to review the insurance coverage and verify its sufficiency. This review should be supported by appraisals or estimates of the replacement value of the inventory and fixed assets.

Goodwill

In 999 out of 1,000 cases, goodwill stated on the books means almost nothing to the purchaser. It is usually the residue of a premium previously paid by the target company over the value of its tangible assets. For the buyer or acquiring corporation's planning purposes, this figure should be totally omitted. It serves only to distort the net book value of the assets being acquired. Courts have defined goodwill as the value paid for going enterprises to reflect the probability that customers will return. Value obviously should be given to goodwill, but this should be reflected more directly in the valuation process (see Chapter 10), rather than as historical financial data.

Accounts Payable

The analysis of the company's balance sheet requires a review of its liabilities as well as its assets. The first liability to consider is the accounts payable. Accounts payable, which originate from trade creditors in the normal course of business, must be distinguished from other nonrecurring creditors. This threshold consideration is necessary to immediately identify the primary creditors of the company, including its key vendors and suppliers. These supplier relationships should be evaluated from the standpoint of the length of their existence, whether any acceptable alternate suppliers are available and special terms or considerations. In many cases, existing terms will change with the transfer of ownership, or some key suppliers may not continue to ship when they realize that a secured lender has become a senior creditor.

Trade creditors are usually very sensitive to any changes in company ownership. Their concern is magnified in transactions which are highly leveraged. This is especially true in the case of corporate divestitures where the operation passes from strong financial hands into a highly leveraged financial structure where a secured lender has a priority lien on inventory and other assets over trade creditors. Under these circumstances a company loses its power to exert pressure on the key suppliers through its parent. Special payment terms and quick delivery or turnaround time may no longer be available to a new owner. Therefore, after the transaction is consummated, one of the first responsibilities of new ownership will be to meet with the important suppliers and trade creditors to get the relationship started on the right foot. Although most suppliers will cooperate because they do not want to lose the business, many will be more cautious in setting credit limits.

To analyze the accounts payable it is necessary to get a detailed current aging of all trade payables. This aging should reflect trade debt which is not substantially beyond the terms provided by the suppliers and vendors. For example, if there is a significant amount of trade debt which is beyond 60 or 90 days, this will have a negative impact on relationships with suppliers and the company's ability to generate needed working capital from trade sources. The buyer should also compute and evaluate the "purchases to trade payables ratio" for the last several months and fiscal periods to determine any negative trends. (This key ratio is discussed in detail later in this chapter.) Any deterioration may have a negative impact on the future availability of working capital.

If the trade debt is already "stretched out," the seller must be questioned to determine if there are any pending lawsuits filed by trade creditors to collect their debt. In the case of turnaround situations, this is very common and must be effectively dealt with to avoid unexpected attachments of the company's assets. In some cases, the company may have valid reasons for its failure to pay arising out of non-performance or disputed merchandise. In this event it may be appropriate to reduce the liability by specific amounts.

Notes Payable

The seller should provide a detailed schedule of all notes payable by the company. The schedule should include the name of the party to whom the note is payable, the date of the note, its original amount, current balance, interest rate, periodic payment, due dates and any other special terms, conditions or payment provisions. It should also specify which assets of the corporation, if any, are encumbered by any of these obligations. Special attention must be given to restrictive clauses or covenants in any of the notes or security agreements which would impact future financing flexibility of the company. Discussions should also be held with the seller or his representative as to which of the notes are to be assumed by the buyer. Although the notes listed on this portion of the balance sheet are short-term (one year or less) in nature, there may be a current portion of long-term notes included. This amount should be specified and correlated with the analysis of long-term debt.

Accrued Liabilities

The balance sheet's accrued liabilities consist of short-term obligations such as vacation and sick benefits, taxes which are due but have not yet been paid and other miscellaneous liabilities. In normal situations, these liabilities do not present any great problems to the prospective buyer. In turnaround situations or in the case where large layoffs or terminations are contemplated, however, the buyer may unknowingly assume substantial accrued vacation and benefit liabilities which were incurred under the previous owner's stewardship. In such cases, adjustments may be made to reflect an equitable allocation of these liabilities.

The buyer must also look very carefully at the accrued tax liabilities to ensure that these are not delinquent. This can be confirmed by reviewing the payroll tax returns for the most recent quarter and also the most recent payroll tax deposits. It must be emphasized that if payroll, sales or income taxes are seriously delinquent, there can be a substantial negative impact on operations.

Long-Term Debt

As with the short-term notes payable, the seller should provide a detailed schedule of long-term debt which sets forth its conditions, restrictions and payment schedule. Any provisions which would preclude the assumption of this debt by a new buyer should be carefully evaluated. In some cases, attractive long-term liabilities which are assumable can be an *asset* to the buyer. For example, if long-term debt has low interest rates with long-term payouts, as in the case of older mortgage debt, it is sometimes possible to discount this debt below its face value in repaying it to the original lender.

Deferred Taxes

If the company has had a continuous program of capital improvements and has utilized accelerated depreciation in amortizing these assets, there will be a deferred tax account in the liability section of the balance sheet. This is a liability which is not paid as long as the company continues to spend money for new capital investment and to amortize capital improvements. However, in cases where capital expenditures slow down or cease, the company may have to begin amortizing this liability. The subsequent impact on cash flow caused by the payment of deferred taxes must be carefully considered by the buyer when formulating a decision on the continuance of the target's capital improvement program.

Unrecorded Liabilities

In addition to the obligations which have been discussed, there are many liabilities of the company which are never recorded on its balance sheet. These must be clearly identified and quantified so that the necessary adjustments can be made to the financial statement. Such liabilities include: pending litigation, warranty contracts, sales allowances or credits, and equipment or other leases and contracts. The buyer should obtain copies of all documents pertaining to the above liabilities and carefully analyze the potential impact of these on company resources. Particular attention must be given to binding leases on assets, facilities or equipment which may no longer be economically useful to the company. These amounts should be quantified and discounted as a business liability. Warranty costs are another potential claim on company assets which should be considered. The best means of ascertaining this cost is to evaluate past period warranty reserves and expenses and discuss the performance of recently shipped material with customers.

Equity

All classes of equity securities, including preferred and common stock, should be reviewed with the seller. The division of ownership of the stock in the case of privately held companies and the respective voting rights of each shareholder should be specified. The inexperienced buyer, after a substantial investment of time and effort, will often discover, to his disappointment, that minority shareholders have the right to block a sale of the company or its assets. Any such roadblocks to the consummation of a transaction should be discussed as early as possible in the evaluation of the company.

Closely related to the equity are stock option plans for company employees. If such plans exist, copies of all documentation should be provided by the seller and investigated by the buyer. Although the buyer may not be legally required to continue such plans, the expectations of key employees may preclude plan termination. To do so would have a harmful effect on employee morale.

ANALYSIS OF THE INCOME STATEMENT

The foregoing analysis of the company's assets and liabilities is a very important step in the analytical process conducted by a prospective buyer. However, most companies are bought on the basis of their continued operation as a going concern. This assumes that the company's assets are worth not only what they would generate if the business were to be liquidated, but also some incremental value determined by the amount of future earnings these assets could generate. This incremental value of the company's assets, if any, will now be considered as we move to a detailed analysis of the income statement. The objective of this exercise is to formulate an adjusted historical income statement based on revised assumptions attendant the change of ownership. It will also enable the buyer to generate a proforma income statement and cash flow based upon historical operations and his outlook of the future.

Factors Influencing Sales

The key to the bottom line of any business is the top line, the revenue that the company can generate. This, in turn, will depend upon the company's relative position in the overall marketplace in which it competes. If there is any one area in the due diligence process which should be emphasized by a prospective buyer, it is in the analysis of the marketplace. The marketplace is where the fate of a company will ultimately be determined. Therefore, the buyer must become intimately familiar with all the forces which will impact the company's competitive position in that marketplace.

Market Segments. The buyer must define, as precisely as possible, the specific market segments, or niches, for the company's products and services. What is the size of these segments and how fast are they growing or shrinking? What are the geographic boundaries of this marketplace as far as the company is concerned? Having defined the size of this marketplace and the role of the company within it, the buyer is now in a position to estimate the target company's approximate share of the market and whether it increased or decreased over the past few years.

Technological Change. The marketplace is the arena where decisions are being made daily by customers and competitors. These decisions will have a definite long-term impact on the company's future. Markets are constantly changing as customers strive to improve their operations or competitive positions. Thus, there is a universal need for improved efficiency and lower costs. As a result, the target company is always vulnerable to technological change or competitive innovations which may have a negative impact on sales. The mere fact that certain practices have worked in the past is no assurance that they will continue to work in the future. Any such changes must be addressed and considered in the projection of future revenues.

The reason for this attention to the company's marketplace is to make a more meaningful evaluation of historical and projected sales. This can only be done if all factors — past, present and future — are considered. The sources of information for this research are numerous. The primary source is the company itself. Opinions of key management personnel who have lived with this company for some time are the starting point. There are also numerous sources of written material, including trade association releases, economic studies by local financial institutions and industry studies by securities firms. Beyond the written word, there is no substitute for going out and making contact with as many people as possible. Suppliers, customers, competitors, lending institutions and anyone else knowledgeable about the industry should be consulted. Of course, the buyer must be discrete and careful not to violate the seller's confidentiality in these discussions.

Competition. Another key ingredient of any market analysis is a detailed study of the competition. Who are the major competitors and what are their relative strengths and weaknesses? Have there been any recent trends which give certain competitors a significant edge in the marketplace? Although it is impossible to directly control the actions of competitors, it is vitally important that their strengths, weaknesses, advantages, and disadvantages be fully assessed. Strong competitors often employ predatory pricing practices against newly acquired companies with a small share of the market especially if they perceive a weakened financial condition.

Economic Conditions. In addition to competitive factors, there will be other external forces impacting the demand for the company's products or services. Foremost among these are the general economic conditions. Although it is difficult to forecast, some consideration must be given to the impact of interest rate fluctuations, government spending priorities and regional economic dislocations. In particular, the effect of these variables on the specific industry in which the company participates should be closely studied. Are there any identifiable trends which would indicate either a positive or negative influence on demand? For example, if the company is a manufacturer or distributor of building materials, will future interest rate movements be positive or negative for the company's outlook?

Regulatory Climate. In addition to economic considerations, the regulatory environment in which the company operates must be scrutinized. Are there trends which would either increase or decrease the regulatory constraints now operating on the company? And, if so, what will be the consequences for the business of the target? For example, is there increasing sensitivity to environmental considerations which would have an impact on demand for the company's products or services?

Customer Base. Aside from market forces, the second most important factor affecting the company's sales is the make-up of its customer base. The seller should provide a list of the company's ten largest customers and their respective percentage of company sales for the past five years. In discussions with the seller, the buyer should determine if there are any impending changes which will affect the customer base. If one or two customers are responsible for a disproportionate amount of the company's sales, this should be a danger signal to a potential owner. Regardless of the closeness or solidity of the relationship with these customers, the company is always vulnerable to sudden shifts in demand from or changes in the management of these customers. Such an eventuality could have a disastrous effect on revenues, and it may take a substantial amount of time for the company to recuperate. If high leverage is employed to acquire the company, its cash flow may not be sufficient to support operations after the loss of business.

The Sales Forecast. Perhaps the single most important set of assumptions a prospective buyer will make are related to the sales forecast. It is the foundation upon which all other key assumptions related to the structuring and financing of the acquisition are based. Therefore, it is imperative this exercise be conducted with extreme caution and study. The starting point for this forecast is an analysis of the firm's sales history. Conditions in the marketplace, including customer needs and competitive forces are always changing. Therefore, historical sales do not provide an absolute indication of future sales. However, they do provide the starting point from which future sales are projected. Assumptions related to the national and local economic outlook must also be incorporated in the sales forecast. If a company is engaged in a cyclical industry, for example, there should be some allowance for cyclical swings in the sales volume.

In addition to adjusting the historical sales base to generate a forecast, it is useful to base future sales on the company's projected share of the market. Assumptions regarding the share of the market which the company will achieve must consider the realities of competitive pressures in the marketplace. The rate of growth of the market segments in which the company is engaged will also have some bearing as to the rate of growth of company sales.

Since the sales forecast is such an integral and important part of the overall decision, estimates should be generated by the buyer to supplement the budget projections of the current owner. The buyer must remember that, because of their desire to paint a rosy picture for prospective buyers, projections by the current owners are often overly optimistic. Accordingly, these projections should be verified in the marketplace by the buyer.

Cyclical or Sick? With regard to cyclicity, it is very important for the buyer to distinguish between a "cyclical" business and a "sick" business. A "sick" business invariably has one or more basic flaws which may, or may not, be curable. Examples of incurable flaws are obsolete products or services, inefficient plants, and increased competition from lower cost producers. Curable flaws include poor management and control of the business. Cyclical businesses, on the other hand, are usually only demand-sensitive due to economic slow-downs. And if the target company has a dominant share of the market, it can survive the down cycles. This is true even with highly leveraged capitalizations with properly structured debt.

Cost of Sales

Once the target company's sales have been analyzed in some detail, it is necessary to move to the estimated expenses related to those sales. The cost of sales is generally divided into three major categories:

- The cost of materials related to the products;
- The cost of any direct labor which must be utilized in production; and
- The indirect expenses which must be incurred in the manufacture of the products.

Materials. In connection with the cost of materials, it is necessary for the prospective buyer to investigate the major suppliers of the company. Although this matter has been previously discussed in the analysis of trade creditors during the balance sheet evaluation, it is of such significance that it merits additional treatment in connection with the income statement. If there are several suppliers willing to provide these products at competitive prices, there is no problem. However, if there are special relationships, contracts or arrangements with key suppliers which may or may not be terminated upon the transfer of ownership, these issues must be effectively dealt with at this time. Additionally, the buyer must evaluate any factors which would cause a significant increase in the cost of these materials and whether these costs can be passed on in the marketplace. If the competitors are in a position to avoid such cost increases or minimize their impact, the target company may be in a precarious competitive position.

Labor. The second component of the cost of sales is the direct labor expenses incurred in the production process. If the company is engaged in the production of products which require a substantial amount of both skilled and unskilled labor, the buyer must be concerned about the availability and cost of local labor. A related concern is the presence or threat of organized labor and its consequent impact on labor cost and production interruptions. It could be that one of the motivating factors behind the seller's desire to sell the company is the threat of organized labor. Of course, where the target company's production processes are more automated, considerations of the availability and cost of labor become less important.

Manufacturing Overhead. The final ingredient impacting the cost of production is the factory overhead or "burden." Included in this category are items such as rent, utilities, indirect labor, supervisory personnel and employee benefits. Unless there is the need for newer or larger facilities, it is unlikely these expenses will change significantly from their historical levels. An exception to this is the case where substantial increases in energy costs are possible. Another important consideration in the analysis of these expenses is the degree to which they are "under-absorbed" in the case of lower sales volume. Since these expenses consist primarily of fixed costs, a substantial decline in sales will have a relatively large negative effect on the cost of sales and gross profit margin.

The combination of the above categories of costs related directly to the cost of producing the product will determine the net contribution of each sale to the company's overhead and operating expenses. In most manufacturing businesses, this contribution, or gross profit margin, should be at least 40 percent of each sales dollar. Anything less than this will usually not generate large enough profit margins, especially if the company has a substantial amount of debt. In distribution companies, where sales volumes and asset turnover factors are much greater, gross profit margins of 15 percent to 20 percent may be reasonable.

Selling Expenses

Selling expenses include all costs associated with the marketing of products or services. Examples of such expenses are salaries of marketing and sales personnel, advertising expenses, travel and entertainment expenses incurred in the course of selling, and any related administrative expenses. An analysis of the selling expenses also entails a review of the effectiveness of the channels of distribution currently employed by the company in the movement of its products to the marketplace. Are the products sold directly by company sales personnel or through third parties (e.g., distributors and manufacturer's representatives)? The buyer should not necessarily assume that current practices are best. Rather, he should question the seller as to why certain marketing techniques are employed. In his analysis of the marketplace, the buyer should confirm that the current channels of distribution are, in fact, the most efficient ones. An in-depth analysis frequently reveals that selling expenses can be reduced by utilizing alternate channels of distribution. If this can be verified, the reduced level of selling expenses should be incorporated into the proforma income statement and cash flow.

General and Administrative Expenses

General and administrative expenses are perhaps the area in which the greatest number of adjustments can be made after ownership of a company is transferred. If the seller is a private, closely held corporation, it is highly probable that the current owners took very large salaries and bonuses in order to minimize the tax consequences of taking compensation in the form of dividends. A new buyer may elect to forego a higher salary in order to generate more working capital or to service any debt incurred in the acquisition. Private sellers also frequently "employ" relatives or friends who perform inefficiently, if at all. If this is the case, some allowance can be made in the projection of future expenses to reflect the discontinuance of this policy.

If, on the other hand, the buyer is not going to be involved in the day-to-day management of the company's operations, it will be necessary to provide funding for a full-time manager. In such a case, the buyer must evaluate the role of the current owner in operational management. After doing so, he may conclude that there is not sufficient cash flow to support an absentee owner.

Interest Expense

Since the company's financial structure may be completely altered as a result of the acquisition, the firm's historical interest expenses may be irrelevent. In determining the impact of interest expense and debt service after the financing structure has been finalized, however, it is necessary to have an estimate of income before interest and taxes. The income and cash flow included in this estimate will determine the nature and extent of financing to be used in the acquisition.

If the acquisition is highly leveraged, it is frequently a major shock to operating management to work under the burden of higher interest charges. However, in some corporate divestiture transactions, the parent company has charged its subsidiaries or divisions for the cost of capital employed in the business. This "cost of capital" expense is often equivalent to new interest charges resulting from acquisition debt. In those cases, the adjustment for incumbent management is much less severe.

KEY FINANCIAL RATIOS

There are a number of key financial ratios which can assist a buyer in the analytical processes attendant the acquisition of a going concern. Ratio analysis not only provides a direct measurement of specific financial relationships, it also renders a useful projection of trends. Many of the ratios are also important tools which assist in the formulation of proforma financial statements. The following paragraphs will briefly explain several key financial ratios and their role in the overall analysis.

Current Ratio

The current ratio is a measure of the company's liquidity and its ability to meet its current obligations. It is computed as follows:

$$\text{Current Ratio} = \frac{\text{Current Assets}}{\text{Current Liabilities}}$$

The current ratio is one measure of the "cleanliness" of the target company's balance sheet. (See Chapter 5.) While a current ratio of 3:1 or greater is preferred, it should be at least 2:1.

A current ratio which has declined over the past few fiscal periods indicates reduced liquidity. This does not necessarily indicate that the company has problems. It may be financing rapid growth with short-term borrowing and/or trade credit. The buyer should be satisfied, however, that any decline in the current ratio can be attributed to an acceptable reason.

The difference between the current assets and current liabilities constitutes a firm's net working capital. This sum is used as a guideline by asset-based lenders in financing buyouts. To the buyer and the lender a purchase price at or below net working capital is exceedingly attractive if it does not exceed the perceived liquidation value of current assets.

Quick Ratio

The quick ratio is further measure of the company's liquidity and ability to meet financial obligations within a short period of time. It is computed as follows:

$$\text{Quick Ratio} = \frac{\text{Cash + Marketable Securities + Accounts Receivable}}{\text{Current Liabilities}}$$

This ratio is important to the leveraged buyer since all current assets employed in its determination are highly financeable. The higher the quick ratio, the more financeable the deal.

Average Collection Period (ACP) Ratio

The ACP ratio is the average number of days that the current accounts receivable are outstanding, based upon the latest 12 months of sales. It is both a measure of the company's liquidity and the efficiency of its utilization of assets. It is computed as follows:

$$\text{ACP (days)} = \frac{\text{Trade Accounts Receivable}}{\text{Annual Credit Sales}/360}$$

This is a very important ratio from the standpoint of the buyer. If the ACP ratio is substantially in excess of normal credit terms, it could be an indicator of either poor collection procedures, poor credit policies, or both. If the problem is attributable solely to inefficient collection procedures, more effective collection efforts could yield a substantial amount of working capital. For example, a receivable base of $5,000,000 with a current ACP of 60 days could generate $1,250,000 in additional cash if the ACP was improved to 45 days. This ratio is equally important to the determination of working capital requirements in the formulation of proforma cash flow.

Inventory Turnover

The inventory turnover ratio is a measure of the efficiency with which the company utilizes its inventory resources and its ability to meet current order demand. It is measured as follows:

$$\text{Inventory Turnover} = \frac{\text{Cost of Goods Sold}}{\text{Period Ending Inventory}}$$

If, due to seasonal or other factors, inventory levels are below average at the end of a fiscal period, a more accurate indication is given by using an average inventory value. High inventory turnover can indicate one of two things. It could mean very good inventory management or undercapitalization resulting in missed sales opportunities. A low ratio, on the other hand, can be indicative of poor inventory management, significant amounts of obsolete inventory, or both. In any case, the buyer must probe beneath the surface to isolate the real reason for the current turnover rate and justification for improving it in the future. As with the ACP ratio, the inventory turnover ratio is used extensively to determine working capital needs for inventory in the formulation of proforma cash flow.

A refinement of the inventory turnover ratio is a ratio of the gross profits during a period to the period ending inventory. This provides a more accurate measure of the relationship between profitability and inventory levels which is particularly useful in trend analysis.

Debt Ratio

The purpose of this ratio is to measure the degree of leverage in the company's current financial structure. It is computed as shown on the following page.

$$\text{Debt Ratio} = \frac{\text{Total Liabilities}}{\text{Total Assets}}$$

A debt ratio of 0.5 would indicate that the company's assets are 50 percent leveraged. As noted in Chapter 5, if the leverage is already in place in the target company, it becomes difficult, if not impossible, to satisfy the existing lenders, new lenders, and the seller. Therefore, it is preferable that the target company have a debt ratio of 0.30 or less.

A trend which shows an increasing debt ratio could indicate that the company cannot generate sufficient retained earnings or outside equity to finance its growth. When the growth is too fast, it could spell trouble if structured as a leveraged deal.

Return on Sales

Of all the profitability ratios, the return on sales ratio is the most meaningful. It is a measure of residual profits on each dollar of sales and is computed as follows:

$$\text{Return on Sales} = \frac{\text{Net Income}}{\text{Total Sales}}$$

The acceptable standards of this ratio will vary with the type of business (manufacturing, wholesale distribution, retail, service). It is particularly useful in trend analysis. A declining ratio could indicate poor management, intensified competition, uncontrollable cost increases, or a combination of all these factors. The buyer must dig to find the real reason for any negative trends and determine if they can be reversed.

Debt Coverage Ratio

The debt coverage ratio is a measure of how the company, under its revised financial structure, can operate under the burden of existing and new debt. It is computed as follows:

$$\text{Debt Service Ratio} = \frac{\text{Earnings Before Interest \& Taxes (EBIT)}}{\text{Annual Debt Service}}$$

This ratio is utilized extensively in the analysis of various financing structures and their impact on the company's cash flow. The acceptable ratio will vary with each company and the stability of its income stream. Most lenders and investors in leveraged deals require a debt service ratio of at least 1.1. If the company is in a cyclical industry or is subject to periodic profit squeezes, the coverage requirement will no doubt be higher, perhaps as much as 1.5.

Purchases to Trade Payables (PTTP) Ratio

The PTTP ratio is a good indicator of the condition of the company's trade credit. It is computed as follows:

$$\text{PTTP (days)} = \frac{\text{Trade Accounts Payable}}{\text{Annual Material Purchases}/360}$$

If this ratio substantially exceeds the normal credit terms offered by trade creditors, it indicates that there is little or no room for further extension of the payables and has a resultant impact on working capital. The experienced leveraged buyer prefers companies that are paying trade creditors on a relatively current basis. This is another aspect of the "clean balance sheet" criteria which is so important in leveraged situations.

At the completion of the analysis of the balance sheet and income statement, the buyer can begin the all important task of constructing the proforma financial statements. (See Chapter 11.) These projections will verify the feasibility of the proposed investment and have a significant influence on how the deal is structured from a financial standpoint. Once the financial structure has been proposed, the buyer can compute the effect of the acquisition financing on interest expense and formulate the proforma balance sheet and cash flow.

This analysis also provides him with the information to determine a value for the company. The various approaches to valuation analysis are the subject of the next chapter.

10 VALUING THE COMPANY

At the conclusion of the target company analysis, the buyer should have a thorough understanding of the firm and its business. In some areas, he may know more about the business than the seller. This is particularly true with respect to what is happening in the marketplace and the relative strengths of competitors. The reason for this surprising circumstance is that most sellers are too busy running the day-to-day business and just don't have the time to perform an objective evaluation of these external factors.

The buyer's perception of the company's financial position, historical earnings, and potential earning power are embodied in the three financial statements constructed following the preliminary evaluation process. These are the adjusted balance sheet, the adjusted income statement, and the proforma income statement. These documents provide the data from which the buyer can determine the value of the company.

In all probability, the buyer has already conducted a "back of the envelope" valuation during the initial qualification stage. This, however, was based strictly upon the limited financial information he had in his hands at the time. Now, after completing the preliminary analysis, he has refined this financial data and is in a position to more accurately value the business.

The purpose of the valuation is to enable the buyer to set some realistic limits on what he is willing to pay for the company. In most cases, he will have a fairly good idea of what the seller expects. Hopefully, it is not significantly higher than the buyer's estimate of value. Because any differences must be resolved in the preliminary negotiations, it is important that the valuation is completed before meeting with the seller to negotiate.

SOME DEFINITIONS OF "VALUE"

Before addressing some of the methods of valuing a business, it is important to understand that the term "value" has more than one definition. Moreover, it often means different things to different people, depending upon their perspectives. For example, the buyer's definition of value differs from that of the collateral lender. Here are a few descriptions of "value."

Fair Market Value

As defined by the Internal Revenue Service, fair market value is "that price at which a willing buyer will buy and a willing seller will sell a certain item of property, neither being under any compulsion to buy or sell and both having a reasonable knowledge of all relevant facts." This is the meaning of value most often referred to by buyers and sellers.

Present Value

Perhaps the best technical definition of value, for both the buyer and seller, is "the net present worth, in current dollars, of expected future cash flows generated by the business over a specific period of time." Under this definition, the value of the future benefits of the business is adjusted for the length of time it takes to receive them. It is based upon the premise that a dollar is worth more if received today than if received a year from today.

Liquidation Value

Liquidation value is "the aggregate value of a company's assets, if sold at auction, minus its liabilities." This definition of value also comes complete with its own variations. An "orderly liquidation" can take place over an extended time frame and usually results in higher proceeds of sale. A "forced liquidation" is implemented quickly and usually generates lower proceeds of sale. Liquidation value is the measure often used by the secured lender in his loan underwriting decisions. Occasionally, it is meaningful to the buyer who will implement a partial liquidation of a company's assets as part of the overall acquisition plan.

Replacement Value

Replacement value is "the expected cost to replace the assets of the business, less the existing liabilities." This concept is often used by insurance companies which insure assets and buyers who weigh the alternative of starting the company from scratch, and it is an important factor in establishing the magnitude of "hidden values" in specific assets.

The foregoing definitions of value clearly indicate that it is a relative term with many meanings. The real meaning of value, therefore, is truly in the eyes of the beholder. Hence, it should not be surprising that the buyer, seller, lender, and investor(s) have different interpretations when they are discussing issues related to the "value" of the company or its assets.

METHODS OF VALUATION

The valuation of a business is both an art and a science. It is inherently inexact due to the numerous complex factors involved in the process that lend themselves only to subjective assessment. Examples of such factors are management skills and external economic conditions. Only experience and sound judgment can give the proper weight to these issues in the valuation equation. On the other hand, valuation is a scientific process that entails the use of specific techniques to derive a value. These approaches are commonly used by appraisers in their valuation of a business as a going concern.

There are seven specific methods or techniques for valuing a professionally managed business. These fall into three major groups, depending upon the source of the financial data utilized in the process: the "balance sheet methods," "earnings and cash flow methods," and "comparable sales methods." There is no one method or formula that works best. The technique that is most appropriate depends upon the nature and circumstances of the particular business. It is often necessary to employ a combination of these methods and to give more weight to those that are the most appropriate. This process of "correlating the values" then yields a final estimate of value. It is important for the buyer or seller to be familiar with these methods and how they can be used to estimate value.

To facilitate this understanding of the valuation process, each method will be briefly discussed in the following sections in terms of the basic concepts, advantages, and limitations.

Balance Sheet Methods

Book Value. The simplest and most straightforward method of estimating a company's value is to take the net book value as it appears on the most recent balance sheet. Book value is the difference between the firm's total assets and liabilities as recorded on its books of account. In cases where the company has significant intangible assets on its books (e.g., goodwill, patents, and capitalized R&D expenses), it is advisable to delete these items from the asset base. This adjustment results in the "tangible book value" or "tangible net worth per books."

The primary shortcomings of book value are: (1) the statements do not accurately reflect the true economic value of certain assets and (2) they omit certain very real liabilities. This unreliability stems from the fact that traditional accounting methods are based on historical costs rather than current economic values. Another disadvantage of book value is that it does not give any consideration to the earning power of the company.

In spite of its shortcomings, book value is the starting place for determining a realistic purchase price. Moreover, it is the standard against which values determined by other methods are compared. It is common among Wall Street investors to discuss stock prices on the basis of their discount or premium relationship to book value. Likewise, in discussing the price of an acquisition, book value is the common denominator to which both buyer and seller relate.

Tangible Net Worth at Market Values. One of the objectives during the target company analysis was to make adjustments to the balance sheet that would indicate the true economic value of assets and liabilities. The result is a revised balance sheet which reflects the "tangible net worth of the company at market values." Depending upon the nature and magnitude of adjustments, this number may be higher or lower than the company's book value. In addition to the deletion of intangible assets, other adjustments which would diminish book value are (1) uncollectible notes or accounts receivable, (2) obsolete inventory, plant and equipment, or (3) unrecorded liabilities. On the other hand, adjustments which can, and usually do, raise the value relative to book are higher replacement values of inventory, plant, and equipment.

One advantage of this method is that it is more indicative of the true economic value of the assets being purchased. The seller has a right to be compensated for any increase in value of company assets during his ownership. Conversely, the buyer should not have to pay for assets which are overstated on the books or to assume hidden liabilities. If this technique is properly employed to develop true values, economic justice prevails for buyer and seller.

On the negative side, this approach does not take into account the value of intangible assets which result from the company's ability to earn in excess of a fair economic return on its asset base. This approach, similar to the book value, fails to take into consideration owner practices diminishing shareholder equity, including taking excessive compensation, fringe benefits, and dividends. This is more prevalent in closely held corporations. If such practices have been material, some premium over book value and economic net worth may be in order.

Earnings and Cash Flow Methods

The major drawback of balance sheet valuation methods is that they ignore the earning power of assets. It is more or less assumed in the book value method, for example, that the earning power of assets is reflected in their adjusted historical cost basis as stated on the books. However, it is more likely, especially with a highly profitable company, that its unique mix of assets coupled with customer goodwill can collectively generate more earnings than they can individually. The general class of pricing techniques based upon earnings and cash flow take these factors into consideration.

Excess Earnings. This is a residual method which allocates the company's operating cash flow in the following order of priority: (1) allowance for depreciation of assets based upon economic values and expected lives, (2) reasonable amortization of intangible assets based upon their expected useful lives, (3) a realistic return on the company's investment in major categories of assets, including net working capital and fixed assets, and (4) income required to service long-term debt.

After this allocation, any residual earnings are designated as "excess earnings" (i.e., those in excess of earnings needed to provide for depreciation and amortization on a realistic basis, those needed to provide a reasonable return on identifiable assets of the business, and those needed to pay interest and principal on debt). These "excessive earnings" are capitalized at a rate commensurate with perceived risk to impute the value of goodwill. The perceived risk and resultant capitalization rate should be based upon the relative certainty or uncertainty that excess earnings will continue in the foreseeable future.

The major advantage of this method is that it considers the relative earning power of all assets and attributes some reasonable value to earnings which are not derived from identifiable assets. It is also very flexible in that economic lives and capitalization rates can be adjusted to reflect changing economic conditions.

Income Capitalization. The income capitalization method involves selecting an appropriate rate, which is the same as "the expected rate of return," with which to capitalize the company's net income. It is based on the formula:

$$\text{Value} \times \text{Net Income}/R$$

(Where R is the capitalization rate.) This rate is derived by considering the relative risk of an investment with the company versus the risk attendant alternative investments. For example, if an investor can get a 15 percent return on marketable long-term government bonds, he should obviously demand more (a higher cap rate) from an investment in a company with no liquidity and an irregular earnings pattern. A higher cap rate might be offset if the company has excellent growth prospects and commensurate potential for capital appreciation.

Although it is a useful exercise to derive a cap rate based upon perceived risk, this method has a serious drawback in that it assumes an all cash purchase by the buyer. While the acquisition may be paid for in cash, much of this cash is often generated from borrowed funds which have a higher cost associated with them. Therefore, to be more accurate, it is necessary to deduct from the income stream those incremental interest expenses attributable to the acquisition financing in order to derive the net income *after* the interest expense. This income should then be capitalized at the appropriate investor equity rate of return to determine imputed equity value. The debt financing must then be added back to the imputed equity value to derive the aggregate value. This refinement of the income capitalization method, by breaking down the value into debt and equity layers, more accurately reflects the impact of the different cost of capital for debt and equity.

Discounted Cash Flow. The discounted cash flow method requires a forecast of cash flow for a specified number of years. The present value of this cash flow is then computed by discounting it using the appropriate discount factor. Any value of the assets of the business expected to remain at the end of the cash flow period is also valued on a discounted basis. The value of the company is the present worth of the cash flow plus the present worth of residual assets less any liabilities expected to remain.

The discounted cash flow technique can be an excellent tool with which to value LBO prospects. By discounting annual cash flows *and* any residual value of the company after five to ten years, the buyer can determine either the net present value (NPV) or internal rate of return (IRR). The residual value is estimated by assuming a sale of the company at an appropriate multiple of book value or earnings in the year of sale.

Price/Earnings Ratio. This method is related to the "income capitalization method" in that the P/E ratio is the reciprocal of the capitalization rate. For example, a P/E ratio of 5 represents a cap rate of 20 percent. This approach compares the P/E ratios of publicly traded companies with similar businesses to that of the company to be valued. If like businesses are selling at 15 times earnings, the value of the company is assumed to be 15 times its current earnings.

Although this method is easily understood, its use must be tempered by the following considerations. First, it is difficult to find truly comparable companies. If there is a public company engaged in the target company's business, it is often commingled with other unrelated businesses. Thus, the P/E ratio for that company may be somewhat distorted. Secondly, public shares represent fractional interests not directly comparable to a 100 percent interest in the target company. There is usually a premium assigned to a controlling interest in a company. Finally, if the target company is privately held, the earnings may be distorted due to tax objectives of the owner(s). A company to which it is being compared, on the other hand, usually seeks to maximize its earnings.

Comparable Sales Method

The last method employed to determine price is based upon the sale of a comparable business within a reasonable time frame. Such methods are used extensively in appraising real estate, especially where there is little difference in the types of property under consideration. With closely held companies, however, there is a real question as to comparability from one firm to another. Unlike real estate, companies tend to be very individualistic and their values are strongly influenced by the talent, experience, and motivation of owners or key management personnel. Nonetheless, the comparable method should be considered as one of the reference points in the determination of value where meaningful data exist.

Sales of Ownership Interests. To the extent such companies are truly comparable, sales of partial, controlling, or complete interests in companies which are comparable with the target company are value indicators. Likewise, recent offers for partial or complete interests in the target company are quite useful. Actual sales of interests in the target company are also worthy of consideration.

To the extent sales of interests in comparable companies can be found, or valid offers for the target company exist, a marketplace judgment on value is available. Such sales or offers may be inflated or deflated by special circumstances, but they nevertheless are value indicators. If minority interests in the subject company have been sold in arm's-length transactions, it may be possible to develop helpful clues as to the value of the entire property.

While suitable public companies can often be found for purposes of comparing sales, earnings, dividends, and the like to similar figures for privately held firms, it is very difficult to find public firms that can be said to have comparable managements, plants, and general prospects. There is considerable question as to whether the stock of any publicly owned company is truly comparable to that of a closely held firm. On the other hand, it is difficult to obtain reliable information on the sale of interests in privately held firms. Even when one is fortunate enough to find such information, there is a real question as to its comparability with the firm being appraised. Closely held firms tend to be very individualistic and are strongly influenced by their owner-managers.

Valid offers for all of or a controlling interest in the target company are certainly useful in analyzing its fair market value. However, there are usually few, if any, such offers to consider. Moreover, the form of such offers may tend to decrease their usefulness. For example, in a proposed stock for stock exchange wherein a larger company has offered to buy a privately held firm using the larger company's stock as payment, it is necessary to value the buying company's stock. If that stock is frequently traded in a broad market, the task may be simple. If, however, the buying firm has a thin market for its shares, many judgments may be necessary to determine the real value of the offer.

Finally, actual sales of interests in closely held firms are sometimes made at less than fair market value. Such sales typically involve minority interests sold to key employees at bargain prices to provide incentives to these people. When minority interests are sold to non-employees, there are usually personal reasons for the sales, such as a desire to benefit relatives of the majority owner. Such sales generally do not represent fair market value. Even when minority sales appear to have been made in arm's-length transactions, it is necessary to theorize as to how much discount they represent relative to the price per share of the controlling interest.

CORRELATING THE VALUES

The selection and relative utility of the above methods will depend upon the type of business and the data available. As a general rule, the buyer should attempt to derive a value from as many of these approaches as possible. This will result in a value range which can be adjusted and weighted as specific circumstances dictate. This process of "correlating the values" requires the buyer to think through all the major factors which might enhance or diminish the feasibility of specific approaches to price determination.

THE LEVERAGED BUYER'S DEFINITION OF VALUE

By using one or more of the foregoing techniques, the buyer or seller can derive a "value" for the company. This is often used as the selling or asking price. But it must be remembered that the concept of value includes more than just the selling price. Value is best defined as the present value of future benefits. To the extent that the seller finances the deal at below-market rates, his benefits (value) are decreased and the buyer's increased. In many cases, therefore, there are two dimensions of value: price and financing terms. In some cases, the financing terms may be even more important than the price. To use an extreme example, if a buyer and seller agree on a price of $10 million, of which the entire amount is paid over a twenty-year period with interest payable at 8 percent on the unpaid balance, the value of the company to the seller is substantially less than $10 million.

To the leveraged buyer, therefore, the value of a business might be defined as follows:

> *"That unique combination of price and terms of financing which will enable the company to pay for itself over a reasonable period of time and yield a competitive return on the buyer's investment of time and money."*

The buyer's perception of value is based not only on price, but also on the cost of capital, whether it comes from outside sources or the seller. This is true for any leveraged buyer, whether it is a large public company which borrows on its own credit lines to finance an acquisition, or a private entrepreneur who borrows against the assets of the target company.

The extent of this second dimension of value will depend upon many factors, including the company's asset mix and projected cash flow, interest rate levels, and the motivation of the seller. All of these factors are brought together in the next two steps involved in acquiring a company: structuring and financing the acquisition.

11

STRUCTURING THE DEAL

11

MORE ON ESOP LBO'S
- Conditions and Requirements
- Contributions, Cash Flow
- Other Benefits
- Disadvantages

TESTING THE FINANCIAL STRUCTURE
- Information Needed to Prepare Proforma Financial Statements
- Other Uses of Proforma Financial Statements
- Preparing Proforma Financial Statements

THE ROLE OF THE COMPUTER

FINANCIAL STRUCTURE OF THE BUYOUT

One of the unique characteristics of leveraged buyouts is that *two* major events in the life of the target company take place simultaneously: a transfer of ownership *and* a major recapitalization. The recapitalization process involves participation of outside financing sources and makes the LBO transaction process significantly more complex than a typical corporate acquisition. In the latter case, the process is simply an exchange of cash or stock between the buyer and seller. If the buying corporation must raise capital to finance the acquisition, it is usually based upon *its own* financial statements. Furthermore, in most cases it is committed to by the lenders far in advance of negotiations with, or even identification of, the target company.

As a result, the leverage (if there is any) in a typical corporate acquisition shows up on the balance sheet of the buying corporation. In a leveraged buyout, there is only one place that the new debt can show up: on the balance sheet of the target company. This transformation of the target company from a business with a relatively "clean" balance sheet to one which is top-heavy with new debt results in not only a new financial structure, but a new way of life.

The Three Layers of Financing

The financial structure of a leveraged deal can be understood by visualizing the right hand side of the balance sheet as three horizontal layers, each of which represents a certain class of financial participation. (See Table 11-A.) Within these layers there may be several sub-layers further refining the degrees of risk associated with different loans and investments. In structuring the transaction, each participant involved in the financing will seek the "horizontal layer" that best represents his risk and reward criteria. In some larger transactions there may be as many as a dozen different layers represented by various classes of securities. Through these debt and equity securities, the respective needs of each participant are satisfied. These requirements include current yield expectations, security interests, priority calls on assets in case of liquidation, and existing or future conversion rights to equity ownership.

Vertical Strips in the Horizontal Layers

In recent years there have been two major developments in leveraged buyout financing that have altered the traditional "horizontal layer" approach to financial structure. First, the trend toward larger transactions has required more institutional financing participants in any given deal. Thus, it has been necessary to create a larger number of securities to satisfy the respective needs of each participant, resulting in a substantially more complex structure. Secondly, insurance companies and pension funds are now willing to take greater risk. Therefore, the distinction between subordinated lender and equity investor has become less clear. The result has been that some investors are willing to invest in a wider risk spectrum by taking securities in more than one horizontal layer. This "vertical strip" approach to financial structure is illustrated in Table 11-B.

Whether the financial structure is viewed from a "horizontal" or "vertical" perspective, each of the parties having claims against or ownership of the target company's assets have specific objectives. The ultimate financial structure is one through which the objectives of the buyer, seller, lenders, and investors can be achieved. To successfully structure the deal, the buyer must be thoroughly familiar with the requirements of all the players.

TABLE 11-A

The Three Layers of Financing

Type of Financing	Investors
Senior Debt	A
	B
Subordinated Debt	C
	D
Preferred Stock	E
	F
Equity	G
	Management

TABLE 11-B

Investing In Vertical Strips

<table>
<tr><th>Type of Financing</th><th colspan="4">Investors</th></tr>
<tr><td>Senior Debt</td><td colspan="2">A</td><td colspan="2">B</td></tr>
<tr><td rowspan="3">Subordinated Debt</td><td colspan="4">C</td></tr>
<tr><td colspan="4">D</td></tr>
<tr><td>E</td><td>F</td><td>G</td><td>H</td></tr>
<tr><td rowspan="2">Preferred Stock</td><td>E</td><td>F</td><td>G</td><td>H</td></tr>
<tr><td>E</td><td>F</td><td colspan="2">I</td></tr>
<tr><td rowspan="2">Equity</td><td>E</td><td>F</td><td colspan="2">I</td></tr>
<tr><td colspan="4">Management</td></tr>
</table>

OBJECTIVES OF THE PLAYERS

The typical leveraged buyout or acquisition has a number of players represented on the right hand side of the target company's balance sheet. Each has specific needs and requirements that must be satisfied or the deal will not come together. The deal must be structured from a financial and legal standpoint in a manner that satisfies the various needs and requirements of all the players.

The Buyer

As was stated in Chapter 1, the nature of the buyer may be different in each deal. It might be an outside investor, an entrepreneur, incumbent management, or any combination of these. It might even be an established operating company seeking to make an acquisition with outside capital sources. Regardless of who is actually wearing the buyer's hat, he wants to structure the deal in a way that will maximize ownership interest. Accordingly, the financing selected for the transaction will seek to minimize equity dilution. All acquisitions are financed from one or more of the following sources: (1) the financial resources of the buyer, (2) funds borrowed from third party lenders, (3) purchase money notes from the seller, or (4) equity capital provided by outside private or institutional investors. The best way to minimize dilution is to borrow from lenders that do not require equity participation. This group includes senior lenders and the seller.

The degree of dilution of the buyer's equity will depend upon a number of factors including price, financial resources, the financial characteristics of the deal, and willingness of the seller to participate as a lender. The buyer who wishes to minimize equity dilution will emphasize the use of debt financing from senior lenders and/or the seller and personal financial resources in devising a suitable financial structure. If these sources are not sufficient, or if a lesser degree of risk is sought, it will be necessary to include subordinated debt or equity players in the structure with the consequent dilution of ownership interest.

The Seller

Unless he is a private individual for whom the deal has significant tax ramifications, the seller is usually interested in getting paid quickly and in cash. Aside from having immediate use of the proceeds, this approach allows the seller to avoid the risks attendant the deferral of payments. Although he may have a lien on the assets as a lender, this security interest is usually subordinate to that of senior lenders. And because the seller is no longer controlling the operation, the company's destiny is in the hands of the new owner. Unless the buyer is a proven operator, the seller may be reluctant to keep this residual capital at risk in the form of purchase money notes.

In certain cases, however, the seller may be forced to participate as a lender if he wants to complete the transaction. This is often the case when (1) the company is too small to attract institutional equity investor interest, (2) the asset base is difficult to finance, (3) the price is too high, or (4) the company has operating problems. In some of these situations, the seller may have good reason to be concerned with the adequacy of future cash flows to meet the operational needs of the company and to service the new debt incurred in the acquisition.

Senior Lenders

As will be seen later in this chapter, the senior lender can be in either a secured or unsecured position with respect to the company's assets. The major difference between these two approaches centers around the relative importance and value of the collateral pool versus the cash flow of the target company. In either case, however, the senior lender's major objectives are to make a competitive return on exposed funds and be assured he has a priority call on company assets or cash flow in the event there is trouble. Since this type of lender usually does not participate in the upside (equity), he wants to avoid any risks on the downside.

As market prices for companies have increased in recent years, many senior lenders have had to advance funds beyond their normal collateral limits in order to make the deal work. To compensate for this increased level of risk, these senior lenders have required "equity kickers" in the form of warrants to purchase stock in the target company. Thus, even the usually clear line between senior debt and subordinated debt has become somewhat blurred.

Subordinated Lenders

Unlike most senior lenders, subordinated lenders are usually willing to take additional risks in return for which they require equity participation. Their objective is to maintain a balance between risk and reward. In seeking this balance, the main focus is on the predictability of the cash flow as it relates to the service of debt securities. In addition, subordinated lender participation is based upon their assessment of the upside potential of the "equity kicker." Because of their equity participation, subordinated lenders can charge a lower and fixed rate on debt securities. They are also more comfortable than senior lenders with longer term notes.

Equity Investors

If the resources available from the foregoing players are not sufficient, it will be necessary to involve outside equity investors to complete the transaction. These may consist of private investors or institutional investors such as venture capital firms and insurance companies. Although in some cases equity investors may also participate as subordinated lenders, their primary objective is to get a high rate of return on investment. They too will focus on the adequacy of cash flow as well as the ability of the company to increase the value of its equity over a period of five to ten years through the amortization of its acquisition debt, the capitalization of increasing income streams, or both.

TYPES OF LEVERAGED BUYOUT TRANSACTIONS

There are two major types of leveraged buyouts. In the vernacular of the financial community, they are called "secured" and "unsecured" transactions. Each has its own characteristics, cast of players, advantages, and disadvantages.

Secured Transactions

The secured transaction is always characterized by the presence of a senior lender who takes a security interest in some or all of the assets of the target company. In return, this lender provides funds to finance a portion of the acquisition price. This structure usually necessitates that the company's asset base consist of good collateral values.

The primary advantage of secured transactions is that the major secured lenders, also known as asset-based lenders, will tolerate higher leverage if the asset values are sufficient. This often results in a lower subordinated debt or equity requirement and, consequently, less dilution of the buyer's equity interest. On the negative side, maximum encumbrance of the assets at the outset of the deal to finance the purchase price leaves precious little room to finance unexpected working capital or fixed asset requirements. Additionally, interest rates charged by most secured lenders tend to be higher.

Unsecured Transactions

In an unsecured transaction, none of the lenders, including the senior lenders, have a security interest in any of the company's assets. This type of structure is more prevalent in larger transactions where the combination of secured financing proceeds, subordinated financing from the seller, and buyer equity is insufficient to meet the purchase price. Typically, the leverage on unsecured deals is justified more by cash flow criteria than collateral values. In such cases, institutional investors, usually large insurance companies or venture capital firms, fill the "gap" between the purchase price and senior debt financing with a combination of subordinated, preferred stock and common stock. One of the conditions of participation by insurance companies is that all senior debt remain unsecured and on a *pari passu* basis with the subordinated lenders. This means that in the event of liquidation, all lenders will share the proceeds proportionate to their respective investments. However, the senior debt is usually the first to be retired from future cash flow.

There are three major advantages to the unsecured transaction. First, an unsecured transaction will usually result in the seller being completely cashed out. This often makes the deal more attractive from the seller's standpoint. Secondly, unsecured deals are not usually as highly leveraged with debt as secured deals, thus leaving more cushion in the cash flow for future business contingencies. Finally, because none of the assets are secured, the financial exposure of the trade creditors is significantly reduced, making them easier to deal with.

If there are any disadvantages to the unsecured transaction, they accrue to the buyer. This type of financing structure requires more participation by institutional investors acting as subordinated lenders or equity investors. Due to their higher return on investment criteria, these investors will always take a significant piece of the equity. Thus, the buyer suffers a dilution of his equity interest. This may also occur in a secured transaction where equity gap financing is required from outside sources. However, dilution does not occur to the same extent as in the unsecured transaction since the "pure lender" provides a larger portion of the financing requirements.

Because of the increased involvement of the institutional equity investors, the buyer also loses some operating control over the business. These investors may wield considerable influence in the major policy decisions of the company with seats on the board. And the restrictive covenants in subordinated loan agreements often restrict management's financial and operational flexibility in dealing with contingencies. In effect, management is indirectly "employed" by those who provide the higher risk portion of the acquisition financing.

Another drawback to the buyer and/or incumbent management team is the desire by many institutional equity investors to exit from the deal within a relatively short period of time (5 years). This often means an upstream merger with a public corporation or a public offering by the target company itself. In many cases, it was the avoidance of these very circumstances (large corporate bureaucracy and/or responsibility to public shareholders) which motivated the management to initially pursue the deal. Thus, the objectives of the institutional investors regarding the liquidation of their investment after five years may be in direct conflict with the desires of the management group, which often prefers to see its return in the form of annual cash flows and operational autonomy.

DETERMINANTS OF FINANCIAL STRUCTURE

The financial structure should reflect the best balance of the needs, objectives, and circumstances of all the parties to the transaction. It is derived through negotiations between the respective players, which are conducted during the process of financing the deal. In addition to the objectives of the various participants, there are other factors which will have a significant impact on the ultimate financial structure.

Size of the Deal

The size of the deal, as reflected by the purchase price, will often dictate the type of structure. With occasional exceptions, the larger deals generally tend to be unsecured transactions. The reason for this is the sheer magnitude of the deal which requires the financial muscle of insurance companies either alone or as part of a syndicated group. Insurance companies almost always insist upon all of the company's assets being unencumbered. Smaller deals, on the other hand, are usually "secured" since it is difficult to attract large institutional investor interest.

Role of the Sponsor

A related ingredient is the role of the sponsor or investor. If the buyer is a management team doing a management buyout, a financially or operationally oriented sponsor may be involved as a part of the buying group. Such sponsors have established relationships with certain lenders and equity investors which have preferences as to deal structure.

Quality of the Asset Base

The nature and quality of the asset base is another factor which may affect structure. Generally, the higher the quality of the asset base and the larger the amount of "hidden asset values," the more likely it is that the deal will be structured on a secured basis. The reason for this is the ability of the buyer to generate greater leverage on the assets. This reduces the need for subordinated debt or outside equity. Accordingly, there is a greater possibility that the acquisition can be financed without the participation of lenders and investors who insist upon the assets remaining unencumbered.

Relationship of Price to Book Value

The relationship of price to book value can similarly impact structure. The greater the price premium over book value, the more likely the deal will be structured as an unsecured transaction. The price premium, which may be more than justified by high, consistent cash flow, usually requires a higher porportion of subordinated debt and participation by "unsecured" lenders. An exception to this might occur when the book value drastically understates the true economic value of the assets. In such cases, it may be possible to finance the transaction on a secured basis.

Management Track Record

One characteristic that all lenders look for is a proven management team. In some cases, however, certain lenders are willing to participate in deals that have questionable management skills, provided that a strong, operationally oriented sponsor is involved as the buyer. These are typically asset-based lenders who are given additional comfort by securing their loans with the target company's solid asset base.

Seller Motivation

Finally, the seller's motivation will often dictate financial structure. A corporate seller under pressure to divest a subsidiary or division has natural timetables (e.g., the end of a fiscal year) which may cause it to be more willing to participate as a subordinated lender. This factor may enable the buyer to structure the deal as a secured transaction and retain a higher percentage of equity.

HOW TO DEVISE THE PROPER FINANCIAL STRUCTURE

There is no one "right" or "best" financial structure which can be universally applied to all transactions. Each deal is different and has its own unique set of circumstances and players. Therefore, the "right" financial structure is the one best satisfying the needs and objectives of all the parties involved in the transaction. To arrive at this optimum financial structure, the buyer must take the initiative. He should follow a specific procedure or "road map" which will ultimately lead to the proper structure. In discussing this procedure, it will be assumed that the buyer's primary objective, other than completing the transaction, is to minimize the dilution of equity. Of course, if the deal has an obvious short-fall of financing requirements, it will be necessary to share the equity with outside investors.

The logical starting place is to attempt to do the deal using one's own financial resources. On the basis of this assumption, the following steps should be taken:

Step 1: Determine the maximum amount of equity capital that can be invested by the buyer and his immediate investment group.

Step 2: Determine the difference between the estimated selling price plus the anticipated expenses of the transaction and the amount of equity capital. The difference represents the "financing gap," the approximate amount of funds that must be raised from outside sources.

Step 3: Based upon the evaluation of the company's asset base, estimate the approximate amount of funds which can be borrowed on the various classes of assets from a secured lender (using the appropriate advance rates for each class of collateral).

Although loan advance rates vary significantly with each unique asset base, the buyer can assume the following for his present purposes:

Collateral Description	Advance	Value Measure
Accounts Receivable	80%	Book Value
Inventory		
Raw Materials	40%	Book Value
Work-in-Process	0	Book Value
Finished Goods	25%	Book Value
Machinery & Equipment	80%	Liquidation Value
Real Estate	65%	Market Value

The aggregate amount resulting from these computations represents the approximate senior debt which can be borrowed from a secured lender.

Step 4: Determine the difference between the total "financing gap" (Step 2) and the amount of senior debt (Step 3). This difference represents the "equity gap" to be filled with either additional equity or subordinated debt.

Step 5: Based upon previous discussions with the seller, the buyer must make a judgment as to whether he will take back a purchase money note which is subordinated to the senior debt. An interest rate and repayment schedule which reflect the seller's motivation and confidence in the buyer should be factored into this assumption. If the seller has been adamant about "all cash or no deal," assume a subordinated debt or equity investment from an outside investor at rates and terms which the deal can handle, based upon its projected cash flow.

Step 6: Test the proposed structure by developing a set of proforma financial statements which reflect the impact of the financing on the company's income, cash flow, and financial position over a period of time equal to the longest term of any of the debt instruments.

Step 7: If the projected cash flow is not sufficient to service the proposed debt structure, modify the terms of the subordinated debt or increase the proportion of outside equity. Reiterate the proforma financial statements.

Step 8: If the projected cash flow still does not adequately service the most liberal assumptions of subordinated debt terms, it may not be a feasible deal without some seller concessions on price, terms, or both.

CASE STUDIES ON FINANCIAL STRUCTURING OF LEVERAGED BUYOUTS

To illustrate the various generic types of financial structures and the dynamic interrelationships between the factors which determine them, hypothetical case studies of several different types of structures will be presented. The objective of this analysis is to demonstrate the impact of the following on the financial structure.

- The type of seller and his motivations.
- Purchase price relative to book value.
- Criteria of various financing participants.
- Nature and quality of the company's asset base.
- Hidden asset values.
- Financial impact of ESOP transactions.

These five cases illustrate only the major variables and their effects on the financial structure of a leveraged buyout. The analysis is limited to the impact of financing on the latest year of operations on a proforma basis. Needless to say, before any financial structure can be considered viable, it should be analyzed from the standpoint of 5 to 10 year income and cash flow projections. Such projections should be supplemented with "what if" analyses on the impact of higher interest rates, lower sales and higher costs. This financial planning is an indispensable step in determining the optimum financial structure of the acquisition.

Description of the Target Company

To provide continuity and clarity, the same company and beginning financial statements will be utilized in each of five case studies. This company will be called "Buyout Candidate Corporation." Buyout is a 35-year-old company engaged in metal fabrication and forming. In addition, the company is a distributor of various types of metal sheeting and tubing. Its diversified customer base includes both large and small firms engaged in the automotive, aerospace, machine tools, and electronics industries. For the past ten years, sales have grown steadily at an annual rate of 7 percent. Although Buyout has customers in the automotive industry, it has been only marginally impacted by past recessions due to the fact that its products are utilized for maintenance and repair requirements in auto manufacturing. Total sales have decreased only 10 percent in the most severe recession in the last 10 years.

Buyout's current financial position and profit and loss statements for the latest 12-month period are shown as follows:

Buyout Candidate Corporation
Balance Sheet

Assets	
Current Assets	
Cash	$ 500,000
Accounts Receivable	3,000,000
Inventory	3,000,000
Sub-total	$ 6,500,000
Fixed Assets	
Machinery & Equipment	1,500,000
Land & Buildings	2,000,000
Sub-total	3,500,000
Total Assets	$10,000,000
Liabilities & Equity	
Current Liabilities	
Accounts Payable	$ 1,800,000
Accruals	200,000
Sub-total	2,000,000
Long-term Debt	—
Equity	
Common Stock	500,000
Retained Earnings	7,500,000
Total Equity	8,000,000
Total Liabilities & Equity	$10,000,000

Buyout Candidate Corporation
Profit and Loss Statement

Revenue	
Fabrication Sales	$12,000,000
Distribution Sales	8,000,000
Total Sales	20,000,000
Cost of Sales	
Material	7,000,000
Labor	4,000,000
Factory Overhead[1]	2,000,000
Total Cost of Sales	13,000,000
Gross Profit	7,000,000
Operating Expenses	
Selling	2,500,000
General & Administrative	3,000,000
Total Operating Expenses	5,500,000
Net Operating Income	1,500,000
Taxes (@ 40%)[2]	600,000
Net Income After Taxes	$ 900,000

Notes:
[1]Includes approximately $250,000 of depreciation.

[2]Due to the 1986 Tax Reform Act, total corporate federal and state income taxes are assumed to be 40%.

CASE 1: SECURED TRANSACTION/ASSET-BASED LENDER ONLY

Target Company:	Buyout Candidate Corp., a wholly owned subisidary of a public company.
Buyer:	Incumbent management group.
Buyer Constraints:	Combined financial resources of entire management group is $1,000,000, and there is a strong desire to avoid dilution of equity.
Seller:	Large publicly held company.
Seller Motivations:	The primary motivation of the parent company is to raise cash to finance capital requirements for other subsidiaries. Buyout's lower return on assets and clean balance sheet makes it a prime divestiture candidate.
Selling Price:	$8,000,000
Terms:	All cash
Legal Structure:	Purchase of stock
Financing Requirement:	$8,000,000
Buyer Equity:	$1,000,000
Seller Financing:	None
External Financing:	$7,000,000

Case 1: Financing Strategy

The seller's requirement to be paid all cash necessitates that $7,000,000 of financing be raised externally. The buyer's first step must be to evaluate the asset base to determine if there is sufficient collateral to generate loans of this amount. The following appraised values and auction values are assumed.

Asset Description	Book Value	Appraised Value	Auction Value
Accounts Receivable	$3,000,000	$2,850,000	N/A
Inventory			
Raw Materials	2,000,000	2,000,000	N/A
Work-in-Process	500,000	500,000	N/A
Finished Goods	500,000	500,000	N/A
Mach. & Equip.	1,500,000	2,500,000	$1,250,000
Real Estate	2,000,000	4,000,000	3,000,000

External Financing Summary

Collateral	Loan Value	Advance	Loan Amt.	Rate/Term
Accounts Receivable	$2,850,000	85%	$2,400,000	17%/Rev.
Inventory				
Raw Materials	2,000,000	50%	1,000,000	17%/Rev.
Work-in-Process	500,000	25%	125,000	17%/Rev.
Finished Goods	500,000	25%	125,000	17%/Rev.
Mach. & Equip.	1,250,000	80%	1,000,000	17%/5 yr.
Real Estate	3,000,000	80%	2,450,000	14%/25 yr.

Total Debt Financing: $7,100,000

Buyer Equity Required: $ 900,000

Seller Financing Required: None

External Equity Required: None

Case 1: Pre-Acquisition and Post-Acquisition Balance Sheet

Assets	Before	After
Current Assets		
Cash	$ 500,000	$ 500,000
Accounts Receivable	3,000,000	3,000,000
Inventory	3,000,000	3,000,000
Sub-total	6,500,000	6,500,000
Fixed Assets		
Machinery & Equipment	1,500,000	1,500,000
Land & Buildings	2,000,000	2,000,000
Sub-total	3,500,000	3,500,000
Total Assets	$10,000,000	$10,000,000
Liabilities		
Current Liabilities		
Accounts Payable	$ 1,800,000	$ 1,800,000
Accurals	200,000	200,000
A/R Loan	—	2,400,000
Inventory Loan	—	1,250,000
Sub-total	2,000,000	5,650,000
Long Term Debt		
M & E Loan	—	1,000,000
Real Estate Loan	—	2,450,000
Sub-total	—	3,450,000
Equity		
Seller	8,000,000	—
Management	—	900,000
Total	8,000,000	900,000
Total Liabilities & Equity	$10,000,000	$10,000,000

Case 1: Income Statement

	Before	After
Revenue	$20,000,000	$20,000,000
Cost of Revenue	13,000,000	13,000,000
Gross Profit	7,000,000	7,000,000
Selling Expense	2,500,000	2,500,000
General & Admin. Expense	3,000,000	3,000,000
Net Operating Income	1,500,000	1,500,000
Interest Expense	—	1,133,000
Net Income Before Taxes	1,500,000	367,000
Taxes (@ 40%)	600,000	147,000
Net Income After Taxes	$ 900,000	$ 220,000

Cash Flow

	Before	After
Net Income	$ 900,000	$ 220,000
Depreciation (+)	250,000	250,000
Principal Payments (-)	0	-214,000
Available for Working Capital	$ 1,150,000	$ 256,000
Debt Coverage (NOI & Depr./Debt Service)	N/A	1.3

Case 1: Analysis

The preceding financial data indicate that of the $8,000,000 required by the seller, approximately $7,100,000 (or 89 percent) can be borrowed from secured lender(s). The remaining $900,000 (11 percent) must be invested by management. The reason for this high ratio of debt to equity financing is the nature and quality of the assets used for collateral. First, apparently because of good credit and collection policies, 95 percent of accounts receivable qualify as collateral and the lender is willing to advance at an above average rate (85 percent). Secondly, there is a high proportion of raw material inventory which, due to its greater marketability, has higher collateral value. Finally, there is hidden asset value in the real estate, which is purchased at book value but collateralized at 80 percent of appraised value.

On the income statement, the additional interest expense has substantially impacted net income. Although operations are still profitable, there is much less margin for error. More importantly, the buyers must be sure that sufficient funds are available from operations and working capital loans to finance future working capital and fixed asset purchase requirements. Since the buyers utilized maximum leverage to finance the acquisition, the availability of the company's working capital requirements from the revolving loans must be confirmed with a 5 to 10 year income and cash flow projection.

CASE 2: LEVERAGED ESOP TRANSACTION/BANK FINANCING

Target Company:	Buyout Candidate Corp., a wholly owned subisidary of a public company.
Buyer:	Management and employees by means of a newly created Employee Stock Ownership Plan (ESOP).
Seller:	Large, publicly held company.
Seller Motivations:	Due to increasing labor costs, this subsidiary has been losing market share and no longer meets the parent company's minimum ROI level.
Selling Price:	\$9,000,000
Terms:	All cash
Legal Structure:	Purchase of stock
Management Equity:	\$ 500,000
Seller Financing:	None
External Financing:	\$8,500,000

Case 2: Financing Strategy

In this case, the financing process is a more difficult undertaking requiring management to consider more creative approaches to financing the transaction. The reasons are:

- The seller was insistent upon a higher price and on being cashed out at closing.
- The company's increasing labor costs and loss of market share made it unattractive to conventional LBO risk capital financing sources.
- Management lacked sufficient equity themselves to close the financing gap.

For the above reasons, it was not possible to finance the transaction with conventional LBO financing methods. However, a leveraged ESOP structure was feasible because all employees, including management, were willing to take a 5 percent pay cut until certain productivity and profitability levels were attained. This factor plus the inherent tax advantage of ESOP's increased after-tax cash flows sufficiently to attract a bank to make a loan to the ESOP. The following assumptions were made on the bank financing:

Loan Amount:	$8,500,000
Loan Term:	8 years
Interest Rate:	10.2%*
Annual Payment:	$1,600,000

*This interest rate is actually 85 percent of the interest rate that the bank would normally charge for this loan (12 percent). Banks are able to lower rates on ESOP loans because 50 percent of the interest collected on such loans is non-taxable to the bank.

Case 2: Pre-Acquisition and Post-Acquisition Balance Sheet

Assets	Before	After
Current Assets		
Cash	$ 500,000	$ 500,000
Accounts Receivable	3,000,000	3,000,000
Inventory	3,000,000	3,000,000
Sub-total	6,500,000	6,500,000
Fixed Assets		
Machinery & Equipment	1,500,000	1,500,000
Land & Buildings	2,000,000	2,000,000
Sub-total	3,500,000	3,500,000
Other Assets (Goodwill)	—	1,000,000
Total Assets	$10,000,000	$11,000,000
Liabilities		
Current Liabilities		
Accounts Payable	$ 1,800,000	$ 1,800,000
Accurals	200,000	200,000
Sub-total	2,000,000	2,000,000
Long Term Debt		
ESOP Loan		8,500,000
Sub-total		8,500,000
Equity		
Seller	8,000,000	—
Management	—	500,000
Total	8,000,000	500,000
Total Liabilities & Equity	$10,000,000	$11,000,000

Case 2: Income Statement

	Before	After
Revenue	$20,000,000	$20,000,000
Cost of Revenue	13,000,000	12,800,000[1]
Gross Profit	7,000,000	7,200,000
Selling Expense	2,500,000	2,400,000[1]
General & Admin. Expense	3,000,000	2,900,000[1]
Net Operating Income	1,500,000	1,900,000[3]
Debt Service[2]	—	1,600,000
Net Income Before Taxes	1,500,000	300,000
Taxes (@ 40%)	600,000	120,000
Net Income After Taxes	$ 900,000	$ 180,000

Cash Flow

	Before	After
Net Income	$ 900,000	$ 180,000
Depreciation (+)	250,000	250,000
Principal Payments (-)	0	—[2]
Available for Working Capital	$ 1,150,000	$ 430,000
Debt Coverage (NOI & Depr./Debt Service)	N/A	1.34

Notes:

[1]As part of the ESOP buyout plan, all employees agreed to a 5 percent pay cut until certain productivity levels were achieved.

[2]In ESOP transactions, both principal and interest are deductible for income tax purposes.

[3]To the extent cash pension or profit sharing contributions were suspended, and/or replaced with the ESOP, this figure would be that much higher.

Case 2: Analysis

This case study illustrates the dynamics of a leveraged ESOP transaction. The use of an ESOP to finance the deal effectively reduces the after-tax cost of capital by allowing the target company to retire debt with pre-tax dollars. Another factor that futher reduces the cost of capital is the lower interest rates that lenders can charge because 50 percent of the interest on ESOP loans is non-taxable. A lower cost of capital was essential, not only because the seller insisted upon a higher price, but also because the deal could not be financed by conventional means.

Another factor that made the ESOP a feasible alternative was the willingness of employees, including management, to take a 5 percent reduction in direct compensation until the company achieved acceptable levels of profitability. The most significant impact of this was to increase operating income by $400,000 annually and cash flow available for debt service to over $2,000,000. Such willingness by employees to sacrifice current income has a very positive influence on lenders and, no doubt, increases their interest in financing the deal.

ESOP's are particularly useful in cases where employee productivity is critical to the success of the transaction. When employees are also owners, they work more effectively because they are now working for themselves.

CASE 3: SECURED TRANSACTION/ASSET-BASED LENDER PLUS SELLER

Target Company:	Buyout Candidate Corp., a closely held private company.
Buyer:	A management group headed by the general manager of the company.
Buyer Constraints:	The management group can raise a total of $500,000 and has a strong desire to avoid outside equity investors.
Seller:	A private individual who is the sole shareholder of the company.
Seller Motivations:	The owner of the company is retired from any active involvement in management. His primary objective is to liquify and diversify his assets, but he also wants control of the company to remain in the hands of existing management.
Selling Price:	$8,000,000
Terms:	Negotiable
Legal Structure:	Purchase of stock
Financing Requirement:	$8,000,000
Buyer Equity:	$ 500,000
Seller Financing:	$2,000,000 to $2,500,000
External Financing:	$5,000,000 to $5,500,000

Case 3: Financing Strategy

The seller's willingness to finance up to 31 percent of the purchase price and the buyer's equity of $500,000 results in an additional financing requirement of $5,000,000. The buyer's desire to avoid outside equity investors again dictates borrowing from a secured lender. The following appraised values and auction values are assumed.

Asset Description	Book Value	Appraised Value	Auction Value
Accounts Receivable	$3,000,000	$2,550,000	N/A
Inventory			
Raw Materials	1,000,000	1,000,000	N/A
Work-in-Process	1,000,000	1,000,000	N/A
Finished Goods	1,000,000	1,000,000	N/A
Mach. & Equip.	1,500,000	2,000,000	$1,000,000
Real Estate	2,000,000	2,000,000	2,000,000

External Financing Summary

Collateral	Loan Value	Advance	Loan Amt.	Rate/Term
Accounts Receivable	$2,550,000	80%	$2,040,000	17%/Rev.
Inventory				
Raw Materials	1,000,000	50%	500,000	17%/Rev.
Work-in-Process	1,000,000	25%	250,000	17%/Rev.
Finished Goods	1,000,000	25%	250,000	17%/Rev.
Mach. & Equip.	1,000,000	80%	800,000	17%/5 yr.
Real Estate	2,000,000	80%	1,600,000	14%/25 yr.

Total Debt Financing: $5,440,000

Buyer Equity Required: $ 500,000

Seller Financing Required: $2,060,000

Seller Financing Terms: 12%/10 year term

External Equity Required: None

Case 3: Pre-Acquisition and Post-Acquisition Balance Sheet

Assets	Before	After
Current Assets		
Cash	$ 500,000	$ 500,000
Accounts Receivable	3,000,000	3,000,000
Inventory	3,000,000	3,000,000
Sub-total	6,500,000	6,500,000
Fixed Assets		
Machinery & Equipment	1,500,000	1,500,000
Land & Buildings	2,000,000	2,000,000
Sub-total	3,500,000	3,500,000
Total Assets	$10,000,000	$10,000,000
Liabilities		
Current Liabilities		
Accounts Payable	$ 1,800,000	$ 1,800,000
Accurals	200,000	200,000
A/R Loan	—	2,040,000
Inventory Loan	—	1,000,000
Sub-total	2,000,000	5,040,000
Long Term Debt		
M & E Loan	—	800,000
Real Estate Loan	—	1,600,000
Subordinated Loan	—	2,060,000
Sub-total	—	4,460,000
Equity		
Seller	8,000,000	—
Management	—	500,000
Total	8,000,000	500,000
Total Liabilities & Equity	$10,000,000	$10,000,000

Case 3: Income Statement

	Before	After
Revenue	$20,000,000	$20,000,000
Cost of Revenue	13,000,000	13,000,000
Gross Profit	7,000,000	7,000,000
Selling Expense	2,500,000	2,500,000
General & Admin. Expense	3,000,000	3,000,000
Net Operating Income	1,500,000	1,500,000
Interest Expense	—	1,124,000
Net Income Before Taxes	1,500,000	376,000
Taxes (@ 40%)	600,000	150,000
Net Income After Taxes	$ 900,000	$ 226,000

Cash Flow

	Before	After
Net Income	$ 900,000	$ 226,000
Depreciation (+)	250,000	250,000
Principal Payments (-)	0	-375,000
Available for Working Capital	$ 1,150,000	$ 101,000
Debt Coverage (NOI & Depr./Debt Service)	N/A	1.3

Case 3: Analysis

This case differs from Case 1 in two respects. First, the quality and value of the collateral is lower for lending purposes. This illustrates the significant financing impact of a higher percentage of unqualified receivables, a higher proportion of work-in-process and finished goods inventory, and reduced market values of fixed assets. All of these factors result in a sizeable gap between purchase price and proceeds available from the secured lender.

To fill this financing gap entirely from their own capital would require a substantial investment ($2,560,000) from management, which they do not have. An alternative is to fund most of the equity requirement through a venture capital investor, but this would result in a significant dilution of management's ownership. A second alternative, and the other feature which differentiates this from the first case, is for the seller to carry back a subordinated note in the amount of the financing gap. This is a viable approach since, unlike the first case, the seller's motivation is different. In addition to converting his ownership into cash, this private seller has an emotional interest in preserving management continuity and rewarding them for their past loyalty.

This case illustrates two significant changes in circumstances which have a dramatic effect on the financial structure of the acquired company. The nature and composition of the assets reduce the amount that can be borrowed. In the absence of additional buyer equity or a willingness by the seller to "fill the gap," the deal would not be feasible. However, the seller's involvement as a subordinated lender not only makes the deal feasible, but also reduces the cost of overall debt service to the buyer. In addition, the buyer may be able to borrow more funds for working capital if the current assets are managed more efficiently.

CASE 4: SECURED TRANSACTION/ASSET-BASED LENDER PLUS VENTURE CAPITAL CO.

Target Company:	Buyout Candidate Corp., a privately held company owned by a family trust.
Buyer:	Operating manager plus outside investor.
Buyer Constraints:	Manager has $100,000 in capital which can be invested. He is willing to include other investors in the ownership if it will enable him to own a significant piece of the company.
Seller:	A family trust for which a bank and members of the family are co-trustees.
Seller Motivations:	None of the surviving family members have the desire to be involved with the company, and the bank lacks the management expertise to monitor the operation. They mutually decide to sell the business at book value and the real estate at market value.
Selling Price:	$9,000,000
Terms:	All cash
Legal Structure:	Purchase of assets
Financing Requirement:	$9,000,000
Buyer Equity:	$ 100,000
Seller Financing:	None
External Financing:	$8,900,000

Case 4: Financing Strategy

The buyer's lack of financial resources and the seller's desire to be cashed out require the participation of outside equity financing sources. Several venture capital firms have expressed interest in providing the financing requirements in excess of the proceeds from a secured lender and the buyer's equity. The following is an analysis of collateral values for secured lending purposes.

Asset Description	Book Value	Appraised Value	Auction Value
Accounts Receivable	$3,000,000	$2,850,000	N/A
Inventory			
Raw Materials	1,500,000	1,500,000	N/A
Work-in-Process	750,000	750,000	N/A
Finished Goods	750,000	750,000	N/A
Mach. & Equip.	1,500,000	2,000,000	$1,000,000
Real Estate	2,000,000	3,000,000	3,000,000

External Financing Summary

Collateral	Loan Value	Advance	Loan Amt.	Rate/Term
Accounts Receivable				
Inventory				
Raw Materials	$6,000,000*	50%	$3,000,000	15%/Rev.
Work-in-Process				
Finished Goods				
Mach. & Equip.	1,000,000	80%	800,000	15%/5 yr.
Real Estate	3,000,000	80%	2,400,000	14%/25 yr.

Total Debt Financing:	$6,200,000
Buyer Equity Required:	$ 100,000
Seller Financing Required:	None
External Equity Required:	$2,700,000

*In this situation it is assumed that the bank trustee, which oversees the company, has referred the buyout financing opportunity to one of the bank's commercial lending officers. Banks traditionally advance less than asset-based lenders and have a blanket encumbrance against current assets. Hence, the lower advance rate of 50 percent against current assets.

Case 4: Pre-Acquisition and Post-Acquisition Balance Sheet

Assets	Before	After
Current Assets		
Cash	$ 500,000	$ 500,000
Accounts Receivable	3,000,000	3,000,000
Inventory	3,000,000	3,000,000
Sub-total	6,500,000	6,500,000
Fixed Assets		
Machinery & Equipment	1,500,000	2,000,000
Land & Buildings	2,000,000	2,500,000
Sub-total	3,500,000	4,500,000
Total Assets	$10,000,000	$11,000,000

Liabilities	Before	After
Current Liabilities		
Accounts Payable	$ 1,800,000	$ 1,800,000
Accurals	200,000	200,000
Secured Bank Loan	—	3,000,000
Sub-total	2,000,000	5,000,000
Long Term Debt		
M & E Loan	—	800,000
Real Estate Loan	—	2,400,000
Subordinated Loan	—	2,200,000
Sub-total	—	5,400,000
Equity		
Seller	8,000,000	—
Management	—	100,000
Investor	—	500,000
Total	8,000,000	600,000
Total Liabilities & Equity	$10,000,000	$11,000,000

Case 4: Income Statement

	Before	After
Revenue	$20,000,000	$20,000,000
Cost of Revenue	13,000,000	13,000,000
Gross Profit	7,000,000	7,000,000
Selling Expense	2,500,000	2,500,000
General & Admin. Expense	3,000,000	3,000,000
Net Operating Income	1,500,000	1,500,000
Interest Expense	—	906,000
Net Income Before Taxes	1,500,000	594,000
Taxes (@ 40%)	600,000	238,000
Net Income After Taxes	$ 900.000	$ 356,000

Cash Flow

	Before	After
Net Income	$ 900,000	$ 356,000
Depreciation (+)	250,000	250,000
Principal Payments (-)	0	-147,000
Available for Working Capital	$ 1,150,000	$ 459,000
Debt Coverage (NOI & Depr./Debt Service)	N/A	1.66

Case 4: Analysis

In this case the higher purchase price is a reflection of the premium of real estate market value over book value. This factor, the lower collateral value of the assets, and more conservative advance rates allowed by the commercial bank, necessitate a financing requirement substantially in excess of the buyer's equity. Accordingly, a venture capital company must participate in the financing to the extent of $2,700,000.

It should be noted that the venture capital firm participates both as a subordinated lender and an equity investor. There are two reasons for this. First, as a subordinated lender, the venture capital firm can dictate financial and management controls through its indenture, or loan agreement. Covenants governing minimum working capital and operating ratios are more difficult to establish as a pure equity investor. Secondly, the subordinated loan or, alternatively, a redeemable preferred stock can be amortized over a period of years, resulting in a return of a significant portion of the total invested capital.

This buyout is structured as a "purchase of assets" rather than a "stock purchase." By structuring the deal in this manner, it is possible to "step-up" the value of the real estate and machinery and equipment by $500,000 each.

CASE 5: UNSECURED TRANSACTION/BANK, INSURANCE CO., VENTURE CAPITAL CO.

Target Company:	Buyout Candidate Corp., a publicly held company.
Buyer:	Investment group and incumbent management.
Buyer Constraints:	Because the management group has only $200,000 in capital, it must involve a sponsor which invests its own capital and arranges the overall financing.
Seller:	Public shareholders of Buyout Candidate Corp..
Seller Motivations:	Shareholders have been increasingly disenchanted with the performance of Buyout's stock, which has sold at a discount from book value. They see a private buyout as a means of selling their shares at a price which is more reflective of intrinsic value.
Selling Price:	$9,200,000
Terms:	All cash
Legal Structure:	Purchase of assets
Financing Requirement:	$9,200,000
Buyer Equity:	$ 200,000
Seller Financing:	None
External Financing:	$9,000,000

Case 5: Financing Strategy

The price premium over book value and the lack of seller financing make a "secured" transaction unfeasible in this case. Because of the higher price, there must be more equity and cheaper debt financing. This can only be accomplished through an "unsecured" transaction. The following is a summary of the financing participants and their respective share of the total financing requirement.

Financing Participants

Investor	Type of Investment	%
Commercial Bank	Revolving Credit Line	22
Insurance Companies (2)	Senior Notes	38
	Subordinated Notes	16
	Preferred Stock	12
	Equity	5
Investment Group Sponsor	Equity	5
Management	Equity	2
		100

Case 5: Pre-Acquisition and Post-Acquisition Balance Sheet

Assets	Before	After
Current Assets		
Cash	$ 500,000	$ 500,000
Accounts Receivable	3,000,000	3,000,000
Inventory	3,000,000	3,000,000
Sub-total	6,500,000	6,500,000
Fixed Assets		
Machinery & Equipment	1,500,000	2,000,000
Land & Buildings	2,000,000	2,500,000
Sub-total	3,500,000	4,500,000
Other Assets (Goodwill)	—	200,000
Total Assets	$10,000,000	$11,200,000

Liabilities	Before	After
Current Liabilities		
Accounts Payable	$ 1,800,000	$ 1,800,000
Accurals	200,000	200,000
Unsecured Bank Loan	—	2,000,000
Sub-total	2,000,000	4,000,000
Long Term Debt		
Senior Notes	—	3,500,000
Subordinated Notes	—	1,500,000
Sub-total	—	5,000,000
Equity		
Preferred Stock	—	1,000,000
Common Stock		
Subordinated Lender	—	500,000
Seller	8,000,000	—
Management	—	200,000
Sponsor	—	500,000
Total	8,000,000	2,200,000
Total Liabilities & Equity	$10,000,000	$11,200,000

Case 5: Income Statement

	Before	After
Revenue	$20,000,000	$20,000,000
Cost of Revenue	13,000,000	13,000,000
Gross Profit	7,000,000	7,000,000
Selling Expense	2,500,000	2,500,000
General & Admin. Expense	3,000,000	3,000,000
Net Operating Income	1,500,000	1,500,000
Interest Expense	—	1,010,000
Net Income Before Taxes	1,500,000	490,000
Taxes (@ 40%)	600,000	196,000
Net Income After Taxes	$ 900,000	$ 294,000

Case 5: Analysis

This case is an example of an "unsecured" transaction where none of the lenders takes a secured interest in any of the assets. The primary reason for structuring the buyout in this manner is the premium of purchase price over book value and the lack of management equity. This premium increases the overall financing requirement above that which the collateral base will support on a secured lending approach. In the absence of seller gap financing and management equity, it is necessary to raise additional subordinated debt and equity capital.

Unlike the "secured" transaction, no lender has any specific claim on any of the assets. There are priority claims on assets in the event of bankruptcy, depending on how the debt instruments are worded. However, the most distinguishing features of these different debt "layers" are their maturity dates. The bank debt, usually a combination of a revolving credit line and a 5 year term loan, is amortized first. After this comes the senior notes, subordinated notes, and preferred stock (if it is redeemable).

Another difference between this case and the four previous cases is the fact that the two life insurance companies each participate in four different "layers" of financing: senior notes, subordinated notes, preferred stock, and common stock. This "vertical participation" in two or more securities by one lender is commonplace in "unsecured" deals. Because of their substantial financing commitment, the insurance companies end up owning the majority of the equity in the acquired concern.

MORE ON ESOP LBO'S

Despite the deluge of current media attention on Employee Stock Ownership Plans (ESOP's) in the corporate finance world, the concept is more than a decade old. Louis Kelso, the attorney and economist credited with inventing the ESOP, had strong beliefs in capitalism but felt not enough Americans were sharing in its benefits. Senator Russell Long, then head of the Senate Finance Committee, came from a family political tradition that believed in sharing the wealth. When the two met in the early 1970's, and Kelso introduced an idea that would both broaden ownership and increase productivity, the foundation for today's ESOP's was laid.

The idea is to make the worker an owner of the company. The mechanism to do this is the existing pension laws of the United States. Using these laws, but amending them to provide for something new — the ESOP — the employee can have a vested interest in the destiny of his company. Congress recognizes the ESOP as a technique of corporate finance as well as an employee benefit plan.

Like other pension and profit sharing plans, an ESOP includes a trust set up to provide employees benefits at retirement. Unlike the traditional plan, an ESOP invests in the shares of the employer corporation rather than a diversified portfolio of stocks and bonds. In addition, the ESOP has the ability to borrow money to finance the purchase. It is this ability to borrow that makes the ESOP a useful tool in leveraged buyouts.

Conditions and Requirements

To obtain approval, and thus corporate tax deductibility from the IRS, the ESOP basically must meet the same plan requirements that govern other pension and profit sharing plans. The requirements include nondiscrimination, vesting, and a number of other rules covered under Section 401 of the Internal Revenue Code. Under the nondiscrimination rule, for example, the plan cannot result in disproportionately higher benefits to directors, major shareholders, or the highest paid employees.

Generally, shares in the ESOP are allocated to the employee's account according to his salary as a percentage of total payroll. These shares accrue to him over the term of his employment under an IRS-approved vesting schedule. If the employee separates from the company before the shares are fully vested, his shares are forfeited and reallocated to the remaining workers. Upon termination, usually at retirement, the employee receives the shares and can choose to keep them or to sell them to realize his pension benefits. In a privately held company, the corporation must agree to buy back the shares for a limited period if the employee wishes to "put" the shares to the corporation.

The shares an ESOP acquires must be voting common or preferred stock convertible into voting common. Where there is more than one class of stock, these shares must be of the best category with respect to dividend and voting rights. In a publicly traded company, participants must be allowed to vote all allocated shares on all issues requiring shareholder approval. In closely held companies, (i.e., companies that do not have a "registration-type class of securities") participants must be allowed to vote all allocated shares on the following issues: merger or consolidation; recapitalization; reclassification; liquidation; dissolution; sale of substantially all assets of a trade or business; or similar transactions specified in IRS regulations. All unallocated shares are voted in the manner specified in the plan document. In most cases, this will be an ESOP administrative committee or the ESOP trustees. This requirement can often be a useful anti-takeover device for public companies since employees are unlikely to vote for an unfamiliar new boss.

Contributions, Cash Flow

In the traditional pension plan, investments are made after the sponsoring corporation makes a cash contribution to the plan. In an ESOP, shares can be acquired in a number of ways. As in the traditional plan, shares can be purchased on the open market or from other shareholders after a cash contribution is made to the ESOP. Since the cash paid into the ESOP is a contribution to a qualified employee benefit plan, it is fully tax deductible to the company.

The sponsoring corporation can also issue and contribute shares directly into the ESOP. Again, the tax deduction is generally equal to the fair market value of the shares, but this time without the use of any cash. This transaction will actually generate cash flow since it lowers the company's tax bill without any cash contribution to the plan. To the extent cash pension or profit sharing contributions are suspended during the period of debt service, more cash flow is also available.

Finally and significantly, when planning on the use of an ESOP in a leveraged buyout transaction, the ESOP can borrow money to finance the purchase of company shares. Under this scenario, annual cash contributions are made by the company to the ESOP to repay the debt. The contributions can be structured to match the ESOP's loan repayment schedule. Contributions to the ESOP are tax deductible even though the funds are being used to repay the principal portion of the ESOP loan. This ability to repay an ESOP/LBO loan with pre-tax dollars is the major advantage over conventional LBO financing techniques where the debt must be paid with after-tax dollars.

Annual contributions to a non-leveraged single-plan ESOP — that is, one that does not borrow — are limited to 15 percent of total payroll. Special non-leveraged 25 percent plans can be designed with a "double-plan" approach. In the case of a leveraged ESOP, the limit is raised to 25 percent of payroll for the repayment of principal on the ESOP loan and an unlimited amount for the payment of interest.

Other Benefits

In addition to the virtual tax "subsidy" on principal repayment of an ESOP loan, the company may also get a discount on the interest it pays on the debt. Under the 1984 Tax Act, 50 percent of interest received on an ESOP loan is tax free to the lending institution. With this significant tax benefit, financial institutions can reduce the rate they charge on ESOP loans. In many cases, the rate may be as low as 85% of what the interest rate would have been had the loan been a non-ESOP loan.

Overfunded pension plans may be used as a source of acquisition debt because of the exemption available to an ESOP from the inclusion in income of pension reversions.

Another 1984 Tax Act benefit to ESOP transactions provides that a shareholder in a privately held company who sells shares to an ESOP can avoid paying capital gains tax on the sale if he "rolls over" the proceeds of the sale into stocks and bonds of U.S. corporations, and if the ESOP owns 30 percent or more of the stock as a result of the transaction. This increases the "yield" to an investor by almost 39 percent on each dollar of gain. Sometimes sellers are willing to share these tax benefits with the buyers through a lower purchase price, since the owners often come out with a lot more after-tax using the ESOP vehicle.

Finally, it should not be forgotten that the major benefit of an ESOP is often the increased productivity that results from the motivated work force. This comes from giving the workers a "piece of the action."

Disadvantages

Thus far, only the advantages of using an ESOP have been examined. The drawbacks of this financing technique must be investigated to get a full sense of how an ESOP works. One negative relates to the accounting treatment of an ESOP transaction. Another may be the repurchase liability, the obligation arising from the "put" an employee has to the sponsoring company. Most important is the dilution of ownership that an ESOP transaction may cause.

Under SOP 76-3 of the Financial Accounting Standards Board, a number of rules impact the financial statements of a company engaging in an ESOP transaction. The ESOP loan, which is usually guaranteed by the sponsoring corporation, appears as debt on the balance sheet of the company, and not as a footnote as in other loan guaranty situations. The outstanding balance of the ESOP loan is shown as a reduction of net worth.

Furthermore, shares held by an ESOP are considered outstanding for the purposes of calculating earnings per share. Earnings per share (EPS), the public's measure of performance, will therefore suffer initially in a leveraged ESOP transaction. With conventional debt, principal is deducted from cash in the funds flow statement. Principal repayment reduces cash but has no effect on earnings. With an ESOP transaction, repayment of the trust's debt is an expense in the form of employee benefits and, therefore, deductible.

In a leveraged buyout transaction the repurchase liability is a potential problem. Upon leaving the employer, an employee receives the shares he has accumulated over the term of his employment with the company. If his company's shares are publicly traded, he can hold or sell these shares on the open market. If, on the other hand, the company is private, he has the right, as discussed earlier, to "put" his shares to the company to realize cash for his stock. With the obligation to buy shares from its employees, the sponsoring company may, over time, build up a significant liability. For an ESOP/LBO, where the resulting company is closely held, a feasibility study should be undertaken to determine whether this liability severely impacts the deal's financing structure. The requirement to distribute and repurchase shares from employees other than at retirement may be postponed until the ESOP debt is fully repaid.

Another problem with ESOP's is that it is very difficult to get the participation of outside investors if the ESOP is a leveraged purchase and external equity is needed at the outset. The reason is the uncertainty created by the Department of Labor (DOL) regarding the fair allocation of equity between investors. Employee stockholders bring notes to the table through the ESOP, while other investors provide risk capital in the form of cash. Yet, both groups are viewed by the DOL as providing equal value in equity contributions. In many cases, this difficulty of providing risk capital investors with a greater proportionate share of equity may preclude them from achieving their own internal ROI objectives and, thus, from participating in a particular deal. In spite of this obstacle, over $3 billion in multi-investor ESOP transactions were completed in 1987.

The last and most fundamental disadvantage in using an ESOP as part of the initial purchasing group is the dilution of ownership. In an LBO, the buyer's purpose in entering into the transaction is to gain ownership and control. Using an ESOP dilutes this ownership. While traditional debt will squeeze the company's cash flow, it may allow management to retain full ownership. In the final analysis, the issue of whether to use an ESOP in an LBO transaction requires an examination of the benefits of additional cash flow against the dilution present in ESOP financed scenarios. Many times this analysis will yield some very surprising results, and is well worth considering as a viable alternative to more conventional approaches to financing the deal.

TESTING THE FINANCIAL STRUCTURE

An integral part of devising the proper financial structure is to test it against the company's ability to generate sufficient cash flow. For any given financial structure to be feasible, it must be clearly demonstrated that the demands imposed by the proposed financing on the company's present and future financial resources can be satisfied. The procedure for veryfying this fact is the preparation of proforma financial statements (income statement, balance sheet, and cash flow statement) which are based upon assumptions developed in the analysis, valuation, and financial structuring of the deal.

This involves a considerable amount of "number crunching" by the buyer or his designated representatives. Although this is a very laborious process, especially if it is necessary to run several different iterations or "what if" analyses, it is an absolutely essential step in the deal process. The process can be greatly simplified by using a microcomputer and software specifically designed to help structure and finance LBO's (see "The Role of the Computer" at the end of this chapter). To make decisions and commitments without performing this analysis is a significant gamble on the part of the buyer. Indeed, since lenders and investors almost always want to see the impact of projected cash flow on their investments, it is unlikely that the transaction could be consummated without it.

Information Needed to Prepare Proforma Financial Statements

If the buyer has properly conducted the analyses, valuation, and structuring steps of the process, most of the basic information and assumptions which will go into the projections is readily available. The balance sheet should be adjusted to reflect any write-ups or write-offs in the assets owned by the target company. Whether these or historical (book) values are used will depend upon the particular legal structure of the transaction. (See Chapter 13.) The liability side of this starting balance sheet should reflect the proposed financial structure, including all debt and equity accounts. The income statement should reflect any adjustments in future revenue and expenses.

Using these statements as a starting point, the buyer is now prepared to start the process of preparing a proforma income statement, balance sheet, and cash flow statement. It should be noted that these statements are interdependent, that is, any one complete statement cannot be prepared unless the other two are also prepared. Due to the many interrelationships between these statements, they are not prepared sequentially. The process involves frequent switching from one statement to another.

Other Uses of Proforma Financial Statements

In addition to their vital role in testing the financial structure, proforma financial statements are also important tools in other aspects of the analysis, financing, and negotiation of the acquisition. First, they enable the buyer to analyze the impact of possible contingencies on the company and on the investments of the financial participants. This "what if" analysis should show the effects of lower sales, increased labor or material costs, and rising interest rates on income and cash flow. Another reason to have basic and supplementary proforma statements is that they form the cornerstone of the "financing package," an important tool in selling lenders and outside investors on the deal. Any such package is only as good as the financial projections and the quality of their preparation.

The projections can also be very effective tools for negotiating with the seller, lenders, or investor. Well-prepared proforma statements will demonstrate that the buyer has done his homework and will improve his credibility. They will also serve to strengthen the buyer's position in the negotiations. Since sellers will invariably use them to support their own position, however, a buyer should not allow the seller to obtain a copy of these computations.

Finally, these projections will be the starting point in an operating plan against which the company's progress can be measured after the deal has closed. Of course, there will be periodic updates and revisions to the initial plan. But any successfully operated business is characterized by prudent financial planning. And the time to start is now, before the deal is closed.

The financial projections should be completed in two distinct phases or time periods. The first set of projections should be done on an annual basis over a 10 to 15 year period or, preferably, for the same number of years as the maturity of the longest debt instrument. If this projection indicates feasibility, it should be refined on a monthly basis for the first year or two following the closing.

Preparing Proforma Financial Statements

Step 1: Develop the sales forecast.

The sales forecast is the foundation of any financial plan. A poor or unrealistic sales forecast will result in a meaningless financial document which will render the remainder of the projections an exercise in futility. Therefore, it should be prepared with a great deal of thought and should be based upon a thorough analysis of the economic outlook, the market, the company's products, and the competition. The forecast should segregate major revenue categories (e.g., different product lines and service income) to which specific costs can be related. It should also reflect any known cyclical forces inherent in the company's industry and major markets.

Step 2: Develop the cost of sales.

As much as possible, costs (e.g., materials, labor, overhead) must be related to specific product or revenue categories. These estimates should be based upon historical data adjusted for any known increases or decreases. For example, if a low cost contract from a material supplier is about to expire, this must be reflected in increased material expenses in the future.

Step 3: Compute the gross profit on sales.

Step 4: Estimate future operating expenses.

Historical selling expenses should be reviewed very carefully in terms of their sufficiency to meet projected revenue. Any adjustments to advertising, commissions, travel, and entertainment should be noted.

General and administrative expenses should be estimated on the basis of expected costs to the company as a stand-alone business. This may result in additional expenses for electronic data processing, legal, accounting, and other services which were previously borne by a corporate parent or buried in a blanket "intercompany" charge.

Engineering and research and development (R&D) expenses should be based upon realistic estimates of the future product development and customer support needs of the company. They should be consistent with the sales forecast.

Step 5: Compute the earnings before interest and taxes (EBIT).

EBIT is a key point of departure for analyzing the effect of financial leverage on the company's operations. Once this calculation is completed, it is time to move to the balance sheet and cash flow statement in order to measure the impact of new interest expenses on the company's net income.

Step 6: Project key balance sheet accounts and list the assumptions upon which they are based. These include:

- Accounts Receivable — utilizing the appropriate "ACP ratio" (see Chapter 9) and the level of forecasted sales, compute the estimated ending balances for accounts receivable for each period.
- Inventory — utilizing the appropriate "inventory turnover ratio" (see Chapter 9) and the estimated "cost of sales," compute the estimated ending balance of inventory for each period.
- Accounts Payable — utilizing the appropriate ratio for "accounts payable days" (see Chapter 9) and the forecasted "cost of materials," compute the estimated ending balance of accounts payable.

- Accrued Liabilities — utilizing the same percentage growth rate as that used for "sales," project the estimated accrued liabilities for each period.
- Fixed Assets — utilizing the beginning account balances and assumed depreciation schedules, project the book value of fixed assets for each period after making any adjustments for future purchases or sales of capital equipment.
- Loan Balances — for loans with specific repayment schedules, project the ending loan balances for each period.

Step 7: Adjust the EBIT to reflect any changes in the depreciation charges, as determined in Step 6 above.

Step 8: Determine the impact on cash flow from "changes in working capital" by netting the difference between changes in current assets from changes in current liabilities (see Step 6).

Step 9: Determine the impact on cash flow of any purchases or sales of capital equipment.

Step 10: Determine the cash flow impact of any loan amortization (Step 6).

Step 11: Estimate the interest expense by multiplying the average loan balance for each loan by its appropriate rate of interest. Use the beginning balance for any non-amortizing working capital loans.

Step 12: Estimate the net income before taxes (NIBT) by subtracting from EBIT (Step 7) the estimated interest expenses (Step 11).

Step 13: Estimate the cash flow from operations by adding to NIBT (Step 12) any depreciation charges (Step 6) and any interest expenses which have been deferred.

Step 14: Estimate the net cash flow for period 1 by netting cash flow from operations (Step 13), changes in working capital (Step 8), net purchases or sale of equipment (Step 9), and loan amortizations (Step 10).

Step 15: Add the net cash flow (Step 14) to the beginning cash balance on the balance sheet to determine the new cash balance. If this new balance is negative, increase the balance of the working capital loan (A/R or inventory) which has been designated as the first priority in subsequent loan draws. Reflect this increase on the balance sheet. If the new cash balance is above the minimum required, reduce the appropriate working capital loan by the surplus and reflect this decrease on the balance sheet.

Step 16: If the increase or decrease in the loan balance is significant, recompute the interest expense (Step 11) and repeat Steps 12 through 15.

Step 17: Balance the balance sheet by inserting the NIBT (Step 12) adjusted for any income taxes and investment tax credits.

Step 18: Repeat Steps 8 through 17 for each of the periods being projected.

THE ROLE OF THE COMPUTER

It is quite obvious that the foregoing process, although extremely important, can be quite laborious and time-consuming. This is especially true when a number of "what if" iterations are necessary. Much time and effort can be saved by using a financial model which automatically computes all of the financial projections after key assumptions are input.

Any standard spreadsheet can be used to prepare a financial model that will perform the multitude of repetitious calculations referred to previously. However, the user should be prepared to invest substantial time and energy to perfect a working model.

Another approach is to purchase a program that already works. One such program is LBO Plan II, developed by Business Publications, Inc. This program, which utilizes a Lotus 1-2-3 template, takes the user step-by-step through the structuring and financing process and produces up to 12 years of proforma statements. A more complete description of LBO Plan II is contained in Appendix P while Appendix G shows a printout of some of the schedules that are produced.

12

FINANCING THE ACQUISITION

The main feature which distinguishes a leveraged buyout from a typical corporate acquisition or merger is the involvement of a group of financing participants in addition to the buyer and seller. Just as the third dimension renders the study of geometry a more difficult task, the addition of financing participants substantially complicates the dealmaking process. Not only is it necessary to meet the demands of lenders or investors themselves, but their legal representatives must also be comfortable with the terms of the transaction. This greater number of voices, some of which are expressing conflicting needs, dramatically increases the risk of the deal "falling out of bed."

The successful buyer, then, is the person who can cope in this increasingly complex environment and reconcile his personal needs with those of the seller, financing sources and their respective representatives. This is no easy task. It requires the utmost understanding, patience and, above all, persistence.

To improve the chances of successfully closing a deal, it is essential that the buyer understand the needs and requirements of the financing participants. Unless these needs are satisfied, there will be no deal. From the leveraged buyer's standpoint, the "golden rule" is most aptly stated as: "He who has the gold makes the rules." This chapter will give the buyer additional insight into the minds of those who have the gold — lenders and investors. This will significantly improve the chances of successfully financing and subsequently closing the deal.

FINANCING SOURCES AND CAPITAL MARKETS

To financial institutions, a leveraged buyout is nothing more than another investment opportunity. It must therefore compete with other potential investments in terms of expected returns, levels of risk, and liquidity. Today's investor has many alternatives to make liquid investments in common stocks or, if he is looking for a higher yield, corporate and government bonds. To convince this investor to make a risky investment in a leveraged buyout, that in most cases would probably be locked up for at least 5 years, it is necessary to offer a very attractive potential rate of return. At the same time, short-term financing sources must in some way be compensated for the higher risk of leveraged acquisition financing. This is usually in the form of a higher rate of interest, a secured interest in the assets, or both. In the absence of these incentives, the short-term lenders will seek less risky investments in the credit markets.

The participants in the leveraged acquisition financing process fall into three major categories: (1) senior lenders, (2) subordinated lenders and (3) equity investors. Within these primary groups or "layers" of financing there are a variety of "mini-layers" which represent a complete spectrum of loans and securities issued by the financing participants. This concept is more clearly illustrated in Table 12-A.

Although institutional lenders and investors are similar, there are some distinct differences. All are alike in that they function as financial intermediaries who "rent" money from various sources and earn a profit on the "spread," i.e., the difference between return on investment and cost of money. The only notable exceptions are the pension funds whose money has no direct cost. The differences

Table 12-A
Leveraged Buyout Financing Chart

Layer	Lenders/Investors	Loans/Securities
Senior Debt	Commercial Banks Asset-Based Lenders Insurance Companies Sellers	1. Revolving lines of credit — unsecured 2. Revolving lines of credit — secured by accounts receivable and inventory 3. Fixed asset loans secured by machinery and equipment and real estate 4. Senior notes — unsecured
Subordinate Debt	Insurance Companies Pension Funds Venture Capital Funds Sellers	1. Senior subordinate notes 2. Junior subordinate notes
Equity	Insurance Companies Venture Capital Firms Sellers Private Investors Management	1. Preferred Stock 2. Common Stock

among these institutions lie in their risk profiles which are dictated by a number of factors, including source of funds, cost of funds, stability of cash flow, and regulatory constraints. These and other related considerations will determine the type of loan or security issued, underwriting criteria, rates, terms, restrictions imposed, and control exercised.

CAPITAL CONTRIBUTION AND EQUITY PARTICIPATION

To understand the manner in which the lenders and investors which comprise the three layers of financing participate in a leveraged acquisition, it is helpful to analyze the relative contribution of each to the total financing requirement and their respective equity interest in the buyout. These numbers, of course, will vary substantially, depending upon the specific circumstances of each deal as well as type of structure. The percentage of capital contributed to the financing and the resulting equity ownership for typical "secured" and "unsecured LBO's is shown in Table 12-B.

Table 12-B
Financing Contribution vs. Equity Ownership

Example 1 — Secured Transaction with Seller Financing

Lender/Investor	% of Financing	% of Equity
Asset-Based Lender	60%	0
Seller	30%	0
Entrepreneur/Management	10%	100%

Example 2 — Secured Transaction without Seller Financing

Lender/Investor	% of Financing	% of Equity
Commercial Bank	50%	0
Venture Capital Co.	40%	60%
Entrepreneur/Management	10%	40%

Example 3 — Unsecured Transaction

Lender/Investor	% of Financing	% of Equity
Commercial Bank	30%	0
Insurance Company or Pension Fund	50%	40%
Venture Capital Co.	15%	40%
Entrepreneur/Management	5%	20%

As these examples illustrate, the senior lender provides a significant portion of the acquisition financing and receives none of the equity in the company. There are exceptions to this which will be discussed later. In general, however, this lender is rewarded in the form of interest on notes. As a result, the senior lender cannot justify taking a substantial risk in the investment.

Risk Allocation and Control

The potential risks taken by financing sources are controlled in two ways. First, a lender may require a lien on all or a portion of the assets which secures a priority right to such assets above all other lenders, investors, and creditors. Secondly, if a secured interest in the assets is not taken, the senior lender will advance funds only to the extent which the company's cash flow can easily retire the incurred debt.

The subordinated lender clearly takes a secondary position to the senior lender as to a claim on assets in the event the business is liquidated. For taking this increased risk, the subordinated lender is rewarded either through a higher rate of interest on the subordinated note, an "equity kicker," or both. In today's financial environment, it is rare to find the subordinated lender who is willing to satisfy this incremental risk solely with a higher rate of interest. As a hedge against future inflation, this lender also wants to share in any increases in value of the company. These equity kickers or "sweeteners" take many forms. They may be in the form of a convertibility feature in the debt instrument, warrants or options to purchase stock at a negotiated price at some future date, or simply "cheap" common stock which is purchased at the closing. Thus, the subordinated lender is normally not a pure lender. This player is both a lender and an investor and, as a result, takes on the characteristics of each. Participation in the transaction is evaluated on the basis of total yield which consists of both current income and future increases in the value of the company.

Within the general category of subordinated debt, there are various classifications of securities which, to a greater degree, reflect the risk profile of various lenders. Thus, there may be varieties of "senior subordinated debt" and "junior subordinated debt" instruments to satisfy the needs of specific lenders or investors. The more "junior" securities have a lower priority call on assets in liquidation and, as a result, carry a higher risk as well as a higher potential return.

Pure equity investors are those who desire to take a greater risk for a greater reward. These are distinguished by the fact that they are willing to stand last in line for any claim on assets in the event of liquidation and receive no current yield on the investment until the company is able to pay dividends. In a highly leveraged capitalization, the latter is quite unlikely, or if it does happen, will not do so for a long time.

There are cases, however, where a pure equity player does receive a current return. This occurs primarily when the equity investor also provides time and operational management expertise to the company. For example, certain sponsors with strong operational experience and orientation often take management fees for their continuing services. And, of course, management is rewarded on a current basis with salaries and incentive bonuses. In both cases, those receiving the fees or salaries are often substantial equity interest holders.

As is the case of subordinated lenders, there are different risk profiles of equity investors and a number of securities can be designed to meet these various risk preferences. The least risky type of equity security, if there is such a thing, is preferred stock. Technically, preferred shareholders have a priority call over the common stockholders on assets or dividends. These, however, are not significant factors for the following reasons. If a company must liquidate, it is doubtful that anything would be left for the preferred shareholders. Preferred stock may be convertible into common or redeemable over a period of time to satisfy specific investor's needs. The investor may also utilize restrictions contained in preferred stock covenants to take control of the company under certain adverse conditions.

PROFILE OF MAJOR FINANCING SOURCES

With this brief background on the various classes of financing participants, the major institutional lenders and investors will be discussed individually in greater detail. This analysis will first consider the organizational structure and regulatory environment and their impact on funding sources, cost of funds, and lending policy. The discussion will then focus upon the specific underwriting criteria for each lender or investor as it pertains to leveraged acquisitions.

Commercial Banks

One of the big factors behind the surge in leveraged buyout activity is the increased participation of commercial banks as senior lenders. It wasn't always this way. Until the 1980's, banks have been reluctant to lend money beyond a relatively low leverage threshold. But changes in the financial markets have significantly impacted the way they now look at LBO's. To understand this metamorphosis in lending policy, it is first necessary to look at how banks operate.

Effects of Deregulation. Banks are highly regulated. Their actions are governed by the Comptroller of the Currency, the Federal Reserve Board, or state banking agencies. Both national and state chartered banks derive the funds which they lend from consumer and business depositors in the form of checking accounts, savings accounts and certificates of deposit in varying maturities. Traditionally, banks have relied upon interest-free checking accounts and artificially low interest savings accounts to make up a substantial portion of their deposit base. With this low cost base of deposits, and the regulatory freedom to employ high leverage on their equity base, banks have shown attractive returns on equity even if they made very conservative loans. The banker takes his risk on the overall asset and liability management policy decisions — the degree of leverage on the balance sheet — and hedges this risk by underwriting relatively "risk-free" loans.

In recent years, however, with the proliferation of money market funds and changes in the regulatory environment, there has been a substantial erosion in this base of core deposits. The result has been increased competition for depositor funds and a higher cost of funds to the bank. Another significant development, at least for the large money center banks, has been the intensive competition from the commercial paper market for their prime customers. Because these large, credit worthy companies can borrow for less by selling commercial paper, banks have seen a significant reduction in loan demand from this market segment. The combination of a higher cost of funds and reduced loan demand has made the banks more aggressive lenders on leveraged buyouts. LBO's offer the banks the opportunity to capture a more attractive yield on their loans by charging up-front fees along with higher interest rates.

In spite of these fundamental changes in the financial markets and the regulations governing them, banks are still the most conservative of all lender participants in leveraged acquisitions. Traditionally "balance sheet lenders," banks rarely extended credit to companies whose debt/equity ratio exceeded 2 to 1. As a result of the aforementioned changes in the financial markets, however, some of the larger money center banks have become quite aggressive and have participated in financings with a debt/equity ratio of 10 to 1 or more.

Lending Policies. To mitigate their risk exposure in highly leveraged capitalizations, banks will look very carefully at the historical and projected cash flows and limit their advances to some conservative multiple, say 3 to 5 times. This is especially true in the case of "unsecured" transactions, where the bank has no source of repayment other than cash flow. In these situations, there is usually sufficient subordinated debt and/or equity in the deal to give comfort to the bank.

Wherever possible, the bank will attempt to secure its loan with some or all of the assets of the target company. The loan advance rates, also called loan to value ratios, are generally lower than in the case of traditional asset-based lenders. For example, banks may loan only 60 percent to 70 percent on accounts receivable, and also have more stringent requirements for them to be considered eligible or "qualified." Banks also prefer to take a blanket lien on all unencumbered assets and put a limit on the total credit line, subject to annual or semi-annual review. A further condition might be a regular amortization or "clean-up" of certain segments of the total credit line as well as severe restrictions on future capital expenditures, bonuses, management fees, or dividends.

If the bank acts as a new secured lender in the acquisition and there are existing liens on the assets to be encumbered, it will be necessary to remove these to enable the bank to perfect its security interest. This will generally take place when the existing lender is taken out with the proceeds of acquisition financing. For most lenders, including banks, there is a general reluctance to see a significant percentage of the new loan proceeds going to pay off another lender. The alternative is to convince the bank that its loan is adequately secured with a secondary lien on the assets, a difficult task at best. In any event, the presence of a substantial amount of pre-acquisition debt in the target company renders the financing process difficult, complex, and usually, not feasible.

The greatest advantage offered by a bank is the lower cost of money to the buyer. In general, banks charge from one to two points over the current prime rate as compared to the standard two to five points over prime charged by asset-based lenders. This is primarily the result of the lower cost of money to the banks and the effect of compensating balances. The latter is a sometimes difficult requirement for the cash-short leveraged deal and, if significant, may offset any savings due to the lower interest rate.

The bank's preferred manner of exiting from a leveraged deal is to be paid out as the company matures and no longer requires short-term debt. This usually occurs within a three to seven year period, depending upon the profitability, growth, and working capital needs of the company.

Asset-Based Lenders

From an organizational standpoint, there are three different types of asset-based lenders: the independents, those which are bank-affiliated, and those owned by large corporate conglomerates. The independent commercial finance companies are the oldest type of asset-based lender. They proliferated in the post-war years in response to the capital needs of small, growing businesses. Since the late 1960's, the number of independents has diminished considerably as large corporate conglomerates and bank holding companies sought to diversify through acquisition.

In recent years there has been an increasing trend for commercial banks to either start up or acquire commercial financing operations. Although these are most frequently organized as wholly owned subsidiaries, in some cases they are a part of the bank itself. The reason for this increasing trend toward bank-affiliated commercial finance companies is the previously discussed fundamental change in the regulations governing financial institutions and the attendant erosion of low-cost core bank deposits. This has caused banks to shift from an orientation toward lower risk, lower-yield loans to higher risk, higher-yield loans in order to satisfy their return-on-equity objectives.

Differences Between Banks and Asset-Based Lenders. In spite of the fact that the line of distinction between banks and commercial finance companies has grown increasingly fuzzy, there are still some fundamental differences between the two which dictate their respective lending attitudes and policies. This is the primary reason that commercial finance operations are often legally and physically segregated from bank lending activities.

The first of these differences is the source and cost of funds. Unlike banks, the commercial finance company has no direct access to depositors and, as a result, must generate funds either from banks or open market instruments (e.g., commercial paper). These sources are more expensive and more volatile than the bank's typical mixture of deposits. In addition to the higher cost of money, the commercial finance company incurs greater overhead in the evaluation, administration and control of collateral. It takes a lot of people, many of whom are highly skilled and well-paid, to appraise fixed assets, perform periodic audits, and monitor inventory and receivables. These costs add an estimated 200 basis points to the asset-based lender's cost of money.

The second major difference between banks and commercial finance companies is a logical consequence of the first. Due to its higher incremental cost of money and increased overhead, the commercial finance company must charge a higher rate of interest. The rate charged usually is set at two to five points over the prime lending rate posted by the major money center commercial banks. Many borrowers incorrectly assume that this higher interest rate is directly related to the higher risk of greater advance rates of the loan. As will be seen, however, most asset-based lenders do not view their loans as "risky." Such lenders will not make a loan which, in their opinion, cannot be completely repaid from the liquidation of their security interests. However, there may be some implicit relationship between price (interest rate) and risk since competition between lenders for particularly attractive and less risky deals may at times result in lower rates.

One method often used to lower the interest rate is to bring in a bank to participate in the loan. Thus, if the bank provides 50 percent of the funds at prime plus 1 and the commercial finance company provides 50 percent of the funds at prime plus 3, the overall, or "blended," rate is prime plus 2. This technique is more often used in the larger transactions with the commercial finance companies responsible for collateral administration. One of the possible difficulties with this arrangement is the relationship between the two lenders. Some banks will only participate in a framework which will allow them to demand repayment of their portion of the loan at any time they perceive that the risk exceeds acceptable levels. Understandably, most commercial finance companies attempt to avoid these kinds of participation arrangements.

The final difference between traditional commercial bank lenders and asset-based lenders is their respective criteria for determining the amount to lend and their respective attitudes toward loan repayment sources. Although both types of lenders will evaluate prospective loans on the basis of the ability of the target company to service the debt with its cash flow and the sufficiency of the collateral base, they do not place equal emphasis on these factors. While banks look primarily to cash flow and secondarily to collateral in making lending decisions, asset-based lenders focus primarily on the liquidation value of the collateral. Of course, they also analyze the impact of new debt on historical and projected cash flows, but only to assure themselves that this is a viable business as recapitalized. To restate a common criteria of all lenders, the asset-based lender is not interested in financing liquidations. Once convinced that the business can make it, lending decisions are based primarily upon the nature, quality, value, and marketability of the different classes of collateral.

Lending Policies. The amount of money which the asset-based lender will lend on any given deal will be determined by his perception of the value of the company's assets and the particular advance rate for each class of asset in the collateral pool. In Chapter 10 several definitions of the term "value" were presented. To the asset-based lender, the only meaningful definition of value is "liquidation value." The major concern is "what can be obtained for these assets if they must be liquidated or sold in the open market and not in the ordinary course of business." A further refinement of this definition is related to the period of time over which the assets are sold. "Orderly liquidation value" is the amount which can be realized if sold over a reasonable period of time. "Auction value," also called "hammer value," is that value which can be realized quickly in an auction, or as some say, "under the hammer." Both orderly and auction liquidation values are used by asset-based lenders in underwriting the loan. Generally, the lender will use the higher orderly liquidation values for more liquid assets. Auction values are more often used for less liquid fixed assets and when the lender's overall policies are more conservative.

In addition to the lender's perception of asset values, the amount of funds which can be borrowed will be determined by the so-called "advance rate." This rate is expressed as a ratio of the loan amount to the collateral value of each type of asset. In fact, it is often called the "loan-to-value ratio." The advance rate is a measure of the lender's confidence in the ability of the collateral, if sold, to generate sufficient proceeds to pay off the loan. The extent to which it is below 100 percent represents a cushion, or uncertainty factor, which the lender believes is necessary to ensure his loan will be repaid in the event assets must be liquidated. The advance rate is based upon the estimate of the collectability of the assets with allowances made for changes in values, costs incurred in the liquidation, or a combination of these factors. The liquidity of the assets will also affect the advance rate. Generally speaking, the more liquid the collateral, the higher the rate of advance, because the values are more certain and can be realized more quickly. Another factor which may influence a lender's rate of loan advance is the familiarity, or lack thereof, with specific types of collateral. The greater his knowledge of the marketability of various assets, the more he will usually lend on them.

Securing the Collateral. Once the asset-based lender has determined how much he can lend on various types of assets, he must perfect a security interest in all the assets. With the adoption of the Uniform Commercial Code in most states, this process has been greatly simplified. It involves filing a form (UCC-1) in the various states and counties where specific assets are located. Upon filing, the transaction becomes a matter of public record and serves notice to all existing and potential creditors that the lender has a first lien on the assets which allows him to foreclose and take title to the assets in the event of default.

Prior to the bankruptcy laws which became effective in 1979, secured lenders could move very quickly to take title to assets, even in the event of bankruptcy. The new laws, which are much more debtor-oriented, provide for an "automatic stay" or "freeze" of the assets, even though they are secured. Thus, the secured lender may have to wait several months before title to the assets can be effected. For this reason, these lenders will take an even closer look at projected cash flows in order to be more certain of the company's viability.

Monitoring the Credit. After the security interest has been perfected and the loan(s) funded, the asset-based lender monitors the credit to ensure there is always sufficient collateral to cover the loan. This is accomplished through regular reports on each current asset category detailing their amounts and relationships to loan balances. With respect to fixed assets, the lender will keep up to date on fluctuations in collateral values through in-house or independent equipment and real estate appraisals. The lender controls the risk in the deal by maintaining the flexibility of lowering advance rates in the event of an economic downturn or a perceived increase in risk within the company. Thus, as values of specific collateral (particularly inventory) decline, the lender may adjust the advance rates and reduce loan advances or require amortization in order to get loan-to-value ratios in line with desired levels. This usually occurs when economic conditions are deteriorating and the lender wants to protect against loan losses. On the other hand, in more prosperous times, asset-based lenders will occasionally lend money in excess of their established advance rates for temporary periods.

Insurance Companies

The next major group of participants in leveraged buyout financing consists of insurance companies. These companies, which may be owned by stockholders (stock companies) or policy holders (mutual companies), control a significant share of investment capital in America. Their main function is to underwrite the risk against loss of life, health or property in return for premium income. Premiums are then invested in a wide variety of securities and other assets, including stocks, bonds, mortgages, and real estate. Returns on these investments are then used to pay off any claims.

Early LBO Investors. Insurance companies have been active participants in corporate financing for many years, primarily through the purchase of marketable securities and privately placed debt securities. A natural outgrowth of this activity in private placements was their involvement in acquisition financing in the 1960's, where the publicly held corporation was the focal point of the credit decision. In the mid-1970's, the more aggressive insurance companies (particularly the larger ones such as Prudential, Equitable, and Teachers) began to seek a way to hedge their fixed income investments against inflation. At the same time, lower overall commitments to real estate loans created surplus funds to invest in other securities. The leveraged buyout, offering both a fixed return and equity participation, proved to be one of the vehicles in which these funds could be invested to provide returns that would keep pace with inflation.

Unlike commercial banks which are regulated primarily by the Federal Government, insurance companies are regulated at the state level. This results in rather diverse regulatory schemes which reflect the statutory provisions of state law. Regardless of regulatory constraints, all insurance companies are characterized by a relatively predictable cash flow and a lower cost of funds due to regular premium payments. Using highly scientific and exacting actuarial methods, insurers are also able to accurately predict their claim requirements. The net result is that insurance companies are able to charge a lower, fixed rate of interest on all or most of their investments in buyout and acquisition financings.

Lending Policies. Insurance companies usually participate in more than one and frequently in all levels of financing except the revolving senior debt. They condition their presence upon all lenders remaining in an unsecured position. And, although they often function as a senior lender along with banks, they are usually paid out over a longer term. They also fund a significant portion of many acquisitions through various types of subordinated debt, preferred stock and common stock securities. As a general rule, an insurance company receives its return on investment through both current income (interest on subordinated debt and dividends on preferred stock) and capital appreciation upon the ultimate sale of common stock. The targeted return is approximately 150 percent of the marketed yield on BAA bonds.

Insurance companies which finance leveraged buyouts and acquisitions are well staffed with highly skilled financial analysts. Most of these individuals received their training in the department of the insurance company which specialized in private placement of corporate debt. In underwriting this intermediate and long-term financing, strong emphasis is placed upon the company's cash flow and its ability to service the proposed debt structure.

Because the insurance companies active in leveraged buyouts and acquisitions tend to be the larger ones, they are usually interested in larger deals. The rationale is that it takes just as much time, and possibly more, to do a $5 million deal as it takes to close a $500 million deal. Moreover, the sheer size of their asset base and annual cash flow necessitates that large chunks of capital be invested. This is accomplished most effectively with larger deals. For example, Prudential, a very active player in buyout and acquisition financing, has over $100 billion in assets with an annual cash flow of over $10 billion. A firm of this magnitude is usually not interested in any deal in which it cannot invest at least $1 million and prefers deals starting at $5 million. Indeed, total financing of a $50 million to $100 million deal by a single insurance company is not uncommon.

As a natural consequence of size, insurance companies tend to do deals involving professional management teams of public companies or corporate divestitures rather than transactions involving private investors and entrepreneurs. Although these deals are most often brought to the insurance company by sponsors who understand the process of structuring and financing a buyout, it is not unusual for the insurance company to take an active role in modifying the structure or interfacing with the other parties in the financing.

Manner of Participation. As was previously noted, "unsecured" transactions usually consist of a number of different securities within the senior debt, subordinated debt and equity layers. The reason for this is to satisfy the divergent needs of different insurance company lenders and investors. These different needs arise primarily from policies toward risk and regulatory constraints. For example, an insurance company which is more conservative would invest exclusively or primarily in senior term notes, and as a result, receive a relatively small portion of the equity interest. On the other hand, a more aggressive institution might take all or mostly junior subordinated debt with a relatively high percentage of preferred or common stock.

Typically, the insurance company provides from 60 percent to 80 percent of the funds in a combination of senior notes, subordinated notes, preferred stock, and common stock. For this commitment, it receives approximately 50 percent to 70 percent of the ownership. This will vary significantly with each deal and the extent of the involvement by other equity investors.

Venture Capital Firms

"Venture capital" is a term ascribed to those funds exposed to the greatest degree of risk in the investment. For taking this higher risk, the venture capitalist almost always participates in the ownership or ownership rights of the company.

Until the post-war years, most venture capital in the United States came from private sources, primarily wealthy American families or foundations such as the Rockefellers, Whitneys, or Carnegies. In 1958, legislation was passed which created a new class of venture capitalist, the Small Business Investment Company (SBIC). SBIC's operate on an equity capital base, created by private or public investors, which can be leveraged up to 300 percent by borrowing from the Federal Government at fixed interest rates for up to 15 years. The program has rather stringent regulatory constraints which are administered by the Small Business Administration. They have been a significant factor in equity capital formation for small businesses since inception. Equally important is the fact that SBIC's marked the beginning of a bona fide venture capital industry which resulted in the training of many full-time professionals.

The availability of these professionals made possible the next major development in the industry — the widespread participation in venture capital by major financial institutions, including insurance companies, pension funds, endowment funds, and bank trust departments. This phenomenon began in the early 1970's and has continued through the 1980's, resulting in billions of dollars in new venture funds being raised. Most of this money has been invested in limited partnerships where institutions serve as limited partners and the professional venture capitalist acts as the general partner. These partnerships usually have an expected ten-year life cycle during which the funds are invested, liquidated, and capital gains returned to investors. Unlike the SBIC's, these institutional funds are not subject to any government regulatory controls.

Investment Policy and LBO's. A majority of the venture capital funds have historically been invested in start-up or early stage financings of companies with significant growth potential. These companies usually are engaged in high technology industries such as electronics, data processing, and biotechnology. This type of investment offers maximum potential return. It also entails the greatest risk of loss, since the investor is taking both a business and financial risk.

Many venture capitalists view their investment portfolios in much the same manner as other investors. They seek not only diversification of investments but also diversification of risk. The objective is to find investments at both the high and low end of the risk spectrum. At the high end are the high tech start-ups, while leveraged buyouts are considered much lower risks because they entail only a financial risk.

At the same time, the stable cash flow characteristics of seasoned companies enable the venture funds to receive a current yield on all or a portion of their invested capital. With earlier stage financings this is not possible because the companies are usually operating at a substantial loss and need to preserve working capital. For these reasons, leveraged buyouts and acquisitions have been and continue to be an appealing investment vehicle for venture capitalists. It should be noted, however, that a minority number of firms, approximately 30 percent of the total, are actively involved in leveraged deals on a continuing basis.

The cost of funds is a more nebulous concept when it comes to the venture capitalist. One measure is the return on investment one can obtain (commensurate with the risk) versus other investment alternatives and competitive venture firms. In other words, it is the rate that must be earned to continue to attract outside investment capital. Another measure is the actual cost of borrowed funds. This measure is appropriate only for SBIC's which borrow a portion of their investment capital from the SBA. The cost of these funds will depend upon when the debentures are issued. For example, 15-year debentures at 6 percent interest were issued in the early 1960's, while more recently rates were much higher, usually in the low teens. Another factor which impacts the cost of funds is the percentage of the pool fund that is borrowed. The actual carrying cost of funds will not affect the total targeted return on investment so much as it will the manner in which it is invested. Those firms with a higher carrying cost of capital will tend to invest more heavily in securities which can yield a current return. Those funds which do not have significant interest costs, such as the more recently formed institutional pools, are more flexible as to the type of securities they own.

Differences Between Venture Capitalists and Insurance Companies. It has become increasingly difficult to draw a clear line of distinction between the role of an insurance company and a venture capitalist in a leveraged deal. In the past, insurance companies have satisfied their yield requirements primarily through current income on senior and subordinated debt securities with a small participation in equity kickers. In recent years, however, they have encroached further into the equity layer which has traditionally been the domain of venture capitalists and management.

In spite of these increasing similarities, there are still some definite characteristics which distinguish these two classes of institutional investors. Some of these distinctions are:

- The venture firm rarely invests in senior securities and its investment is always tied to some form of equity participation.
- While the insurance company depends upon current income for two-thirds or more of its total expected yield, venture firms often receive one-third or less from current income. In other words, venture firms take more of the low or non-yielding preferred and common stock securities while insurance companies take more of the senior or subordinated notes.
- The venture firms engaged in buyouts tend to be more actively involved in the dealmaking process as a sponsor or lead investor and are more inclined to stay involved in the company's affairs after the deal is closed.
- The venture capitalist will participate in either a "secured" or "unsecured" transaction.
- The venture firm has a shorter investment horizon than the typical insurance company investor.

Exit Strategy. Since it can be a very important issue to the buyer, this last point deserves some additional comment. As discussed earlier in Chapter 8, there are three primary means by which investors can cycle their investment in the company into cash or more liquid marketable securities: (1) a public offering, (2) a merger with or acquisition by another public company, or (3) a redemption of outside investor interests. Where the buyout group consists of professional managers of a previously publicly held company, the first two exit vehicles for the venture capitalist may not be very attractive to management. Their main objective may be to remain a private company with some control over their destiny. This aspect of the deal should be given careful consideration in the buyer's initial negotiations with the venture capital investors. There should be a clear understanding of how and when the venture firm plans to exit and the potential impact on the company at that time.

From an underwriting standpoint, since the venture capitalist is primarily an equity investor, he is not constrained by the collateral ratios of the asset-based lender or the debt coverage measures of the banks or insurance companies. He must, however, be convinced that the cash flow is sufficient to support the price and proposed financial structure. Furthermore, because the venture capitalist is substantially at risk without a secured interest, he will usually conduct an extensive due diligence procedure including in-depth checks on management, markets, customers, and suppliers. After all studies are concluded, the deal is priced and structured to yield at least a 35 percent compounded annual rate of return over the investment horizon with a feasible means of exiting from the investment. The particular securities used will depend upon a number of factors, including current yield requirements, control criteria, and tax considerations.

Seller Financing

In many transactions, the seller plays an important role in the financing process. Historically, transactions in which the seller financed a portion of the purchase price by means of purchase money notes on an installment schedule were quite common. This was especially true if the seller was a majority shareholder of a closely held company. By taking a note for at least 70 percent of the purchase price, the seller was able to defer the payment of capital gains taxes on that portion of the purchase price. In 1981, however, the federal regulation governing installment purchases was changed. It is no longer necessary for the seller to carry back 70 percent or more of the purchase price. The portion of the purchase price related to the note is now deferred from capital gains taxation without regard to the amount. The net result has been the elimination of the need for the seller to finance the sale of the company strictly for tax purposes.

Seller Requirements. In spite of these tax law changes, the seller continues to play an important role in financing leveraged deals. Today, however, other reasons for the seller's participation in the financing must be strong enough to overcome the diminished tax incentives. These other reasons almost always relate back to one single factor — the seller's motivation to sell the company for the desired price. If the seller is highly motivated, for any of the reasons to be discussed, it is quite likely that he will finance a portion of the transaction, provided two conditions are met. First, he must be convinced that his financing participation is necessary to complete the deal. Secondly, and this is extremely important, he must be convinced that the buyer is capable of preserving the value of his (the seller's) residual investment, the purchase money note. Without these assurances seller financing will be difficult, if not impossible, to achieve.

One of the key determinants of the seller's willingness to cooperate is his perception of the buyer's integrity and ability. In most cases, the purchase money note will be subordinated to the senior lenders. This puts the seller substantially at risk if the company is not successful for a long enough period to amortize the note. In fact, because of the relatively high leverage, the seller must look at the buyer as his operating partner. The buyer's success or failure in operating the company will determine if the seller will ever get paid. If he fails, it is unlikely that the seller will receive any of his residual investment, even though he may be secured by a second lien on all the assets.

Under these circumstances, it should come as no surprise that the seller, whether private or corporate, will be very cautious with whom he does business as a lender. Before taking a "naked note" he must be thoroughly convinced that the buyer has unquestioned integrity and will not do anything to waste or deplete the asset base. Furthermore, he must be absolutely sure of the buyer's business acumen. The seller must be confident in the buyer's ability to manage or oversee the management of the operation to insure profitability.

When Seller Financing is Necessary. The seller's participation may be an essential factor due either to internal circumstances related to the company itself or external conditions related to the economic environment. The main internal circumstance which often limits institutional financing and necessitates seller financing is a weak asset base. Companies engaged primarily in services with few "hard" assets other than receivables are prime examples. Inconsistent cash flows are another factor that scares off institutional lenders and investors. Companies in highly cyclical industries, for example, are more likely to require seller financing.

External economic and financial factors may also force the seller to play an active financing role. Economic conditions may be such that institutional lenders and/or investors are not actively seeking to make loans or equity investments and are more conservative in their underwriting standards. Interest rates may be so high that a smaller amount of senior and subordinated debt can be supported by the company's cash flow, leaving a gap between the purchase price and the available debt and equity funding. In such cases, the buyer must come up with additional equity, which may result in further dilution, or he must convince the seller that his participation in closing the gap is essential. Ironically, limited credit and high interest rates may present the best possible circumstances for the buyer. Sellers may be more apt to give favorable terms on their financing, such as long maturities, deferred principal payments, ramped-up amortization schedules, balloon payments, and low interest rates during difficult economic times.

Seller Security. There are two measures that a seller can take to minimize his risk in financing a portion of the leveraged buyout transaction. One is to ask the buyer for outside collateral such as marketable securities or real estate. Another is to require personal guaranties from both the buyer and management. How adamant the seller is about receiving these additional assurances will depend upon the dynamics of the deal. If the seller is highly motivated and the buyer has an excellent track record, outside collateral and personal guaranties may not be that critical. In general, buyers should expect to give personal guaranties to senior lenders, but should exercise caution in doing so to the seller. Remember, the seller knows much more about the business and its ability to service debt than the buyer.

Aside from the protection of their economic interests, both private and corporate sellers have other reasons to be concerned about the buyers they finance. The private seller, even after the sale, is still emotionally attached to his employees, customers, and suppliers. Thus, in his eyes, the ability, or lack thereof, of the company to meet its future obligations is a direct reflection on him. The corporate seller, on the other hand, is more conscious of the impact of the financing on his operating results. At the time of the sale, the corporate seller's auditors set up a reserve for the purchase money notes, based upon their discounted value. Usually, this reserve reflects only the financial parameters of the note (i.e., the variation of interest rate below market and special terms) since it is assumed that the note will be collected over the specified term. If, in the future, the buyer is delinquent in the payment of interest and/or principal, the public auditors may require that the entire note be written off. This charge flows directly to the bottom line and may have a significant negative effect on current operating results, an anathema to the top management of public corporate sellers.

Advantages of Seller Financing. The seller's participation in financing a portion of the acquisition is frequently very important to the buyer. It can often make or break the deal. And there are distinct advantages in dealing with the seller as a lender as opposed to dealing with institutional lenders. First, because he has no official "cost of money," the seller can offer interest rates much below those found in the open market. He can also be quite flexible on terms of repayment and can structure the loan to fit the company's projected cash flow. If the deal encounters problems, it is easier to renegotiate and stretch out the terms of the loan. The seller will usually have fewer negative covenants which can restrict future flexibility of the company, although he will almost always make some provision against potential wasting of assets or excessive buyer compensation or dividends. In some cases, the note may be structured as a "covenant not to compete," for which the payments are fully deductible to the buyer. Finally, by getting the seller to fill the "gap" with a subordinated note, the buyer avoids the dilution of his equity. The alternative of raising the funds from outside equity investors would result in a significant dilution of buyer ownership.

The importance of establishing and building credibility with the seller should now be quite apparent. The buyer must never forget that, while he is qualifying the seller, the seller is also qualifying him. The buyer's effort from the outset should be focused to give the seller every opportunity to say "yes" when confronted with the decision to finance the deal.

UNIVERSAL UNDERWRITING CRITERIA

Just as a buyer has specific criteria for qualifying a deal, the various financing sources have comparable guidelines. While the entire spectrum of requirements may vary from one class of lender/investor to another and also between similar types of lenders or investors, there are certain fundamental criteria which every deal must possess in order to ensure a financing commitment. These requirements apply without regard to type of lender or investor.

Management Qualifications

The first concern of anyone lending to or investing in the acquisition of a company is the quality of the management team. Regardless of how great the potential of the business, without capable management it will not likely succeed and provide a safe return of, and an acceptable return on, invested capital. The "team" aspect of management is emphasized here because no single individual possesses all the management skills necessary to run any business with significant size or potential. There must be breadth of management abilities in the areas of marketing, finance, engineering, and production. Whether the buyer/entrepreneur's involvement in the operation of the company is passive, part-time, or full-time, it is imperative that proven management is either in place or can be retained. If not, the buyer will have a very difficult time convincing the financing sources to lend to or invest in the transaction.

For this reason, management buyouts where proven operational managers are already in place are much easier deals for lenders and investors to digest. In such situations, the overall business risk is reduced, not only because incumbent management has a visible track record, but also because of their familiarity with the particular operation. Therefore, if the buyer intends to play an operating role, but does not have the luxury of a captive acquisition vehicle, every effort should be made to select a target company which can utilize his specific industry knowledge or managerial talent in the operation of the target company. The lack of directly related experience will create doubt in the minds of the lenders and investors and may preclude them from financing the deal.

Buyer's Financial Risk

A second related criterion required by almost all lenders is some financial commitment from the buying group. This includes operating management and/or private investors who sponsor the deal. The extent of this commitment will vary with each deal and the financing participants involved. Most lenders and investors want the buyers to have sufficient money at risk so that in the event of failure there would be a meaningful loss. Institutional financing sources feel those who stand to make the most if the company is successful should be willing to endure some pain if the venture turns sour. On the other hand, they do not require a financial investment to the extent that it will place a severe strain on management and inhibit their ability to run the company. As a rule of thumb, most lenders and investors like to see at least one-third of the buyer's net worth at risk.

The risks taken by a buyer may take many forms. The most obvious, of course, is cash. The buyer may also pledge marketable securities or real estate to a lender involved in the financing. Personal guaranties for all or part of the senior debt are also used, especially when the lender perceives it is collectable. In rare cases, the lender may waive direct equity investments or guaranties by the buyer if there is a substantial cushion in the loan-to-value ratios or debt coverages.

Viability of the Business

Finally, all lenders and investors want to be convinced that the business of the target company is viable. They will look at many of the same factors that are reviewed by the buyer in the analysis of the target company. Questions concerning proprietary products, market niches, share of market, and the ability to pass through cost increases are all considered by the money sources before they invest. The impact of these and other business risk considerations on the cash flow is the key area of lender and investor concern. In general, the financing participants in a leveraged deal want to avoid any significant business risk and to restrict their exposure to the financial risk of leverage. Even the secured lenders, whose investments are well protected, will look closely at the viability of the business since they are not in business to orchestrate liquidations.

THE FOUR CLASSES OF COLLATERAL

The four major classes of collateral which serve as security for the asset-based lender, in descending order of desirability, are (1) accounts receivable, (2) inventory, (3) machinery and equipment, and (4) real estate. As one moves down this list of assets, liquidity decreases and perceived risk to the lender increases. Each class of collateral will be considered in terms of liquidity, lender preferences, restrictions, advance rates, and loan terms.

Accounts Receivable

The most preferred security of the asset-based lender is the trade accounts receivable. Since most sales are based upon 30-day terms, receivables are highly liquid and their real value is often close to book value. The lender looks at receivables from the same perspective as the buyer. He looks at the quality and credit-worthiness of the customer base. Just as the buyer is concerned about over-dependence on a few customers, the lender is wary of over-concentration of receivables, especially if the credit is questionable.

The lender will, in his field audit, look for any factors which result in a diminution of the value of the receivables. This would include the uncollectable accounts which can be determined by analyses of the aging and the historical reserve for bad debt. The receivables should reflect a bona fide amount due to the company which represents the unconditional and final sale of a product or service for which title has passed to the customer. The lender evaluates the effect of this factor on collectability by an analysis of the sales contracts with customers and the historical rate of customer returns and allowances. All of these considerations will determine the lender's loan advance rate, which usually ranges from 70 percent to 90 percent of eligible accounts receivable.

Not All Accounts Receivable Qualify. "Eligibility" is the key word. A lender will often disqualify certain receivables which, in his opinion, are considered a higher risk and have a lower chance of being collected. The primary category of ineligible accounts are those which are older than 90 days from the date of invoice, unless extended terms or "dating" of invoices is a common practice in the industry. On the other hand, in businesses where accounts are usually collected within 30 days, the lender may disqualify all receivables over 60 days. Some lenders also have an accelerated disqualification rule, which means that if the delinquent accounts over 90 days from a given account exceed a certain portion (e.g., 10 percent) of the total customer account, all accounts receivable from that customer are disqualified. This rule can have a devastating effect on either acquisition funding or cash flow after the deal is closed. Other types of ineligible receivables are "contra accounts" (accounts which are also trade creditors of the company), foreign accounts receivable (unless they are insured), progress billings, and conditional sales. All of the foregoing accounts are deducted from the receivable base and the advance rate applied to the remainder to determine the loan amount.

One method that buyers often employ to minimize the impact of ineligible accounts receivable is to have the seller guarantee their collection. Sellers are often willing to do this because of their familiarity with the customers and confidence in their ability and willingness to pay. However, most guaranties are limited to the receivables on the books as of the closing date. Therefore, once these initial receivables have been collected, and if historical payment patterns prevail, the buyer will experience a squeeze on cash flow because some of the newly created accounts are again ruled ineligible.

Loans secured by accounts receivable are technically demand notes. Thus, they appear as short-term debt on the borrower's balance sheet. In reality, however, these loans are constantly revolving as old receivables are collected and new receivables pledged. These "evergreen" or "revolving" loans theoretically can remain outstanding indefinitely, provided there is a sufficient collateral base.

Inventory

The next balance sheet asset the asset-based lender considers for collateral is inventory. Inventory is not as attractive as security because of its relatively reduced liquidity. Moreover, its value, for lending purposes, may be difficult to ascertain. The value of this form of collateral will depend upon the particular mix of inventory types and their marketability. Even after adjustments by auditors, many inventories are carried on the books in excess of their realizable value. On the other hand, if the company utilizes the LIFO method of accounting for inventory, there may be a substantial amount of "old" inventory on the books at prices far below current realizable market value. In such cases, the lender can justify a much higher advance rate, sometimes even 100 percent of the book value.

Classes of Inventory. For lending purposes, inventory is segregated into three distinct categories: raw materials, work-in-process, and finished goods. Each has its own advance rate, depending upon the disparity between book value and liquidation value and its liquidity. Although it takes the longest to convert into a more liquid account receivable, raw material inventory can often represent good collateral values if it is composed of highly marketable commodity items, such as standard size metal tubing or sheeting. Advance rates can go as high as 60 percent for marketable raw materials with relatively stable values.

Work-in-process is the least desirable of all inventory categories. Other than for its scrap value, inventory in this state is of little or no use to anyone. Even if the work-in-process inventory has very short periods for its conversion to finished goods, lenders will only lend on the inventory "as is" and will not increase their advance rates. These usually range from zero to 20 percent and are based primarily upon scrap values. Lenders do not like to take an active, direct role in converting work-in-process inventory to finished goods. In one such case, a lender who took control of a printing company's assets through foreclosure and converted work-in-process to finished goods was presented with a claim by the union for unfunded pension benefits as a successor in the interests of the company owners.

The final category of inventory, finished goods, can also vary substantially in terms of its collateral value. If the products are highly specialized with a limited market, lenders are reluctant to lend anything. On the other hand, commodity items with a broad market can justify advance rates in excess of 50 percent. Finished goods for which there are firm orders, but are being held for specific shipment dates, could warrant larger advance rates. It depends upon the lender's perception of how long it will take to convert them into an accounts receivable.

Because inventory is such a variable and subjectively valued asset, it often is the "swing vote" in making or breaking a deal from a financing standpoint. Where a buyer or seller perceives one value, the lender might see something altogether different. One method successfully employed to bridge the gap and enable the lender to advance more against inventory is to have the seller promise to buy back any unsold inventory. If the seller is confident in the inventory value, this "put" to a certain segment of the inventory is often able to generate the extra funds needed to close the deal.

Loans secured by inventory may be evergreen, like the accounts receivable loan, but more often the lender likes to see an amortization schedule which reduces the overall advance rate over a period of time. The lender is more likely to require an amortization if the inventory is electronic components, which are subject to technological obsolescence, than would be the case with standard metal parts.

Machinery and Equipment

In terms of their relative attractiveness to the asset-based lender, the third class of assets on the balance sheet is machinery and equipment. Machinery and equipment is less attractive than current assets as collateral primarily because of its lack of liquidity. Unlike accounts receivable, most of which can be converted into cash within 90 days, or inventory which can often be reduced or liquidated in the ordinary course of business, the sale of machinery and equipment may take a longer period of time to accomplish. The financeability of the machinery and equipment will depend upon the degree to which it can offset these concerns in the lender's mind.

Lender Concerns. The most important of the lender's perceived risks, marketability, will depend upon several factors. First is the relative price of the assets. Generally speaking, the higher the price for a piece of machinery or equipment, the more limited is the market. A second determinant is the breadth of the market or the number of users for which the machinery and equipment has utility. An asset which is general purpose in nature and can be utilized by a large number of potential users is much more desirable than highly specialized equipment which has more limited applications. For example, a standard metal working machine which can be used in a variety of industries is more financeable than a specialized conveyor system which is highly specific to one industry or a certain type of company. Another factor which may be important is the attachment of the equipment to the physical plant in a way that makes its removal an extremely expensive proposition. This reduces both the value and liquidity of the asset.

The capital equipment sector of the United States and world economies is dynamic in terms of its ability to discover new and more productive equipment. In some industries technology is moving so rapidly that equipment purchased within the past two years may be significantly inferior to recent models. This often results in the rapid deterioration in the market value of used, but relatively new equipment. To the machinery and equipment lender, the possibility of technological obsolescence must be carefully examined and factored into loan underwriting decisions. To the extent that machinery and equipment assets are subject to this type of risk, they will be less attractive as collateral. A good example is the computer industry. There the quantum level improvements in capability and reduction in hardware costs each year create a very soft market for used equipment. As a result, secured lenders are reluctant to lend on such assets, except for very short terms and at relatively low advance rates.

Another factor leading to a sudden drop in the value of machinery and equipment is the overall health of a specific industry in which the equipment usage is highly concentrated. If the industry is in a prolonged slowdown, it may result in the simultaneous failure of many firms which have the same type of machinery and equipment. This will create an oversupply of equipment and the subsequent low demand may yield substantially lower prices. For example, machinery and equipment which is highly specific to the oil drilling industry declined in market value in 1982 due to a large oversupply of assets for sale. In such situations, the lender who once was in a comfortable position on collateral coverage may suddenly become undercollateralized.

To protect against the above risks on loans secured by machinery and equipment, the asset-based lender must carefully evaluate the industry, the company, and the specific assets in question. This risk is controlled by his determination of value, the advance rate, and the loan repayment terms. The most important of the above variables for both the buyer and the lender is the determination of fair market value.

Fixed Asset Valuation. To the buyer's advantage, fixed assets, of which machinery and equipment are often a significant portion, are usually understated on the books of the target company. In an inflationary economy, the replacement value for machinery and equipment assets is much higher than the original cost. The large disparity between replacement value and net book value of these assets is called "hidden asset value." The machinery and equipment is often perceived quite differently by the buyer and lender. While the buyer looks at current replacement value of the assets, the lender looks at "auction value." Because it is the most easily defined market and because the lender wants to be repaid quickly in the event of default, this value is more reflective of what the assets are worth under actual conditions of liquidation. In addition, the auction value represents the most conservative estimate of value, toward which any lender naturally gravitates.

The valuation of assets is done by a professional appraiser who may be employed by the lender or an independent third party. Appraisers maintain up-to-date data banks on auction values for various types of machinery and equipment throughout the country. Therefore, they can often give an accurate appraisal without personally inspecting the items to be valued if given the proper information. Such data includes description, model number, serial number, date of purchase, purchase price, depreciation reserve, and other relevant facts. The appraiser will most often physically inspect the equipment to make sure it is in working order. Having defined a value of the machinery and equipment through the appraisal process, the asset-based lender further controls risk by advancing funds at a rate less than 100 percent of auction value. This advance rate is usually 80 percent. The remaining "cushion" serves to cover unforeseen declines in value and liquidation expenses.

Loan Terms. A final means by which the lender controls risk on machinery and equipment loans is the term of the loan. The greater the perceived risk, the shorter the term and the more rapid the amortization of the loan. Terms usually range from 5 to 10 years, but can be as short as 3 years or as long as 15 years. A key determinant of the loan term is the lender's perception of the expected life of the assets and the inherent risk of technological obsolescence. These loans are generally written with fixed monthly or quarterly reductions of principal and interest on the average outstanding balance. In some cases, the amortization will be based on a longer schedule with a balloon payment at the end of a shorter term. This device is especially appropriate where cash flows are tight in the early years and some relaxation of debt service is necessary. To allow this, the lender must be convinced that the collateral values will be sufficient to cover the remaining loan balance at the balloon date. In practice, such loans are usually rewritten at maturity with new amortization schedules which reflect the expected life of the assets at the time.

Real Estate

The last class of assets, and the least desirable to the asset-based lender, is real estate. Since the manner in which an asset-based lender views real estate as loan collateral is very similar to the assessment of machinery equipment, the specific criteria will not be repeated. Instead, the discussion will focus on the major differences between real estate and machinery and equipment and why this collateral is not particularly appealing to most asset-based lenders.

It is important to remember that loans secured by real property have not been the domain of the classical asset-based lender. Most of these loans have been financed by the traditional real estate lenders such as insurance companies, savings and loans, banks, and for a brief period in the early 1970's, real estate investment trusts. Although these institutions usually have ample funds, their underwriting criteria for single tenant, special purpose industrial properties, which are typical in buyout transactions, are based primarily upon buyer equity. Except for the relatively few insurance companies that invest in buyouts, there are few traditional sources of real estate financing for leveraged buyouts or acquisitions. By default, therefore, the asset-based lenders are the only available source and they don't like these types of loans.

Real estate collateral is less attractive than machinery and equipment for three reasons. First, it is immovable and its value primarily determined by location. Second, the properties are often large in size and special purpose in design and layout. This makes them difficult to sell or lease in the event of foreclosure. Finally, the lender often incurs expenses for security and rehabilitation in order to remedy the vacancy problem created by the default. It should be no surprise, then, that lenders accustomed to liquidating accounts receivable in 90 to 120 days are reluctant to lend on real estate. Responses on real estate loan requests range from outright refusal to an extremely conservative advance.

How to Get More from Real Estate Assets. Since real estate asset values are often understated on the books, this presents an interesting dilemma for the buyer. If the purchase price bears a reasonable relationship to book value, the real estate may represent significant "hidden asset values." He must find a way to generate adequate financing on these assets to effect a transaction. There are several methods by which this can be achieved. Under the first approach, the buyer purchases all of the target's assets, except the real estate. Title to the realty remains with the seller who then leases the property back to the target company. Ownership rights can be granted to the buyer through an option to purchase at some future date. This procedure is more prevalent with private sellers who are more real estate oriented and want to retain ownership. In fact, it may be difficult to persuade some private sellers to grant a purchase option to the buyer. A related technique is to have the seller become the real estate lender by taking back a purchase money note secured by a first mortgage on the real estate. This is especially appealing to corporate sellers because the note is secured by the property itself as opposed to an unsecured subordinated note or a secured junior subordinated note.

Because most buyers are private individuals or investment groups (including management), they are often interested in transferring ownership of the real estate from the target company to their own personal accounts. This allows them to take advantage of the tax benefits of depreciation and future appreciation in property values. It can be accomplished simultaneously with the closing, but may also be done subsequent to the closing if interim financing, either from the seller or an outside source, can be secured. With the new provisions of the 1986 Tax Act, however, there is not as much incentive to separate out the real estate under different ownership.

A final method of financing real estate is a more conventional approach. It is made possible by the emergence of the intermediate term lender (ITL). Whereas the traditional asset-based lender shuns loans secured by real estate, and, to a certain extent, machinery and equipment, the ITL aggressively seeks them. This player fills a definite niche in the marketplace for leveraged acquisitions and understands the marketplace for all types of fixed assets, including machinery, equipment, rolling stock, and real estate. His underwriting methods for determining loan amounts and terms are both similar to and different from other asset-based lenders. They are similar from the standpoint of appraisal techniques and the emphasis on liquidation value. Where the typical asset-based lender will rely solely on collateral, however, the ITL will give strong consideration to historical and projected cash flow. If the cash flow is sufficient to meet or exceed debt coverage criteria, the ITL will base his loan primarily on this parameter. Thus, it is possible to have a loan which is in excess of 100 percent of the collateral values, if there is enough cash flow. By using both a collateral and cash flow approach, the ITL can often lend more than a typical asset-based lender. Because of their familiarity with fixed asset values and expected economic lives, these lenders are also more flexible on terms.

As prices for leveraged buyouts increased, real estate assets became an increasingly important vehicle to finance the needed cash demanded by sellers. This was accomplished, in numerous cases, by syndicating the real estate to a group of private investors at a higher price than the buyer himself paid for it. Much of the appeal for such investments came from the tax benefits derived from rapidly depreciating the assets. With the limitations of the 1986 Tax Act on using "passive losses" to offset income, this technique may diminish in importance.

SECURING THE FINANCIAL COMMITMENT

In a leveraged buyout or acquisition, the financing step assumes a special importance in the overall dealmaking process. This is not to say that the other steps — finding, qualifying, analyzing, valuing, and negotiating — are unimportant. But, without a firm commitment and subsequent funding by lenders and investors, the deal has absolutely no chance of closing. Therefore, it behooves the buyer to focus a significant amount of time and energy on obtaining an acceptable financing commitment.

Much has already been discussed about securing the necessary financing for an LBO. However, because it is such a vital part of the transaction, some of this will be re-emphasized to put the entire financing process in perspective.

Above all, the buyer — whether it is an outside entrepreneur/investor, or an incumbent manager — must realize that financing the leveraged buyout is a *process,* not an *event.* For most outside buyers, it starts long before the deal at hand has even surfaced. And it doesn't end until the documents are signed at the closing. In the meantime, anything can happen. Unexpected events often occur which threaten to unravel the financing. These often put the buyer's relationship with his financing sources to an extreme test before the deal ultimately closes.

For this reason it is important for the buyer to establish close *personal relationships* with his financing sources. These relationships should not only be based on mutual needs, but also on respect for each other's integrity and business judgment. These relationships form the foundation which can withstand the inevitable trials of the LBO funding process.

After personal relationships, the next important thing for the buyer to have is *knowledge of his lenders and investors.* What type of deals do they like, what type don't they like, what are their underwriting criteria, their approval procedures, etc. He must find a way to extract promises out of the financing sources and convert them into firm commitments. To accomplish this, the buyer must have the final essential ingredient necessary to successfully finance the leveraged buyout: *knowledge of the target company.*

Armed with these three weapons, the buyer is in a strong position to exert some control over the financing process. This involves several contacts with lenders and investors throughout the dealmaking effort. In effect, the buyer's financing sources must be viewed as "partners" who are to be contacted at critical points in the deal. It officially begins during the qualification stage, when the buyer calls his financing sources to discuss the general parameters of the deal. If the lenders and/or investors signal a green light, the buyer takes the next step and meets with the seller. Then, after performing his preliminary due diligence, the buyer must put his case together and meet with his key financing source. At this point he needs clear direction from the lender or investor. Is it a deal they *can* do? Is it a deal they *will* do? What has to happen next to convert the "can" to a "will"?

The process continues as the financing sources conduct their own due diligence review, field audits and, if necessary, appraisals. During this time, the buyer must maintain close communications and deal with any major concerns of the lenders. Above all, he must maintain contact with the seller and keep him posted on the progress of the financing.

In financing a leveraged buyout, there may be one or more sources who participate. The final number and type of financing sources will depend upon several factors, including the price, characteristics of the deal, how much equity the buyer has to invest, and whether the seller is willing to finance a portion of the deal. In the simplest transaction, the buyer's (or management's) equity plus senior debt is sufficient to pay the seller what he wants. In today's market, however, prices have increased to the point where additional equity and/or mezzanine financing is required. Obviously, these more risky financing components are more critical to the deal than senior debt. These key sources should be the first consulted, because without their participation, there will be no interest from senior lenders.

THE FINANCING PACKAGE

Although initial communications with lenders and investors will be verbal, it will ultimately be necessary for the buyer to summarize the deal in writing. The product of this effort is called the "financing package." The "package" is one of the tools used by the buyer to communicate with his financing sources. It cannot supercede or take the place of solid relationships and verbal dialogue, which are critical aspects of the financing process. But, in most cases, it is necessary to summarize the facts for the money sources.

The purpose of the financing package is twofold. First, it should present all relevant information needed by lenders and investors to make a decision on whether or not to participate. Secondly, it should present both the buyer and the deal in the best possible light to potential lenders and investors to improve the chances of a favorable response.

The degree of detail contained in the package is a controversial issue in financial circles. Some lenders and investors prefer very "thick" packages complete with detailed market studies. Others are content with shorter summaries with little verbiage, as long as they include the relevant information on the deal. The ultimate choice of the "short" or "long" version will be determined by the buyer's perception of the preferences of those financing sources which have been contacted. Other determinants will be the buyer's time resources and the availability of supplementary information, such as market studies. If one does prepare a detailed package, it is important to summarize the key information or make it easy to find. It is difficult to retain the interest of a lender or investor who is required to dig through a voluminous report to find the important information. For this reason, the abbreviated package may be the most practical.

Regardless of size, any financing package must contain the following information if it is to accomplish its purpose.

- Historical Financial Statements — these should include a recent balance sheet and income statements for the past five fiscal years.
- Proforma Financial Statements — projected balance sheets, income statements, and cash flows for the next 5 to 10 years or the period of the longest piece of debt.
- History and Background — this should include information on the company, its owners, and their motivation for selling.
- Market and Industry Analysis — this should describe dynamics of the industry, the company's relative share of the market, and a study of the strengths and weaknesses of key competitors.

- Strategic Plan — the buyer should explain his strategic approach to gaining or maintaining market share.
- Collateral Information — schedules of major assets, including accounts receivable aging, inventory lists, capital equipment lists, and descriptions of facilities. Any appraisals should also be included.
- Financing Summary — summary of the proposed financing as the buyer sees it.
- Biographies of Key Management — this should include the entrepreneur (buyer) as well as key members of the operating management team.

Appendix H contains a suggested outline that any buyer (incumbent management or outside entrepeneur) may use in preparing the financing package. It includes a brief narrative of the objectives that the buyer should try to accomplish in each major segment of the proposal.

It is important for buyers to understand that a fancy package alone will not ensure the necessary commitments. In fact, an overly impressive package may create concern among lenders or investors that the deal is being "shopped" and, as a result, they won't even read it. This is particularly true when the buyer had had no prior discussions with the financing source before sending the package. Thus, the "package" should be viewed as a written communication tool to be used at the appropriate time in his dialogue with lenders and investors.

FINANCING LBO'S IN A HIGH PRICE ENVIRONMENT

The leverage buyout market basically follows the overall market for public corporate securities. In periods of high interest rates, valuations of public and private companies usually decline for two reasons. First, because investors can get a more competitive yield on fixed income securities, they require a higher return (lower price) on equity investments. Secondly, higher interest costs diminish the target company's net cash flow and thus reduce its value. Conversely, when interest rates decline, stock values in general and LBO values in particular generally increase.

As interest rates dropped in the mid-1980's, valuations of all corporate securities, both public and private, rose accordingly. This placed the leveraged buyer in a new, higher priced environment that required some new, innovative approaches to structuring and financing deals. As prices expanded, buyers had to create new means of raising additional capital if they didn't want to pull it out of their own pocket or dilute their equity interest.

Asset Sales

The obvious and "least costly" approach was to realize more value for the assets by immediately selling them. It started with a sale and leaseback of fixed assets, usually real estate, at fair market value to third parties. The cash raised from sale/leasebacks was then given to the seller or used to pay down acquisition related debt. As deals became larger and more expensive, the asset sale concept was extended to include entire pieces of the business that were often sold to other leveraged buyers. In some respects, the leveraged buyout process became a race to acquire and then quickly sell off various components of a company until the debt was reduced to a manageable level. This is quite a departure from the original LBO concept of allowing the target company to reduce its own debt over a period of five to ten years primarily through its operating cash flow.

Expansion of Mezzanine Financing

Other than quick asset sales, the major impact of higher prices on LBO's was the expansion of the role played by mezzanine financing. Senior lenders limit the amount of their participation on the basis of cash flows and collateral values. While these variables may improve somewhat in good economic times, it is not nearly enough to offset the significant increase in prices. And LBO investors, if possible, prefer to limit their equity to 10 percent or 20 percent of the purchase price. The mezzanine financing sources, that have proliferated in both number and dollars available, are anxious to participate. As a result, most of the increase in the multiple of earnings or book value paid by leveraged buyers has been financed by these sources. The dramatic rise in junk bond financing in the larger deals is strong evidence of this development. But the same phenomenon has occurred in the smaller and medium-sized buyouts.

Another significant factor has been the increased participation by classical senior lenders in the mezzanine layer. It was stated earlier in this chapter that senior lenders most often receive no equity in the buyout because they take the least amount of risk. While this may have been true when prices were at lower levels, the market now dictates that senior lenders "stretch" their normal advance rates or collateral limits if the deal is to be financed. To compensate for this additional risk, many asset-based lenders demand a share of the equity.

New Financing Techniques

To cope with the increasing disparity between price and cash flow, buyers and their mezzanine financing sources have devised a number of new approaches to LBO financing. Foremost among these is the *zero coupon bond.* This is a debt instrument bearing no current interest, but the accrued interest is paid along with the principal at maturity. It is particularly useful in structuring deals where cash flows are expected to show steady and predictable gains and there is sufficient realizable value in the underlying assets to cover the accrued interest. When issued for cash in a typical LBO financing, a zero coupon bond bears an "original issue discount" equal to the difference between its issue price and its amount payable at maturity. This difference is amortized over the term of the obligation.

Another approach to resolving cash flow shortfalls in the early stages of a buyout has been for mezzanine lenders to structure debt with deferral periods of one to three years or more on either interest, principal, or both. This technique is not necessarily new, but has been used with increasing frequency as prices have risen.

The increased participation of mezzanine financing sources — and some senior asset-based lenders — in underwriting the risk capital needs of LBO's has not been without cost to both outside and inside buyers. Lenders have demanded more equity in return for the higher level of risk to which they are exposed. As the equity pie must be divided up into a larger number of smaller pieces, a natural consequence is that less is left for the entrepreneurs and managers.

Sellers Retain Residual Interests

Sellers also have had to adjust to living in a higher priced LBO market. While, as a group, sellers have been the prime beneficiaries of the rise in prices, they have also found that there are limits to how much the target company can borrow and investors are willing to commit. If prices get too far ahead of cash flow, the seller is not be able to do a deal with the leveraged buyer. Rather than take a lower price from a non-leveraged buyer or financing the deal with an inordinant amount of subordinated debt, many sellers have chosen to retain a residual interest in the target company. This may take the form of retaining approximately 20 percent of the stock or receiving warrants for future purchases of stock in the new buyout entity. Although this is more prevalent in larger divestiture transactions, an increasing number of private sellers are also using this approach.

PHASE III
CLOSING THE DEAL
(Chapters 13-15)

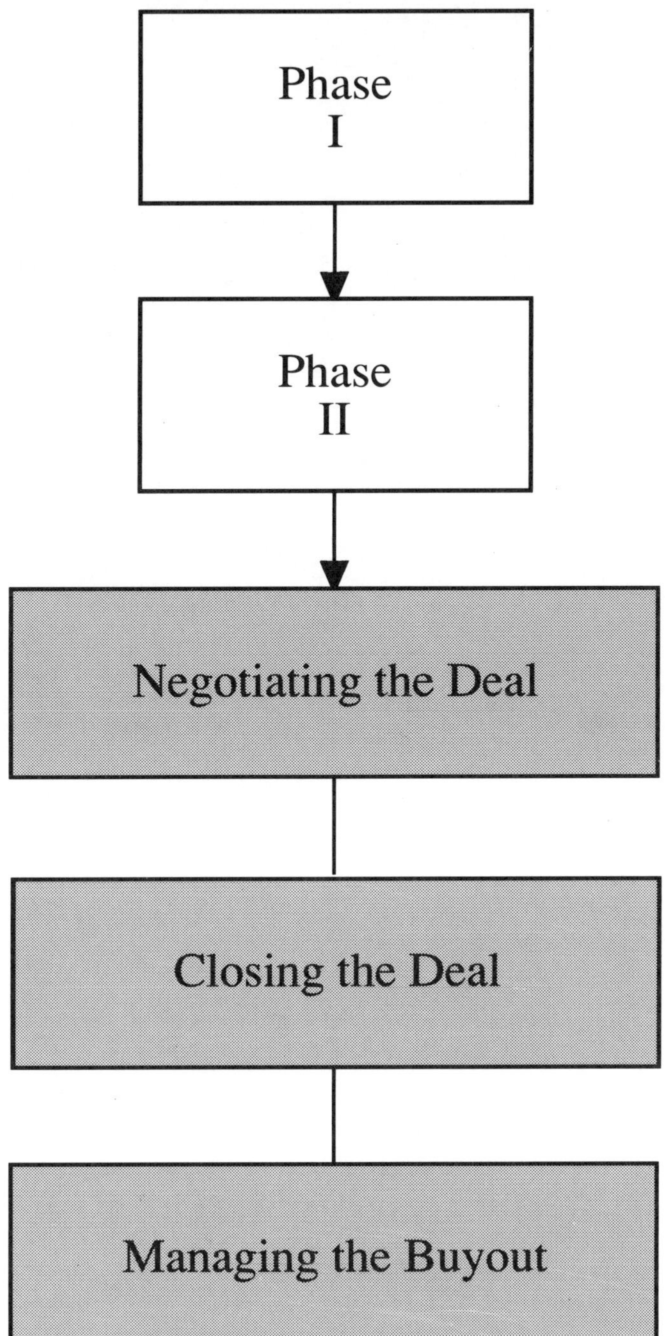

13

LEGAL AND TAX CONSIDERATIONS

To this point, examination of the leveraged buyout process has primarily focused on business and financial considerations. Very little has been said about the legal and tax aspects of the transaction. This is not to suggest that these issues are not significant. Quite the contrary, they are critical factors as to how the transaction will be structured. In many cases, legal or tax considerations become the focal point of the deal and can strongly influence its successful closing or ultimate demise. This chapter will focus on these matters and their impact on the transaction. Additional legal, tax, and securities factors affecting leveraged buyouts are set forth in Appendix A.

MEMBERS OF THE BUYER'S TEAM

The buyer, whether an outside entrepreneur or incumbent management, is always the prime mover in making the deal. However, there are times in the dealmaking process where outside professional help is needed. This might include help with obtaining the financing commitments by using an investment banking firm. It may even be necessary to hire an appraisal firm to establish collateral values of assets for lenders and allocate the purchase price. But there are two professionals in particular who are absolutely indispensable to the buyer. They are his attorney and his Certified Public Accountant (CPA).

Since the skill and experience of the lawyer will be a significant determinant of the buyer's success in closing a deal, this professional is generally regarded as the most important of the two. For this reason, it is important to take a closer look at the characteristics of a successful "deal-oriented" lawyer.

The Lawyer

The primary goals of the buyer's attorney are to close the deal while protecting the client's legal rights and remedies. To achieve these objectives, the deal lawyer must have a number of attributes and qualifications, some of which differentiate him from many other lawyers. First and foremost, he must have the requisite knowledge and experience in business combinations and reorganizations. This not only includes a solid understanding of the intricacies of acquisition contracts, but also a high degree of familiarity with various forms of institutional lender and investor documentation. Included in this area are notes, collateral security agreements, inter-creditor agreements, and bankruptcy law. (A list of typical closing documents with which the deal-oriented attorney must be familiar is shown in Appendix I.) The deal lawyer should also be knowledgeable on the rapidly changing tax regulations and their effect on leveraged buyouts. A lawyer who is also a CPA is a definite plus in this regard.

Aside from the technical skills, a good deal lawyer has a positive outlook and seeks to find solutions rather than uncover problems. Instead of finding reasons for "killing a deal," the qualified attorney is oriented to "making the deal," provided that it doesn't compromise his client's legal position. He should also be adept at the art of working with other people, especially when it comes to subordinating his own ego to those of counsel representing the seller and the lenders. Finally, the deal lawyer must be able to work well with the client in the negotiating process. Naturally, the more deals a buyer and his counsel do together, the more efficiently they will work as a team.

The experienced acquisition attorney knows what has to happen and when it must take place. Along with the buyer, he maintains the momentum of the deal, especially with regard to those aspects involving legal counsel for the seller and lender. These professionals usually prepare and follow a transaction timetable outlining the various tasks to be accomplished, the person responsible for them, and the target completion dates. An example of a buyout timetable is shown in Appendix J. Although this is an example of a rather complex transaction, it provides some insight into the scope and detail of the closing process and the importance of competent legal counsel.

The CPA

Although this team member may not be as vital as the lawyer, the CPA also plays an important role. Depending upon the size and complexity of the deal, he can participate in the process in any one of three ways. First, some of the "Big 8" accounting firms have professionals who provide consulting services to current or potential clients on private buyouts and acquisitions. This service is mainly oriented toward management teams contemplating a buyout and includes advice on structuring and financing a transaction. These services are often provided for a nominal charge to the buyer, with the understanding that the new company will employ the firm as its auditor and/or tax accountant. Due to potential conflict of interest, it may not be feasible for a CPA firm which is the auditor for public corporate sellers to also represent the buyout group.

A second service offered by the CPA firm is to consult for the buyer in the due diligence process. Most often this takes the form of a "businessman's review" which is not nearly as large in scope as a full certified audit. This less detailed review is designed to analyze the accounting and control systems and compliment the buyer's evaluation effort. Emphasis is on verification of historical financial data and disclosure of any material factors in the accounting methods which will impact value, cash flow, or financeability. (An example of the procedures and tests of the "businessman's review" is shown in Appendix F.)

The final area of service which may be provided by the CPA is the analysis of the tax ramifications of various alternative acquisition structures. As will be seen, there can be significant tax consequences to both buyer and seller, depending on how the deal is structured from a legal standpoint. The buyer must have a complete knowledge of these tax consequences so they can be integrated into the negotiations with the seller, investors, and lenders. The qualified CPA possesses the essential technical knowledge of the tax code, as well as applicable revenue rulings and tax court decisions to provide reliable information for the buyer.

HOW TO FIND QUALIFIED ADVISORS

The buyer has many important decisions to make throughout the leveraged buyout process. None, however, is more important than his selection of the key advisors that are essential to his success. Yet many entrepreneurs and managers approach this important task in a nonchalant manner, basing their decision more on prior relationships with the advisors rather than professional qualifications.

To put the importance of advisor selection in perspective, it is similar to a CEO's decision on hiring a Chief Financial Officer. Would a competent CEO hire a person for this important position merely because he has some knowledge of accounting and has known him for several years? Absolutely not! He would most likely conduct his search among individuals that he *doesn't already know.* He would carefully screen and check any candidate's qualifications and record of accomplishments.

In the same manner, the buyer must view the selection of his key advisors as his most important "hires." The lawyer, in particular, will be his most trusted advisor during the dealmaking process. The buyer should use the same principles in selecting his advisors as a CEO does in hiring his CFO. In particular, he should:

- Network for possible leads.
- Carefully screen and interview the best candidates.
- Conduct reference checks.
- Select on the basis of qualifications, not how "inexpensive" their fees might be.

Networking for Leads

The role of a competent advisor is something for which buyers can't place a "help wanted" ad, and most highly qualifed lawyers and accountants don't advertise their services. They don't have to because they're too busy. So the normal approach for developing a list of qualified prospects is to *network.* The best place for the buyer to start is with his own contacts. But he must recognize that just because someone has a law degree, it does not guarantee he is capable of working on a leveraged acquisition. And not all CPA's have the necessary experience to conduct a businessman's review or to analyze the tax consequences of a deal.

For these reasons, it is best to network among sources who are connected with the merger, acquisition, and leveraged buyout field. This includes intermediaries, investment bankers, asset-based lenders, and, most important, other buyers. Business newspapers and magazines, such as the *Wall Street Journal* and *Business Week,* have regular "tombstone" ads of recently completed LBO's as well as articles and news releases. These are excellent sources to contact and merely ask: "Who was your lawyer?" and "Would you recommend him?" It won't take long to develop a long list of prospects.

It would be preferable to find advisors who are located reasonably close to the buyer or where he expects to buy the company. But this becomes less of a factor as the deal gets larger in size. In no case, however, should distance outweigh professional competence. The buyer may end up spending more on travel and telephone, but the end results will be worth it.

Screening and Interviewing

It is difficult for some people to look upon the selection of professional advisors in the same manner as hiring key employees. Perhaps it is because they are easier to fire. But regardless of how quickly they can be fired, the wrong advisor can cause irreparable harm to the buyer's efforts. For this reason, the selection process should be approached in the same careful manner as hiring a key employee.

Initial screening can take place over the telephone by discussing the advisor's prior experience in LBO's. It may be that he is "overbooked" already and cannot take on additional clients. If so, the buyer should move on to the next prospect. But if the lawyer or CPA is interested, the buyer should not be reluctant to approach this conversation as a "preliminary interview" and ask relevant questions. In addition, he should ask for several references. Although this is just a telephone conversation, it will enable the buyer to determine the advisor's level of interest, professional experience, and if there is good personal chemistry between them. Once the buyer has narrowed down the field, he should personally visit with the "finalists" before making his selection.

Conduct Reference Checks

The buyer should also not be hesitant to conduct reference checks. Although lawyers and accountants will rarely give a reference who will say anything bad about them, discussions with other clients will provide some insight into their specific areas of expertise and responsiveness. Of course, responsiveness is a function of how much business a particular client brings to the advisor. It may not be accurate to assume the same level of service for the small, one-time buyer.

Don't Select the "Cheapest" Advisor

If there is one area where the buyer should not try to economize, it is in selecting professional advisors on the basis of their billing rates. This does not mean that he should go out and hire the most expensive lawyer or CPA he can find. It does mean that the advisor's billing rate should not supercede the other factors — qualifications, experience, and personal chemistry — in the ultimate selection process. In fact, it may be "cheaper" in the long run to hire a more "expensive" advisor. This is because they are more experienced and, hence, more productive. Most important of all, their experience will improve the buyer's chances of closing the deal.

In his interview and selection process, the buyer should establish the rate at which the advisors bill and any other factors related to their compensation. If it is a brand new relationship, he should be prepared to pay an up-front retainer against which future fillings are charged.

THIRD PARTY FEES

This brings up the larger issue of what fees the leveraged buyer will have to pay and, more importantly, how to control them. Fees from outside professionals and lending sources are a reality of the LBO process. Although the buyer is seeking to leverage his capital in buying the company, it is unrealistic for him to start looking for a deal without setting aside some funds to pay fees to key advisors when their services are needed. How much he pays will depend upon a number of factors including size and complexity of the deal, the buyer's particular experience, and the type of financing sources utilized. Generally speaking, fees total anywhere from 1 percent to 5 percent of the total purchase price. The following is a brief description of the different types of fees that the leveraged buyer typically encounters in his quest for a deal.

Types of Fees

Intermediary Fees. These were previously discussed in Chapter 4. In most cases, the intermediary represents the seller and is paid by him. However, it is not unusual for the seller to either refuse to pay the fee or not guarantee it in writing. In such cases, if the buyer wants to see the deal, he must "protect" the intermediary's fee, i.e., promise in writing to pay it if the seller will not. If the buyer agrees to pay the fee, which usually is 2 percent to 5 percent of the transaction value, this must be factored into the financing assumptions. If it isn't, there will be a shortfall of funds and possibly no deal. Or, if the deal does close, the buyer may be sued by the intermediary for payment of the fee. The one positive feature of intermediary fees is that they are contingent (only payable if the deal actually closes). Thus, the buyer has some control over the situation. If the deal doesn't make sense or can't be financed with enough left to pay the intermediary fee, it shouldn't be done. Another possible solution to a shortfall is for the intermediary to take his fee in the form of a note or equity in the target company.

Legal Fees. This is the most significant and important expense the buyer must face. The magnitude will vary with the size and complexity of the deal and at what point the buyer brings his lawyer into the transaction process. Lawyers are expensive and, as previously stated, the most expensive lawyers are usually the best. In a typical small to medium sized leveraged buyout ($5 million to $50 million purchase price), the buyer should figure on paying at least $25,000 in legal expenses, although it is not unusual for fees to exceed $100,000. They may be much higher if the deal is more complex in terms of legal due diligence and documentation.

One method of controlling or eliminating legal expenses is to include the lawyer as an equity partner in the deal. Most lawyers are reluctant to do this, however, and the buyer must ask himself if he really wants this person as a partner. Above all, the buyer must not sacrifice legal competence in order to avoid paying up-front fees. With an unqualified lawyer, he may never get the deal done.

Accounting Fees. These expenses are usually incurred by buyers who lack the necessary expertise themselves or within their staff to conduct a thorough examination of the target company's books and records. This step, which usually occurs in the final due diligence activities, is most important to ensure that the buyer is getting what he's paying for. Like lawyers, CPA's bill by the hour and can be quite expensive. A typical "businessman's review" might cost in excess of $25,000. Of course if the buyer is sophisticated and has the requisite accounting knowledge, he may be able to reduce or completely avoid this expense.

Tax considerations are also an important consideration in an LBO. With rapidly changing tax laws, it is important for buyers to get competent tax advice at various points in the deal. Although this can be expensive, it can be more costly to proceed on the basis of faulty assumptions.

Financing Fees. One of the attractive features of LBO's to lenders is that they can get a higher yield by charging up-front "commitment fees." These are usually charged by the senior and mezzanine lenders when they issue their formal commitments to fund the loan(s). Such fees usually range from ½ percent to 2 percent of the total financing and, in many cases, must be paid when the commitment is made. Some lenders may only require the fee to be paid if the loan is funded.

Lenders may also incur substantial expenses for their own due diligence, appraisals, and legal documentation procedures. In some cases, the buyer is expected to pay these regardless of whether the loan is ultimately funded. Again, such expenses will vary with deal size, but it is not unusual for these fees to exceed $25,000.

If an outside investment banker is employed to arrange the financing, the buyer will also have to pay for his services. Fees charged will depend upon the type of financing raised. Senior debt normally costs 1 percent plus expenses while mezzanine or equity financing fees are usually based upon the Lehman (5-4-3-2-1) scale.

Appraisal Fees. The buyer may want to have an independent appraisal of the company or its assets for financing purposes or documentary support for the allocation of purchase price. Appraisal fees for lending purposes are often paid to the lender's in-house appraisal team or an outside firm designated by the lender. Appraisals for purchase price allocations are often restricted to larger deals where this matter becomes more material and the transaction runs a higher risk of challenge by the IRS. With the 1986 tax law changes, the rules for allocation have been tightened considerably and, as a result, may lessen the need for outside appraisals.

Consulting Fees. If the buyer is unfamiliar with a certain industry, manufacturing process, etc. he may want to call in outside experts to help with the due diligence effort. Another possible need is for specialists in certain areas such as employee benefits and pensions plans, the analysis of which is critical to the transaction. Such experts also charge for their time and expenses and, in some cases, their fees can be substantial. The buyer must weigh the importance of these analyses and opinions against the cost incurred in getting them.

Controlling Fee Expenses

As the preceding paragraphs show, fees for outside experts who may be necessary to complete the transaction are both manifold and costly. The problem is that most of the providers of these needed services work on a non-contingent basis. Their fees must be paid regardless of whether or not the deal closes. This doesn't present a problem if the deal closes, because the payment of transaction fees is included in the overall financing requirements and ultimately is paid by the target company. But, as we have seen, many deals die before they ever close for a number of uncontrollable reasons. In these cases, the buyer may face a substantial fee liability. Therefore, it is in his best interest to control fees to minimize these liabilities.

How can this be done with professionals and institutions who expect to be paid for time expended on a project? The first step is to act carefully and not authorize these firms to "start the meter" before it is absolutely necessary. This is particularly true with legal and accounting fees. If the buyer follows the procedures outlined in this book, he will avoid the premature engagement of lawyers, accountants, and other outside experts. He will know when help is necessary and when it is not. This is the most important factor in controlling fee expenses.

Another possibility is to convert some of the providers from a non-contingent to a contingent fee basis in exchange for equity. By rewarding them with potential ownership rights for their time, the buyer can lower his "sunk costs" before the transaction closes. On the negative side, this complicates the ownership picture and often gives rise to disputes on what the services provided were really worth. Also, some firms, especially the larger legal and accounting firms, have policies prohibiting this.

Financing fees can often be minimized by negotiating up-front with lenders. If the buyer has good credibility and is a possible repeat customer for the lenders, they will often waive advance fees, or at least change them to a contingent basis. The buyer should not be reluctant to discuss fees with lenders *before* going too far with any transaction. Misunderstandings can be both costly and embarassing.

Because the payment of some fees are a reality of the LBO process, the buyer must have financial resources available for this purpose. It is the equivalent of working capital for a business. Neither can function effectively without it. The analogy to a business applies equally as well to how the buyer controls his fee expenses. Smart businessmen spend only when it's necessary. Likewise, smart buyers authorize fee services only when it makes sense.

THE LEGAL STRUCTURE OF A PRIVATE BUYOUT

From a legal standpoint, the transaction is considered a "buyout" if the buyer is a newly formed business or corporate entity created specifically to acquire the stock or assets of the target company. It is considered an "acquisition" if the buyer is a pre-existing business entity, although a new legal entity (such as a subsidiary) may be formed to acquire the assets of the target company. The buyout is usually accomplished by a private investment group formed specifically to "buy out" the stock or assets of the target company. The acquisition is usually accomplished by a corporation with an operating history that wishes to acquire the target company's stock or assets. In orther words, private buyers do buyouts (sometimes called "private buyouts") and corporations do acquisitions.

The buyout or acquisition may be leveraged or unleveraged, depending upon the objectives and financial resources of the buyer as well as the financial characteristics of the target company. For the purposes of these discussions, however, the transaction is assumed to be leveraged with new acquisition debt.

In the simplest legal form, a leveraged buyout or acquisition consists of the formation of a new corporation which purchases the stock or assets of the target company. Another alternative is to have the buying corporation, whether it is an existing operating company or a newly formed company, form a wholly owned subsidiary (Newco), which is then merged with the target company. If Newco is the surviving subsidiary of the buying corporation, the transaction is called a "triangular merger." However, if the target company is the surviving subsidiary of the buying corporation, the transaction is called a "reverse triangular merger." (See Table 13-A.)

ASSET VS. STOCK DEALS

The financing of the buyout is accomplished by the issuance of new debt and equity securities to lenders and investors in return for their proportionate share of the total funding. These funds are then paid to the nominal seller, who's identity will depend upon whether the transaction is structured as a purchase of assets or stock. If it is a purchase of assets, the nominal seller is the target company itself, which either returns the proceeds of sale for the benefit of its shareholders, or is liquidated and the proceeds distributed to shareholders. If the transaction is a purchase of stock, the nominal sellers are the shareholders of the target company. In the case of a corporate divestiture, there is only one shareholder, the parent company.

It is apparent from the preceding paragraphs that the ultimate legal structure of the buyout or acquisition, whether it is a purchase of assets or stock, can have significant implications for the buyer and seller. If there is a secured lender involved in the deal, it may also affect his ability to perfect a security interest in the assets. The following sections will examine the pros and cons of asset or stock transactions for the buyer, seller, and secured lender.

Buyer Considerations

There is no "best way" to legally structure the buyout or acquisition from the buyer's standpoint. It all depends upon the unique circumstances surrounding the deal, and each deal is different. Unless there are compelling reasons not to do so, however, the buyer always prefers to purchase assets instead of stock. The main reason underlying this preference is that it enables him to avoid responsibility for undisclosed and unknown liabilities. Under a purchase of assets and assumption of liabilities, the buyer purchases only those assets and assumes only those liabilities specified in the acquisition agreement. Any subsequent liabilities which surface are the sole responsibility of the seller. If there is a purchase of capital stock, all present and future liabilities become the responsibility of the buyer.

As a practical matter, however, it is often difficult for the buyer to completely escape liability. Even in asset deals, courts will sometimes permit certain unpaid creditors to recover from a buyer regardless of deal structure. In California, for example, the courts have ruled in favor of product liability claims against companies which have disclaimed any such liabilities in the acquisition of assets. It should be noted, however, that an asset purchase arrangement does focus the attention of the seller on potential plaintiff actions and stimulates him to make a full and complete disclosure of liabilities. If there are strong reasons for purchasing stock, the buyer can obtain protection against undisclosed liabilities through representations and warranties from the seller. However, the seller will usually insist upon some limitations on future claims.

Sometimes the corporate entity of the target company has, in addition to its assets and liabilities, some charactertistics that have value to the buyer. In such cases, these advantages, which can be preserved through a purchase of capital stock, far outweigh the previously discussed advantages of an asset purchase. The most common of such "corporate benefits" are highly favorable leaseholds, mortgages, franchises, or other contracts. Such agreements often contain clauses prohibiting assignment by the corporation. Thus, in a sale of assets, these valuable rights would not be transferable to the buyer. A purchase of stock, in most cases, will not disturb the integrity of these agreements. The situation may also arise where the target company is encumbered by a burdensome contract, such as an expensive labor contract. In this case, an asset purchase would be one means of circumventing the obligation.

Tax Issues. Under present law, the buyer has the option, under certain circumstances, to treat a stock purchase as an asset purchase under Section 338 of the Internal Revenue Code. Section 338 requires an acquiring corporation to exercise a statutory choice within 12 months of a purchase of 80 percent or more of a corporation's stock and voting power. The election pursuant to IRC 338(a) results in the target corporation being treated as having sold all of its assets at the close of the acquisition date in a single transaction. In addition, the new corporation is treated as a new entity which purchased all assets of the acquired company as of the beginning of the date after the acquisition date. The price at which the sale is deemed to be made is an amount equal to the grossed-up basis of the purchasing corporation's stock in the target corporation on the acquisition date adjusted pursuant to applicable regulations for liabilities of the target corporation and other relevant items (presumably comparable to former IRC Section 334(b)(2) provisions).

If the election is made, the target corporation's tax attributes are terminated and the acquiring corporation is allowed to treat all the assets in the corporation as purchased. Therefore, the step up in basis of the assets reflects the purchase price paid for the stock. Before the 1986 Tax Reform Act, this provision enabled many leveraged buyers to increase the depreciable base of assets with no tax penalties other than the recapture of investment tax credits (ITC's) and accelerated depreciation. With the repeal of the so-called *General Utilities Doctrine* in 1986, however, there will be an additional tax at the corporate level on the difference between their new stepped-up vaiue and their original basis. As a result, Section 338 elections may no longer be economical, except in cases where the target company has net operating losses which can offset the gain recognized from the election.

Alternative to making the election is the ability of the acquiring corporation to choose to avoid purchase treatment and achieve a complete tax attribute carryover for the acquired assets. While tax attribute carryover may be achieved, as opposed to a step up in basis, tax planning for achieving both of these benefits is no longer available.

Other Issues. Other factors for the buyer to consider in the legal structuring of the transaction is the impact of bulk sales law requirements, sales taxes, and lender requirements. By far the most important of these are the lender considerations, which will be shortly discussed in detail. The bulk sales laws of most states require notification to creditors if the assets of the target company consist primarily of merchandise inventory. If proper notice is not given, the creditors may have a right to the acquired assets in the event that their claims are not satisfied. Most sellers are sensitive about disclosure of a deal before it is signed and closed, primarily because of the impact on key customers and suppliers. In these cases, the seller may wish to circumvent the bulk sales disclosure. The buyer may waive this requirement provided the seller indemnifies the lender in the event of non-payment of the liabilities by the buyer. The lender's willingness to cooperate will be contingent upon his perception of the credit-worthiness of the seller.

Seller Considerations

In almost all cases, the seller prefers to sell stock rather than assets. Many of the reasons which make the purchase of assets attractive to the buyer make it unattractive to the seller. Foremost among these is the exposure to contingent liabilities which may be unknown at the time of closing. The purchase of stock and the absence of specific warranties to the contrary transfers all liabilities, both known and unknown, to the buyer. Although, from a legal standpoint, they do not flow to the buying corporation if the target company is kept as a subsidiary, new liabilities diminish the buyer's expected value in the target company.

If the seller insists upon a stock transaction, the buyer can protect himself from liabilities through adequate representations and warranties. However, the typical attitude of the seller is "we'll open our books to you and your professionals and disclose our liabilities to the best of our knowledge, but we are not going to be responsible for what we don't know." The buyer will seldom go along with such a complete exposure to contingent liabilities. Since his main concern is the possibility of large claims, a middle ground is often struck by means of the seller warranting against claims or losses in excess of a certain cumulative dollar amount, usually $25,000 or $50,000. The seller will generally limit such warranties to a two or three-year period, provided they are within the statute of limitations. Tax claims are an exception for which the buyer always seeks protection for longer periods.

Another reason for the seller's preference for a sale of stock rather than assets is the possibility of sales taxes on the sale of fixed assets and ordinary income tax on the sale of certain classes of inventory. Also, the documentation is simpler. In a stock purchase, the sellers simply deliver and endorse their share certificates to the buyers in return for the consideration. In an asset purchase it is necessary to have a detailed bill of sale executed by the target company and the execution of a detailed list of liabilities assumed by the buyer. In addition, consents and assignments from third parties such as landlords, lenders, suppliers, lessors, and contract customers may be required in order to avoid the termination or acceleration of important contracts.

Secured Lender Considerations

In many deals, it is neither the buyer nor the seller who ultimately determines the legal structure of the transaction. The determination is often made by the senior lender. This is particularly true where this player is secured. Since this lender is usually advancing a significant portion of the acquisition price, the "Golden Rule": "He who has the gold makes the rules," is once again applicable.

In a stock transaction, the borrower is the buying corporation which passes the proceeds of the loan directly to the selling shareholders in exchange for their stock in the target. An alternative is to make payment directly to the target company which then pays dividends to its shareholders. In either case, the collateral for the secured loan(s), if any, is the target company's assets. Thus, there arises the situation where the borrower is not the same legal entity which has title to the collateral serving as security for the loan(s).

This makes it more cumbersome, and risky, for the secured lender to perfect his security interest in the collateral. To do so, the new subsidiary, the newly acquired target company, must first guarantee the borrowings of its parent and, secondly, pledge its assets as collateral for the loan(s). Yet none of the money flows into the company; it flows directly to its shareholders. Or if the money is funded to the target company, it doesn't stay there. This presents a potential problem for secured lenders. If the company must file a bankruptcy petition within the next year and the courts deem that the acquisition was inadequately capitalized and technically doomed to failure from the beginning, the security interest in favor of the secured lender can be set aside. The transaction will be deemed a "fraudulent conveyance," although fraud, in the ordinary sense of the term, was not perpetrated by any of the parties.

Unless there is a substantial cushion of subordinated debt or equity to reduce the risk of failure, therefore, the secured lender will almost always insist upon the deal being structured as a purchase of assets. Since the buyer in an asset transaction is buying only assets and assuming liabilities, the assets are owned by him. Hence, the borrower and owner of the assets is the same legal entity. This facilitates the granting of a security interest to the secured lender.

If the seller participates with the secured lender in the financing, it will be necessary for the documentation to include inter-creditor agreements which clearly delineate the relative rights and remedies of each lender and the priority of claims on the assets.

Other Considerations

Notwithstanding the desire and influence of secured lenders, there is a clear "battle line" between buyers and sellers on their respective preference for how the deal is structured. For all the foregoing reasons, sellers prefer to sell stock and buyers prefer to buy assets. These preferences were further magnified by the passage of the 1986 Tax Reform Act, which repealed the *General Utilities Doctrine*. Under the new law, the shareholders of corporations selling assets now must pay a double tax if the proceeds are distributed. Although sellers can adjust their prices to reflect this higher tax bite, this may prove to be more difficult to accomplish in actual negotiations. Thus, it would appear that the 1986 Tax Act provisions will further entrench the seller in his position of preferring stock sales.

However, there may be one compelling reason for both buyers and sellers to reconsider their traditional advocacies on whether to structure the deal as a stock or asset purchase. It relates to a landmark Supreme Court ruling in 1983 which expressly rejected the *sale-of-business* doctrine. This doctrine, which has been observed for years in the federal courts, had insulated sellers of controlling interests in closely held companies from any liabilities under federal securities laws. The net effect of the court's decision in the *Landreth Timber Co. vs. Landreth* case enables a disenchanted buyer to sue the seller under federal securities laws in cases where the transaction is structured as a purchase of stock if he can prove fraud in the disclosure process.

This powerful remedy available to the buyer may cause sellers to weigh the risk of potential litigation against the inherent advantages of selling stock rather than assets. Under the Securities Act of 1933, the buyer can recover the purchase price plus interest from sellers who have made "an untrue statement of a material fact or have omitted a material fact necessary in order to make the statements." At the very least, this development should motivate sellers to make sure that all material facts have been fully disclosed and take a stronger stand in their representations and warranties.

LEVERAGED BUYOUTS OF PUBLIC COMPANIES

Historically, most leveraged buyouts or acquisitions have involved either the private seller of a closely held corporation or the corporate seller of one of its subsidiaries or divisions. In recent years, however, there have been a large number of cases where the sellers are the shareholders of a publicly held company. The dramatic increase in this type of transaction, which is usually much larger and more complex than the traditional buyout, is a direct consequence of the condition of the stock market. For many companies, particularly those with more mundane and non-glamorous businesses, the market value of their shares has been far below the underlying value of the assets or business. This rather peculiar set of circumstances has made these companies excellent candidates for "going private" via a leveraged buyout. The values which can be justified by the leveraged buyer look very attractive to the long-suffering public shareholder, whether he is a control shareholder or an individual with a nominal equity interest.

More recently, a new devise has been increasingly utilized to put cash into the hands of public shareholders while also providing them with a residual interest in the company. This recapitalization technique is called the "leveraged cashout." It differs from a traditional LBO in that management engineers an exchange of equity for new debt, the proceeds of which are paid to shareholders, who also retain a nominal interest, say 20 percent, in the company. It has the two-fold advantage of allowing managers, rather than outside sponsors, to control the recapitalization while also enabling shareholders to participate in the future growth of the company.

"Cash Merger" Buyouts

By far the most popular approach to structuring leveraged buyouts of public companies has been the "cash merger," which was popularized by the investment banking firm of Kohlberg, Kravis & Roberts in the early 1980's.

The "cash merger" buyout, in many respects, is not unlike any other acquisition for cash. The only differences are the nature of the acquiring company, its shareholders, and the financing of the transaction. The cash merger technique usually includes one or more corporations in effecting the acquisition. The number of corporations is ultimately determined by future tax considerations, since it is often desirable to defer an immediate decision on liquidation but allowing for it at a later date. Usually, however, the acquiring company establishes a new acquiring subsidiary which it later merges into the target corporation. As a result of the merger, the target company becomes a wholly owned subsidiary of the acquiring corporation, and the target company's shareholders receive cash in payment for their shares. In such a cash merger of a subsidiary into the target company, the old shareholders are not secondarily liable, and more importantly, the buyers get 100 percent of the stock.

Some of the key managers are typically invited into the investment group and are usually given three to five year management contracts. The financing needed to effect the merger is raised by selling equity securities in the acquiring company and debt securities in the subsidiary. The debt of the subsidiary is assumed by the target corporation and becomes its obligation, notwithstanding the fact that the obligations under the debt instruments are not necessarily secured by any assets of the target corporation.

Conflicts of Interest

In all buyouts or acquisitions where incumbent management participates, potential conflicts of interest can arise. Some aspects of this conflict have already been discussed in Chapter 8. The management group has a fiduciary responsibility to the seller as well as personal economic interests conflicting with those of the seller. Where the seller is a private shareholder of a closely held company or a corporate parent of a subsidiary, this problem can be mitigated by management's early and clear declaration of its position on the buying side of the bargaining table. Another effective means of dealing with this situation is to involve a sponsor who acts as the spokesman for the buying group in direct negotiations with the seller. In this case, management's role is more passive and the risk of direct confrontation between this group and the owner/seller is diminished.

The conflict of interest problem is significantly magnified when management is also a shareholder in a public company. Because there may be a large number of widely dispersed shareholders in such cases, it is impossible for the buyer to negotiate with a single person who represents all of the sellers' interests. (The only exception would be a control shareholder situation.) In most cases, these shareholders also have a significant economic interest in the buyout. In actual fact, the insiders who wish to participate in the ownership of the company as a private entity are the very same persons who, as fiduciaries, are obligated to protect the interests of outside shareholders.

To protect outside shareholders from selling out at prices below the economic market value of their holdings and to protect insiders from potential claims, the Securities and Exchange Commission (SEC) has formulated rather extensive disclosure requirements governing such transactions. These requirements, which are spelled out in SEC Rules 13(e)(3) and 13(e)(4), basically cover the following aspects of a transaction:

- The vote of the insiders should be "neutralized" so that the decision to effect the transaction lies entirely in the hands of the outside shareholders.
- The price must be fair.
- The transaction must be structured and conducted in a manner which both demonstrates and promotes fairness.

The specific information required to be disclosed to shareholders includes: (1) the purpose of the proposed transaction, (2) potential conflicts of interest with management, (3) employment agreements, (4) management equity participations, (5) tax benefits to management, (6) contemplated sales of assets or subsidiaries, (7) projections of future earnings, (8) other material evaluations supplied to outside lenders and investors, and (9) opinions of outside independent consultants as to fairness.

Dealing with Dissenting Shareholders

Despite the extensive disclosure requirements designed to ensure that outside shareholder interests are considered, there are invariably some minority shareholders who object to the proposed transaction. While these dissenters cannot be totally ignored, the law does not permit an insignificant minority group to prevent a transaction of which the majority approves. The term "insignificant minority" is relative and depends upon the state or jurisdiction whose laws govern the transaction. In some states the requisite vote to proceed is only a simple majority (51 percent) whereas in other states the requisite shareholder consent may be as high as 80 percent.

If the requisite vote is prohibitively large, the transaction may proceed through the use of the so-called "cramdown merger" technique. Using this method, the deal can be closed while those shareholders who voted against it retain the right to appeal the fairness of the transaction through established judicial procedures. Depending upon the legal structure of the transaction and the state in which the seller is located, these "dissenters rights" may or may not involve statutory appraisal proceedings.

In this regard, "cash merger" transactions usually have the right of statutory appraisal proceedings. This procedure enables dissenting shareholders to receive a higher value for their shares if such is deemed appropriate after a court-supervised appraisal. The courts may also determine that the dissenting shareholders are entitled to all cash for their shares rather than a combination of cash and notes. In addition to statutory protections, dissenting shareholder considerations are important to the buyer or buying group because institutional lenders and investors often condition their financing commitments on some maximum allowable percentage of dissenting shareholders.

DEBT OR EQUITY?

The tax consequences of the legal and financial structure are also extremely important considerations. In buyouts or acquisitions which are substantially leveraged, one of the primary attractions is the reduction in the cost of capital attributable to the deductibility of interest by the company. In effect, the federal government subsidizes a portion of the acquisition cost because a substantial amount of income is offset by interest payments. In recent years, however, there is increasing concern among various acquisition financing professionals of the potential consequences of either existing or proposed regulations. In particular, Sections 279 and 385 of the Internal Revenue Code address the issues of what properly constitutes "debt" or "equity" in the capital structure. This is quite significant with respect to leveraged buyouts and acquisitions since a reclassification of "debt" as "equity" would result in substantially higher taxes to the newly capitalized company. Without going into considerable detail, the following paragraphs describe the rudiments of each section and its impact on the legal and financial structure.

Section 279 has been a part of the Internal Revenue Code since the late 1960's. Its purpose was to prevent classifying as debt securities those securities which are, in effect, equity securities. For example, when subordinated debt is issued with related rights to equity, either through a conversion feature or an option, interest on it is not deductible if: (1) the new company's debt to equity ratio exceeds 2:1 or (2) the new company's projected earnings are less than three times the proforma interest charges. The concept of a unit investment, which may be proportionate shares of several different debt and equity securities, is frequently mentioned in the code. An example would be a vertical strip of the various securities which are often purchased by insurance companies.

An extreme interpretation of Section 279 would result in the classification of the entire "strip" of securities (i.e., the entire investment) as equity, with the resultant reduction in deductible interest. Although this regulation has been in effect for some time, the appearance of large buyout transactions in the 1980's has caused increased sensitivity by large institutional investors to the possibility of challenge by the IRS. To avoid potential problems on this section of the code, institutions have been careful to clearly label their securities as either debt or equity rather than use "hybrid" securities. All equity is purchased "up front" in the form of common stock. This remedy has created a separate problem for insurance companies domiciled in the state of New York where statutes prohibit an insurance company from owning more than 5 percent of a company's common stock. On the other hand, the investment can only be justified with a larger percentage of equity. The traditional solution to the problem is the issuance by the company of a junior preferred stock which is convertible into common stock upon sale. To comply with the provisions of Section 279 and the New York requirements, these insurance companies now receive common stock with "exploding warrants" which increase their percentage ownership at the time the stock is sold.

A related, but separate, addition to the code is Section 385. This very complex section had been in the formative stages for 11 years before the Treasury proposed implementing its first regulations. After widespread criticism of both their complexity and potential negative impact on capital formation, the regulations were withdrawn and reintroduced with minor revisions in early 1982. Many groups, including small business owners and large institutional lenders and investors, bitterly opposed the highly restrictive and entangled provisions.

Their efforts succeeded in effecting withdrawal of the highly controversial regulations in November 1983. As a result of the withdrawal, the determination of whether an instrument constitutes debt or equity will be determined on a case by case basis in accordance with judicial decisions.

IMPACT OF THE 1986 TAX REFORM ACT ON LBO'S

History is repleat with major legislative initiatives to reallocate the tax burden among the various classes of private and corporate citizens in the U.S. Within the last decade it has happened with increasing frequency, the latest being in 1986. Dubbed "The Tax Reform Act of 1986," this legislation has had a significant impact on mergers and acquisitions in general and LBO's in particular.

Many of the changes in the 1986 Act will have a profound effect on the way leveraged buyouts are structured and perhaps on overall activity. To get a clearer picture of these effects, it is necessary to take a closer look at the major provisions of the Act that will impact mergers and acquisitions.

Modification of Tax Rates

One of the major provisions of the Tax Reform Act of 1986 was to revise income and capital gains tax rates for both individual and corporate taxpayers. For individuals, the maximum tax rate on ordinary income was lowered to 28 percent from 50 percent while taxes on capital gains were increased from 20 percent to 28 percent. On the corporate side, the income tax rate was lowered from a maximum of 46 percent to 34 percent while capital gains rates were raised from 28 percent to 34 percent. Essentially, these rate modifications: (1) eliminated any preferential treatment for capital gains over ordinary income for both individuals and corporate taxpayers, and (2) for the first time in recent memory, reduced individual tax rates below those of corporations.

For leveraged buyers, the lower corporate rates reduce the value of interest deductions and thus increase the "tax cost" of the acquisition relative to unleveraged buyers. While the net after-tax cash flows increase for both leveraged and unleveraged buyers, they increase more for the latter. All else being equal (which it usually isn't), this will make it even harder for leveraged buyers to compete with cash-rich corporate buyers. And because individual tax rates are now lower than corporate rates, there is a stronger incentive for buyers to structure deals using "pass through" entities. These include S corporations, limited partnerships, and master limited partnerships.

On the seller's side, the increase in capital gains rates at both the corporate and personal level diminishes the after-tax proceeds of a sale. However, this is more than offset by the lower corporate income tax rates which allow more income to fall to the bottom line. For example, consider the following case of a company with a pre-tax income of $1 million:

	Old Law	New Law
Pre-tax income	$1,000,000	$1,000,000
Tax rate	46%	34%
Taxes	(460,000)	(340,000)
After-tax income	540,000	660,000
P/E multiple	16	16
Value	8,640,000	10,560,000
Capital gain rate	20%	28%
Capital gain taxes	(1,728,000)	(2,956,800)
After-tax proceeds	6,912,000	7,603,200

Using this example, the seller actually receives 10 percent more than he would have prior to December 31, 1986 (all other things being equal, of course).

Repeal of the *General Utilities Doctrine*

An obscure provision of the old tax code, referred to as the *General Utilities Doctrine,* enabled corporations which sold assets and then distributed the proceeds to shareholders to avoid taxes at the corporate level. Shareholders, of course, were taxed at their individual capital gains rate for the difference between the net proceeds and their basis in the stock. The 1986 Tax Reform Act repealed this pass through exemption and, as a result, reduced the after-tax proceeds to shareholders of corporations which *sell assets* and subsequently liquidate. Consider the following example of a corporation with the same $1 million in pre-tax income:

	Old Law	New Law
Pre-tax income	$1,000,000	$1,000,000
Tax rate	46%	34%
After-tax income	540,000	660,000
P/E multiple	16	16
Pre-tax proceeds	8,640,000	10,560,000
Corporate capital gains rate	0	34%
Corporate capital gains tax	0	(3,590,400)
Proceeds to corporation	8,640,000	6,969,600
Shareholder capital gains rate	20%	28%
Shareholder capital gains tax	(1,728,000)	(1,951,488)
Net shareholder proceeds	6,912,000	5,018,112

This analysis shows that, if the deal is structured as a purchase of assets, selling shareholders will receive $1,775,520, or 27 percent, *less* under the new law than they would have under the old law. Furthermore, by structuring the deal as a stock sale, shareholders would receive $2,423,502, or 52 percent, *more* than if they sell assets. Clearly, the 1986 Tax Reform Act offers strong economic incentives to sellers to structure their deals as sales of stock rather than of assets.

The impact on LBO's is significant. Under the old rules, the seller was basically indifferent to selling assets or stock from an *economic* standpoint. He still had *legal* reasons for preferring stock deals. But, because the buyer could step-up the depreciable values of the assets in asset sale transactions, he could afford to pay the seller a higher price. These economic benefits often overshadowed the disadvantages of asset sales for the seller. Now with a strong economic incentive for the seller *not* to sell assets, the buyer will be unable to step-up their value and reap the rewards of higher depreciation write-offs. In effect, Uncle Sam has said: "Either the seller gets less or the buyer has to pay more in taxes."

The same loophole had been closed with respect to a purchase of stock followed by an election pursuant to Section 338 of the Internal Revenue Code to liquidate the company. This was previously discussed under *Assets vs. Stock: Buyer Considerations*. With the repeal of *General Utilities,* any election under Section 338 to liquidate the company treats the acquisition as if it were a purchase of assets rather than stock, and imposes higher taxes as a consequence.

Yet another effect of the loss of the *General Utilities Doctrine* is to increase the "tax cost" of certain liquidating sales of "unwanted assets" to third parties. As prices have risen for LBO's in general, this technique has become a more integral part of the overall strategy to quickly reduce acquisition related debt.

Purchase Price Allocation Rules

The 1986 Act also changes the rules regarding the allocation of purchase price. On one hand, it reduced this from a major to a minor issue in negotiations between buyer and seller, due to the equalization of corporate income and capital gains tax rates. On the other hand, the new law generally requires that the "residual method" of allocation be used by both the buyer and seller. This method, as opposed to the "second tier method" which was more prevalent prior to 1986, maximizes the allocation to goodwill and other nonamortizable intangible assets rather than other depreciable assets. The net result is a reduction in the buyer's after-tax cash flow.

NOL Carryforwards

Prior to the 1986 Tax Reform Act, leveraged buyers skillfully blended businesses with excellent cash flows and those with tax loss carryforwards to maximize after-tax cash flow. The revised rules severely limit the extent to which this can be done and, in effect, eliminate the use of NOL carryforwards in LBO's. Specifically, the Act limits the use of the tax loss of one company to offset the earnings of another in any given year to an amount equal to the loss corporation's equity multiplied by the yield on tax-free municipal bonds.

In conclusion, the 1986 Tax Reform Act has impacted mergers and acquisitions in general by increasing the after-tax cost to the buyer, reducing the after-tax proceeds to the seller, or both. It has had an even greater effect on leveraged buyouts by diminishing the after-tax value of debt financing relative to equity. Moreover, it has placed a strong incentive for buyers to utilize "pass through" ownership vehicles and for sellers to structure the deals as stock sales rather than as asset sales.

TABLE 13-A
LEGAL STRUCTURE OF A BUYOUT

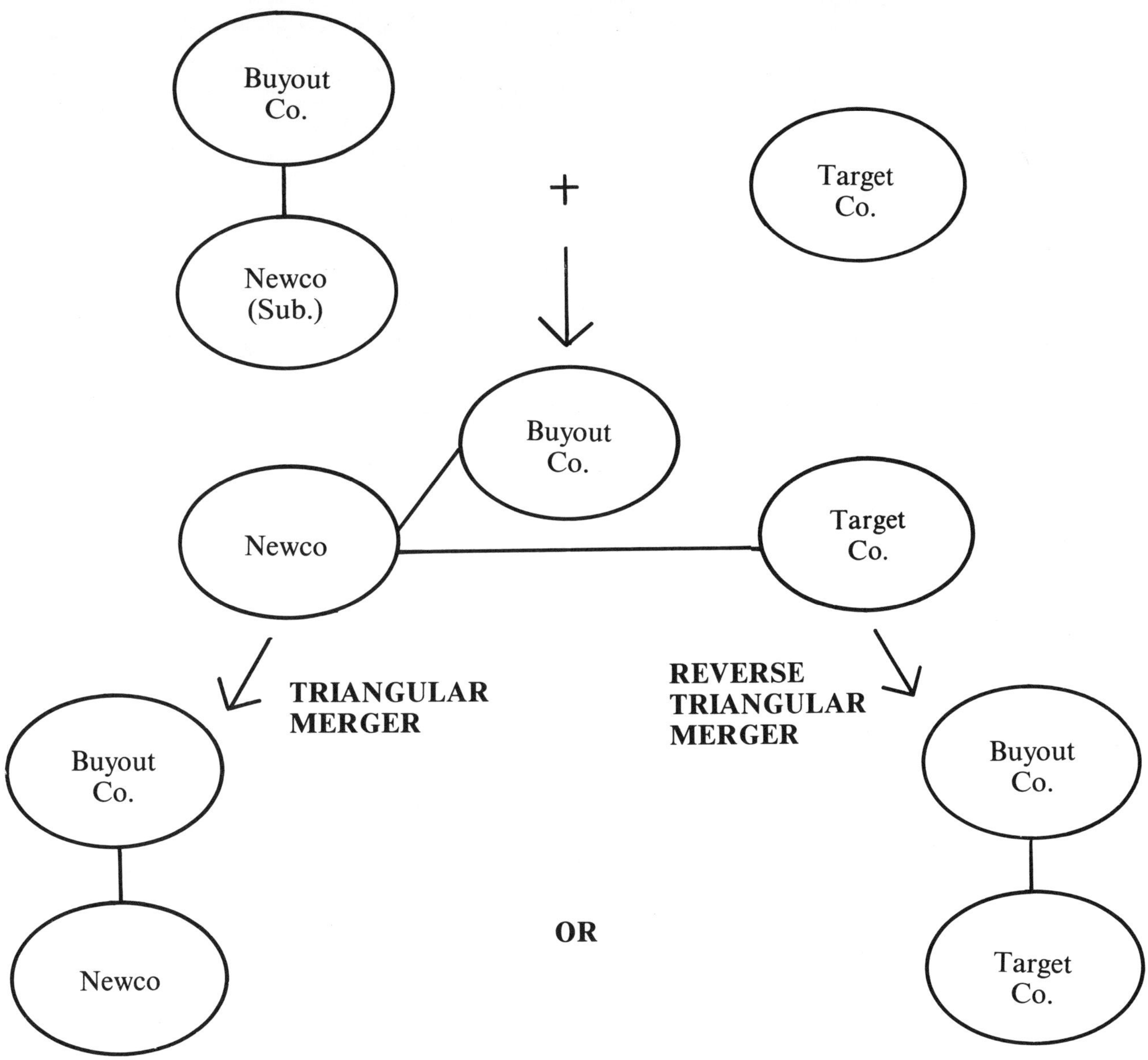

14

NEGOTIATING AND CLOSING THE DEAL

NEED SATISFACTION AND THE NEGOTIATING PROCESS
- The Buyer's Needs
- Management's Needs
- The Seller's Needs
- Needs of the Financing Participants

OTHER KEY PLAYERS IN THE NEGOTIATIONS
- The Role of the Intermediary
- The Role of Legal Counsel
- Do Lawyers Really Kill Deals?

REVIEW OF THE NEGOTIATING PROCESS
- The First Meeting
- The Second Meeting
- The Third Meeting (Preliminary Negotiations)
- The Fourth Meeting

KEY ISSUES IN THE NEGOTIATING PROCESS
- Representations and Warranties
- Management Fees
- Personal Guaranties
- Covenants Not to Compete
- Intercreditor Agreement

"GOLDEN RULES" OF NEGOTIATION FOR LEVERAGED BUYERS

COUNTDOWN TO CLOSING

Most people, including the buyer and seller of a business, view the negotiating process as a contest in which there is a clear winner and a clear loser. To a certain extent, negotiations often entail one of the participants gaining an upper hand on the other by means of his relative power in the situation or superior negotiating skills. A buyer, however, must be careful not to overemphasize the "win/lose" attitude in negotiations and the resulting propensity to bury a perceived "opponent."

The primary purpose of negotiations is not to declare a "winner" and a "loser" in a sophisticated battle of wits. Rather, they should be viewed as a vehicle through which the needs of the participants are reasonably satisfied. Thus, the negotiator should view the process as one in which everyone wins. The primary objective of any negotiator should be to avoid the situation where an involved party perceives himself the loser. Such feelings, whether real or imagined, often trigger irrational responses that are usually counterproductive. By emphasizing a "win/win" approach to negotiations, the buyer can dramatically improve the chances for a successful outcome. In reality, the most successful negotiations are those in which all parties have to give as well as receive. Human nature is such that people feel better if they have achieved an agreement through the mutual give and take of healthy negotiations.

NEED SATISFACTION AND THE NEGOTIATING PROCESS

It has been expressed on several occasions that the transaction will close only if the needs of the primary participants — buyer, seller, and financing sources — are satisfied. The process by which these needs are ultimately satisfied is negotiation. To clearly understand the negotiating process and how to utilize it effectively, it is helpful to review human behavior in terms of our basic needs. According to the famous psychologist, Abraham Maslow, all human beings have six levels of needs. These are as follows:

- Physiological
- Safety and security
- Acceptance
- Esteem
- Self-actualization
- Knowledge and understanding

These needs start with the most basic physical requirements and ascend to those related to mental and emotional satisfaction. Since these needs are hierarchical, the most basic needs must be satisfied before a person becomes overly conscious of the next higher need.

While this theoretical model may seem somewhat remote from the realities of negotiating a deal, it is helpful to keep it in mind when encountering the seller. In general, all of the needs either implied or expressed during the negotiating process are related to the middle four — security, acceptance, esteem, and self-actualization. One can safely assume that all parties have met their basic physiological needs and are too preoccupied to be concerned with their need for higher knowledge and understanding.

The Buyer's Needs

Before the buyer tries to decipher the needs of others involved in the deal, he must first understand his own. The old maxim "know thyself" certainly is applicable in the case of an individual or corporation seeking to buy a company. Some aspects of this question were considered in Chapter 2, where the buyer was asked to define his criteria for potential acquisitions based upon a realistic assessment of his experience and financial resources. It will be helpful to review some of these issues in an effort to pinpoint specific buyer needs and how they are expressed and controlled in negotiations.

For a buyer to be effective, his most basic needs must be satisifed before he undertakes the demanding task of buying a company. Specifically, his safety and security needs must be provided for in the form of external income or accumulated financial resources in order for the buyer to operate effectively while seeking, finding, and closing the deal. The main motivation in buying a company is to satisfy the higher needs, primarily those related to self-esteem and self-actualization. Buyer needs falling within these categories are the desire for independence and wealth, as well as the satisfaction of accomplishment associated with successful entrepreneurship.

In negotiations with the seller and financing sources, these needs must be expressed in a controlled manner so as not to leave the impression that one "has to have" the deal. Above all, the buyer must remain calm and objective throughout the negotiating process.

Management's Needs

Incumbent management needs are similar to those of the entrepreneurial buyer expressed above. In fact, as was explained in Chapter 8, management may be *the* buyer in certain situations.

When they first perceive that the company is for sale, management's first concern is for their own security. The change of ownership creates some feelings of uncertainty as to how they will fit in with the plans of the new owner of the company. Unlike outside entrepreneurial buyers, most managers do not have sufficient sources of independent income or capital to sustain themselves.

After reconciling these needs, many managers have the same motivation as the outside entrepreneurs. They desire the opportunity to own a significant stake in the company and create wealth in the process. During the negotiations with an outside buyer or investor, these needs will be expressed as management seeks to solidify its position as the essential operating figures and maximize their ownership position.

The Seller's Needs

The needs of the seller, which must be satisfied through negotiations, will depend upon which type of seller is involved. The private seller has a wide spectrum of needs that are felt, both consciously and unconsciously, when he is in the process of selling his company. On the more basic level, his safety and security needs may be affected by the proceeds derived from the sale and, if he participates in financing the purchase, his expectations of being repaid by the buyer. Needs for acceptance and esteem may be reflected in his desire to protect loyal employees or in his continued participation in company decisions as a consultant or minority shareholder. Very often the private seller's primary motivation to sell his company is based upon his desire to satisfy higher needs such as self-actualization or knowledge and understanding. These are often expressed by the seller's stated intention to pursue other outside interests.

While the private seller's needs are related to both capital and career considerations, the corporate seller is most often governed by capital needs of the business and career-related needs of the key corporate decision makers. The latter needs fall mainly into the categories of security, acceptance, and esteem. They are manifested by the decision makers' desire to improve overall corporate performance via divestiture of the target company. Behind this desire may be the need to solidify positions in the corporate hierarchy and move further up the corporate ladder.

Regardless of the type of seller or attendant motivating factors, the buyer should be aware of and responsive to the manifold needs of different sellers. Before and during the negotiating sessions he should study the seller in order to identify his most important needs and conduct the negotiations in a manner through which they can be satisfied.

Needs of the Financing Participants

As is the case with the corporate seller, the needs of the various financing sources involved in a buyout or acquisition are both institutional and personal. First are the needs of the financial institution itself. Second, decisions of lenders and investors are made by people, not institutions. Accordingly, the needs of these key decision makers must also be considered. These respective insitutional and personal needs may vary, depending upon the type of lender or investor in question.

From an institutional standpoint, all lenders and investors have a need to perpetuate their corporate existence. This is achieved by earning their stockholders or depositors a competitive return on investment. This need is reflected by two not necessarily consistent objectives: (1) the desire to make investments and (2) the desire to avoid losses. In presenting an acquisition financing opportunity to any financial institution or in subsequent negotiations, the buyer must always be aware of these basic institutional needs.

The needs of the individuals representing the institutional financing sources are equally important in the negotiating process. Like their corporate seller counterparts, the decisions and actions of these individuals are mainly career oriented. Thus, the manner in which the individual perceives that his decisions will enhance or hinder his career progress, or satisfy security and esteem needs, will dictate his actions. An exception to these traditional career motivations exists with the managers of venture capital pools, where the individuals also participate in the reward of capital appreciation that results from their lending or investment decisions.

OTHER KEY PLAYERS IN THE NEGOTIATIONS

Aside from the principals, incumbent management and financing sources, there are other individuals who play a key role in the negotiating process. These include the intermediary who brought both sides together and the lawyers who represent both the buyer and seller.

The Role of the Intermediary

Depending upon a number of factors, the intermediary may also play a key role in the negotiation of the transaction. If he is involved at all, his participation is usually in the earlier stages of the deal, when the buyer and seller are endeavoring to arrive at mutually acceptable terms.

One factor that determines how and to what extent the intermediary is involved in negotiations is the nature of his legal responsibilities to either the buyer or seller. In situations where the intermediary has an agreement with the seller, he is legally responsible to the seller as his agent. Less frequently, the intermediary becomes the buyer's agent by means of a written agreement to conduct an acquisition search. In some cases, the intermediary acts strictly as a "finder," and, accordingly, has no legal obligation to either the buyer or seller. Regardless of his legal responsibilities, in all the above situations the intermediary represents himself. He is primarily motivated to close the deal because he receives most, if not all, of his compensation if the transaction closes.

Having considered the basic factors that motivate the intermediary, it is easier to understand the role he plays during negotiations. Where the intermediary has a long standing relationship with the seller and his opinions are valued, he will obviously play an important role. The smart buyer will recognize this at an early stage in the negotiations and seek to utilize the intermediary's influence to facilitate the process. Another factor that will dictate his involvement is the particular role the intermediary has from both a legal and psychological standpoint. If he is acting primarily as a finder, with no agency representation to either buyer or seller, the intermediary is less likely to become involved in the negotiations. His major function is to bring the buyer and seller together and hope they work out a deal. On the other hand, if he is the exclusive agent of either the buyer or seller, he will feel more compelled to partipate in negotiations.

Finally, the intermediary's role in negotiations will be dependent upon his knowledge and experience and the willingness of the buyer to keep him involved. In some cases, especially if the intermediary suffers from a lack of relevant experience, the buyer may request that he disengage himself from the negotiating process with the assurance that he will be paid if and when the transaction closes. In other cases, however, the experienced professional intermediary can serve as a vital link between the buyer and seller. Because of his knowledge of the company and the needs of the respective parties, he is able to simultaneously lower the seller's expectations and persuade the buyer to reach above his previous offers. Thus, the intermediary can have either a negative or positive impact on negotiations depending upon his knowledge and experience.

The Role of Legal Counsel

In any transaction as complex as a leveraged buyout, the lawyers for the buyer and seller are indispensable members of the cast of characters. Many professionals involved in the acquisition process often do not fully understand the role of the attorney in buying and selling a company. When a transaction fails to close, one or more of the principals frequently blames the attorney for "killing" the deal. Although the lawyer takes the blame, it is often the client — or his inability to properly use his legal counsel — that causes the deal to die.

The lawyer performs three basic functions for a client who is acquiring or selling a company. First, the lawyer advises (counsels) the client about the various aspects of the transaction. Second, the lawyer advocates the client's position in negotiations with the opposite party or in ancillary proceedings (for example, with government agencies). Finally, the lawyer documents and implements the closing of the transaction. When a dispute arises out of the transaction, the lawyer may carry out yet another function, that of advocating the client's position in ensuing litigation or further negotiations.

The Counseling Function. The counseling function consists primarily of calling to the client's attention potential risks and problems and, if possible, suggesting means of dealing with them. This consultation takes place continuously throughout the acquisition process. Typical questions that arise in the early stages of a leveraged buyout relate to tax implications, whether to purchase (or sell) assets or stock, lenders' requirements, the risk of latent liabilities, and antitrust and other regulatory issues. Usually the lawyer is able to suggest courses of action or alternatives that avoid or limit many of the identified problems. Most clients have little, if any, difficulty in choosing among alternatives suggested by their lawyers. On these items, although the decision ultimately rests with the client, the client relies heavily on the lawyer's advice.

Almost inevitably, however, there are some potential risks and problems that cannot be quantified or for which no remedy exists. Sometimes the identified risk or problem is highly theoretical or involves a technical legal point for which the lawyer has no solution. Making decisions under uncertain conditions is the role of the entrepreneur or manager.

An imponderable raised by a lawyer is no different from the many uncertainties an executive must balance in the course of running any business. If the buyer is strongly committed to the transaction, an additional risk will probably not dissuade him from proceeding. If, on the other hand, the deal was marginal in the first place, the buyer may decide to abort the agreement. Whether he decides to proceed with the transaction or to abort it, the client has made a business decision.

The Negotiating Function. Negotiations play a key role in any business transaction, but especially in the leveraged buyout, where so many variables can influence the buyer's or seller's interest in proceeding. Because many of these variables change during the course of the acquisition, negotiations are an ongoing process rather than an isolated event. There are two particular points in the acquisition where negotiations become quite intensive. Both the role and degree of involvement of the lawyer are different at each of these two major points.

The first point where negotiations take place is when the buyer and seller discuss price and terms. This is usually early in the deal at the *preliminary negotiation* stage discussed in Chapter 7. At this point, participation by the lawyers is very indirect. During this period, the lawyers stay hidden in the background counseling their clients independently while the clients establish rapport and seek to find a mutually acceptable middle ground. If successful, the buyer and seller arrive at a handshake agreement on purchase price, financing terms (if any), other conditions of sale, and a general timetable for closing.

Although preparation of a "letter of intent," or "offer to purchase," may intervene, the next critical step is drafting a definitive acquisition agreement that incorporates the basic ingredients of the handshake agreement. This leads to the second major point in the negotiations, during which the lawyers for both clients are actively and directly involved.

The buyer's lawyer usually prepares the first draft of the definitive agreement, exercising critical judgment as to how *hard or soft* the agreement should be. Although the buyer's lawyer may be tempted to draft a very one-sided pro-buyer agreement, an artful lawyer will include just enough protections for the seller to avoid turning the negotiations into an adversary proceeding.

Because the definitive agreement is very detailed and specific, it focuses the attention of both buyer and seller on a number of substantial issues that were not addressed in the handshake agreement. In addition, the passage of even two or three weeks may bring changes in external economic or internal operational circumstances that modify the desire of buyer and seller, or both, to complete the transaction. The only way to resolve these new or submerged differences is to get all parties — clients and lawyers — together in the same room for another round of negotiations. Whereas in the initial negotiations the lawyer was in the background, he now moves onto the stage with his client. While before he was strictly an advisor, now he is clearly an advocate of his client's position.

Major issues in these negotiations usually include the content of the seller's representations and warranties, allocations of the risks of contingent liabilities, and allocating tax burdens such as depreciation recapture in the sale of assets. In purchases of subsidiaries or divisions of large public companies, non-competition covenants can be a difficult hurdle to clear. The buyer and seller will, on the advice of their respective lawyers, take opposing positions on these and other material issues that affect their legal and economic interests. Although the lawyers may be able to resolve many apparent disagreements, it is important for the buyer and seller to make sure that they (and not their lawyers) remain in control of the negotiations. These issues often come back to an assessment of business risk and the weighing of potential strategic or economic benefits against these risks. Only the person who stands to gain or lose from taking or not taking such risks should make these decisions. An experienced acquisition attorney will realize this, take the cue from his client and either harden or soften his position in advocating his client's negotiating posture.

Implementing the Transaction. Once the lawyer has properly counseled the client on the legal implications of the transaction and advocated the client's position in negotiations, his remaining task is to make sure the transaction moves forward to a closing. In this stage of the deal, the lawyer moves to center stage while the clients move to the sidelines. The primary responsibility in this regard is to prepare and refine all the documentation necessary to close the deal. This may range from the simple task of cleaning up the acquisition agreement to highly complex legal procedures involving the Securities Exchange Commission and other federal and state regulatory bodies. During this process there will still arise new, unexpected issues that must be negotiated. However, at this point, these issues are often technical legal points that can be resolved by the lawyers without requiring much participation by the buyer and seller. This is especially true if both buyer and seller have a strong desire to close and have conveyed this to legal counsel.

A key factor in the lawyer's success with this phase of the transaction is not only his understanding of the pertinent legal considerations, but also his ability to work cooperatively with legal counsel representing other parties in the deal. In addition to the buyer or seller, other parties represented by legal counsel may be lenders, equity investors, and minority shareholders of the seller. To facilitate the transaction, the lawyer must often subordinate his ego to that of the other lawyers.

Do Lawyers Really Kill Deals?

It is probably a fair criticism of lawyers that, because of their training in advocacy in our adversary legal system, they may lose sight of the primary purpose of a leveraged buyout: a cooperative activity in which the buyer, the seller, and the lenders share a common goal. That goal is to close the deal! As a result, some lawyers, in counseling their clients and advocating their positions, become overly protective. This often gives rise to the frequent criticism that the lawyer is the primary *deal killer* when a transaction fails to close.

The criticism inherent in the accusation that *lawyers kill deals* is not that lawyers consciously advise their clients to abort transactions which both ultimately agree are not in the clients' best interests. Rather it is that lawyers raise so many obstacles and problems that they *prevent* the completion of transactions, contrary to their clients' true desires. This implies that clients are powerless victims of their attorneys' wills and is patently false. The lawyer's role is to advise the client on various legal options and their relative risk. But after doing so, the lawyer should advocate the position of the client in accordance with the lawyer's perception of the client's desire (or lack thereof) to do the deal.

The lawyer should receive explicit instructions from his client. If, for example, the buyer is strongly committed to the acquisition, this fact should be stressed to his lawyer. More importantly, the buyer should insist that the seller give similar instructions to his lawyer. Many deals fall apart because one party or the other is not really committed to the deal, and his lawyer's resistance to compromise shows it.

Although the buyer and the seller expect their lawyers to strongly advocate their respective positions, it is the clients who must be prepared to take charge and make business decisions to clear any impasses that may develop. Just as it is the client's responsibility to decide what to do after being advised by the lawyer that a problem may exist, it is also his responsibility to decide upon which points to compromise and upon which points to insist.

The bottom line is: *lawyers kill deals only if their clients let them.*

REVIEW OF THE NEGOTIATING PROCESS

It has been emphasized throughout this book that negotiating a leveraged buyout is a process rather than an event. There is no one magic meeting at which everything is ironed out forever. In fact, it is not uncommon for negotiations to continue right up to the moment the final closing papers are signed. There are, however, key points within the process where negotiations *should* and *should not* be conducted. These critical junctures have been touched upon in Chapters 6, 7, and 8. But, in order to put the entire negotiating process in perspective and enable the buyer to devise a negotiating strategy, it is helpful to review these points.

Actually there are at least three occasions, and possibly four, where the buyer has the opportunity to meet face-to-face with the seller. At only two of these meetings, however, should any serious negotiations be carried out. The other meetings are held basically to prepare the buyer for effective negotiations.

The First Meeting

The first meeting between the buyer and seller occurs during the qualification stage. The primary purpose is for the buyer to build a solid relationship with the seller and to further qualify the feasibility of a deal. The latter includes the seller's level of motivation and the possibility of financing the transaction.

Generally speaking, it is premature to commence negotiations at this point. The buyer just doesn't have enough facts about either the business or his ability to finance it. The buyer should therefore resist the temptation to begin any negotiations with the seller at this initial meeting, particularly in an effort to "soften him up." If the buyer is convinced that the seller has a bona fide reason for selling and is motivated to do so, he should defer negotiations to a future date.

A possible exception might exist in cases where the seller's stated asking price is clearly excessive or beyond the buyer's preliminary estimates of how much can be financed. If it appears that price and/or terms are going to be a major impediment to the deal, it is appropriate to bring the subject up. To ignore it will only serve to mislead the seller and cause animosity between them in the future. If the issue is an excessive asking price, the buyer might first ask himself what he's doing there! But, since he's already there, he should question the seller as to how "firm" the price is. Above all, he should try to reconcile the difference between the seller's motivation level and the price, if they are both high.

When the major issue is not excessive price, but an apparent financing gap, the seller might be queried on his willingness to finance a portion of the purchase. An indication of no flexibility on either price or terms may well be a signal to the buyer to move on to greener pastures.

The Second Meeting

The buyer's second visit with the seller occurs shortly after the first. This is where the buyer conducts his preliminary due diligence. In many situations, particularly larger deals or those involving corporate divestitures, the seller himself (or the key executive negotiating the deal) will not be present at this meeting. In other cases, however, the seller may be present at least some of the time during these preliminary investigations. When this occurs, the buyer must again be careful not to engage in any premature and counterproductive negotiations.

The buyer's principal goal on this visit is not to negotiate, but to lay the groundwork for future negotiations. He is on a fact-finding mission that will enable him to establish reasonable limits for price and financing terms. Some buyers have a difficult time accepting the specific nature of the task on this trip to visit the company and start to engage in negotiations. This is a tactical error by the buyer and should be avoided.

The Third Meeting (Preliminary Negotiations)

Unlike the first two meetings between the buyer and seller, this meeting is specifically called for the purpose of negotiating the key points of the deal. This does not mean that the buyer is unaware or oblivious to the seller's expectations before this time. On the contrary, the experienced buyer knows well in advance of this meeting just how far apart the two sides are. The seller's price expectations are usually signaled early in the deal, even before the buyer and seller initially meet. And, if they are unrealistic or beyond the buyer's ability to finance, this meeting should never take place.

It is preferable that the preliminary negotiations be conducted only between the buyer and seller without their respective legal counsels. The reason for this is quite simple: the main objective is to agree on the key *business* points of the transaction. Legal points will come later in the transaction, if it proceeds, at which time the lawyers will play an important role. But, for now, their presence in the negotiations only serves to complicate and slow down the program.

The obvious deal points, of course, are the *price* the buyer is willing to pay and the *terms* upon which it will be paid. But another consideration is equally important in the mind of the seller: *contingencies* of the deal. In particular, the seller will be very concerned about any financing contingencies that will determine if the buyer can or cannot complete the transaction. For this reason it is imperative that the buyer have a high level of confidence that his financing sources fully understand the deal, have verbally committed to fund it, and will follow through on their commitment.

The successful buyer will emerge from this meeting with a "handshake" agreement on the principal deal points. These can be summarized in a non-binding "letter of intent" from the buyer to the seller. Although this takes additional time, it serves to minimize any possible misunderstandings on what each party has agreed upon. It also serves as an excellent guide for legal counsel to draft a formal acquisition agreement.

The Fourth Meeting

The fourth meeting between the buyer and seller marks the beginning of the sometimes arduous process negotiating the finer points of the transaction. Since these issues require the intensive participation of legal counsel for each side, they have already been described in the section entitled "Role of Legal Counsel."

This is a very important time in the life of a deal, because momentum can be easily lost due to hang-ups on some relatively obscure issues. To avoid this, the buyer must be attentive to those points or differences that at first may appear insignificant but could eventually turn into "deal killers."

KEY ISSUES IN THE NEGOTIATING PROCESS

In the negotiating process, every transaction usually hinges on several key issues that continually emerge as difficult hurdles for the buyer and seller to clear. Because no two buyout or acquisition transactions are exactly alike, each deal will have its own unique set of hurdles and a different order of importance. In the beginning, little or no thought was given to these matters by either the buyer or seller. But as the closing nears, they have now emerged as a new generation of "deal points." The following are the issues that surface as obstacles in the final negotiations of most leveraged buyouts.

Representations and Warranties

The first of these difficult areas of negotiation involve the "representations and warranties." Although these terms are often used interchangeably, there is a significant legal distinction between a "representation" and a "warranty." A representation is a statement of fact accompanied by a statement that what is being said is true. If it turns out to be false or erroneous, the plaintiff must prove that the representor knew that the statement was not true to support a legal action against him.

A warranty, on the other hand, is a promise that a certain fact will be true. In order to prevail in a legal action for breach of warranty, the plaintiff must simply prove that the warranty was made and wasn't true. Thus, in expressing certain facts regarding the target company, the seller wants to give representations while the buyer seeks to have seller warranties. This can become a particularly delicate issue in the case of transactions involving the sale of assets (as opposed to stock) where the seller is asked to warrant that there are no liabilities other than those that have been previously disclosed to the buyer. The seller is usually reluctant to unequivocally guarantee the truth of such a statement when, in fact, he's not sure of it himself. This difficulty can often be circumvented by imposing minimum limitations on such warranties from both a monetary and time perspective.

Management Fees

A second critical deal point involves the matter of dividends or management fees to the buyer. This issue usually looms larger in cases of leveraged buyouts where the seller carries back a significant amount of financing in the form of purchase money notes. In such situations, the seller is often concerned, and rightly so, that the buyer may make management decisions that erode the collateral of the loan.

To prevent the buyer from "wasting the assets," unsecured lenders — and particularly seller/lenders — often want to impose restrictions on the buyer's future operation of the business. Institutional lenders (e.g., banks and insurance companies) almost always insist upon including numerous negative covenants and working capital ratios in loan documentation. Thus, in an unsecured transaction, it is almost impossible for the buyer to negotiate such covenants out of the deal. In the case of secured transactions where the seller is the subordinated lender, the buyer often can negotiate to eliminate these restrictions. However, the buyer will have to replace them with provisions assuring the seller he will not dissipate the collateral and place some reasonable limitation on his compensation until such time as the seller's note is paid down.

Personal Guaranties

A related, but equally important deal point centers around personal guaranties of loans to institutional lenders and, if applicable, seller/lenders. In cases where the seller finances a part of a deal and the buyer's equity is relatively thin, the seller will usually insist on some form of personal guaranty from the buyer. Most guaranties give the party who holds them relatively strong grounds to take prompt legal action to collect from the guarantor.

Since a highly leveraged deal entails substantially increased risk, the buyer should make every attempt to avoid personal guaranties of subordinated debt, even when the purchase money notes have been sufficiently collateralized by the company's assets. It is reasonable to guarantee acquisition debt to a senior lender that has been secured by accounts receivable, inventory, machinery and equipment, and real estate because it is unlikely the lender will advance loan amounts in excess of its ability to collect in liquidation. This is not the case with subordinated seller notes that are often not covered by excess collateral. The buyer's ability to avoid guaranties on such notes will depend upon a number of factors, the most important of which are his perceived ability to successfully operate the company, the seller's level of motivation to sell, and the size of the transaction.

Covenants Not to Compete

A final key point of the negotiation process is the matter of the so-called "covenant-not-to-compete" (also called the "noncompetition clause"). Buyers will almost always insist on the inclusion of the covenant in the acquisition contract because the ability of the business to continue as a viable concern and generate profit can be adversely affected by the prior owner's emergence as a new competitor. This is especially true in the case of private sellers where the role of the previous owner or management in the operations is a significant factor in the goodwill of the business. In such situations, it is standard procedure for the seller to agree to a "covenant-not-to-compete."

However, in the case of larger corporate sellers, it is often quite difficult for the buyer to obtain an unconditional covenant. This difficulty stems from the reluctance of the seller, often a very large and complex organization, to limit its future options with respect to new acquisitions. The firm's executives may, at some future time, have the opportunity to acquire a larger, more attractive company in the same business. An even more compelling reason could be the fact that one of the corporation's subsidiaries is already engaged in a similar business which, from a technical standpoint, could violate the "covenant-not-to-compete."

Prior to the 1986 Tax Reform Act, there were strong tax incentives for buyers to negotiate a non-compete covenant for any deferred portion of the purchase price. That was because the payments were fully deductible against ordinary income, which under the old law was taxed at a higher rate. For the same reason, the seller preferred to structure deferred payments as debt, which would be taxed at the lower capital gains rates. Since the 1986 tax law basically equalizes the corporate tax rate for ordinary income and capital gains, there are no longer the same tax incentives. Ironically, the new law may actually incentivize *sellers* to use non-compete covenants in cases where they have converted to sub-chapter S corporations. The reason, of course, is that in such cases ordinary income, which is now taxed at a *lower* personal rate, is passed directly through to shareholders.

Intercreditor Agreements

Outside lenders and investors often become a party to final negotiations because of the need to protect their interests. This often presents a significant challenge for lawyers of both the buyer and seller if the seller carries back a subordinated note. In this situation, it is necessary to draft an "intercreditor agreement" which defines the respective rights of outside lenders and the seller. Since institutional lenders often take a very hard line, this may place the seller in a very weak position with respect to his rights as a lender.

"GOLDEN RULES" OF NEGOTIATION FOR LEVERAGED BUYERS

Experience has revealed that there are several fundamental rules of negotiation for a buyer involved in a leveraged buyout or acquisition. If followed, these basic guidelines will improve the buyer's chances of successfully negotiating and closing the deal.

- View negotiations as a "win/win" rather than a "win/lose" situation.
- Identify your own needs, strengths, and weaknesses prior to negotiations.
- Try to determine the needs, strengths, and weaknesses of the seller and other parties with whom you will be negotiating.
- Get a competent deal attorney who is adept at working with counsel for the seller and lenders.
- Negotiate only when you are prepared and do not allow yourself to be drawn into premature negotiations.
- Enter into the negotiations with high, but not unreasonable, aspirations.

- In making concessions, do so as late as possible in the negotiations and always get something in return.
- When the other party makes a concession, take it and avoid any further negotiations on that particular point.
- Don't put yourself in the position where you "must have the deal." (But, if you really must have it, don't let the seller know it.)
- Know your limits and be prepared to "take a walk."

COUNTDOWN TO CLOSING

Although negotiations are usually conducted at specific points in time, they may also take place at unpredictable intervals. In the process of buying a company, many things will occur that cannot be controlled or anticipated. In fact, one caution universally applicable to dealmaking is to "expect the unexpected." During the time between reaching an "agreement in principle" and the closing, one or more unexpected things can happen to kill the deal. Many aspiring buyers, who are otherwise very capable, often lose the deal and their investment of time and money because of their inability to cope with these disappointments. The astute buyer, however, expects the unexpected and, unless it is clearly not in his best interest, finds creative solutions to any unanticipated problems.

These unexpected, and usually unpleasant, surprises may include poor interim operating results, a better offer from another buyer, negative inputs from the seller's legal and accounting advisors, seller's remorse, corporate politics, lowball lender appraisals, and reduced lender advance rates. The key is to make the necessary adjustments, assuming the deal still makes sense from an investment perspective.

If the participants have successfully cleared all hurdles and dealt with all unexpected surprises, the day for which all parties have been waiting will finally arrive. It usually takes about five to six months from the inception to close a transaction. By that time, everyone is usually tired of the deal, but happy to finally see the results of their efforts.

The closing is really not an ending, but a beginning. It marks the first day of a new and exciting life for the buyer, whether it is an outside entrepreneur or incumbent management. Life will never be the same for him or his company. With just a few strokes of the pen, he has taken what was probably a perfectly (financially) healthy company and transformed it into one with an "upside down" balance sheet.

There is a bit of irony in all this. For the last six months, the buyer has worked day and night to raise the debt. Now he will labor for the next six (or more) years trying to get rid of it!

15

AFTER THE CLOSING: MANAGING THE LEVERAGED BUYOUT

The party is over! It's now the morning after the closing. In all probability, the new owners of the company have a "hangover" in the wake of the celebration of their accomplishment. But they aren't the only ones feeling the after-effects of the "big event." The target company has its own version of a "hangover": a balance sheet that is now top-heavy with debt. The ecstasy of doing the deal is history. Both the new owners and the company itself must now face the significant challenge that lies ahead: how to manage all that new debt.

Those who are new to leveraged buyouts often assume that the most difficult part of the process — doing the deal — is now behind them. In their minds, the next task — making it work — is relatively simple. In most cases it doesn't work out that way. While it should be evident that "putting the deal together" is no easy task, the *real* work begins after the closing. The new owners have created a company that, financially speaking, is not in the best of health. In the months and years ahead, they must do whatever is necessary to nurse it back to a healthy condition. And, just as the physical healing process often involves some pain, the company must make some difficult adjustments as it adapts to a new financial environment.

THE AFTERSHOCKS OF THE CLOSING

In and of itself, a change of ownership is a very traumatic event in the life of a company. Uncertainties surrounding the new owner and his policies can cause severe problems during the transition period. As a result, employee morale, productivity, and ultimately, profitability decline. These problems are magnified when a substantial amount of new debt is loaded onto the company's balance sheet. The simultaneous transfer of ownership and a massive recapitalization create a number of "aftershocks" among the major groups of people who are involved — directly or indirectly — with the business. The following paragraphs describe those who are most affected by the significant changes that have just occurred and how the new owners can minimize their negative consequences.

Management

The one factor enabling a company to absorb the "double whammy" of a change in ownership along with substantial new leverage is the fact that there is continuity in the operating management. Because the managers usually own a meaningful share of the business and have some of their own capital at risk, they stand to lose something if the deal doesn't work. This continuity and commitment is the single most important factor attracting outside capital sources to leveraged buyouts.

In spite of their new role as partial owners and the inherent motivation to work harder and smarter, many managers have to make some difficult adjustments in the first few months after the buyout closes. The first may just be getting used to their "new boss." Perhaps a better description is "new partners," but no matter how it is phrased, managers are now responsible to those individuals or institutions which took the greatest risk in financing the buyout. Unless they funded the entire equity themselves, management will have other voices and opinions on the future direction of the business. In most cases, any major differences will have already been aired and resolved throughout the dealmaking and financing process. Nevertheless, it may take some time for the managers and outside investors to establish "territorial rights" that are acceptable to both.

Another difficult adjustment for some managers is adapting to a new financial climate where cash is always in short supply. Most leveraged buyout candidates, by definition, have a relatively debt-free balance sheet *before* the closing. Therefore, managers are often unaccustomed to operating the business under the heavy hand of high leverage, which now has a first call on all available cash. With these new constraints, managers must, first and foremost, become effective cash managers. This is not an easy adjustment, especially for those managers who have worked for a large public company where the primary emphasis is on maximizing earnings growth and the availability of cash has never been a major problem.

Employees

Although the company's employees (other than top management) are insulated from any commotion in the boardroom, they are ultimately affected by the change in ownership and the new financial realities. The emphasis on maximizing cash flow to reduce debt will often dictate additional job responsibilities and perhaps some changes in their benefit and compensation program. Particularly in the case of corporate divestitures, employees may have been beneficiaries of an attractive employee benefit package provided by the parent company. This may have included excellent medical insurance coverage at no cost and generous pension and profit sharing programs. While the new owners should make every attempt not to take away any such benefits, it may not be financially feasible to continue some prohibitively expensive programs. This could have a negative impact on employee morale, unless such losses are perceived as temporary or offset with other potential gains. For this reason, Employee Stock Ownership Plans (ESOP's) have risen in popularity in recent years. These plans enable employees to participate in the ownership — and future growth — of the company.

In some cases, the need to preserve cash flow will require immediate expense reductions in the form of layoffs or wage freezes. Such actions not only hit employees where it hurts the most — their pocketbooks — but also magnify their uncertainties concerning the future. Unless handled properly, expense reductions can have a devastating effect on morale and the operation of the business.

Customers

Customers may also become uneasy when a business changes hands. This is particularly true when there is a strong personal loyalty to the seller himself, which often occurs in the sale of a privately held company. Although the involvement of incumbent management in the new ownership mitigates against this problem, the buyer should never underestimate the fact that the company is more vulnerable to a loss of major customers when ownership changes hands.

This can present a serious problem for the new owners. In its highly leveraged condition, the loss of a major source of revenue can have a devastating effect on cash flow and seriously affect the company's ability to service its debt. Therefore, management should consider major customer reaction to the buyout and, if necessary, take any steps to retain their support.

Competitors

Any precarious situations with customers are not helped by the company's major competition, whose salesmen often fan the flames of uncertainty with stories on the company's "shaky" financial state. Some competitors may also seize the opportunity to make life very difficult for the company by reducing their prices. The objective of predatory pricing tactics, of course, is to either gain market share at the expense of its leveraged competitor or seriously impair its already weakened financial condition. This is more difficult to accomplish if the buyout company has a dominant share of the market or possesses some strategic cost or marketing advantages over the competition.

Suppliers

In previous chapters there have been several references to the possible negative reaction of key suppliers of the target company to its new, highly leveraged balance sheet. This is particularly true in cases where secured lenders have a lien on the company's assets. Although trade creditors will continue to supply the leveraged company, they may tighten credit limits or even put the company on a "COD only" basis. Such actions can have a significant impact on the company's cash flow in cases where the creditor represents a substantial portion of its outstanding accounts payable.

Again, management continuity will often help ease the concerns of important trade creditors. However, managers should understand that such problems are very often "bumped upstairs" in the creditor organization into the hands of unfamiliar decision makers. Therefore, if management anticipates any problems with suppliers whose lack of trade credit would have a significant financial impact, they should either plan for the worst scenario or meet with them prior to the closing to establish some acceptable groundrules.

PREPARING FOR LIFE AFTER THE CLOSING

The "aftershocks" of the closing should come as no great surprise to the buying group. These are natural consequences of the significant changes that have just taken place within the company. Each problem can be dealt with in a manner that will preserve the operational integrity of the business. The key to successfully dealing with these important issues is to *anticipate* them rather than *react* to them. If the buyer waits until after the closing to focus on these repercussions, it will be a much more difficult task to deal with them in an effective manner.

It is well documented that many mergers and acquisitions yield disappointing results because insufficient attention has been given to integrating the operations after the closing. Poor planning results in diminished productivity of the newly combined organization. While LBO's usually don't have to deal with the problems of integrating two operating companies, the need for planning is just as important. That is because the first year or two is the most critical time period in the life of the newly capitalized company. If the new company survives the first two years, the odds are dramatically improved for its long-term success.

The Operating Plan

One of the key components of a successful leveraged buyout is a detailed operating plan formulated by the buying group. This is more than a rehash of management's latest budget. It is a comprehensive analysis of what steps must be taken to ensure that cash flow will be sufficient to service the debt of the newly acquired company. As a result, the operating plan focuses not only upon the company's income statement, but also its asset base. The buyer must determine which assets can be disposed of in order to raise cash and how to make the remaining assets work harder.

The formulation of an operating plan actually begins when outside investors, in cooperation with incumbent managers, prepare the proforma financial statements to determine the feasibility of the buyout and to secure the financing commitments. These initial projections should incorporate the basic strategic operating assumptions — specific actions that can and will be taken to make the company operate more efficiently after the closing. The operating plan may be subsequently refined as management and outside investors dig more deeply into what further steps can be taken to enhance cash flow.

While the initial projections are done on an annual basis over a 10 to 15 year period to test the financial feasibility, the buyer must then look at the first year or two under a microscope. The reason, of course, is that the company is exposed to the greatest degree of financial risk during the first 12 to 24 months following the transaction. It is important to carefully project revenues and expenses on a monthly basis to determine the impact of budget variances on cash flow. In the past, such variances may have been inconsequential; however, with a highly leveraged balance sheet, they may impact the ability of the company to remain solvent.

IMPLEMENTING THE OPERATING PLAN

Just as members of the buying group should plan well in advance for life after the closing, management should waste no time in implementing the operating plan. Procedures to maximize cash flow should be put into effect immediately. To the extent that such actions impact employees, customers, or suppliers, management must clearly communicate any changes and the rationale behind them. The following is a brief discussion of the major aspects of the operating plan that management should implement immediately.

Asset Management

Previous references have been made about the opportunity to generate cash and reduce debt by making the retained assets work more efficiently. The best starting place is with cash itself. Although more businesses are attuned to cash management techniques today, the leveraged company, in particular, cannot afford the luxury of idle cash. Those individuals responsible for financial management should take advantage of the "float" by drawing down on the company's credit lines only when needed to cover outstanding checks. This will result in an "overdraft" on the books which reduces borrowings and the interest expense related to such borrowings. As a general rule, the business should be able to maintain a $100,000 overdraft for each $5 million in sales.

Credit management is another area offering opportunities to generate extra cash. As was explained in Chapter 9, reducing the average days for which accounts receivable are outstanding converts these assets into cash that can be used to reduce debt. To do so, management must have a well organized credit and collection program that limits high credit risk customers and persistently calls on accounts exceeding payment terms. Those responsible for credit and collections should be compensated directly on their ability to limit bad debt expense and reduce the average collection period.

Inventory is another asset that can be reduced to generate cash. Obviously, there are limits to which inventory levels can be lowered before it starts having a negative impact on the customer. But by careful coordination between sales and production management, materials can be scheduled for shipment on a "just in time" basis. It requires more work and more planning, but the benefits of reducing working capital requirements may be worth it. Another possible approach to reducing inventory investment, especially in distribution businesses, is to utilize suppliers who are willing to work on a consigned stock arrangement. Although such arrangements are the exception rather than the rule, it does occur in cases where new suppliers are highly motivated to capture a share of the company's business.

Very often, the best operating plan will be to "shrink" the business by disposing of unprofitable or marginally profitable product lines. This often means that certain fixed assets such as equipment and real estate are no longer needed and can be liquidated for cash. Of course, if such assets are secured by a senior lender (which usually is the case), the lender must cooperate to effect a lien release. In most cases, the lender will insist that the proceeds of liquidation be used to reduce the outstanding debt.

Finally, trade credit can be utilized in some situations as a source of working capital. This occurs when the company has payed its bills promptly before the buyout occurred. Under these circumstances, it may be possible for the buyer to "stretch" the payables a week or so beyond their current terms. Before doing so, however, management must be convinced that such actions will not precipitate a limitation or withdrawal of credit terms from key suppliers. Nothing can devastate the company's cash flow quicker than its major creditors imposing COD terms.

Another factor to consider in the management of trade credit is the timing of any major changes in how quickly bills are paid. If management plans to stretch out the company's trade debt, it should not be done shortly after the transaction closes when vendors are most likely to be apprehensive about the financial integrity of the new owner. Such policies should be implemented several months following the closing and then only on a gradual basis.

Price Increases

In some cases, cash flow can be increased immediately by raising prices or charging for services that were previously given away. Obviously, before making any such moves, the potential impact on sales must be carefully analyzed. It may be that the gains in revenue from price increases are more than offset by the loss of business.

One might assume that incumbent management, if it is doing the job properly, has adjusted prices to their optimum level. However, some managers are reluctant to raise prices because they fear the possible loss of business. The involvement of "outsiders" in the buying group may have a beneficial effect by helping management take a fresh, new look at potential price increases. While these outsiders may be less familiar with the dynamics of the marketplace, they do lend an element of objectivity to any discussions of the matter. They may provide just the impetus needed to give management the necessary courage to take the step.

The key issues in dealing with price increases are the company's relative strength in the marketplace and the reaction of competitors. If it has a dominant market share and its competitors have traditionally been "followers," increasing prices may not be so risky. However, if the company has strong, well-capitalized competition, it may not be advisable. Timing of any price increases is also important. Generally speaking, they should not be made immediately after the closing unless absolutely necessary. This gives nervous customers more reason to change their sources and opportunistic competition more material for negative propaganda. It is better to wait until the recent change in ownership and the company's leveraged balance sheet are no longer major issue.

Overhead Reductions

Reducing overhead, particularly laying off employees, is always a painful process. In some cases, though, it is necessary if the business is to survive. If personnel reductions are necessary, there are certain procedures for managers to follow in order to minimize the impact on other employees and on operational performance.

First of all, payroll reductions should be planned as far in advance as possible. This starts with the operating plan jointly developed by incumbent managers and outside investors. Second, the buyer must carefully analyze the financial impact of such reductions, including severance costs and the payment of accrued benefits. Finally, any reductions should be done at one time and not carried out over an extended period. Communication with both terminated and retained employees should be both frank and honest. No purpose is served by telling tales that aren't true.

WHEN THE GOING GETS TOUGH. . .

If everything goes according to plan, the road will be relatively smooth. In many cases, however, it doesn't work out that way. The road gets quite "bumpy" and the ride is somewhat uncomfortable. Cash is tight, competition gets more aggressive, or interest rates increase. But, by staying with it, the buyer can usually weather the storm and stay on the original plan of reducing the level of debt in the company.

There are some situations though, where the ride gets downright rough and the very survival of the business is at stake. Cash is very tight, trade creditors may be screaming, and lenders may be threatening to turn off the life support system (credit lines). Such conditions may be precipitated by a sudden change in the marketplace, like the loss of major customers, or the onslaught of a recession. Regardless of its genesis, those who own the company must now get a firm hold on things or their investment may soon evaporate into thin air. They are in effect, managing a turnaround.

Maintaining Objectivity

It is most critical that members of the buying group maintain their objectivity in such situations. This may be more difficult for incumbent managers, because they are so close to the situation and are more emotionally involved. As a result, outside investors must assume a stronger role and sort out the facts.

There are three major questions that members of the buying group must ask and answer:

- Is the change that precipitated the crisis temporary or permanent?
- What immediate steps can be taken to ease the drain on cash while not destroying the business itself?
- What are the long-term alternatives and their financial impact?

Taking Action

If the underlying fundamentals have changed so dramatically that the business is no longer viable, the owners have no choice but to minimize their losses through a liquidation, preferably an orderly liquidation with the cooperation of senior lenders. In most cases, however, the business is salvageable. The key question is "how much will it cost to salvage it?" Management must carefully construct a detailed workout plan along with contingent actions if things don't go according to plan. This will enable the ownership group to quantify the additional funds needed and negotiate with lenders and investors.

Depending upon the severity of the problem, the original investors may have to advance additional funds to keep the company alive. If the situation is only a temporary cash flow squeeze, this may be avoided by convincing the senior lender to "overadvance" funds beyond its normal lending limits.

It may be necessary to dramatically reduce expenses, liquidate assets, restructure debt, or any combination thereof. The important factor is to have a sound plan that is effectively communicated to trade creditors and, if necessary, key customers. Lack of communication with these key resources only serves to intensify their uncertainty and may cause them to prematurely take action that would threaten the continuing viability of the company.

Managing Trade Credit

Trade creditors, in particular, must be handled delicately during periods when cash flow is tight. This is best accomplished by classifying them into the following groups that describe their relative importance to the company's operation:

"A" Group: This group includes creditors that are immediately and absolutely essential to the continuation of the business and cannot be replaced.

"B" Group: These creditors are also important, but are not immediately needed to supply the business.

"C" Group: This group includes all vendors not essential to the continuity of the business or who can be replaced by other sources.

Obviously, creditors in the "A" Group must receive top priority. If they cannot be paid on regular terms, management must negotiate a mutually acceptable payment schedule in advance. If it is subsequently apparent cash flow will not be sufficient to meet this schedule, the creditor should be given advance notice. Similar, but less binding, arrangements should be made with creditors in the "B" Group, while those in the "C" Group should be told that payments will be made when the cash flow problems are resolved. If possible, an estimated payment date should be given, but no firm promises made to the less important creditors. However, it is important to satisfy such creditors to the extent that they will not obtain a judgment against the company. This could precipitate an involuntary bankruptcy, usually the last resort of all workout alternatives.

MONITORING THE LBO

The model leveraged buyout combines a business with certain financial attributes with a proven management team so the probability of serious problems are minimized. And, if problems do occur, who is better prepared to deal with them than management, who also own a stake in the company they have run for several years? While these factors may give some degree of comfort to outside investors, it is naive to completely delegate responsibility for overseeing their investment to incumbent management. Someone must monitor the performance of management and the company. This is usually the investor himself or, if it is a larger firm, one of its principals or representatives.

Depending upon the characteristics of the company and its management, the monitoring function may be very intense or quite passive. At a minimum, the outside investors should be represented at the board level. It is also preferable to have some representation on key policy committees, particularly in the first year or two of the buyout. This representation will assure outside buyers that management is doing an acceptable job of running the company and protecting their investment. It also gives incumbent management another objective opinion on major policy issues that determine the company's future success.

LIST OF APPENDICES

APPENDIX A

LEGAL, TAX AND SECURITIES ASPECTS OF LEVERAGED BUYOUTS

By
Darrel A. Rice, Esq.
Winstead, McGuire, Sechrest & Minick, P.C.
Dallas, Texas

LEGAL, TAX AND SECURITIES ASPECTS OF LEVERAGED BUYOUTS

By
Darrel A. Rice, Esq.
Winstead, McGuire, Sechrest & Minick, P.C.
Dallas, Texas

September 15, 1988

TABLE OF CONTENTS

Page-A

TABLE OF CONTENTS
(Continued)

TABLE OF CONTENTS
(Continued)

TABLE OF CONTENTS
(Continued)

TABLE OF CONTENTS
(Continued)

TABLE OF CONTENTS
(Continued)

TABLE OF CONTENTS
(Continued)

Page-A

TABLE OF CONTENTS
(Continued)

Exhibits

LEGAL, TAX AND SECURITIES ASPECTS OF LEVERAGED BUYOUTS

By
Darrel A. Rice, Esq.
Winstead, McGuire, Sechrest & Minick, P.C.
Dallas, Texas

September 15, 1988

I. Definition of Leveraged Buyout.

The definition of the term "leveraged buyout," or "LBO", is only a generalization, and may include a wide variety of acquisitions of businesses in which the seller could receive cash and debentures or even preferred stock in consideration of the sale of stock or assets of a business, or the acquisition of a business in a merger transaction. The essence of the leveraged buyout technique is the acquisition of a business in a transaction where the purchaser's equity risk is small in relation to the purchase price, and the bulk of the purchase price is provided by borrowing from one or more outside lenders and/or from the seller in the form of a deferred purchase price.

Leveraged buyouts utilize "leverage," which is the use of borrowing power to obtain an equity interest. This creates debt to equity ratios which may be much higher than most companies bear, and are structured to allow payment of a substantial portion of the purchase price from the cash flow of the acquired company. A common element in all leveraged buyout transactions is that the principal source of the repayment for the financing will be the after-tax cash flow generated by the acquired business. Typically, the buyers, who frequently include management of the acquired company, put up no more than about 10% of the purchase price in permanent equity capital and finance the rest with debt which the company intends to repay from cash flow from operations and/or proceeds from sales of assets. Accordingly, the lenders in an LBO look primarily to cash flow and secondarily to the sale of assets of the acquired business as a source of repayment of their loans. The purchaser generally has no legal commitment to invest funds beyond the initial investment.

II. Participants.

A. Seller. The seller is frequently a large or mid-size company which is selling a division or a subsidiary, although sellers in leveraged buyouts include private owners of closely-held or non-public companies and shareholders of public companies.

B. Buyer. Buyers of a business in a leveraged buyout may include individual investors or entrepreneurs, managers or management groups of a subsidiary or division of a corporation divesting itself of a business, employee groups (including employee stock ownership plans, or "ESOPs"), venture capital investment groups, privately or publicly held corporations, and large LBO funds sponsored by major investment banking firms or LBO specialists.

C. Secured or Senior Lender. The secured or senior lender provides debt financing, through loans or the purchase of debt securities, including revolving lines of credit (unsecured, or secured by accounts receivable and inventory), fixed asset loans secured by machinery and equipment and/or real estate, or senior unsecured notes. Secured or senior lenders typically include commercial banks, asset-based lenders, and insurance companies.

D. Mezzanine Lender. A mezzanine lender is usually a "subordinated lender," i.e., a purchaser of subordinated debt, and the investment is subordinated debt securities, generally either convertible or with an "equity kicker" such as common stock warrants. Subordinated lenders may frequently include insurance companies, pension funds, commercial finance companies, other non-bank financial institutions, or Sellers.

E. Equity Investors. Equity investors make an investment in leveraged buyouts which is generally common stock. In some LBO transactions, there is a preferred stock equity layer, usually purchased by one or more of the lenders, or an affiliate of the lenders. Equity investors may frequently include management, insurance companies, LBO funds, private investors, or investment banking firms.

III. Legal Counsel.

A. Role and Selection of Legal Counsel. The role of legal counsel, whether representing the buyer, seller, senior or subordinated lender, or equity investor in a leveraged buyout, is to structure the transaction in a manner most favorable to his client. The leveraged buyout is generally a single "deal" and a search for counsel which will best represent a party in the buyout should focus on the attributes which suggest counsel is "deal oriented." Counsel selected should possess (i) experience in business acquisitions and combinations, (ii) experience and knowledge of the intracacies of the documents, including not only the acquisition agreement but loan documentation and other investor documentation, (iii) ability to negotiate, (iv) ability to reach solutions to difficult problems which may arise not only during the negotiation phase, but throughout the entire transaction, and (v) ability to set a transaction events timetable and see that the events in such timetable timely occur.

B. Timing of Involvement of Legal Counsel. To be most effective, counsel should be involved in the acquisition process at the earliest possible opportunity. Involvement in evaluation of the potential acquisition candidates enables counsel to advise as to potential "pitfalls" regarding tax and liability issues. Also, it provides counsel with insight as to purposes for which an acquisition or sale is being sought and facts necessary to effectively negotiate an acquisition agreement and draft and review the other documents necessary to effectuate the transaction in a manner which meets the objectives of the party represented. Counsel becomes of utmost importance in monitoring the events of the acquisition process after signing of the definitive acquisition agreements to ensure that those events necessary to meet the closing schedule occur in a timely manner.

IV. Overview of Leveraged Buyouts.

A. Introduction. The leveraged buyout market is extremely vigorous and has grown dramatically over the past few years. An increasing number of privately-owned investment firms specializing in leveraged acquisitions, as well as major investment banking firms, insurance companies and banks are involved in LBOs. Many large LBO funds have been formed, including an apparently unprecedented $5.6 billion LBO fund lined up during 1987 by Kohlberg Kravis Roberts & Co. from institutional investors, including pension funds, banks, and insurance companies. *See*, Fortune, July 4, 1988. LBOs have revolutionized the manner in which companies are bought and sold and have significantly affected the way in which institutions invest their capital. According to a recent article in the *Wall Street Journal*, more than 500 companies, including well-known companies such as Hertz, R. H. Macy, Levi Strauss, and Safeway have gone private in the past three years through LBOs. Apparently, in some industries, such as grocery chains and textiles, almost no big public companies remain. Anders, "Leveraged Buy-Outs Make Some Companies Tougher Competitors," Wall St. J., Sept. 15, 1985 at 1, col. 6.

Leveraged buyout transactions can be categorized in several broad classes: buyouts of public companies (including "going private" transactions), buyouts of subsidiaries or divisions of public companies (frequently by existing management of the subsidiary or division), buyouts of companies (whether public or private) by employee stock ownership plans ("ESOPS"), and buyouts of private companies. Generally, a buy-out is structured to provide either an acquisition of assets of the target company ("T") or acquisition of stock from the shareholders of T, or to provide for acquisition of T by the use of a merger, frequently with a wholly-owned acquisition subsidiary of the buyer.

B. Acquisition of Assets. As an example of an LBO using an asset acquisition, see Exhibit 1 attached hereto. In this example, Buyer forms a corporation ("Newco") and purchases assets of T. Financing of the purchase price is provided by a senior lender whose loan is secured by accounts receivable and inventory, and a subordinated lender who provides "mezzanine financing" in the form of convertible subordinated debt. The assets of T are acquired from T for cash by transferring the acquired assets, subject to any liabilities specifically assumed by Newco under the asset purchase agreement. T may then make a liquidating distribution to its shareholders or use the proceeds to acquire a new business or enter into a new venture.

C. Acquisition of Stock. As an example of an LBO using a stock acquisition, see Exhibit 2 attached hereto. In this example, Buyer frequently forms Newco as a holding company to acquire the stock of T from T's shareholders. Financing of the purchase price is provided by a senior lender whose loan is secured by accounts receivable and inventory, and by a venture capital investor who provides "mezzanine financing" in the form of convertible preferred stock.

D. Merger Transactions. In a triangular merger an existing corporation (or possibly a newly-formed corporation) will form a new acquisition subsidiary ("New Sub") to acquire T. New Sub and T are then merged.

1. <u>Straight Triangular Merger</u>. In a straight triangular merger New Sub will survive the merger. Exhibit 3 attached hereto illustrates a triangular cash merger transaction, in which the shareholders of T receive cash in exchange for their shares.

2. <u>Reverse Triangular Merger</u>. In a reverse triangular merger, T survives the merger.

E. <u>Going Private Through "Cash for Assets" Transaction</u>. In a "cash for assets" buyout, a private, non-operating, unaffiliated company will acquire for cash the assets of a publicly-held company, usually at a premium over the market price but at a substantial discount from the book value of the assets. The buyer will usually finance a substantial portion of the purchase price with debt which will be secured by the assets acquired. The transaction requires approval of shareholders obtained pursuant to a proxy statement filed with and approved by the Securities and Exchange Commission. Upon consummation of the transaction, the shareholders of the publicly-held company will hold stock in a company whose only asset is cash and thus will be treated as a personal holding company unless the cash is invested in municipal securities. The surviving shareholders may wish to make application to operate as a closed-end Registered Investment Company under the Investment Company Act of 1940. One unique aspect of the cash for asset transaction is the management agreement which the buyer and the management of the acquired company may make. Often, management of the company whose assets were acquired will form a partnership and enter into a long- term management agreement with the buyer whereby the partnership will provide management services to the buyer. Thus, senior officers retain their management positions in the company. The cash for assets transaction may be quite appropriate where there is a control shareholder group seeking a bailout.

F. <u>Going Private Through a "Cash Merger" Transaction</u>. In a cash merger transaction, the acquiring company will generally form a subsidiary to acquire the target corporation (see paragraph D, above). Upon consummation of the acquisition the target will become a subsidiary of the parent and the shareholders of the target corporation will receive cash in exchange for their shares. In many instances management of the target corporation will be given management contracts to maintain continuity of the organizational structure.

Generally the debt of the subsidiary is assumed by the target and becomes its obligation. A cash merger transaction will usually result in larger selling prices and gives less consideration to the seller's tax implications. The cash merger deal is somewhat less complex than the cash for assets transaction since there is no ultimate goal of complying with the Investment Company Act of 1940 as a registered investment company.

G. Organizing the Buyer. Regardless of whether the buyer in an LBO transaction is an individual, a corporation, a partnership, or a group of individuals or other entities, it is frequently advisable to organize a new holding corporation to sign the purchase agreement and close the transaction. In a stock acquisition, the holding company will generally acquire the stock of the operating company, and the operating company whose stock is acquired will thereby become a subsidiary of the holding company. In an asset acquisition, a second corporation is generally formed as a wholly-owned subsidiary of the holding company, which subsidiary will acquire the assets being purchased, subject to any liabilities assumed under the asset purchase agreement. This newly-formed subsidiary of the holding company will thereby become the operating company.

The use of the holding company structure may be advantageous in certain situations involving a stock acquisition, by allowing deferred acquisition debt to be placed at the holding company level, rather than on the balance sheet of its shareholders, who are the principals in the acquisition. The holding company structure may be advantageous in an asset transaction, by allowing the deferred acquisition indebtedness to be kept off of the non-consolidated balance sheet of the operating company, with any borrowings by the operating company appearing as working capital borrowings by the operating company. However, this type of situation generally involves a guarantee by the operating company of the holding company's debt incurred to pay the balance of the purchase price, with such guarantee being secured by the assets of the operating company. This "upstream" guaranty may cause concern on the part of the senior lender, due to the potential for attack on the validity of the "upstream guaranty" as a fraudulent conveyance. See "Senior Lender Considerations--Fraudulent Conveyances, Voidable Preferences, and Other Security Interest Concerns" below.

V. Financing--Participants and Structure.

A. Participants. LBO financing is frequently provided by more than one entity, and frequently includes a senior lender, a "mezzanine" financer (or subordinated lender), and equity participants, generally including management of the acquired company and frequently including LBO investment banking firms, and perhaps other forms of financing such as a deferred portion of the purchase price evidenced by a note to the seller.

1. Senior Lender or Senior Lending Group. The senior lender provides capital in the form of debt financing and typically obtains a security interest in the assets of the target company. If possible, guarantees from principals in the transaction are also obtained. In some instances (where the profit or cash flow prospects for the company are extremely favorable) such lender may finance the acquisition without taking a security interest in any property. The senior secured debt in large LBOs is typically syndicated to a number of senior lenders, in order to mitigate risk and comply with regulatory loan limits. The lead lender, or agent bank, may earn significant fees by retaining a disproportionate amount of origination, agent, and other fees as the senior debt is participated or syndicated to other lenders.

2. "Mezzanine" Investor or Subordinated Lender. The "mezzanine" investor or subordinated lender provides capital to effect the buy-out and in return will generally obtain an equity position in the acquired company through convertible preferred stock, convertible debt, or through non-convertible preferred stock or debt with an "equity kicker" such as warrants.

3. Equity Participants. The equity participants provide equity capital, usually in the form of common stock or preferred stock. In LBOs by management, the lenders usually require management to provide a specified minimum amount of equity capital as a condition to the loans. The sponsor or promoter of the LBO transaction usually contributes or is responsible for raising a significant portion of the equity capital for Newco.

4. Sponsor or Promoter. A leveraged buyout of a large public or private company may frequently require the management investors to team up with an investment banking or merchant banking firm which specializes in LBOs. This investment banking or merchant banking firm is frequently referred to as the LBO "promoter" or "sponsor." An LBO sponsor who has a proven track record in assisting LBO transactions will provide credibility to a transaction. The LBO sponsor must have the necessary knowledge, along with its financial, tax, and legal advisers, to analyze the target company, and to structure the acquisition and the financing for the LBO transaction. The most critical element in completing the leveraged buyout will be the financing, and the sponsor's skill at raising money for LBO transactions is the primary reason for the involvement of sponsors in the transaction. Furthermore, because of the conflict of interest which management of a company may have when pursuing an LBO transaction, the sponsor is perhaps in a better position to negotiate the terms of the transaction with the independent directors or disinterested members of management of the target company. The larger LBO transactions are more likely to be originated by a "sponsor" or "promoter". The investment banks tend to compete vigorously for large LBO transactions because of the potential profits which may be obtained from future mergers and acquisitions advisory work, subsequent assets sales, and potential initial public offerings.

5. Other Variations. There are numerous other variations by which the financing may be structured, including without limitation, Seller financing, involvement of multiple lenders, equity or debt offerings, "junk bonds", and "bridge financing" by investment banking firms or merchant banking organizations.

B. Terms and Structure of Financing. Many factors affect the terms and structure of the financing of LBO transactions, including the size of the transaction, the nature of the underlying business being acquired, and the identity and business objectives of the parties. One of the most significant factors affecting the terms of any particular LBO transaction is the dollar amount of the purchase price.

1. <u>Transactions Up to $25 Million</u>. Transactions of less than $20 million to $25 million tend to be structured based on book value rather than earnings, and involve only a single lender. Senior secured debt may represent as much as 80-95% of the acquisition financing, with equity investors putting up 5-10% of the capital required, and frequently the seller taking back a subordinated seller note of as much as 10% of the purchase price.

2. <u>Transactions of $25 to $200 Million</u>. Transactions larger than $20 to $25 million, and up to $150 to $200 million tend to be structured based upon a multiple of cash flow, or earnings before interest and taxes ("EBIT"). Although there may be some reliance on asset values, most loans tend to be structured on the basis of cash flow and/or business "going concern" values of the transaction. In these LBO transactions, a senior lender generally works in conjunction with a subordinated lender in concurrently funding the acquisition price on the closing date. Subordinated debt may consist of private subordinated debt from a single lender, or publicly offered or privately-placed debentures or "junk bonds." The typical capital structure may involve 65-70% senior debt, 25-30% subordinated debt (possibly including a subordinated note payable to the seller), and 5-10% equity from the equity investors, who may include management as well as established LBO firms or merchant banking firms which may act as sponsors of the transaction.

3. <u>Transactions Larger Than $200 Million</u>. Larger transactions may involve a smaller percentage of the financing provided by the senior secured lender, with an additional layer of senior subordinated financing constituting as much as 15-25% of the acquisition cost, and junior subordinated debt providing 10-15% of the acquisition funding. Many of the largest transactions involve public companies which are acquired in "going private" transactions. The purchase prices in these transactions tend to be highly impacted by stock market conditions, especially price-earnings multiples. <u>See</u> Michael J. Litwin, "Financing the Leveraged Buyout", <u>Leveraged Acquisitions and Buyouts 1988</u> (Harvey E. Benjamin, Michael B. Goldberg), 107.

4. Asset-Based vs. Cash Flow Lending. Conventional asset-based lending techniques, which involve lending only against a company's assets (including accounts, inventory, and fixed assets) may not be competitive in transactions larger than $25 or $30 million, due to the current competitive environment in which acquisitions may be made based on high multiples of book value and earnings. As a result, many lenders appear to be underwriting loans based primarily on cash flow and business valuation techniques, rather than traditional asset-based lending techniques, in transactions larger than $25 to $30 million.

C. Steps Taken in Example Stock Transaction. In a typical stock acquisition LBO, the stock purchase agreement provides for the acquisition by Buyer from Seller of all the outstanding capital stock of the Operating Company. In this example, a corporation is the Seller, and is selling its wholly-owned subsidiary (the "Operating Company") to a newly-formed corporation organized by a group of investors for the purpose of effectuating the LBO transaction. Financing is provided by a senior lender, and a subordinated lender, whose loans are secured by first and second liens, respectively, on the assets of the Operating Company. A portion of the purchase price is deferred, and is evidenced by a subordinated note payable to the Seller.

Step 1. Because of concerns about the validity of an "upstream guarantee" by a subsidiary of the debt of its parent under fraudulent conveyance laws, as discussed below, the lenders typically wish to make most or all of their loans to the Operating Company, secured by its assets, and guaranteed by its parent corporation. To facilitate this loan structure, the Holding Company at the closing of the LBO transaction issues (a) a demand note in the amount of the payment of the purchase price due on the closing date, secured by a pledge of the stock of the Operating Company, and (b) a subordinated installment note, payable to the order of the Seller, in the amount of and reflecting terms of payment of the deferred portion of the purchase price. The demand note and the subordinated seller note represent payment of the full amount of the purchase price for all of the outstanding common stock of the Operating Company, based on the purchase price, as defined in the stock purchase agreement. The Seller then transfers to the Holding Company all of the outstanding common stock of the Operating Company, thereby making the Operating Company a wholly-owned subsidiary of the Holding Company. *See* Step 1 in Exhibit 4 attached hereto.

Step 2. In Step 2, described in Exhibit 4 attached hereto, the senior lender and the junior (subordinated) lender make loans to the Operating Company secured by liens on all the assets of the Operating Company.

Step 3. At the closing, and concurrently with Steps 1 and 2, the Operating Company uses the proceeds of the loans from the senior and subordinated lenders to repay intercompany advances owed to Seller by the Operating Company. The balance of the loan proceeds, to the extent not retained or made available for working capital, is advanced by the Operating Company to the Holding Company, the new parent of the Operating Company. The proceeds of such advance are then used by the Holding Company to pay the demand note to Seller. At the conclusion of the Closing, Seller has received the entire purchase price in cash on the closing date, except for that portion of the purchase price for which payment is deferred, and evidenced by the subordinated note payable to Seller. *See* Step 3 of Exhibit 4 attached hereto.

Obviously, the use of loan proceeds to pay intercompany advances due to the Seller by the Operating Company only applies if there is existing debt to Seller from its subsidiary. However, this is frequently the case, because the Seller's equity often includes debt from its subsidiary. In the example set forth in Exhibit 4, the subsidiary pays this debt using proceeds from borrowings from the lenders, thereby reducing the purchase price and downpayment by an equivalent amount. As an alternative, the intercompany debt can be contributed to capital as a part of the acquisition.

D. *Steps Taken in Example Asset Transaction*. In a typical asset transaction LBO, the asset purchase agreement provides the right of the holding company, as buyer, to require the Seller to convey the assets to be acquired, subject to specific liabilities to be assumed, to a newly-organized subsidiary (the Operating Company). In an example asset transaction similar in structure to the example stock acquisition discussed in 3. immediately above, the same two note system described above for a stock transaction may be followed. The steps in the transaction for the acquisition of assets are then as follows:

> <u>Step 1</u>. At the closing, the Holding Company issues (a) a demand note in the amount of the portion of the purchase price due on the closing date, and (b) a subordinated installment note, payable to the order of Seller, in the amount of and reflecting the terms of payment of the deferred portion of the purchase price.
>
> <u>Step 2</u>. At the closing, the Holding Company acquires the assets, and contributes them to the Operating Company, subject to any assumed liabilities, as a contribution to capital. Assets acquired are transferred to the Operating Comany by deeds, bills of sale, etc.
>
> <u>Step 3</u>. The Operating Company, which now owns the assets, (a) makes a borrowing from the senior and subordinated lenders, secured by accounts receivable, inventory, and fixed assets, and (b) guarantees to Seller the payment of the subordinated note issued by the holding company to the Seller to evidence the deferred portion of the purchase price.
>
> <u>Step 4</u>. The Operating Company uses a portion of the loan proceeds to make an advance, or to pay a dividend to, the Holding Company; the Holding Company uses these proceeds to pay in full the demand note payable to the Seller. Any dividend must pass the applicable corporate law surplus test.

E. <u>Warrants</u>. Lenders in LBO transactions today frequently utilize warrants to increase loan yields to better compensate them for assuming the greater risk in financing LBOs at larger purchase price multiples. A warrant is simply an option to purchase for a specified time and at a defined price a certain number of shares or specified percentage of a company's common stock, usually on a fully diluted basis, after giving effect to the issuance of new stock purchased by the warrant holder, and protecting the warrant holder against dilution by the issuance of shares to others. Both the issuance of the warrants and the issuance of the underlying shares of common stock upon exercise of the warrants are subject to federal and state securities laws. Generally, the shares are not issued at the closing, but are reserved by the company to meet outstanding warrant obligations.

The warrant may be issued either at the holding company level or the operating company level, although lenders may sometimes prefer the warrant to be issued at the holding company level, with the debt at the operating company level. If the purchase of the warrant is also coupled with a purchase of preferred stock or other securities of the holding company by the lender, subject to applicable regulatory restrictions on equity ownership by banks or other regulated lenders, the lenders may bolster their argument that the warrant is not additional "interest" on their loans, thereby strengthening their position against attack on the basis of alleged violation of state usury laws.

Federal banking laws permit bank holding companies and their subsidiary banks to make general voting equity investments only in very limited circumstances. Regulation Y issued under the Bank Holding Company Act prohibits a holding company from owning, directly or indirectly, more than 5% of the voting stock of a corporation unless the corporation is engaged in certain types of limited permitted businesses. A national bank itself may hold stock only under the very limited circumstances described in the National Banking Act, generally involving equity acquired in a "workout" situation, and subject to a five-year divestiture rule.

In financing the mezzanine portion of an LBO transaction, a bank holding company affiliate may seek to obtain an amount of equity which exceeds 5% of the common stock of the entity being financed. A possible method of accomplishing this goal is to divide the equity into voting and non-voting common stock, with the affiliate taking the permitted portion of voting stock and the balance of its equity in the form of non-voting stock. However, the rules and policies of the Federal Reserve Board with respect to these so-called "non-voting equity investments" are complex, and a complete discussion of these limitations is beyond the scope of this outline.

One alternative for dealing with these limitations on equity investments from the lender's perspective is the acceptance of warrants which are freely assignable. There is limited precedent indicating that banks are permitted to accept such warrants provided that they ultimately sell them rather than exercise them. Consideration must also be given to the issue of usury. <u>See</u>, "Mezzanine Financing (Including Subordinated Lender) Considerations--Usury Problems" below. Any federally insured lender considering the acceptance of warrants should consult counsel with respect to the issue of legal permissibility as well as usury.

Once a warrant is issued, the holder of the warrant can realize value by exercising the warrant and holding the stock for dividend or distribution income, or the holder may transfer the warrant or the shares purchaseable under the warrant in a private sale permitted under the securities laws, and any applicable bank holding company laws and regulations. A warrant holder may also exercise the warrant and either (a) sell in a public offering, if it has a contractual right to registration of its shares, or to participate in a registered offering by the issuer, or (b) participate in the sale of control of the issuer.

In addition, a commonly used technique for allowing the realization of the value of the warrant is to establish a "put" or "call" mechanism in the warrant purchase agreement, which is signed and delivered at the closing of the LBO transaction. A "put" is an option which gives the holder of the warrant the right to sell the warrant (or the stock purchased upon the exercise of the warrant) back to the issuer during a specified time at a price defined in the warrant. A "call" is an option which gives the issuer the right to buy back the warrant (or the stock purchased upon the exercise of the warrant) from the holder during a specified time at a price defined in the warrant. The time during which the "put" and "call" can be exercised is negotiable, and may frequently range from five to ten years for "put" options and six to ten years for "call" options.

The put and call option prices are also a matter to be negotiated in each LBO transaction. Put and call option prices may be determined based on a multiple of book value, market value if the stock is publicly traded, appraised value if the stock is not publicly traded, some multiple of EBIT, or a combination of the foregoing. Generally, puts or calls cannot be exercised if the purchase of the warrant would cause the company to be in default under the financing or loan agreements, or under applicable corporate statutes restricting the payment of dividends or redemption of securities. In some cases, the lenders agree in the financing documents to finance the purchase of the warrant if sufficient cash flow coverage is available to service the additional debt.

Most holders of warrants acquired in connection with LBO transactions will require some sort of registration rights, in order to comply with applicable securities laws in connection with the sale of the underlying warrant shares. Most warrants have "piggyback" registration rights, which allow the holder of the warrant to participate in a public offering initiated by the issuer. In addition, it is common for the warrant holders to have "demand" registration rights which allow the lender to force the registration for sale to the public of the stock which is purchased upon exercise of the warrant, although typically this demand right is available only after the company's initial public offering.

VI. Senior Lender Considerations.

A. Documentation.

1. Commitment Letter. This letter, from the lender to the borrower by which the lender commits to lend certain funds to borrower, stipulates the terms and conditions upon which such loan is to be made. In addition, the lender may specify certain requirements which must be met before the loan will be made. The commitment letter will provide a date upon which the commitment to lend will end and may also provide for fees to the lender for making the commitment.

2. Loan Agreement and Note. The Loan Agreement will evidence the terms of the loan (including payment schedule, interest rate and other terms), property in which a security interest will be taken to secure the loan, representations and warranties of the Borrower, affirmative and negative convenants, default provisions, enforcement provisions, and any rights of assignment under the loan agreement. The Note is a negotiable instrument which is given by the borrower to the lender evidencing the funds which have been advanced by the lender to the borrower.

3. Security Agreement. The Security Agreement documents the security interest in the property of borrower which is taken by the lender to secure payment of the debt. Filings under the Uniform Commercial Code may be made in various states where the collateral taken is governed by the Uniform Commercial Code. In addition, deeds of trust may be taken to obtain a lien on the real property which is given as collateral for the debt.

4. Guaranty. A Guaranty may be required by the lender. Such Guaranty would require that in the event of default by the borrower (or in certain other specified conditions) payment of the debt would be made by another related party who executes this Guaranty. Such related parties may include the controlling individuals of a corporation, other corporate entities which may be a parent or subsidiary of the borrower, or any affiliated company controlled by individuals who are also in control of the borrower.

5. Subordination Agreements. Where there are existing loans, the lender of the acquisition funds may require that the lenders under such pre-existing loans subordinate their debt to the lender of the acquisition funds. Also, controlling persons who have borrowed from the corporate entity may be required to subordinate such borrowings to the lender of the acquisition funds. Seller financing, if any, is usually subordinated to the senior lender, and the seller may retain a secondary lien security interest, or mortgage, subordinated to the lien of the senior lender, to serve as collateral for the portion of the purchase price financed by the seller.

B. Fraudulent Conveyances, Voidable Preferences, and Other Security Interest Concerns. The lender must also consider whether the security interest in the property taken as collateral for the loan will be given priority in the event the borrower should declare or become subject to bankruptcy subsequent to the date of the loan. The three most significant areas of concern regarding whether a trustee (or the debtor itself in those Chapter 11 reorganization cases where no trustee has been appointed) may avoid a transfer under the Federal Bankruptcy Code are fraudulent conveyances, voidable preferences and equitable subordination. In addition, there may be other provisions under state creditor's rights and insolvency statues which would result in the lender's security interest not having the priority sought by such lender and should be considered by the lender in making any loan (e.g., the applicable state statute governing creditors' rights to upset fraudulent conveyances which are incorporated into the trustee's [and debtor-in- possession's] arsenal of rights under Section 544 of the Federal Bankruptcy Code and which may allow the trustee [or debtor-in-possession] to avoid fraudulent conveyances having occurred several years prior to the bankruptcy).

1. Fraudulent Conveyances. The lender must be certain that the borrower is solvent prior to the grant of the security interest in the collateral, solvent after giving effect to such grant and is financially viable going forward. The Federal Bankruptcy Code at 11 U.S.C §548 provides two instances where a trustee in bankruptcy (or debtor-in-possession) may avoid a transfer of an interest (i.e., the granting of a security interest to the lender in property of the bankrupt) or the incurrence of an obligation (e.g., execution of a guaranty or assumption of indebtedness by the bankrupt) as follows:

   a. Within one year before the filing of the petition, a transfer is made with intent to hinder, delay or defraud a creditor, or

   b. The debtor received less than a reasonable value in exchange for the transfer or obligation and was either:

      (i) Insolvent on the date of the transfer or became so as a result of the transfer or obligation;

      (ii) Engaged or about to engage in in a business in which he was or would be left with unreasonably small capital after the transfer; or

      (iii) Intending to incur or believed it would incur debts beyond the debtor's ability to pay as such debts matured.

   c. Generally speaking, a "transfer" does not occur until the appropriate documentation (e.g., deed of trust, mortgage, security agreement, financing statement) is duly filed or recorded in the proper public places, so it is important to file and record as quickly as possible.

2. Uniform Fraudulent Conveyance Act. Similarly, under the Uniform Fraudulent Conveyance Act ("UFCA"), which has been adopted with some variations in several states, a transfer without fair consideration where the debtor is left insolvent or with unreasonably small capital or the debtor intends or believes that he will incur debts beyond his ability to pay as they mature is fraudulent as to creditors. The UFCA establishes a form of balance sheet insolvency which compares the present fair salable value of the debtor's assets to the amount that will be required to pay the debtor's probable liability on its existing debts as they become absolute and matured.

3. Gleneagles and Other Case Law Applying Fraudulent Conveyances to LBOs. Applying the law of fraudulent conveyances to leveraged buy-outs is an emerging area where little case law exists. Only a few courts have applied the law of fraudulent conveyances to leveraged buy-outs to invalidate transfers by the borrower to a lender in an LBO. However, after the Third Circuit Court of Appeals' decision in United States v. Tabor Corp Realty Corp., 803 F.2d 1288 (C. A. 3rd 1986) ("the Gleneagles case"), lenders must be increasingly cautious to avoid having an acquisition attacked as being a fraudulent conveyance and consequently invalidated. In Gleneagles, the Court of Appeals affirmed the three district court opinions applying the Pennsylvania version of the UFCA. The court held that the lender lacked the good faith encompassed in the UFCA's definition of "fair consideration" because it was aware that (1) the imposition of the secured loan obligations would render insolvent the borrower and its subsidiaries as a whole as well as individually; and (2) that the lender was aware that no lender of the borrowing group would receive fair consideration as defined by the statute. The transaction involved the target borrower "upstreaming" the loan proceeds to the acquirer in exchange for a note. The acquirer then used the loan proceeds to purchase the target stock and to

retire part of the target's debt. The district court had found that the loan proceeds "were merely passed through the borrowers . . . ultimately to the selling stockholders and could not be deemed consideration received by the borrowing companies." United States v. Gleneagles Investment Co., Inc., 565 F.Supp. 556 (N.D. Pa. 1983), affd. sub. nom.; United States v. Tabor Corp Realty Corp., 803 F.2d 1288 (C.A. 3rd 1986).

The Gleneagles case involved an egregious set of facts in which the presence of intentional fraud compelled the court to set aside the mortgages as fraudulent conveyances. Because the Gleneagles facts were so compelling, there is some indication that leveraged buy-outs evidenced by legitimate commercial transactions, will withstand attack under the fraudulent conveyance laws. For example, in Credit Managers Association of Southern California v. Federal Company, 629 F.Supp. 175 (C.D. Cal. 1985), the court refused to set aside the leveraged buy-out as a fraudulent conveyance even though the court found that the corporation did not receive "fair consideration." Furthermore, in response to the argument that the company was left with inadequate capital, the court stated that the law requires only that the company "not be left with 'unreasonably small capital' at the time of the conveyance alleged as fraudulent," notwithstanding that the company was consequently, heavily indebted.

Some uncertainty remains as to how broadly the fraudulent conveyance laws will be applied to leveraged buy-outs. Nevertheless, the lender's objective, to minimize the risk that the target has a fraudulent conveyance defense available, is most directly advanced by ensuring that the target or its subsidiaries that own the assets, directly receive the loan proceeds, thus constituting "fair consideration." The lender will best be able to assert that the target is receiving fair consideration if it structures the loans so that they are made directly to or assumed by the target.

In addition, in cases such as Credit Managers, where "fair consideration" cannot be established, lenders should attempt to avoid fraudulent conveyance problems by analyzing and recording the target's financial condition at the time of the transaction. Such financial status documentation will buttress the lender's ability to defend the transaction against a potential fraudulent conveyance claim. For example, in Credit Managers, the note was executed by the acquirer and the target. The note was secured by the target company's assets. However, the court upheld the transaction, despite finding a lack of fair consideration, because giving great weight to the documented financial analysis, the court recognized that based on the lender's cash flow analysis of the borrower at the time of the buy-out, the lender believed the target had sufficient capital to generate the income necessary to service the debt and make a profit. Thus, establishing records with respect to the Borrower's financial condition such as provisions in the loan documents or certificates regarding solvency, capital adequacy, and ability to pay debts can help the lender demonstrate that no other element of a fraudulent conveyance exists.

4. Voidable Preferences. The Federal Bankruptcy Code at 11 U.S.C. §547 gives the trustee the right to void certain transfers of property of the debtor where the transfer was:

   a. Made to or for the benefit of a creditor;

   b. Made to secure an antecedent debt;

   c. Made while the debtor was insolvent;

   d. Made either

      (i) on or within 90 days before the date of the bankruptcy petition filing, or

      (ii) between 90 days and one year before the date of the filing of the petition if the creditor was an insider and had cause to believe the debtor was insolvent at the time of the transfer; and

   e. Made to enable the creditor to receive more than such creditor would have received in liquidation had the transfer not been made and the creditor received distribution in accordance with provisions of the Bankruptcy Code (i.e., the creditor received a greater percentage of the debt owed to him than did the other creditors in his class).

There is a provision in §547 for safe harbor from treatment as a voidable preference for certain transfers, such as those made in a contemporaneous exchange for new value; those made in the ordinary course of business and not later than 45 days after the date the debt was incurred; those transfers of perfected security interests in inventory or receivables or the proceeds therefrom; certain security interests in property acquired by the debtor where new value is given, if perfected within ten days after the security interest attaches; and certain transfers made for the benefit of the creditor where new value is given. Moreover, generally speaking, it is critically important at all times to duly file and record all security documentation within ten (10) days after any transfer is made.

5. Equitable Subordination. This is a common law principle which has been codified in the Bankruptcy Code at 11 U.S.C. §510 and allows a court to void a transfer or otherwise subordinate a claim or lien where it results in injury to the other creditors and violates the rules of "fair play". The doctrine of equitable subordination enables bankruptcy judges to subordinate even secured creditors to other creditors (principally trade creditors and banks) if it is "equitable" to do so. Generally it is necessary that there have been some misconduct (including running the corporation on the creditor's invested capital) by the investor-creditors. An example of equitable subordination could be an instance in which the holders of an issue of convertible notes have representatives on the board of directors of the issuer and the board has been directing the operation and management of the issuer to the detriment of the other creditors, so that the probability of obtaining a return of their investment is impaired. In this situation, the holders of the convertible notes may be "equitably subordinated" in bankruptcy proceedings so that the trade creditors and banks have priority in payment over the holders of the convertible notes. No distinction is made under equitable

subordination as to whether a creditor is secured or not. The overall problem of equitable subordination will typically relate to strenuous efforts by the board of directors, management, or creditors in "control" of the borrower during the company's financial distress to seek merger candidates or to obtain other financing or take extreme measures to "bail out" the company.

6. General Bankruptcy Concerns. In connection with bankruptcy concerns in general, any financial statements upon which the lender intends to rely in making credit and credit renewal decisions should be certified by the borrower and guarantors as true, accurate and complete in all respects. This may assist the lender in preventing the borrower's discharge in bankruptcy proceedings under 11 USC §523. Any decision to set off in anticipation of a bankruptcy should be reviewed with bankruptcy counsel in advance of the set off.

7. Evidencing Financial Performance. Comprehensive financial covenants will almost always be included in the loan documents in order to show a good faith effort to meet the financial condition tests relating to fraudulent conveyance, fraudulent transfer, and bankruptcy concerns of the senior lender. Inclusion of a revolving credit facility may be desirable in order to demonstrate that debtor has an additional source of funds available to pay its debts.

   In addition to LBO "solvency letters," discussed below, financial condition certificates from financial officers of the debtor and opinions of independent accountants and investment bankers may supplement and validate the lender's own analysis of asset value and cash flow. The stronger the analysis and validation thereof, the greater the likelihood of minimizing fraudulent conveyance risks.

8. LBO Solvency Letters. The fraudulent conveyance statutes discussed above, as well as similar state fraudulent conveyance or fraudulent transfer statutes are designed to protect unsecured creditors against transfers of or security interests in property that defraud such creditors or result in an inequitable outcome to creditors in the event of bankruptcy or insolvency of the

debtor. The due diligence process of lenders in connection with fraudulent conveyance analysis encompass matters relating to solvency which are similar to the condition set forth in the applicable fraudulent conveyance statutes. These generally relate to "fair value," for purposes of determining consideration or value received, "fair value" of assets for determining solvency, "solvency" itself, based on an evaluation of assets and liabilities, the existence or non-existence of "unreasonably small capital," or the "ability to pay debts as they mature" on the part of the borrower.

Lenders had been requesting accounting firms to provide them with "solvency letters" addressing these issues, as part of the lender's due diligence in underwriting the loan transaction. The issuance of these letters aroused a great deal of controversy, resulting in an AICPA interpretation, effective in February 1988, which precludes accountants from giving any form of assurance on matters related to solvency. In some instances, accountants appear to be providing more limited services for prospective lenders, including agreed upon procedures tailored to lender's desires for testing financial information. However, the accountants in connection with these services disclaim any assurance or opinion as to the borrower's solvency, adequacy of capital, or ability to pay its debts.

A substitute for "solvency letters" from accountants is a "solvency letter" or "solvency opinion" provided as a service of valuation and appraisal companies. There are several major valuation and appraisal firms, which are providing solvency letters on a regular basis. It appears that lenders in LBOs are frequently requiring these solvency letters as a condition to executing loan agreements to finance LBO transactions. The typical analysis includes valuation of both tangible assets, such as equipment, and primary financial characteristics such as price-earnings ratios, discounted cash flow, balance sheets, and income statements.

C. <u>Environmental Liability</u>. Congress enacted the Comprehensive Environmental Response, Compensation and

Liability Act ("CERCLA"), 42 U.S.C. § 9601, et seq., in 1980, which enables the Environmental Protection Agency ("EPA") to clean up hazardous waste sites using Superfund money and then to recover the cost of the cleanup from the "responsible parties." "Responsible parties" as defined by the statute includes "the owner and operator of a facility" and "any person who at the time of disposal of any hazardous waste substance owned or operated any facility." 42 U.S.C. § 9607. Because CERCLA is broadly construed, lending institutions and thus, lenders providing LBO financing, that make secured loans to the owner or operator of such a "facility" are also subject to liability under the statute.

The statutory definition of "owner or operator" specifically excludes a "person who, without participating in the management of a facility, holds indicia of ownership primarily to protect the security interest in the facility." The definition thus suggests that a lender may protect its interest as long as it refrains from exerting control over the affairs of the borrowers sufficient to fall within the "owner or operator" definition, which would trigger statutory liability. The several courts that have considered whether a secured lender is an "owner or operator" within the statute have not subjected lenders to CERCLA liability. However, the courts have indicated that where the lender becomes entangled in the borrower's operational, production, or waste disposal activities, in contrast to merely protecting the collateral, liability may be imposed. United States v. Mirable, No. 84-2280 (E.D. Pa. Sept. 6, 1985). The CERCLA "owner or operator" test appears to be entanglement and/or active participation in management.

Similarly, merely foreclosing on collateral will not be enough to render a secured lender an "owner or operator." The In re T. P. Long Chemical, Inc., 45 Bankr. Rep. 278 (Bankr. N.D. Ohio 1985) court held that the ownership of collateral was distinct from control over the borrower's operations and was therefore insufficient to impose liability on the lender. The court suggested that even if the lender had repossessed the property, the only "indicia of ownership" that would be involved would be that of the lender protecting its security interest, which is consistent with the statutory exemption.

Thus, because these cases indicate that CERCLA liability can accompany a security interest in real property, lenders providing LBO financing should scrutinize carefully the property to which the security interests are attached. Further, lenders financing LBO transactions must be careful of the extent to which they participate in the management of the facility in their attempts to protect their security interests. Lenders should refrain from participating in the borrowers' operational activities, otherwise the participation could be accompanied by substantial CERCLA liability in the form of environmental cleanup costs.

VII. Mezzanine Financing (Including Subordinated Lender) Considerations.

A. Seniority or Preference of Securities Over Common Stock. Investors or lenders providing mezzanine financing will generally require some form of seniority or preference of the securities which they purchase over the common stock of the issuer, to insure that if the issuer is bought out at an early stage due to lack of significant growth, the investors will receive back their invested capital before holders of common stock receive anything out of the proceeds of the sale. "Seniority" in this situation is a seniority or preference only with respect to common stock, and should not be confused with the "seniority" of the senior secured lender. Seniority in this situation is not generally designed to achieve a senior position with respect to creditors in a bankruptcy, since the preferred stock or notes are almost always subordinated to any bank debt or other senior lenders, and there is rarely enough to pay off even the trade creditors when a small issuer goes bankrupt.

B. Type of Securities Issued. The type of securities generally purchased by the investor or lender providing mezzanine financing are convertible preferred stock, convertible notes, or a combination of notes or preferred stock and warrants. Sometimes a combination of shares of common stock and non-convertible preferred stock are used. The most frequently used type of security seems to be subordinated debt, although convertible preferred stock is sometimes used to provide flexibility for dealings between management and the investors, and to assist in avoiding usury problems which may be present in certain states. Further, the use of convertible preferred stock may be helpful to the founding entrepreneurs in substantiating their claims that they have received their common stock at market prices (not "cheap stock" creating taxable income or possible challenges by blue sky administrators in the event of a subsequent public offering), eventhough the price at which they purchased was substantially below the conversion or exercise price of the senior securities or warrants purchased by the mezzanine investor.

C. Usury Problems. In certain states there are usury laws which fix the maximum rate of interest for loan transactions which may affect the mezzanine portion of a leveraged buyout. Under the law of these states, the purchase of convertible notes or notes with warrants may be interpreted to be a loan transaction such that the present value of an equity feature, including conversion rights or warrants, is considered as "interest" paid in connection with the "loan". If the present value of the equity feature, when treated as "interest", yields an interest rate that is higher than the maximum rate permitted by applicable law, then the transaction may be held by a court to be usurious, and subject the investor to substantial penalties (usually including the forfeiture of all or a portion of "principal" or "interest") as a result. In instances where state usury law is a significant consideration, it may be advisable to use a convertible preferred stock to assist in avoiding characterization of the transaction as a "loan".

D. Subordinated Convertible Debt vs. Convertible Preferred Stock. The differences between the purchase of subordinated convertible debt as opposed to the purchase of convertible preferred stock is not significant for many investors, as they will probably be subordinated to trade creditors or bank creditors in any bankruptcy proceeding. All of the essential requirements of the typical venture capital investor can be met by the use of convertible preferred stock. Assuming that the United States Treasury's debt-equity rules are not adopted in a form which will change the result, the principal disadvantage of using convertible preferred stock instead of a debt security is that the issuer will lose the deduction for interest paid on a debt security. Corporations and small business investment companies ("SBIC's") will gain an advantage by use of preferred stock because they are permitted to exclude from taxable income 100% (in the case of SBIC's) and 80% (in the case of other corporations) of any dividends received on the preferred stock.

E. Optional Redemption Provisions and Mandatory Conversions. Convertible preferred stock purchased by a mezzanine investor, or warrants purchased by a mezzanine lender, will frequently include a "put" or a "call" providing for the optional redemption of stock or purchase of warrants in a single transaction or in installments commencing about five years following the closing, although this time period can vary considerably. The "put" provision gives the investors the right, at their option, to require the issuer to redeem their securities. The primary reason for the put provisions is to allow the investors an "out" or an "escape hatch" in the event the issuer is profitable but does not achieve the projected increase in equity value of the securities purchased. A redemption premium is frequently included in order to allow the investors to achieve a higher return for allowing the issuer the use of their money. These redemption premiums will be viewed as ordinary income for tax purposes. Optional redemption provisions which allow the issuer to call preferred shares for redemption (sometimes at specified premiums), usually after a period of a few years, have the effect of permitting the issuer to force conversion of the convertible preferred stock or exercise of warrants before the investor might otherwise wish to convert or exercise. Optional redemption provisions may be coupled with an automatic conversion feature which gives the issuer the right to effect conversion of convertible securities in connection with a registered public offering at a price per share in excess of a certain amount (perhaps three to five times the per share price of the present financing).

F. Anti-Dilution Protection. Stock dividends, stock splits, and other stock combinations or changes in the outstanding amount of securities of the issuer require provisions in convertible preferred stock, convertible subordinated debt instruments, and warrants to protect the investor from dilution. Anti-dilution protection can become very complicated, especially if the anti-dilution provisions are drafted with a view to protection against the issuance of common stock at a price below the price of the equity in the present issue (or below "market" value, or both). Some investors will obtain from the issuer a proportional adjustment consisting of an automatic reduction in conversion or exercise price of the current issue to the conversion price or exercise price of a subsequent issue, if that price is lower. This kind of a proportional adjustment is intended to guarantee against the issuer having sold its shares at too high a price to the current group of investors.

G. Voting Rights. Voting rights to holders of convertible preferred stock may include the contractual right to one or more seats on the board of directors of the issuer. Control of the board is rarely sought unless the issuer fails to meet its projections and requires further financing in order to "bail it out". In that event, the investors may require control of the board. The right to elect directors, sometimes a majority of the board, may be triggered under a preferred issue in some instances in the event of a "default", which lapses when the default is cured. The definition of "default" is a highly negotiated provision, which may include failure to make a certain number of dividend payments on preferred stock.

H. Liquidity; Registration Rights. Securities that are purchased in offerings that are exempt under Regulation D or Section 4(2) of the Securities Act of 1933 may be resold only under certain conditions. Generally, these conditions include a registered public offering, a Rule 144 sale, or a privately negotiated sale to a sophisticated and wealthy purchaser. Accordingly, investors generally seek to have the issuer grant certain rights that will enable them to require the issuer to register their shares under the Securities Act of 1933 (and state securities statutes). Registration rights generally relate only to common stock, and may be either a "demand" registration (required upon a demand by the investor), or a "piggyback" registration, in which the investors may register some or all of their securities (depending upon the feasibility of the sale of the number of shares desired to be sold, frequently determined by the underwriter) in conjunction with registered public offerings initiated by the issuer. See "Securities Law Considerations" below.

VIII. Tax Aspects.

A. Tax Considerations of Buyer

1. Use of Leverage

As previously noted, the essential characteristic of a leveraged buyout is the substitution of debt for equity in the acquired entity. Financing for the acquisition comes in two basic forms including, (a) loans from financial institutions and (b) seller financing. Within these two major categories are numerous creative forms of financing including profit participations, convertible debt, zero coupon bonds, "junk bonds", etc. The concern of both the buyer and the lender in these transactions is that the net, after tax cash flow of T be sufficent to meet the debt service on the acquisition indebtedness. In this regard, the buyer and lender should determine if, and to what degree, T will be able to shelter its income with noncash expenses (i.e. depreciation, amortization, etc.). From the buyer's perspective, another concern is that the debt is respected as such.

a. Interest Deduction

The substitution of debt for equity enables the leveraged entity to utilize its tax attributes to a greater degree. For example, leverage enables the buyer to deduct the interest on the purchase price indebtedness rather than face the nondeductibility of dividends paid on equity raised for a similar purpose. This interest deduction may then shelter income otherwise generated by T.

Section 279 of the Internal Revenue Code of 1986, as amended (the "Code") restricts the availability of an interest deduction attributable to certain corporate acquisition indebtedness. Corporate acquisition indebtedness includes any obligation evidenced by a bond, debenture, note, certificate or other form of indebtedness if the obligation is issued to acquire stock or assets of another corporation and the debt is (i) subordinated, (ii) subject to equity participation and, (iii) issued by a corporation which is thinly capitalized (debt to equity ratio is greater than two to one or projected earnings do not exceed three times the annual interest to be paid). If the evidence of indebtedness is corporate acquisition indebtedness, then interest on such indebtedness is not deductible to the extent the interest exceeds $5,000,000 less any other interest paid or incurred by such corporation during the year on obligations to provide consideration for an acquisition of a similar nature.

b. Debt v. Equity.

One concern in using leverage is its recharacterization as equity. If this were to occur, the interest deductions could be recharacterized as nondeductible dividends for the payor, and the principal payments could be treated as taxable dividends to the lender with no portion treated as a return of capital. The determination of whether an instrument is debt or equity is based upon statute and case law. Several factors have been utilized in this analysis, including (i) the existence of an unconditional promise to pay on demand or on a specified date a sum in money with a fixed interest rate, (ii) subordination, (iii) ratio of debt to equity, (iv) convertibility, (v) proportionality of debt and equity holdings, (vi) voice in operation of corporation, (vii) rights upon default, and (viii) the name of the instrument.

Section 385 of the Code provides some guidance in classifying an instrument as stock or debt. This Section has been subject to much controversy. Several drafts of regulations for this provision have been published by the Treasury for comment. The most recent draft regulations were withdrawn in July of 1983 and no further proposals have been released since that time.

2. Basis in T.

a. Asset Acquisitions

The principal consideration of the buyer will frequently be tax attributes, such as depreciation, relating to T's assets. If the fair market value of the assets, and thus the purchase price, is greater than the book value of the assets, the buyer will generally prefer to buy assets. In this situation, the buyer will get a step-up in the basis of the assets and the seller of the assets will recognize the taxable gain on the sale. The buyer's aggregate basis in the assets will be the cash paid, plus debt incurred plus any liabilities assumed. Section 1060, enacted by the Tax Reform Act of 1986 (the "Tax Act"), provides that the purchase price must be allocated to the assets first to cash, then among the assets pro rata in amounts equal to their fair market value, and any excess to goodwill.

b. Stock Acquisitions

(i) General

Contrary to asset acquisitions, and except as provided by Section 338 discussed below, a stock acquisition results in the buyer's basis being reflected in the stock acquired in T. The basis in T's assets are unaffected.

(ii) Section 338

Section 338 of the Code permits a purchaser to elect to treat a qualified stock purchase as an acquisition of the underlying corporate assets. A "qualified stock purchase" is the acquisition of eighty percent (80%) of the voting power and eighty percent (80%) of the overall value of T's stock during a twelve (12) month period. If an election is made under Section 338, T is deemed to sell all of its assets. This results in a step-up in basis of T's assets to the purchase price of the stock. Prior to the Tax Act, sales by a corporation which had adopted a plan of liquidation under old Section 337 generally did not result in recognizable gain at the corporate level. However, the Tax Act repeals these nonrecognition provisions, and thus the deemed sale by the corporation of its assets is fully taxable at the corporate level. As a result, T can get a step up in basis only at the cost of full recognition of the gain inherent in the assets (i.e. the amount by which the fair market value exceeds the assets' adjusted basis). Since the buyer will now own T, the buyer will bear the tax cost of such a Section 338 election. Under the new law, an election to treat a purchase of stock as a purchase of assets under Section 338 is likely only to be a benefit in two particular instances, (i) where T has a large net operating loss carryover which can absorb the gain recognized and, (ii) in instances where a subsidiary member of an affiliated group filing a consolidated return jointly makes an election with its parent to prevent gain recognition on the sale of stock.

3. <u>Tax Attributes of T</u>.

a. <u>Asset Acquisitions</u>

An asset acquisition of T, followed by a liquidation of the corporation would essentially eliminate all tax attributes of T, including, net operating loss carry-forwards, tax credits, and many of the other tax attributes described under Section 381.

b. <u>Mergers and Stock Acquisitions</u>

With some exceptions, the tax attributes of T will normally survive the acquisition of assets of a corporation through stock for stock, stock for debt or merger transactions. One significant exception to this general rule is the utility of a net operating loss ("NOL") carryforward of T. The Tax Act enacted new Section 382 which limits the availability of T's NOL if there is a fifty percent change in ownership over a three-year period. If there is such an ownership change, the NOL of T annually available to offset T's income is equal to the fair market value of T (determined by aggregate stock value) as of the date of a change in ownership multiplied by the long term tax exempt interest rate periodically announced by the Treasury.

4. Dividends Received Deduction.

The lender in a leveraged buyout looks to the cash flow of T for repayment of its debt. Where buyer and T file a consolidated return, Section 243 provides that cash flow from T to parent to lender moves without taxation because the dividends from T to parent are excluded from parent's income. If the buyer owns less than eighty percent of T, the dividends from T to parent cannot be completely excluded from parent's income. Section 243 provides a deduction of eighty percent of the amount received as dividends from a domestic corporation. This results in an effective taxable rate on dividends of 6.8%.

B. Tax Considerations of Seller.

1. Corporation.

a. Repeal of Nonrecognition Provisions.

As mentioned above, prior to the enactment of the Tax Act, a corporation generally did not recognize gain or loss (other than depreciation recapture and similar items) as a result of a distribution of assets in complete liquidation. Also, sales of assets after a plan of liquidation was adopted did not result in gain at the corporate level if the corporation completely liquidated within twelve months after the adoption of the plan. The Tax Act, though, amended Section 336 to provide that the corporation must recognize gain or loss on a distribution of property in complete liquidation as if such property were sold to the recipient shareholder at its fair market value. Additionally, sales made after the adoption of a plan of liquidation result in gain at the corporate level. Thus, a leveraged buyout of the assets of T no longer has many of the significant tax benefits previously enjoyed (i.e. step-up in basis without recognition of gain).

b. <u>Golden Parachutes, Options, Rights, Restricted Stock and Extraordinary Dividends</u>.

One aspect of leveraged buyouts is the impact which the acquisition has on the management of T. For example, if golden parachute payments to an officer, director or highly compensated employee exceed three times the average annual compensation of such individual for the five preceding years, Section 280G of the Code imposes a 20% nondeductible excise tax on the amount by which the present value of the parachute payments exceed this base amount or reasonable compensation. The excess parachute payments are not deductible by the corporation.

Participants in leveraged buyouts who hold stock options, stock appreciation rights, restricted stock and similar forms of compensation may be affected by the acquisition of the corporation. For example, the management may be forced to cash-out their position thus resulting in substantial taxable income.

Moreover, if a corporate shareholder in T receives an extraordinary dividend (i.e., a dividend with respect to a share of stock which was not held for more than two years before the dividend announcement date), the shareholder must reduce its basis in the stock of the distributing corporation by the amount of the dividends received deduction allowed for the extraordinary dividend. That is, the Internal Revenue Service is trying to prevent the practice of purchasing shares at an inflated price which reflects a soon-to-be-distributed dividend, collect the dividend at a low tax rate (i.e., 80% is excluded from income), and then sell the reduced valued stock at a loss.

2. <u>Individuals</u>.

a. <u>Sale or Exchange v. Dividend Income</u>.

In 1987 only, long term capital gains were taxed at 28% for individuals, thus avoiding the higher blended rate of 38.5% on ordinary income. After 1987, the capital gain exclusion was repealed, but the determination of whether payments are for the purchase of stock or are dividends is still important for purposes of determining capital or ordinary losses and calculating the amount of income to be recognized upon receipt of a payment for stock. One risk to the shareholders of T is the characterization of payments received from T for their stock in T as dividends under Section 302 and not as payments in exchange for stock. In this event, all of the payment received is taxable, and none of the payment is offset by the shareholder's basis in his stock. Normally, corporate distributions are treated as dividends unless the distributing corporation undertakes a redemption which satisfies one of several tests under Section 302(b) or the payments are in complete liquidation of the corporation. The significant tests under 302(b) would be, (i) a substantially disproportionate redemption of stock, (ii) a termination of a shareholder's interest, or (iii) a redemption from a noncorporate shareholder in partial liquidation of the corporation. In instances where the purchaser and seller are small closely held corporations, Section 304 may be applicable. Under this provision, if one corporation acquires the stock in another corporation, and one or more persons are in control of each of the two corporations, payments for the acquired stock may be characterized as dividends.

In situations where the buying group is shareholders of T and they receive cash, debentures or notes in exchange for some of their shares but continue to have some equity in T, the receipt of cash, debentures or notes may be characterized as the receipt of a dividend in a recapitalization of T. To avoid this event and assure capital gain treatment for a redemption of stock, the shareholder must have an equity ownership in T subsequent to the transaction which is both below fifty percent (50%) and less than eighty percent (80%) of the equity ownership of such shareholder in T prior to the transaction.

b. Original Issue Discount.

If debt instruments issued to a shareholder in exchange for his/her stock have a stated maturity amount which exceeds the stock issuance price, the difference is original issue discount ("OID") (e.g. in instances where the accrual rate exceeds the pay rate). The OID is taxed to the holder (and is deductible to the issuer) as income on a yield to maturity amortization over the life of the debt, regardless of the holder's method of accounting.

c. Installment Reporting.

If the shareholders of the acquired corporation receive a deferred payment obligation in exchange for their stock, they may recognize a gain on the installment method under Section 453. So long as the obligation is not "payable on demand" or "readily tradeable", installment reporting is probably allowed. However, if the debt instrument is convertible into equity tradeable on a public securities market, it is possible that the installment method is not permitted.

d. Recharacterization.

The Internal Revenue Service may attempt to recharacterize a transaction where, in its view, the form does not comport with its substance. This is particularly true in the analysis set forth in (a) above. If a payment treated as in exchange for stock is recharacterized as a dividend payment, the shareholder of T may recognize ordinary income rather than capital gain.

IX. Comparison of Acquisition of Assets v. Acquisition of Stock.

A. Acquisitions of Assets.

1. Unknown or Undisclosed Liabilities; Escrow and Indemnification. In the acquisition of assets the

buyer generally assumes only those liabilities of the corporation which are associated with the assets acquired. There is no assumption of the remaining liabilities of the corporation, unless expressly provided in the asset purchase documentation. Accordingly, in an acquisition of assets, the exposure to the liabilities of the company acquired (particularly unknown, undisclosed, or contingent liabilities) may be significantly reduced, since under the acquisition agreement the buyer assumes only those liabilities which are specifically stated in the agreement.

The negative impact of such contingent or unknown liabilities may be further mitigated by a provision in the purchase agreement to place a portion of the seller's proceeds in an escrow fund to be utilized to liquidate such claims or a provision providing for guarantees and warranties of the sellers that no such liabilities exist and that they (the sellers) will indemnify the purchaser for expenditures made to satisfy any such liabilities which may arise.

2. Re-valuation of Assets. Acquisition of assets results in re-valuation of the assets. To the extent there is a write-up of the assets, additional depreciation may be available. If the assets are to be written down, it may be more beneficial to acquire stock.

3. Depreciation or Investment Tax Credit Recapture. An acquisition of assets may result in the recapture of both depreciation and investment tax credit.

4. Bulk Sales Law. The Unifom Commercial Code Bulk Sales Law provisions may be applicable, requiring identification of and notification to all creditors of the target company in connection with the proposed acquisition.

5. Assignability of Franchises and Agreements. Many valuable franchises, contracts and agreements to which a target may be a party often contain provisions which prohibit assignment. In a sale of assets, consents of lenders, governmental authorities, or others may be required in order to transfer rights under such franchises and agreements.

B. Acquisition of Stock.

1. Net Operating Losses. In a stock purchase the net operating losses of the acquired company may, subject to significant statutory restrictions, still be available to offset future earnings of the acquired corporation.

2. Exposure to Unknown and Contingent Liabilities. In the acquisition of stock, the purchaser generally assumes not only the stated liabilities of the corporation but any contingent liabilities or unknown liabilities which may be attributable to the occurrence of events prior to the acquisition date but only become known subsequent to such acquisition date. All liabilities (including unknown, undisclosed, and contingent liabilities) remain in the corporation whose stock is acquired, with the result that all such liabilities remain with the buyer by virtue of its stock ownership of the acquired corporation. The risk of exposure to unknown or contingent liabilities may be mitigated by an indemnification agreement from the seller.

3. Franchises or Favorable Agreements. In some cases, the target company holds valuable franchises or highly favorable leasehold estates, mortgage financing, or other favorable agreements. A purchase of stock, in most cases, will not terminate such franchises or agreements, whereas the non-assignability features which are present in many franchises and agreements will require consents to transfer if assets are purchased.

X. Securities Law Considerations.

A. Principal Federal Securities Statutes. Federal securities law applicable to leveraged buyouts is principally embodied in two acts: the Securities Act of 1933 (the "Act") which generally governs registration of securities; and the Securities Exchange Act of 1934 (the "Exchange Act"), which generally provides on-going reporting requirements and certain rules as to trading and other transactions in the stock after it is initially registered.

B. Securities Law Aspects of the Acquisition of a Publicly-Held Target Company.

1. Insider Information. The most significant concern of the acquirer of T, which is publicly held, involves "insider trading" rules under Rule 10b-5, promulgated under the Exchange Act. This rule makes it unlawful for any person in connection with the purchase or sale of a security to use any instrumentality of interstate commerce (mail or telephone would be considered interstate commerce) to engage in any act which operates as a fraud or deceit upon any person. Thus, trading in contemplated acquisition candidates without disclosing material information to the public may be considered a violation of Rule 10b-5.

2. "Going Private". If the leveraged buyout of a public company will cause a registered class of equity securities, subject to the reporting requirements of the Exchange Act, to be held by less than 300 persons or to be delisted and the corporation is to become an affiliate of the newly formed corporation, then the "going private" rules promulgated under the Exchange Act in Rule 13e-3 must be followed and Schedule 13E-3 must filed. The information required by this Schedule includes the issuing class of securities subject to the transaction; the identity and background of the purchaser; any past contracts, transactions and negotiations between purchaser and the target company; the material terms of the transactions; any plans or proposals of the purchaser; the source and amount of the funds or other consideration; the purpose of the transaction; a statement as to whether the purchaser believes the transaction is fair or unfair to unaffiliated security holders; projections of revenue, income (loss), or earnings (loss) per share and other material information.

3. Proxy. The leveraged buyout of a public company in a merger transaction, or by an acquisition of assets requires shareholder approval through the solicitation of proxies in accordance with the Exchange Act. Section 14 of the Exchange Act regulates the solicitation of proxies from holders of securities registered on an exchange and holders of over-the-counter securities registered under the Exchange Act. Any solicitation of

proxies must comply with the requirements of the rules promulgated under Section 14. The proxy must be accompanied by a proxy statement. Such proxy statement and the form of proxy must be filed with the Securities and Exchange Commission 10 days prior to the date the copies are sent or given to the security holders. The proxy statement itself must detail the material features of the proposed acquisition and include a description of the business of the purchaser and the corporation being acquired, the location thereof, and detailed financial information regarding the purchaser and the corporation being acquired.

4. Tender Offer. Section 14 of the Exchange Act also provides for the filing of information for tender offers of securities of public companies. The person making such tender is required to file with the Securities and Exchange Commission a Tender Offer Statement which includes information regarding the source of funds; the identity and background of the person making the offer; any past contracts, transactions or negotiations with the subject company; the purpose of the tender offer and the plans or proposals of the person making such offer; any interest in the securities of the subject company; other information regarding contracts with the subject company and the financial statements of the bidder.

5. Voting Control and Ownership. Section 13(d) of the Exchange Act is designed to monitor changes in the voting control of equity securities of a corporation. Section 13(d) requires that any person who acquires, directly or indirectly, a beneficial ownership of more than 5% of certain classes of voting equity securities must, within 10 days after such acquisition, report such acquisition to the issuer and to the Securities and Exchange Commission. Section 13(g) of the Exchange Act is designed to provide identification of the ownership of securities, rather than to monitor changes in voting control. Section 13(g) provides that any person who is directly or indirectly the beneficial owner of more than 5% of *any* class of security must report such ownership to the issuer and the Securities and Exchange Commission within 45 days after the end of the calendar year of the issuer.

C. Formation of New Subsidiaries. The formation of a new subsidiary for which an equity issue is to be sold through the use of interstate commerce (e.g. telephone or mail) will require registration under the Act unless an exemption is available. Almost all acquiring companies are formed without registration, in reliance upon applicable exemptions, usually the "private placement" exemption or Regulation D, discussed below.

D. Private Placement Exemption. The issuance of securities to the senior lender, subordinated lender and equity investor, as well as the issuance of securities upon formation of new subsidiaries in leveraged buyouts, are frequently accomplished without registration with the Securities and Exchange Commission, in reliance upon applicable exemptions. Exemptions for certain types of securities and certain transactions in securities are available as provided in Sections 3 and 4 of the Act. The federal exemptions most often relied upon are "private offerings" which are not registered with the Securities and Exchange Commission in reliance upon the exemptions afforded by Regulation D or Section 4(2) of the Act.

1. Statutory Private Placement Exemption. Section 4(2) of the Act exempts from the registration requirements of Section 5 of the Act "transactions by an issuer not involving any public offering." This so-called "private placement exemption" does not contain a definition in the statute of what constitutes a non-public offering. The Securities and Exchange Commission and the courts have interpreted the exemption to be available for offerings involving sophisticated offerees and purchasers who have access to the same kind of information that a registered public offering would provide, who are able to "fend for themselves" as knowledgeable investors, and where the offerings are conducted in a non-public manner without general public solicitation.

2. Regulation D. In 1982 the Securities and Exchange Commission promulgated Regulation D, which provides "safe harbor" provisions for certain unregistered offerings. Regulation D is based both on the Section 4(2) "private placement" exemption and the Section 3(b) "small offering" exemption. Regulation D exemptions are discussed below.

E. Regulation D Exemptions. The Securities and Exchange Commission has issued "Regulation D," which governs exemptions from registration for certain limited offerings of securities, and replaces exemptions that were previously available under SEC Rules 146, 240 and 242. Regulation D is actually a series of six rules, numbered 501 through 506, and establishes three exemptions from the registration requirements of the Act.

1. Rule 504 is limited to offerings where no more than $1,000,000 of securities are to be sold in a twelve month period, provided that no more than $500,000 of such aggregate offering price is attributable to offers and sales of securities without registration under a state's securities laws. The advantage of Rule 504 is that there is no ceiling on the number of investors, and if the offering is conducted exclusively in states where the issuer is qualified or registered with the State Securities Commission (and if the state requires the delivery of disclosure documents before the sale), there are no restrictions on the manner of the offering and on resale of the securities offered.

2. Rule 505 provides an exemption for offers and sales not exceeding $5,000,000 in any twelve month period where sales are made for not more than thirty-five nonaccredited investors and an unlimited number of accredited investors.

3. Rule 506, which replaces the old Rule 146, relates to transactions which are deemed to be exempt from registration under Section 4(2) of the Act (the "private placement exemption"). Rule 506 has no maximum dollar amount limitation on the size of the offering. Rule 506 has certain advantages, including that it (a) is available to all issuers for offerings sold to an unlimited number of "accredited investors" and not more than thirty-five "nonaccredited" investors, provided such nonaccredited investors meet certain purchase qualifications, (b) retains the concept of "purchaser representative" so that persons who, acting alone, may lack the requisite knowledge and experience to independently evaluate the risks and merits of the offering may participate, with the aid of another person who is their representative, and (c) eliminates the need to deliver disclosure

documents if only accredited investors participate in the transaction.

4. General Rules. Rules 501 through 503 provide certain definitions and general conditions applicable to all Regulation D offerings, including without limitation the following:

   a. "Accredited Investor". The Rule 505 exemption for offerings up to $5,000,000 and the Rule 506 exemption are limited to offerings in which there are no more than 35 purchasers. However, the "accredited investor" is one of the categories of persons who need not be included in the count of purchasers. The term "Accredited Investor" means persons or entities that are not counted towards limitations on the number of purchasers, and includes generally: (i) banks and savings and loan associations and similar institutions such as credit unions, whether acting for their own account or as fiduciaries; any broker or dealer registered under Section 15 of the Exchange Act; insurance companies; investment companies registered under the Investment Company Act of 1940; business development companies as defined under Section 2(a)(48) of the Investment Company Act of 1940; Small Business Investment Companies; employee benefit plans (within the meaning of ERISA), provided that either (a) the investment decision must be made by a plan fiduciary which is a bank, a savings and loan association, an insurance company, or a registered investment adviser, or (b) the employee benefit plan must have total assets of more than $5,000,000, or (c) the employee benefit plan must be a self-directed plan and the investment decisions are made solely by persons that are accredited investors; (ii) any private business development company as defined under Section 202(a)(22) of the Investment Advisers Act of 1940; (iii) tax-exempt organizations, exempt under Section 501(c)(3) of the Internal Revenue Code, corporations, Massachusetts or similar business trusts and partnerships, not formed for the specific purpose of acquiring the securities offered, with total assets of more than $5,000,000; (iv) directors, executive officers, and general partners of the issuer, or any director, executive officer, or general partner of a general partner of the issuer; (v) any natural person whose individual net worth or joint net worth of that person and their spouse at the time of the purchase exceeds $1,000,000; (vi) any natural person who has an individual income in excess of $200,000 in each of the two most recent years or joint income with that person's spouse in excess of $300,000 in each of these years and who reasonably expects an income of at least such minimum amount in the current year; (vii) trusts having total assets of more than $5,000,000, not formed for the specific purpose of acquiring the securities offered, if the purchase is directed by a sophisticated person; and (viii) any entity in which all of the equity owners are accredited investors as provided above.

b. Limitation on the Manner of Offering. Except as provided for certain Rule 504 offerings, neither the issuer or any person acting on its behalf may make any offers as sales of securities by any form of general solicitation or general advertising, including, without limitation, any advertisement, article, notice, or other communication published in newspaper, magazine or similar media or broadcast over television or radio. However, seminars or meetings discussing the offering are allowed, so long as those attendees have not been invited by any general solicitation or general advertising. The practical impact of this provision is that the issuer must control the number and kind of offerees so as to show that no general solicitation existed.

c. Required Disclosure of Information. Required disclosure of information varies depending upon the size and nature of the offering. There is no specific information requirement if the securities are sold under Rule 504 (which relates to offerings up to $1,000,000) by companies not subject to Exchange Act reporting requirements; in addition, there is no specified information requirement if the securities are sold only to "accredited investors."

The issuer must furnish the prescribed information to all purchasers during the course of the offering and prior to sale: if securities are sold under sold under Rule 505 or Rule 506 to <u>any</u> purchaser who is not an accredited "investor" (Rule 505 pertains to offerings up to $5,000,000, while Rule 506 pertains to limited offerings not subject to a specific dollar limit).

The type of information required to be furnished to purchasers varies depending on whether the issuer is subject to the reporting requirements of Section 13 or 15(d) of the Exchange Act. Effective April 11, 1988, persons making offering up to $2,000,000 must provide the kind of information that would be required in Part II of Form 1-A, except that the issuer's balance sheet, which must be dated within 120 days of the beginning of the offering, is to be audited; for offerings up to $7,500,000, the issuer must provide the same kind of information as required in Part I of Form S-18; and for offerings of more than $7,500,000, the issuer must provide the same kind of information as would be required in Part I of a registration statement that the issuer would be entitled to use.

If the issuers are subject to the Exchange Act reporting requirements, they have a choice as to the manner of satisfying some of the information requirements. The information required includes certain publicly available information or filings under the Exchange Act or the Securities Act, as well as certain additional mandatory information including a brief description of the securities being offered, the use of the proceeds of the offering, and any material changes in the issuer's affairs that are not disclosed in the documents furnished.

In addition, SEC Rule 10b-5 and other anti-fraud rules and statutes require the disclosure of material information about the securities being offered.

d. Limitation on Resale. Generally, securities acquired in a transaction under Regulation D will be deemed "restricted", and cannot be resold without registration under the Act or an exemption therefrom. Securities issued under Regulation D or under Section 4(2) should contain a legend to the effect that they have not been registered under the Act and may not be sold absent such registration or an opinion of counsel that such registration is not required.

e. Filing of Notice of Sales. Any issuer making a Regulation D offering must file with the SEC five copies of notice on Form D.

f. Non-Exclusive Nature of Regulation D Exemptions. The foregoing is only a brief summary of certain selected provisions of Regulation D, and a thorough discussion of the Regulation D exemptions is beyond the scope of this outline. However, it is important to note that any attempted compliance with a Regulation D exemption does not act as an exclusive election, as the issuer can also attempt to use other exemptions. However, it is advisable for issuers to attempt to follow most of the requirements of the Rule 506 exemption even if they intend to make a private placement "outside the Rule" and rely only on Section 4(2), which is the statutory "private placement exemption".

F. Investment Liquidity; Resale of Securities Received In A Private Placement. As discussed above, one of the most important considerations to any investor in a leveraged buyout is the ability to liquidate his investment. Since securities which are received in a private placement or other non-public transaction with an issuer or its affiliate are "restricted", they can only be resold under certain conditions. Section 5 of the Act requires that all non-exempt sales of securities be registered under the Act. Generally speaking, the only exemption that may be available to an investor is the Section 4(1) exemption which exempts sales by persons who are not "an issuer, underwriter or dealer" of the securities being offered. This exemption has caused considerable debate since its adoption, and in order to clarify its meaning the Securities and Exchange Commission in 1972 adopted Rule 144, which establishes objective criteria for determining whether or not a person may resell "restricted securities", which are securities acquired directly or indirectly from the issuer in a transaction or chain of transactions not involving a registered public offering. Rule 144 is a safe harbor provision, and was not intended as the exclusive interpretation of Section 4(1). Accordingly, it is possible to make a privately negotiated resale of securities "outside the rule" under the Section "4(1-1/2)". Although the intricacy of Rule 144 and the Section "4(1-1/2)" exemption are beyond the scope of this outline, certain aspects relating to them are discussed briefly below.

1. Rule 144. Rule 144 imposes the following requirements for the sale of restricted securities by a non-affiliate of the issuer:

   (a) Rule 144 is generally available only for securities of a public company, since the rule generally requires that adequate public information concerning the issuer be available through current filings with the Securities and Exchange Commission under Section 13(a) of the Exchange Act of Section 15d of the Act, as the case may be.

   (b) The seller must have held the shares to be sold under Rule 144 for at least two years, after giving effect to certain "tacking" provisions and "tolling" provisions.

   (c) There are volume restrictions, which limit the number of shares to be sold by such non-affiliate, together with all other sales of restricted securities for the account of such persons within the preceding three months, to the greater of 1% of the outstanding shares of that class or the average weekly trading volume in the class of securities to be sold during the preceding four full calendar weeks if the shares to be sold have been held by the seller for less than three years.

(d) The sales of the shares must be made via "broker's transactions" or to a bona fide market maker of the shares if the seller has held the subject shares for less than three years.

(e) The seller, prior to the execution of the sale, must file with the Securities and Exchange Commission a notice of sale on Form 144, unless he is a non-affiliate who has held his shares for at least three years.

An affiliate of the issuer seeking to rely on Rule 144 must comply with all of the requirements of Rule 144 including the notice, volume and manner of sale requirements, irrespective of his holding period. However, an affiliate need not comply with the holding period requirement with respect to shares which are not "restricted securities."

Because of the intricacies of Rule 144, it is important to discuss certain points relating to potential sales under Rule 144 at the time the investment is made, and to obtain written agreements on some of the more obvious issues.

2. <u>Section "4(1-1/2)" Exemption for Private Resales of "Restricted Securities"</u>. The Securities and Exchange Commission, in no action letters and other pronouncements, has frequently required that private resales of restricted securities meet at least some of the established criteria for exemptions under both Section 4(1) and Section 4(2) of the Act. The requirements of Section 4(1), for sales other than under Rule 144, are not easily determined, and generally require an opinion of counsel in order to effectuate the resale of restrictied securities in reliance upon the exemption. Perhaps the biggest difference between sales "outside the rule" under Section 4(1) and those in reliance upon Rule 144 is that the public information requirement under Rule 144 is not a condition to the availability of the exemption under Section 4(1). However, there is a certain degree of risk in relying upon the Section 4(1) exemption in the absence of public information regarding the issuer. The real problem becomes whether or not counsel for the issuer and counsel for the seller can reach an understanding as to the availability of the

exemption. While Rule 144 generally presumes the availability of a public market for the issuer's securities, Section 4(1) of the Act is designed to accommodate both public and private resales, with the requirements for private resale being a sometimes confusing and nebulous set of guidelines. In 1979 a committee of the American Bar Association published a position paper with respect to private resales of restricted securities. Although a thorough discussion of the 4(1) exemption outside of Rule 144 is beyond the scope of this outline, as a broad generalization the following statements may provide some guidance as to the requirements of the exemption:

(a) A shareholder will be unable to claim an exemption under Section 4(1) if the holder is deemed to have purchased from the issuer "with a view to distribution", sold for the issuer in connection with a distribution, or participated in a distribution by the issuer. In order to avoid one or more of these inferences, the selling shareholder must be able to prove that his or its resales do not represent a further step in the issuer's distributive process. In other words, a selling shareholder who wishes to rely on the 4(1) exemption must establish that his or its securities have "come to rest" in his or its hands, therefore, any resale constitutes a separate transaction from the offering of securities by the issuer, or the selling shareholder must make his or its sale in a transaction similar to a "private offering". For purposes of this discussion, certain guidelines or "rules of thumb" will be suggested for sales before the securities "come to rest" and for sales after the securities "come to rest", as follows:

(1) Resales Before Securities Come to Rest. As a rule of thumb, any sale by a holder prior to holding the shares for a period of three years must be made in a "negotiated private transaction" in which sales are limited to persons who would have qualified for participation in a private offering by the issuer under the Section 4(2) "private placement exemption". Accordingly, the

selling shareholder must sell to one or a limited number of purchasers, without public solicitation, provided that the purchaser (or each of the purchasers) has, either alone or with his advisors, the ability to evaluate the risks of the investment, and is provided with access to the kind of information that would be required of the issuer in a registration under the Act.

(2) Resales After Securities Come to Rest. As a rule of thumb, if a selling shareholder has held its stock for a period of three years or more, this stock can be sold without fear of having the sale viewed as a part of the issuer's stock offering. However, it is important to note that after three years the stock could also be sold by a non-affiliate under Rule 144(k) without limitation on the volume of securities sold.

G. State Securities Law. Virtually every state provides statutes, rules, and regulations regarding transactions in equity securities. Such laws in most instances are similar in nature to federal securities law; however, the individual state securities act should be reviewed in connection with transactions involving securities within that state.

Registration under the state securities acts generally follows the scheme of the federal securities law in that registration is required but certain transactions or securities may be exempt from registration. In addition, many states provide that registration may be taken by coordination with registration under the Act, by notification where the characteristics of the offeror indicate that registration is unnecessary, or by qualification, which requires submission of information to a much lesser degree than would be required were registration under the state securities law undertaken. The exemption scheme of the state securities act varies from state to state; however, many of the exemptions from registration which are granted by state statute are similar to the federal securities law and many of the states have adopted regulations similar to Regulation D promulgated under the 1933 Act.

XI. Conflicts of Interest; Fiduciary Duties of Directors.

A. Conflicts of Interest in Buyout of Subsidiary or Division by Management. Many conglomerates are in the process of divesting themselves of certain of their subsidiaries or divisions which do not fit within their corporate plan. This presents an opportunity for management of such subsidiaries or divisions to buyout their division or subsidiary. Such a buyout presents inherent conflicts of interest, since the management of the division or the subsidiary is inherently familiar with the operations thereof and is most likely able to bargain with knowledge that is unknown to the parent. Such conflicts of interest must be considered by all parties to the buyout transaction.

B. Conflicts of Interest in Buyouts of Public Companies. The primary question in the nature of a conflict of interest which is raised by the leveraged buyout of a public company is whether the public shareholders are having their interests in the public company bought out at a fair price. This question arises from the fact that the company's own assets will substantially provide the financing to purchase the company. In order to be a "fair price", the price must be capable of proving itself in the market place, i.e., once the company is priced by management, any other company can compete with a higher bid if it is interested in purchasing the assets (or stock, in a "going private" transaction). In fact, competitive third party bids have frequently occurred. Other conflicts in the purchase of a public company via an asset transaction include the generation of immediate tax consequences to the public holders since they generally tender their shares for cash, while the insiders may under certain circumstances defer tax consequences. In a merger transaction, a conflict may arise if the insiders will be participating in the equity of the purchasing corporation beyond the customary limits of management participation, or will be receiving long term employment contracts.

C. Techniques to Mitigate the Impact of Conflicts of Interest. In order to mitigate or resolve the conflicts of interest referred to above, there are several possible techniques which may be utilized, all of which are designed to establish an arms-length bargaining procedure or to otherwise show that the potential conflicts have been resolved in an arms-length manner which is fair to the persons potentially injured by the conflict of interest. Some of these techniques are: obtaining an investment banking opinion as to the fairness of a particular transaction, or as to fairness of a price for the acquisition of a public company; obtaining approval of a committee of disinterested directors negotiating on behalf of the minority shareholders; requiring a "super majority" shareholder approval, such as seventy-five percent (75%) or eighty percent (80%) of all shares outstanding entitled to vote; full disclosure of the transactions in the proxy statement or any other documents filed with the Securities and Exchange Commission or others; and use of an outside independent counsel and independent investment banker to assist in structuring, negotiating, and effectuating the transaction.

XII. Leveraged Buyout by ESOP.

A. ESOP as a Vehicle for Financing. An employee stock ownership plan ("ESOP") may play an integral role in financing, in whole or in part, a leveraged buyout of a public or private corporation, or a leveraged buyout of a subsidiary or division of a larger corporation. A leveraged ESOP may be of particular value in financing a leveraged buyout of a company or division of a company which has lost competitiveness primarily because of high labor costs. In a leveraged buyout by an ESOP, the ESOP obtains financing from a lender to enable it to acquire the target. The company which has formed the ESOP makes contributions to the ESOP to fund the ESOP's payments of principal and interest. Qualified lenders may exclude 50% of the interest from gross income for federal income tax purposes.

B. Special Considerations of Leveraged ESOP's. Special limitations pursuant to the Code and the Employee Retirement Income Security Act of 1974 ("ERISA") are applicable with respect to a leveraged buyout by an ESOP. Subject to certain legal limitations, the employer will contribute cash annually to the ESOP in an amount sufficient to amortize the principal and interest on the ESOP loan. The primary advantages of ESOP participation are (1) under federal income tax law, use of the ESOP in effect permits a repayment of both principal and interest on the ESOP debt to be made on a tax deductible basis, and (2) because the employees of such an enterprise will possess a significant equity interest and, thus, share in the potential risks and rewards of the acquired enterprise, the transfer of a substantial economic stake in a going enterprise to employees through a leveraged acquisition by an ESOP may be accompanied by wage concessions and increased productivity, thereby substantially increasing the competitiveness of the acquired business. A myriad of advantages apply in the sale of a closely-held company, such as (i) tax deferral opportunities to selling shareholders, (ii) estate tax advantages, and (iii) liquidity for otherwise illiquid securities. Possible disadvantages of the leveraged buyout by an ESOP include: (i) risk of fiduciary liability and employee morale problems if the value of the stock declines; and (ii) substantial dilution to existing shareholders if newly issued stock is contributed to the trust.

C. Fraudulent Conveyance Concerns in Leveraged Buyouts by ESOPs. In a leveraged buyout transaction, the security interest or guaranty granted by the employer with respect to the ESOP loan can be defeated by Bankruptcy Code § 548, Uniform Fraudulent Conveyance Act §§ 354 and 355, and applicable state fraudulent transfer law. Accordingly, special care must be taken in structuring an ESOP loan used to finance a leveraged buyout.

When a lender makes a direct loan to an ESOP, it typically requires the employer to either grant a security interest in its assets or to guarantee the loan. However, if the loan proceeds are used to purchase employer stock from parties other than the employer itself, it appears that the employer receives nothing in exchange for the security interest or guaranty. If, in addition, the transaction leaves the employer insolvent or lacking capital or with debts beyond its ability to pay as they mature, the security interest or guaranty may be voided as a fraudulent conveyance. The risk of a fraudulent conveyance in an LBO utilizing an ESOP can frequently be reduced by using a "back-to-back" or "mirror" loan structure whereby a loan is made directly to the employer, which lends the proceeds to the ESOP.

In light of the fraudulent conveyance risk, as well as increased scrutiny of ESOP-financed buyouts by the Internal Revenue Service and the Department of Labor, each party to the transaction should obtain independent counsel and separate appraisals of the employer company, including separate solvency letters or opinions. Legal opinions should also be obtained relating to the structure of the transaction and the enforceability of the transaction documents. Further, a lender cannot be certain under existing statutes and case law which approach in valuing assets and liabilities would be used by a court which subsequently applied any of the financial condition tests relating to solvency, etc. under a fraudulent conveyance analysis. Financial statements are sometimes restated using "pushdown accounting" in accordance with APB 16 after giving effect to the ESOP - financed buyout. An accountant's opinion that such restatement is permissible under generally accepted accounting principles should be obtained.

XIII. Special Considerations of the Buyer.

There are many special considerations of the Buyer which may be applicable in leveraged buyouts, in addition to those discussed above. Among a few of these are ERISA (applicable to qualified pension and profit sharing plans) and the Hart-Scott-Rodino Act (anti-trust law). As discussed above, the buyer is also particularly concerned about identifying those liabilities to be assumed, and in protecting against "hidden" liabilities (undisclosed, unknown, or contingent liabilities), and is also particularly concerned about the assignability of key contracts, leases, or franchises. Furthermore, the "Buyer" may technically be Newco, but the real parties or principals to the transaction from the acquirer's side are generally a management group and a promoter or sponsor, and its group of investors. Each of these types of investors has certain special concerns, some of which are discussed briefly below, along with certain issues under the Hart-Scott-Rodino Act.

A. Concerns of Members of Management in Their Role as LBO Equity Investors.

The role of management in the acquisition of a target and its relationship to the sponsor or promoter will vary widely depending on a number of factors, including the size of the company being acquired, the purchase price, the amount of equity being provided by management, and the perceived strength and ability of management. Although management may control the acquisition of a company in an LBO situation, it is more typical for management to have an important, but not a controlling role in the company after the closing of the transaction. It is important for management to have a significant ownership role in any LBO transaction, because (i) equity ownership by management acts as an inducement to obtain bank and investor financing, by providing an indication that the insiders are willing to invest their own money, (ii) the investment acts as an effective incentive for management to devote its efforts to running the company on behalf of all shareholders after the LBO, and (iii) a significant equity investment serves as a strong incentive for the continuing involvement and employment of management by the company, in that their efforts will help protect and enhance their own personal investment. Some of the significant issues that relate to the involvement of management in the LBO as equity participants are briefly discussed below.

1. Percentage of Management's Ownership. Management's equity participation will typically range from as little as 5% to as much as 25% of the outstanding voting stock on a fully diluted basis. Generally, the management participants (which are typically a group of key senior managers) will hold common stock in the newly-formed holding company, and this ownership will be shared with the sponsor and other investors. Ownership may also be shared by virtue of warrants issued to lenders or their affiliates. See "Financing--Participants and Structure-Warrants" above. Management may sometimes have "incentive shares" which are shares that may be purchased or earned by management upon the achievement of certain "milestones" or goals for performance set by the board of directors of the company.

2. Purchase Price for Management Shares. Occasionally the shares of the newly-formed holding company or "Newco" are sold to management at a discount from the price paid by the other equity investors. However, the typical arrangement is for the promoter or sponsor, management, and other equity investors to pay the same price for their shares of Newco stock. Generally, management will make an election under Section 83(b) of the Internal Revenue Code of 1986 with respect to restricted stock to be received in the transaction. In some cases, the company may arrange for bank loans to the managers, or may provide bonuses or loans from the company to finance most or all of the purchase price for Newco stock.

3. Shareholder Agreements Restricting Transferability of Management Shares. In order to provide appropriate incentives to management and insure

that "outsiders" do not become shareholders through purchases of stock from management, it is typical for the management and the other equity investors to enter into a shareholders agreement restricting share transfers by management. Typical arrangements allow certain types of transfers, such as transfers upon death, gifts to certain family members or trusts for tax or estate planning purposes, and pledges of stock to a bank financing the acquisition of the management shares. After some period of time, generally five to ten years, the outright prohibition on transfer may give way to some form of right of first refusal to Newco and the other shareholders. Frequently, the restrictions on transfer are terminated entirely if Newco is taken public.

4. Voting and Election of Directors. Depending upon the circumstances, voting control of Newco may be vested in the sponsors pursuant to the terms of the shareholder agreement. If the equity participation of management is relatively large, it may be appropriate for the shareholder agreement among the shareholders to deal with the composition of the board of directors and voting on certain key issues, with the management group and the sponsors each nominating a specified number of directors to the board.

5. Puts and Calls on Management Stock. Newco will frequently have a call right pursuant to which Newco may purchase the stock of any member of the management group whenever the management group member ceases to be employed by Newco or its subsidiaries. This concept is a type of "golden handcuff" which ties the investment of management to the continued employment with Newco. The price under the call option is frequently based upon a formula which relates to the level of Newco's book value or fair market value at the time of the termination of employment of the member of the management group. This type of call option may be structured so as to allow a concept of "vesting" so that the call right may not be applicable to all terminations, depending upon the number of years of management's service and the circumstances surrounding the termination. Bank loan agreements and other financing documents must be structured to minimize any restrictions on repurchases of the stock of Newco owned by

management. In some LBO transactions, management will be able to put the stock back to Newco at a formula price upon certain terminations of employment.

6. Employment Contracts. In some instances, the LBO management investor will enter into an employment contract with Newco, in order to protect his status as an employee. In addition, lenders sometimes will require contracts for key managers as a condition to their providing funds for the acquisition.

B. Special Concerns of the LBO Sponsor or Promoter.

1. Agreement Concerning Sponsor's Expenses. Because lining up the financing and negotiation of an LBO acquisition is extremely time consuming, and expensive due to accountants' and attorneys' fees and financing commitment fees, many sponsors will not begin to seek commitments for financing without some formal agreement with respect to the sponsor's expenses. The sponsors and management in an LBO transaction will frequently be under strong pressure from the target company to produce evidence of the sponsor's and management's ability to close the deal quickly, and may be requested or required to provide firm commitment letters from banks and other financing sources, which are generally expensive in terms of commitment fees and other up-front fees. As a result of the concerns about expenses incurred by the sponsor, the sponsor will generally seek to have the company agree to pay legal and accounting fees, although the target company will often seek to put a cap on the maximum dollar amount of expenses that it will pay, and may seek to be relieved from its responsibilities to make such reimbursements if the buyout group fails to meet certain conditions, such as arrangement of financing by a specified date.

2. "Break-Up" Fees. In addition to the reimbursement of expenses, the promoter will want to be paid a "break-up fee" for its efforts in the event that the proposed LBO transaction does not close. The break-up fee is generally a fixed fee based on the dollar size of the transaction. Generally, the break-up fee is conditioned upon the termination of the proposed leveraged buyout transaction for

reasons which are not the fault of the buyout group.

3. "Best Efforts" to Obtain Financing. The sponsor will generally require that its obligations be subject to a financing condition, since the definitive financing agreements or binding commitments for financing will generally not exist at the time the acquisition agreement is executed. In addition, the financing agreements almost always contain significant conditions to funding, which pose significant contingencies to closing of the acquisition financing. However, the credibility of the buyout group, and the credibility of its bid for the target will be considerably stronger to the extent that it has obtained either financing commitments from banks or other financial institutions, or a "highly confident letter" from a reputable investment banking firm that financing will be capable of being obtained. In any event, because of the uncertainties surrounding the ability to complete the financing of any LBO transaction, obligations of the sponsors or promoters to raise the financing should be on a "best efforts" basis only, so that any failure to complete the financing will not constitute a breach of its agreement.

C. Hart-Scott-Rodino Act.

In the typical leveraged buyout transaction, Newco will be a corporation organized for the specific purpose of making the acquisition of the target company. The provisions of Hart-Scott-Rodino should not apply to the leveraged acquisition by the newly-formed buyer unless that buyer has an ultimate parent (who is the owner of more than 50% of the voting securities of Newco) which meets the threshhold size test. The "size-of-person" test set forth in Section 18a(a) of the Hart-Scott-Rodino Act states that the notification required to be filed with the FTC and the Justice Department is required only if voting securities or assets of a person with annual net sales or total assets or \$10,000,000 or more are being acquired by a person with total assets of \$100,000,000 or more, or voting securities or assets of a person with annual net sales of \$100,000,000 or more being acquired by any person with total assets or annual net sales of \$10,000,000 or more.

1. Exemption for LBO by Newly-Organized Acquisition Company. Since, prior to the consummation of the LBO, Newco has virtually no assets, and no net sales, a "recent" balance sheet may show that it does not meet the size test. Rule 801.11(e) promulgated by the FTC under the Hart-Scott-Rodino Act directs that an acquiring person without a balance sheet need not include, in determining its size, any cash used by the acquiring person as consideration for the acquisition of assets or voting securities of the acquired person, and any cash used for expenses incidental to the acquisition. Accordingly, Newco may exclude from its assets for determining whether the size test is met, the funds which are used to effect the acquisition.

2. Exemption for Formation of Newco. Another consideration is whether the formation of Newco triggers a "joint venture" notification filing under Hart-Scott-Rodino, pursuant to the joint venture rules. Under Section 18a(a)(3), a notification filing is required if as a result of an acquisition the acquiring person would hold 15% or more of the voting securities or assets of the acquired person, or an aggregate total amount of voting securities and assets of the person in excess of $15,000,000. In appropriate instances, Newco may rely upon an exemption from the Act's coverage under Rule 802.20 of the FTC rules. Rule 802.20 provides a "minimum dollar value" exemption if: (i) the stock acquired does not exceed $15,000,000 in value; and (ii) does not confer upon the acquiring person "control" over an entity with annual net sales or total assets of $25,000,000 or more.

XIV. Conclusion.

This outline touches on only some of the many legal, tax and securities implications of leveraged buyouts. In particular, the negotiation, form and substance of the representations, warranties, and covenants contained in the asset acquisition agreement, stock purchase agreement, or merger agreement are not discussed in this outline. However, as can be seen from this outline, leveraged buyouts entail many legal considerations and the necessity of legal counsel cannot be overemphasized. Early involvement of legal counsel should help to avoid many of the pitfalls which may entrap the unwary person undertaking a leveraged buyout.

Such involvement by legal counsel enhances the planning aspects and helps a buyer, seller, lender, or investor to become more knowledgeable and make more intelligent decisions with respect to a leveraged buyout transaction.

Exhibit 1

EXAMPLE OF LEVERAGED BUYOUT
USING ASSET ACQUISITION

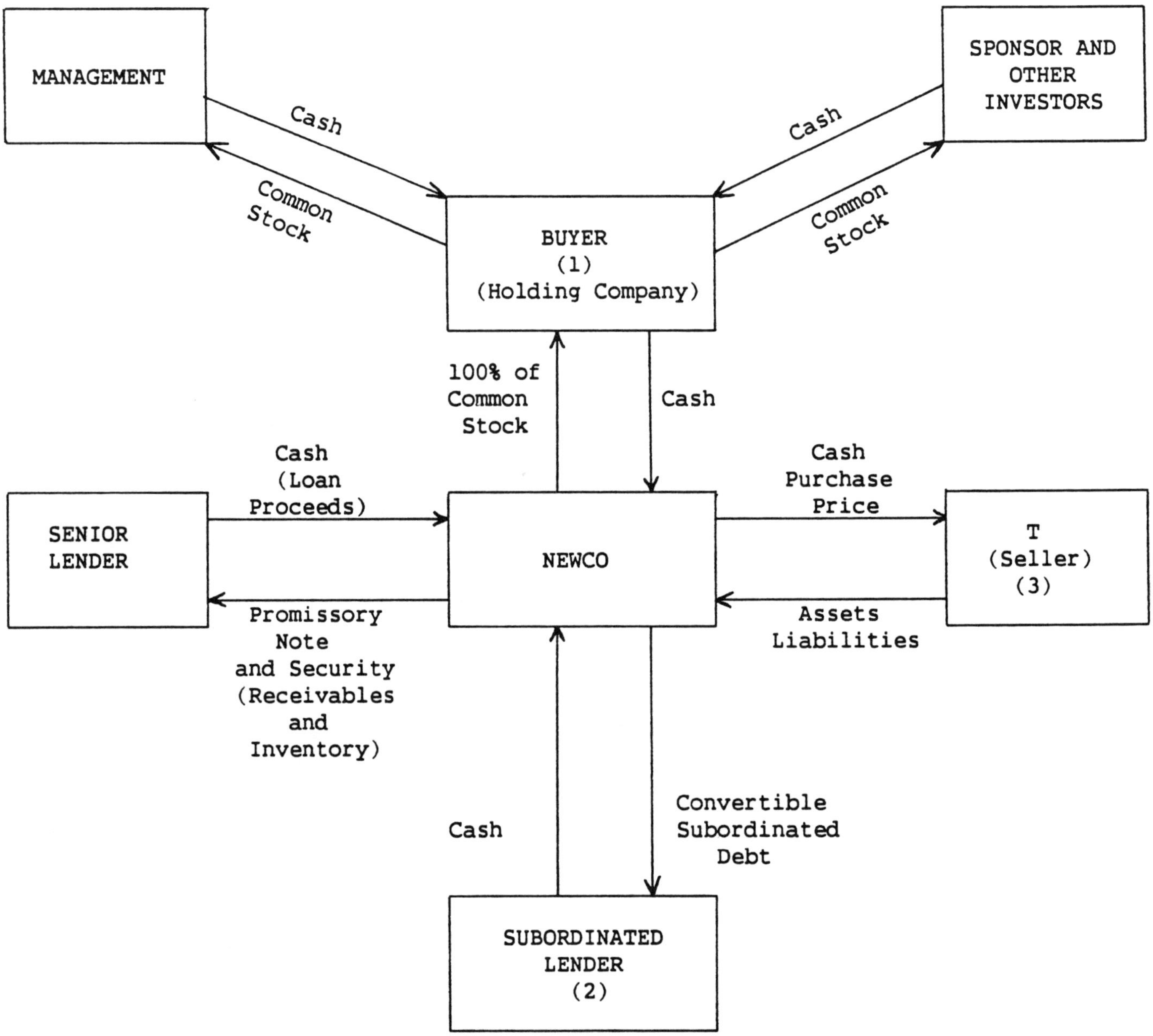

1. Small infusion of cash, usually not more than 5-10% of capitalization is made by Buyer (which is frequently a holding company formed by management, a sponsor, and other investors).

2. Convertible subordinated debt is purchased by the Subordinated Lender.

3. Target sells assets, and Newco assumes only those liabilities, if any, specifically agreed on in the asset purchase agreement. Target now has cash as its assets, and may completely liquidate and distribute cash to its shareholders, use the cash to enter a new business, or become a mutual fund.

<u>Exhibit 2</u>

EXAMPLE OF LEVERAGED BUYOUT
USING STOCK ACQUISITION

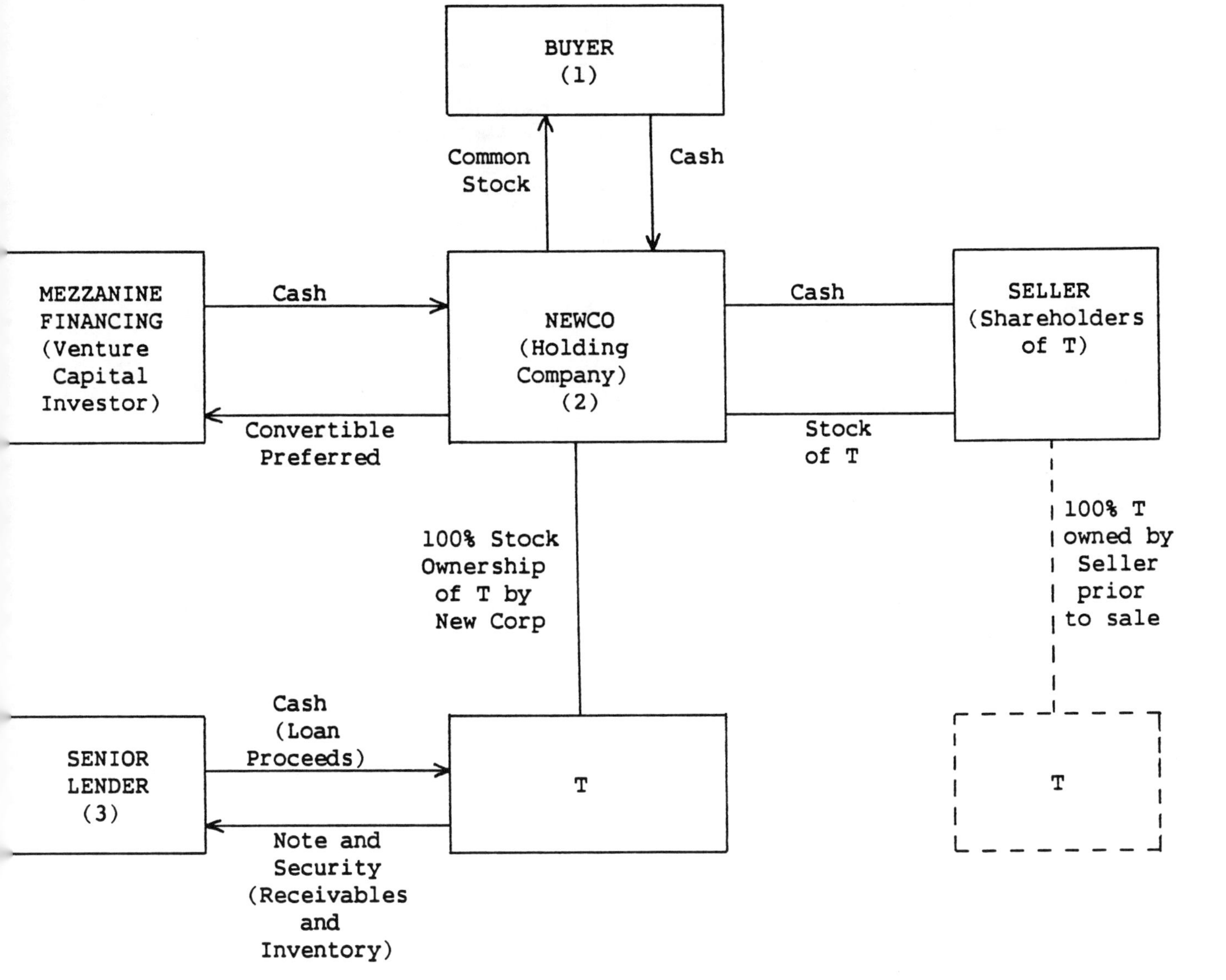

- "Buyer" is frequently a management group, a sponsor or promoter, and other investors. Newco is capitalized with common and preferred stock.

- Newco pays cash to the shareholders of T, and 100% of the stock of T is transferred to Newco, making T a wholly-owned subsidiary of Newco.

- Senior Lender loans to T, secured by accounts receivable and inventory. T may use the proceeds partly as a dividend or advance to Newco, to pay intercompany debt to Seller, to pay existing bank debt of T, or for working capital.

Exhibit 3

EXAMPLE OF LEVERAGED BUYOUT
USING CASH MERGER (TRIANGULAR

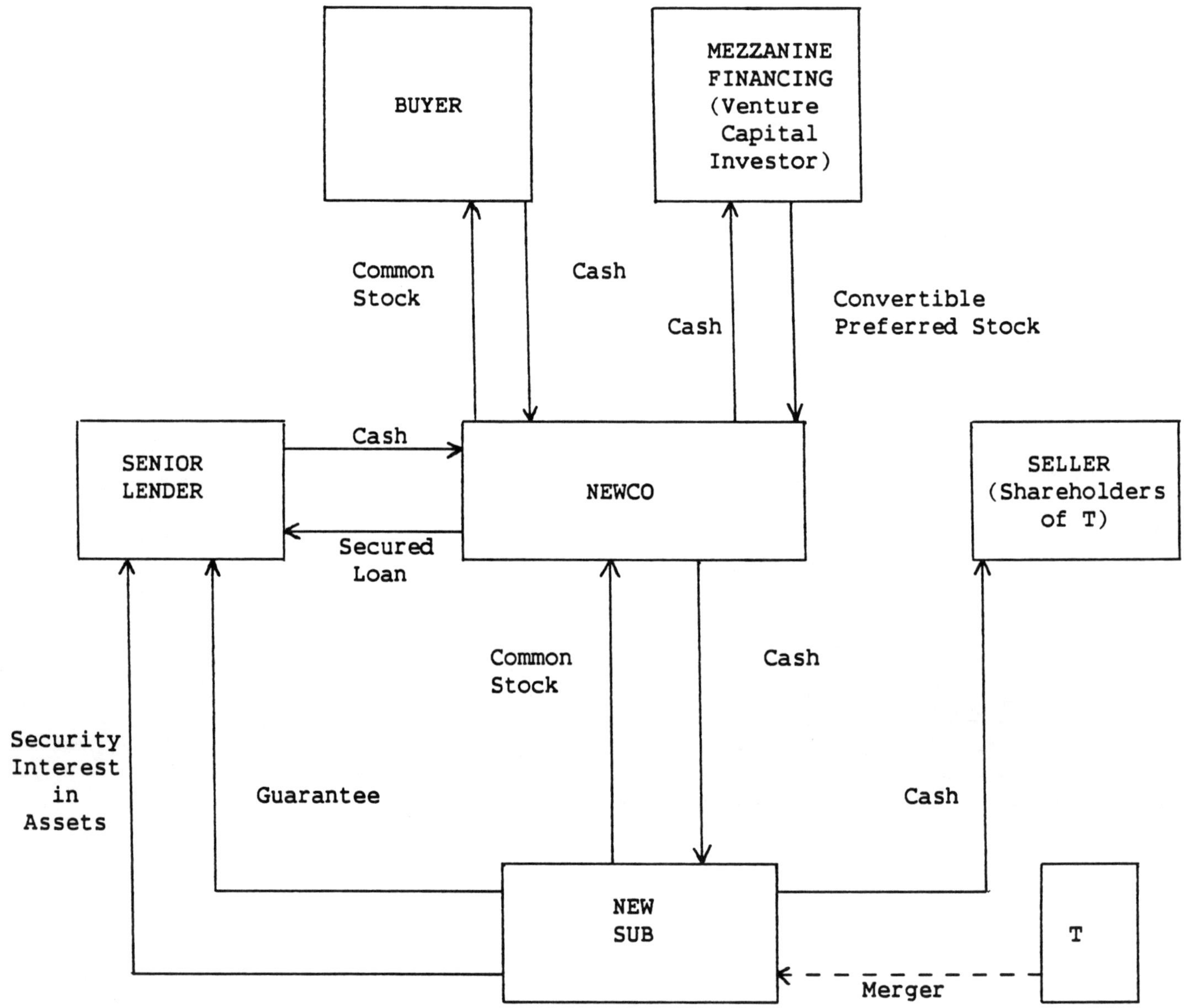

Exhibit 4

STEPS IN A STOCK TRANSACTION
USING A DEMAND NOTE STRUCTURE

Step 1--Purchase of Stock in Exchange for Demand Note and Subordinated Seller Note

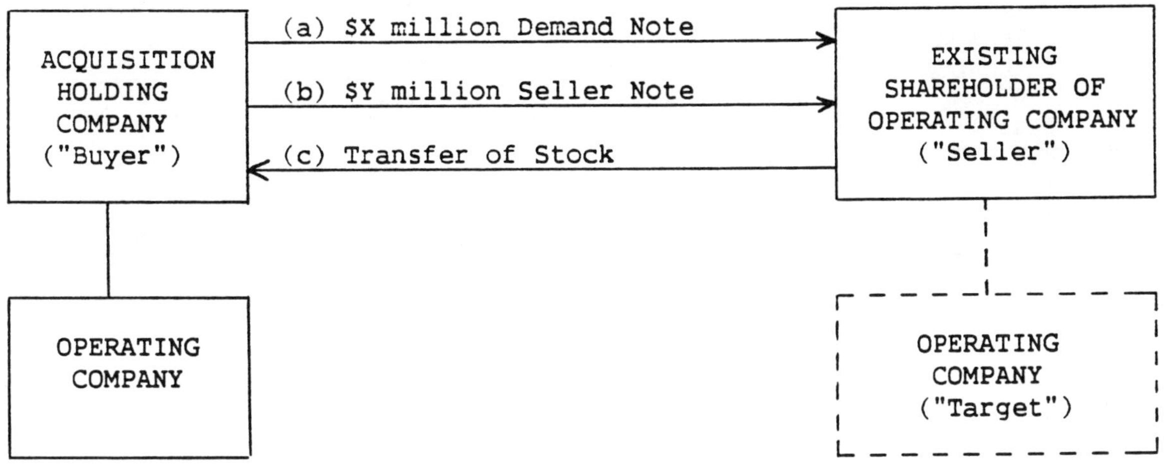

STEPS IN THE TRANSACTION (all occur concurrently)

1. Buyer (a) issues an $X million demand note, payable to the order of Seller, and (b) issues a $Y million subordinated Seller Note, payable to the order of Seller, in payment of the full amount of the purchase price for all of the outstanding common stock of the Operating Company, based on the purchase price, as defined in the stock purchase agreement, and secured by a security interest in the stock being acquired. (c) Seller transfers to Buyer all of the outstanding common stock of the Operating Company, thereby making the Operating Company a wholly-owned subsidiary of Buyer.

Exhibit 4

Step 2--Loans to Operating Company

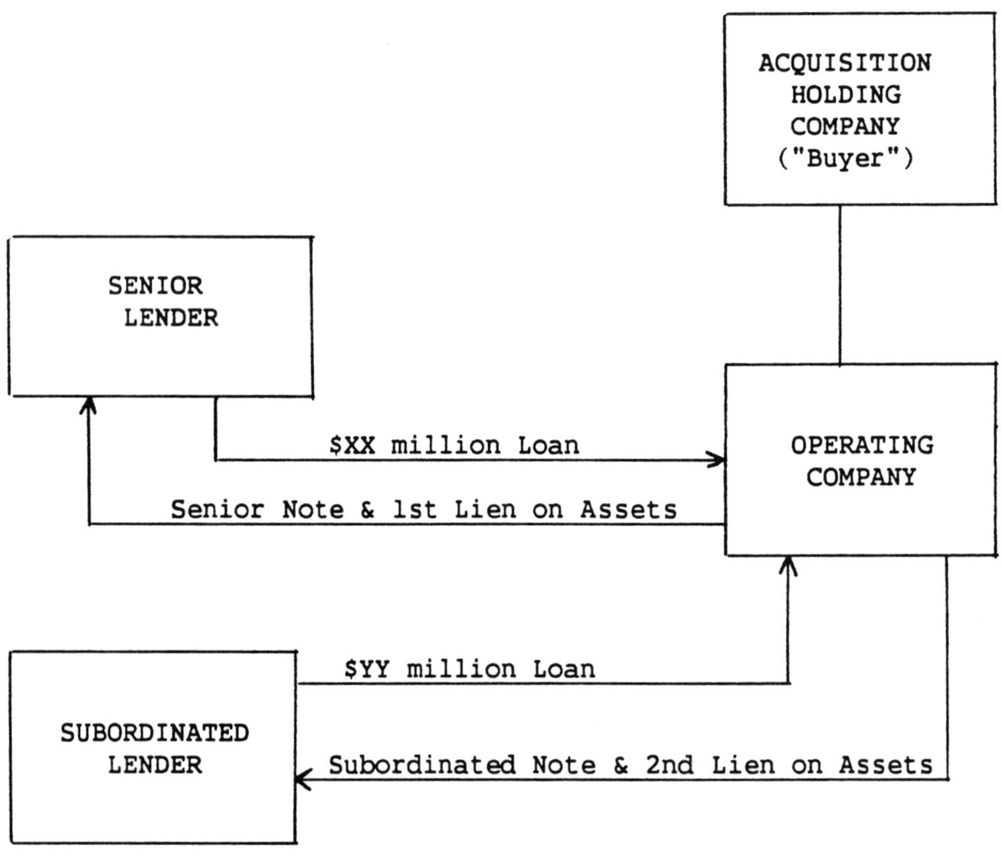

2. Senior lender loans $XX million to the Operating Company, pursuant to a senior loan, secured by a first lien on all assets of the Operating Company. Subordinated lender loans $YY million to the Operating Company, secured by a second lien on all of the Operating Company assets.

Exhibit 4

Step 3--Use of Loan Proceeds to Repay Demand Note and Intercompany Debt

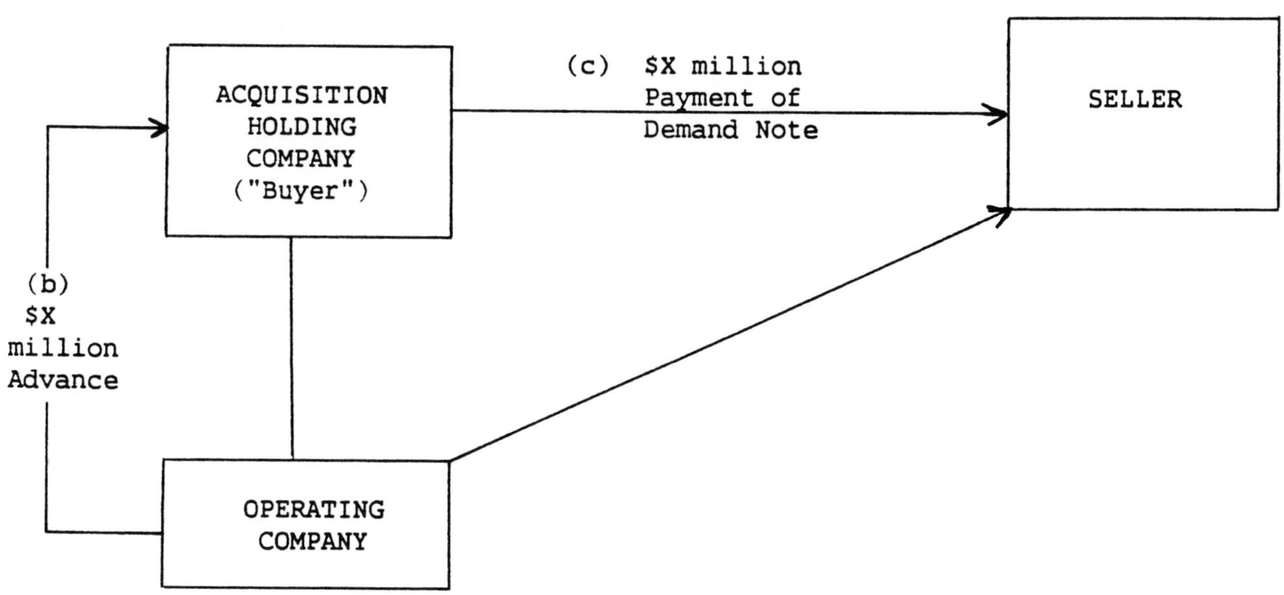

3. Operating Company uses the loan proceeds from the senior and subordinated loans as follows: (a) to repay $AA million of intercompany advances owed to Seller; and (b) to make an $X million advance to the Buyer. (c) The Buyer then uses the proceeds of the advance from the Operating Company to pay the $X million demand note to Seller.

Exhibit 1

EXAMPLE OF LEVERAGED BUYOUT
USING ASSET ACQUISITION

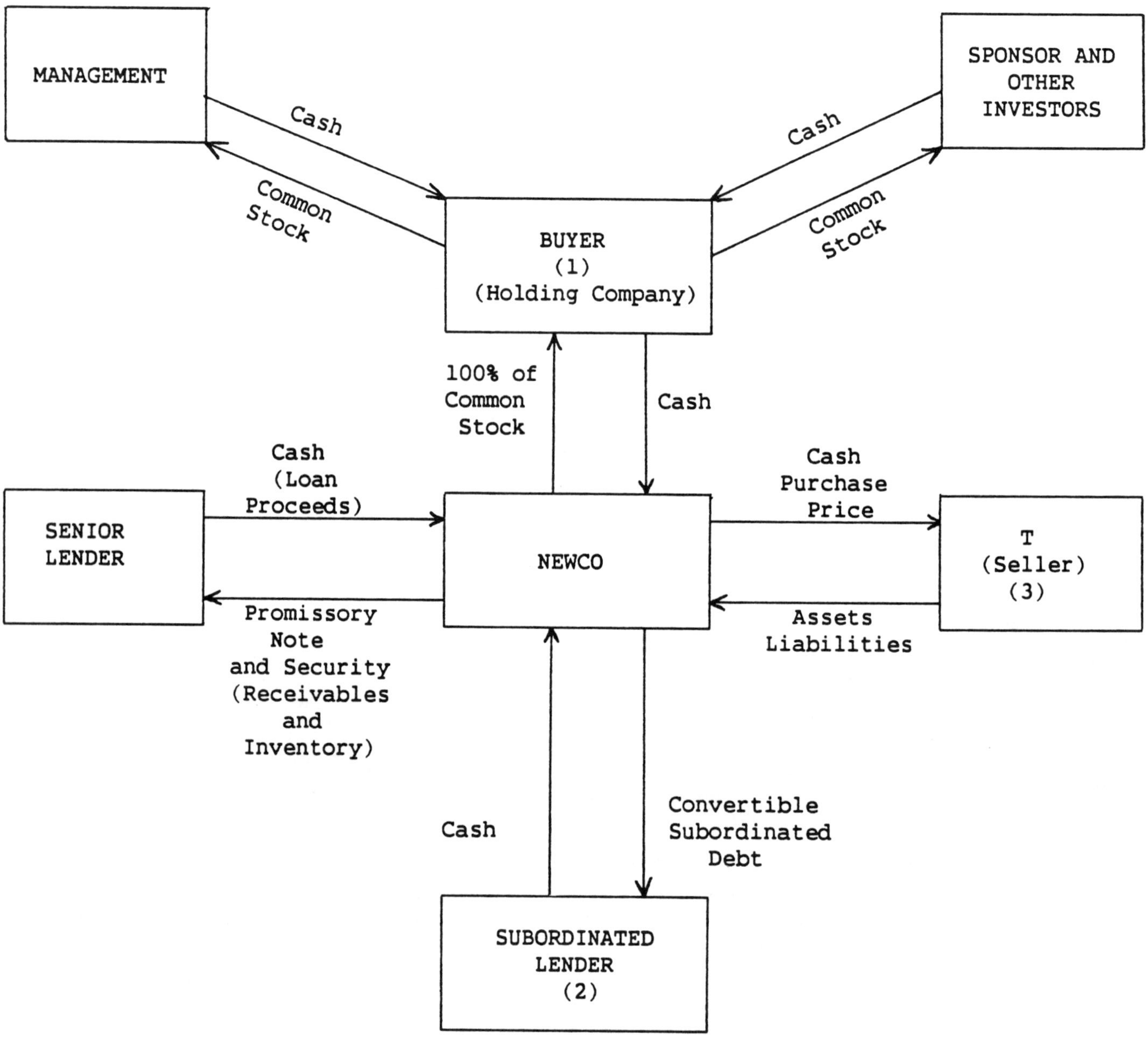

1. Small infusion of cash, usually not more than 5-10% of capitalization is made by Buyer (which is frequently a holding company formed by management, a sponsor, and other investors).

2. Convertible subordinated debt is purchased by the Subordinated Lender.

3. Target sells assets, and Newco assumes only those liabilities, if any, specifically agreed on in the asset purchase agreement. Target now has cash as its assets, and may completely liquidate and distribute cash to its shareholders, use the cash to enter a new business, or become a mutual fund.

Exhibit 2

EXAMPLE OF LEVERAGED BUYOUT
USING STOCK ACQUISITION

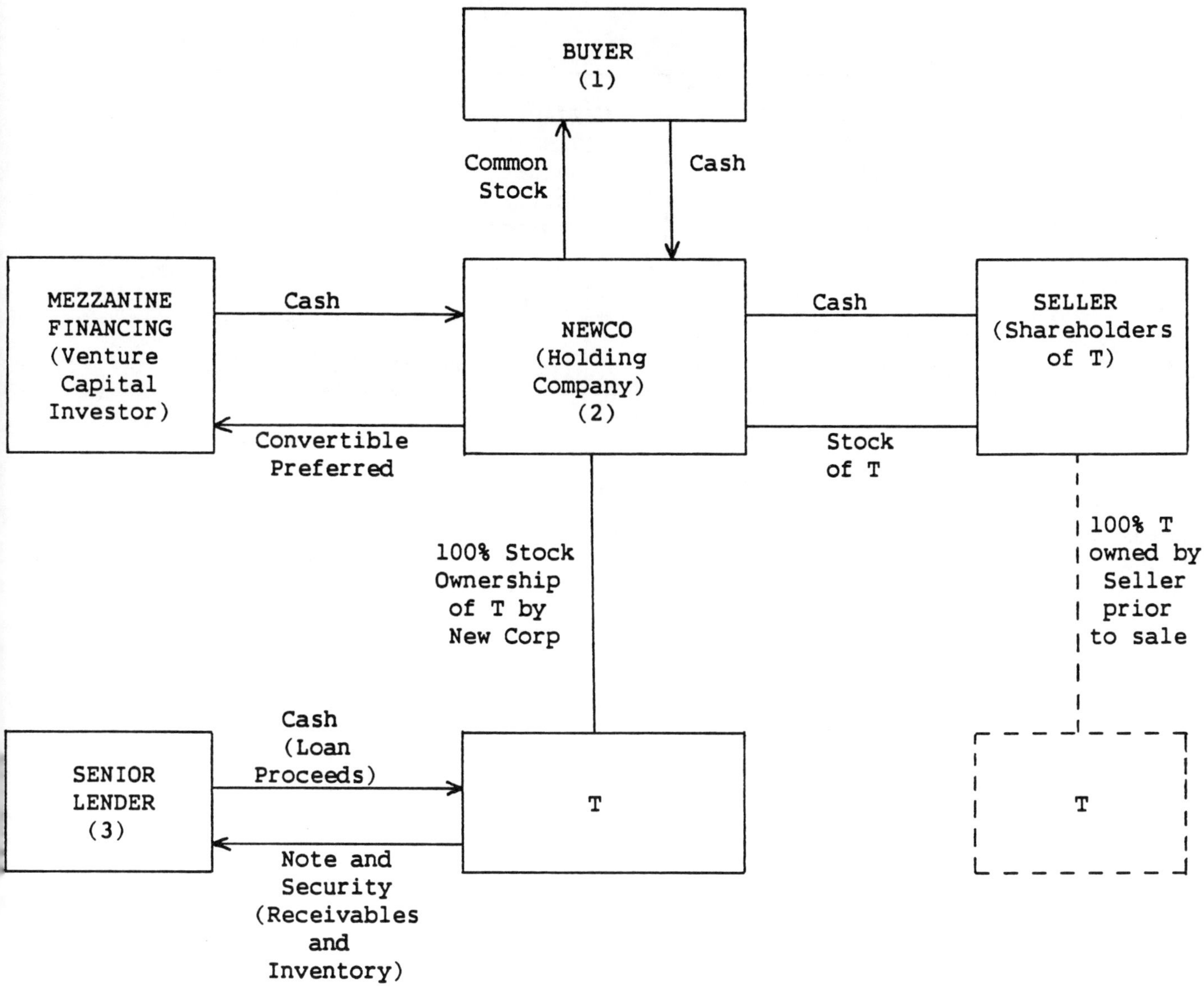

1. "Buyer" is frequently a management group, a sponsor or promoter, and other investors. Newco is capitalized with common and preferred stock.

2. Newco pays cash to the shareholders of T, and 100% of the stock of T is transferred to Newco, making T a wholly-owned subsidiary of Newco.

3. Senior Lender loans to T, secured by accounts receivable and inventory. T may use the proceeds partly as a dividend or advance to Newco, to pay intercompany debt to Seller, to pay existing bank debt of T, or for working capital.

Exhibit 3

EXAMPLE OF LEVERAGED BUYOUT
USING CASH MERGER (TRIANGULAR

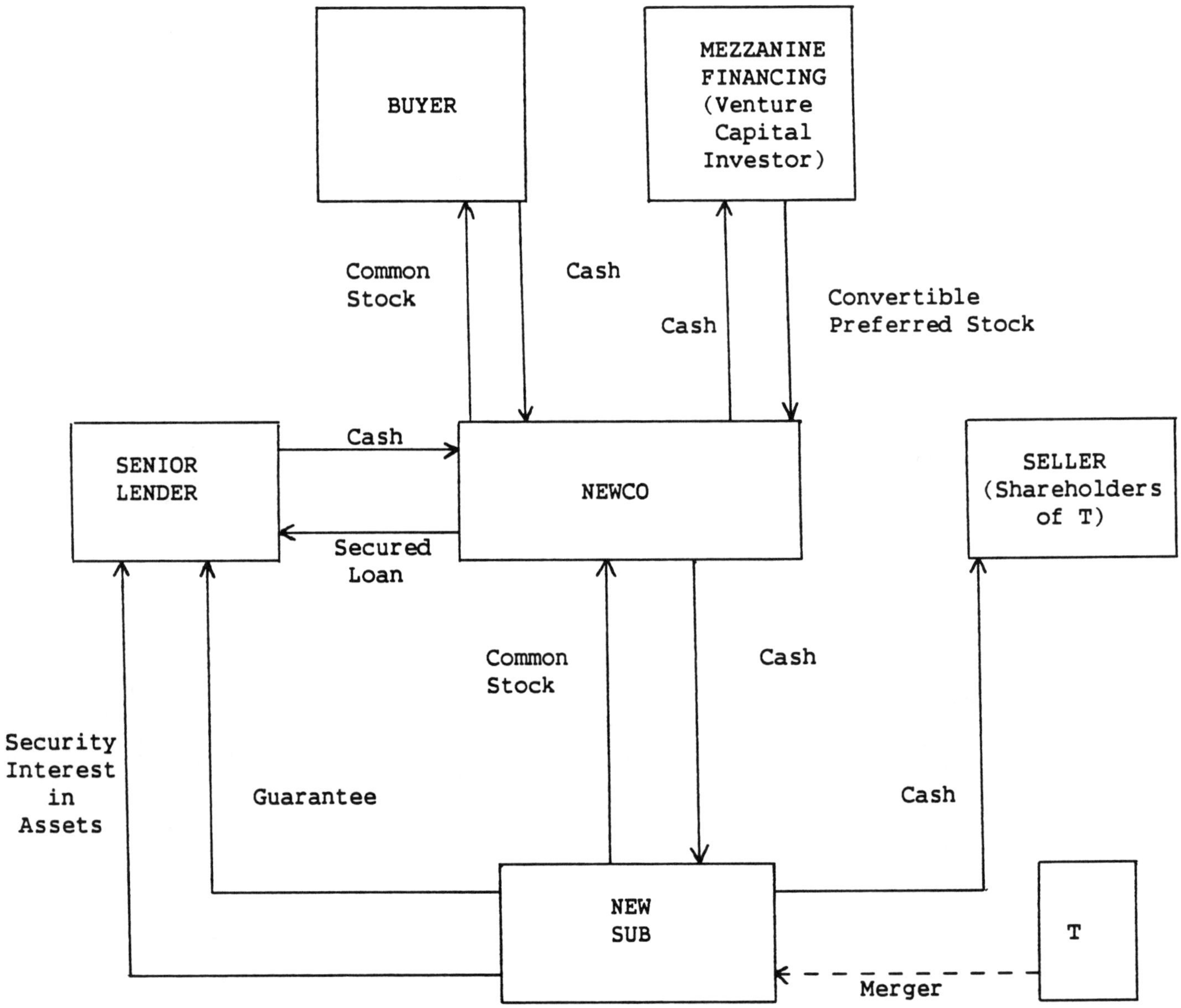

Exhibit 4

STEPS IN A STOCK TRANSACTION USING A DEMAND NOTE STRUCTURE

Step 1--Purchase of Stock in Exchange for Demand Note and Subordinated Seller Note

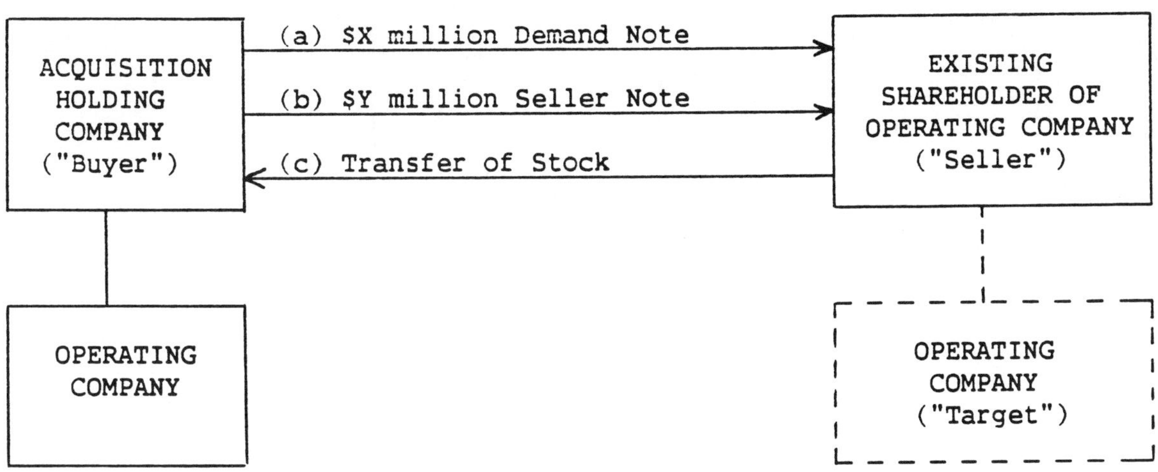

STEPS IN THE TRANSACTION (all occur concurrently)

1. Buyer (a) issues an $X million demand note, payable to the order of Seller, and (b) issues a $Y million subordinated Seller Note, payable to the order of Seller, in payment of the full amount of the purchase price for all of the outstanding common stock of the Operating Company, based on the purchase price, as defined in the stock purchase agreement, and secured by a security interest in the stock being acquired. (c) Seller transfers to Buyer all of the outstanding common stock of the Operating Company, thereby making the Operating Company a wholly-owned subsidiary of Buyer.

Exhibit 4

Step 2--Loans to Operating Company

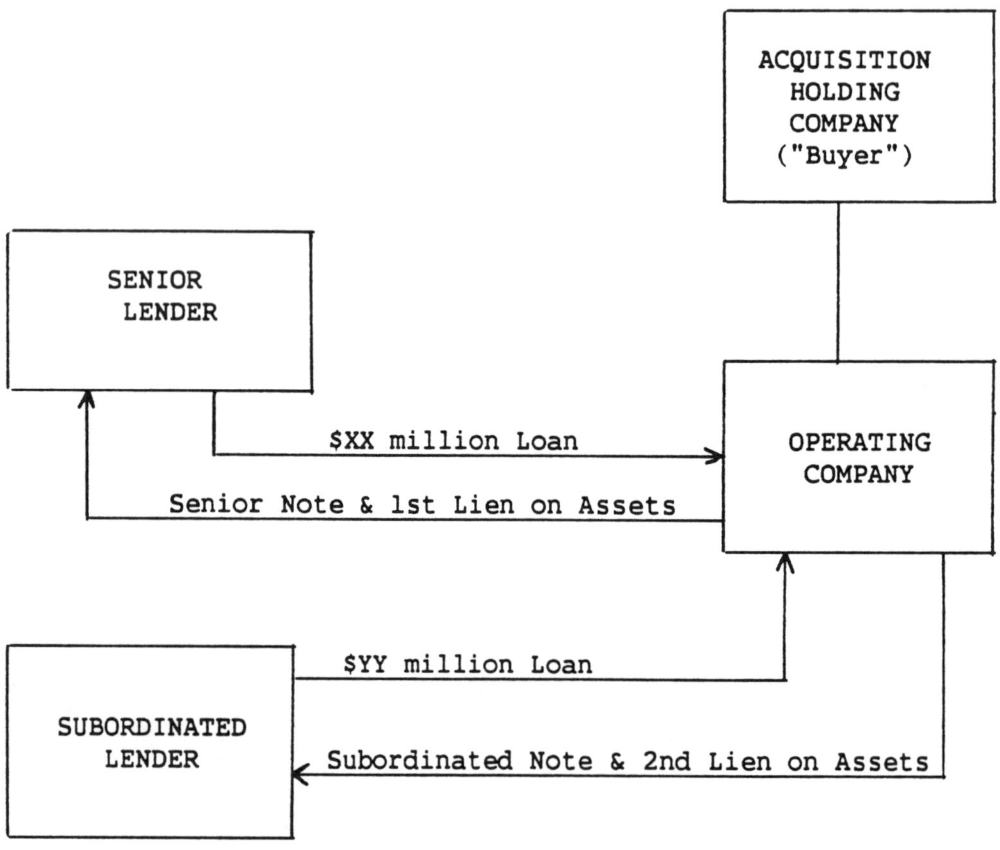

2. Senior lender loans $XX million to the Operating Company, pursuant to a senior loan, secured by a first lien on all assets of the Operating Company. Subordinated lender loans $YY million to the Operating Company, secured by a second lien on all of the Operating Company assets.

Exhibit 4

Step 3--Use of Loan Proceeds to Repay Demand Note and Intercompany Debt

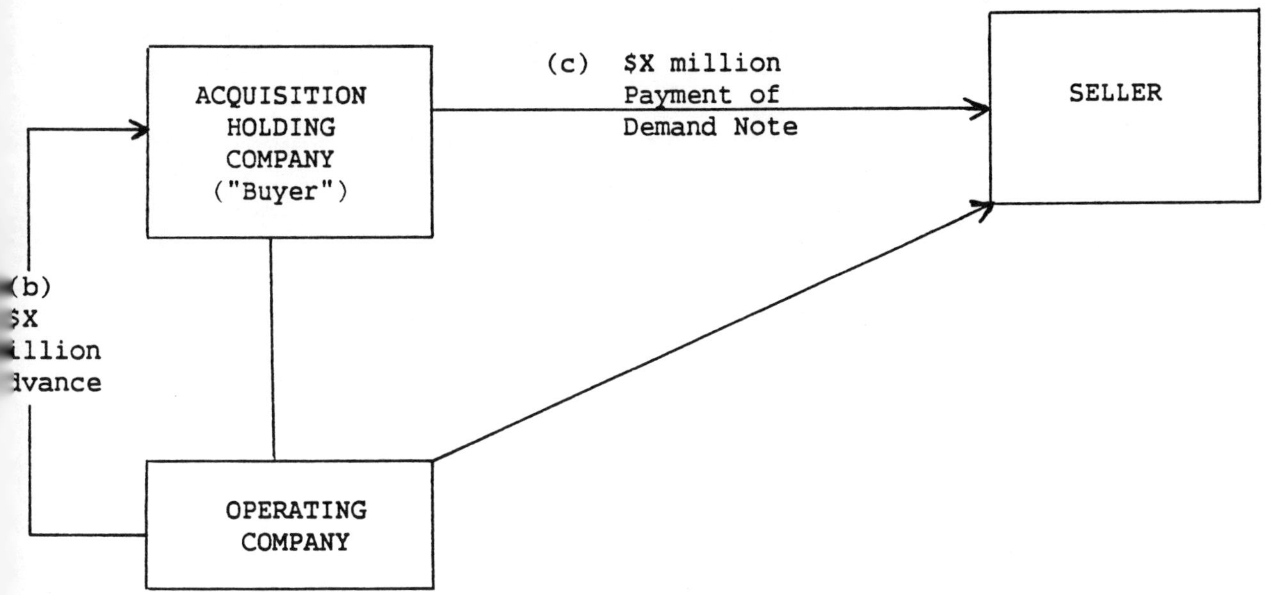

Operating Company uses the loan proceeds from the senior and subordinated loans as follows: (a) to repay $AA million of intercompany advances owed to Seller; and (b) to make an $X million advance to the Buyer. (c) The Buyer then uses the proceeds of the advance from the Operating Company to pay the $X million demand note to Seller.

APPENDIX B

BUYER'S PACKAGE

Wallner & Co.

WALLNER & CO.

Private Investors

Wallner & Co., Private Investors

Wallner & Co. is a privately owned investment firm headquartered in La Jolla, California. The company specializes in private buyouts of public and private companies and corporate divestitures. The company's primary objective is to acquire established operating companies for the personal accounts of its managing partner, Nicholas Wallner, Ph.D., his operating partners and incumbent management groups. Since its founding in 1975, Wallner & Co. has acquired portfolio companies with aggregate sales in excess of $1 billion.

The company is actively engaged in a continuous investment program of acquiring companies with demonstrated operating results, strong balance sheets and quality management teams. We are fully staffed and organized to respond quickly and professionally to timely investment opportunities. Our operating partners and staff are all professional managers from solid operating backgrounds. We are considered one of the most experienced acquisition and operating groups in the nation, and our track record as successful private investors is well known in financial circles. We function as investors only and do not act as intermediaries, brokers, finders, investment bankers or consultants in the merger/acquisition process.

This brochure is written primarily for owners, directors and managers of private and public businesses and corporate subsidiaries and divisions being considered for sale. We also welcome inquiries from control shareholders of public companies seeking liquidity for their holdings. In addition, Wallner & Co. wishes to maintain an active dialogue with other investment groups, financial institutions, investment bankers, venture capitalists, merger/acquisition specialists, finders and business brokers, attorneys, accountants and other members of the financial community.

Selling Your Private or Public Company, Subsidiary or Division

The most important yet frustrating business experience for private, corporate or public owners is the sale of the assets or stock of a going business. For private sellers, a sale is almost always a once-in-a-lifetime decision. For corporate sellers, it is usually part of an overall corporate strategy. For control shareholders in public companies, it is often the only path to liquidity.

The key aspect of a sale is to interest a small number of bona fide buyers who have the experience and capital resources to react quickly, discreetly and professionally.

The buyers are usually either corporate buyers or private investment groups. To achieve a tax-free exchange of stock, the seller should always consider a merger with a larger public or private company if market conditions are right. If the seller wants cash (often obtainable through a tax-free transaction), continued corporate independence and, perhaps, an equity involvement for the owners and/or management, then a sale to a private investment group is a viable alternative. The role of the private group as buyers of operating companies has become a dominant factor in the acquisition field in recent years.

Corporate Divestitures

Corporate sellers are usually motivated by strategic and economic reasons. Product line strategies, product fit and size are major reasons for divestiture. The assets for sale, although usually profitable and trouble-free, may not fit the corporate bench marks of return on assets or equity or of growth in sales or earnings. Sometimes the corporate seller needs cash, has been unable to solve a management problem or may even have antitrust problems which can be solved only by a divestiture. Corporate owners of subsidiaries or divisions frequently find it difficult to supervise their holdings because of the distances involved, especially if these companies represent only a minor part of their overall activity.

Corporate sellers usually want cash for their unneeded or unwanted assets. The most viable buyers for corporate spin-offs are private investment groups and/or management teams. Frequently, private investors and incumbent managers team up to acquire a spin-off because the management group is usually not experienced or knowledgeable enough to structure the acquisition and package the financing alone. Management often has difficulty negotiating an arms length transaction with their own immediate supervisors. Finally, the lenders and sellers almost always insist on outside capital and/or expertise in the deal.

Private Companies

The sale of a closely-held company affects the owner, his family, his estate and his employees. It is usually a deliberate, positive decision, not the result of urgency or distress.

Selling a privately held company can provide estate liquidity for the owner and his family by separating his capital and his career. Other considerations are retirement, health, management succession, multiple ownership and division of interests. The prospect of going public is less viable or desirable than it used to be. The alternative of merging with a larger company often means the loss of identity and independence.

Frequently, the best alternative for a closely held company is to sell for cash or for cash and notes to a private investment group. The sellers thereby preserve the continuity and independence of their company for their management and employees by retaining employee benefit programs, pension and profit-sharing plans, and established relationships with customers, suppliers, accountants, attorneys and banks. They may also contribute to and benefit from the future growth of the company by becoming part of the investment group.

Public Companies

Major shareholders of small to medium-sized public companies frequently have little or no liquidity for their stock, suffer from low price-earning multiples, have few opportunities to raise capital through new offerings, yet still have the burden and high cost of remaining public. These companies have all the problems of being public but enjoy none of the benefits.

The only two solutions to this problem are for the corporation to buy back all of its stock or to sell substantially all of its assets or stock to a private investment group. The first method of going private is usually very costly, risky and time consuming. The sale of assets or stock to private investors for cash is usually easier and quicker. In the case of cash-for-assets transactions, the shareholders of the public company may either redeem their shares for cash or remain as shareholders of the firm, which usually becomes an investment company. Using the cash merger technique, the shareholders end up with cash as in any other acquisition for cash. Both of these extremely effective techniques have been pioneered in recent years by private investment groups.

The Investment Process

The process of acquiring operating companies is a complex undertaking which requires highly specialized skills in various areas of corporate finance and management. The past success of Wallner & Co. in this field can be attributed, in large part, to the excellence of its partners and staff and the unique structure of its acquisition and management organization.

As a general rule, each acquisition is made by a new corporation organized by Dr. Wallner and one of his operating partners. The operating partner in any given investment will depend upon his background and experience as it relates to the target company's operations. A third and very important component of this partnership is the incumbent management team of the proposed investment.

The overall investment process is divided into three distinct phases, each of which requires a different combination of skills provided by Dr. Wallner and his operating partners. The **Selection Phase**, which includes defining, finding, screening, qualifying and evaluating an investment, is shared equally by Dr. Wallner and his operating partners. The **Acquisition Phase** which includes pricing, structuring, financing, negotiating and closing, is directed primarily by Dr. Wallner with the help of outside legal and accounting counsel. The **Monitoring Phase**, which involves major policy decisions and performance measurement is performed by Wallner Management & Co. and an operating partner.

The Selection Phase

The first step in the investment process is to carefully screen identified prospects to determine their suitability under certain criteria. The criteria listed below have been developed by Wallner & Co. to assist in screening prospective acquisition candidates.

Established Business Enterprises. Primarily manufacturers, distributors and retailers of industrial, commercial and consumer products, with dominant market shares in concentrated industries or companies with significant leadership positions in fragmented markets. We prefer relatively mature companies in viable industries which offer the potential to generate exceptional investment returns while also limiting the risk to the investment group.

Proven Operating Performance. A record of profitable operations for at least three to five years. Constant earnings and consistent cash flow are more important than rapid growth, although we prefer companies capable of at least doubling earnings every five years. Size is not a factor. In regard to underachieving companies, we recognize that adverse circumstances sometimes produce historical results not indicative of the true potential of a business. Our focus, therefore, is not necessarily today's circumstances but what a company can become if it is properly managed and capitalized.

Strong Balance Sheets. Tangible, viable assets, a high degree of liquidity and little or no debt. We prefer companies with fast-turning inventories and accounts receivables, undervalued, excess or hidden assets, and relatively low capital intensity.

Quality Management Teams. We prefer mature, experienced and competent operating managers with dedication, integrity and proven records of success. Management must be willing to remain or be easily replaced from the outside. In either case, we believe that management should have a significant equity involvement in the venture.

The Acquisition Phase

After an acquisition candidate meets the criteria of Wallner & Co., an extensive analysis is conducted of the company, its industry, products, competition, management, sales and earnings, balance sheets and cash flow. From this analysis, the company is valued, an offering price is determined and the financing and legal structure for the proposed investment is determined. Wallner & Co., usually represented by Dr. Wallner, then conducts all negotiations between the sellers, the buying group and the financial institutions and their respective legal and accounting counsel.

The financing of an investment is conducted simultaneously with the acquisition phase. Once the buyers and sellers agree on price and terms, Wallner & Co. has the responsibility for arranging the necessary debt and equity financing. The company maintains excellent working relationships with many major lenders and equity sources. These financial institutions include commercial banks, commercial finance companies, insurance companies, pension funds, SBICs and venture capital companies. They usually participate in our acquisitions with senior and subordinated debt and may also become equity partners.

he onitoring hase

The completion of an acquisition signals the beginning of an extremely intensive follow-up to ensure the success of our investments. Wallner Management & Co. and our operating partners devote a substantial amount of time to each investment in an effort to achieve a high probability of success. However, our relationship with management is primarily supportive and we do not become immediately involved in the day-to-day operations. The investors make their contribution through participation on the board of directors. Although the firm participates in management at the board level, we strongly believe in operating autonomy for the management group.

By drawing on the collective experience and capabilities of our operating partners and our staff, we support management in the areas of policy, corporate goals and objectives, long-range planning and strategies, corporate business plans, financial planning, budgets and controls, cash management, credit, data processing, equity and debt financing, mergers & acquisitions, insurance programs, pension and profit sharing and other benefit and incentive plans, and liaison with the company's general counsel and independent auditors.

erger termediaries

Wallner & Co. welcomes the submission of proposals directly by principals, incumbent management teams or through established merger intermediaries such as investment bankers, merger brokers, finders, attorneys, accountants, consultants, financial institutions and other third parties. Those submitting proposals should provide background material on the company, including operating statements for the past five years, a current balance sheet, a brief description of the company's history, markets, products, competitors, customers, suppliers, composition of ownership and resumes of the key management personnel and composition of ownership. A business plan for the next five years, including income statements, balance sheets and sources and uses of funds statements should also be provided.

We prefer that fee arrangements be made between sellers and intermediaries in writing. If this is not possible, we will pay fees to intermediaries, subject to the seller's authorization. We will honor prior participations and fee splits. Material submitted to us and all of our discussions are held in strict confidence and we will indicate promptly the extent of our interest.

WALLNER & CO. Private Investors

Wallner & Co., La Jolla, California

Acquihold Corporation

a company organized by Wallner & Co.
and The Hillman Company

has acquired substantially all the stock of

Foremost Dairies, Inc.

formerly a division of Foremost-McKesson, Inc.

Nicholas Wallner, Ph.D., Willard C. McNitt, J. Terrence Greve, and Blacklog Investments, Inc., an affiliate of The Hillman Company, negotiated this private buyout, arranged the financing and participated as principal investors along with the management.

Effective: December 1, 1982

This announcement appears as a matter of record only.

WALLNER & CO.
Private Investors

Wallner & Co., La Jolla, California

Acquihold Corporation

a company organized by Wallner & Co.
and The Hillman Company

has acquired the stock of

New Magnin, Inc.

dba Joseph Magnin Co., Inc.

Nicholas Wallner, Ph.D., Willard C. McNitt, J. Terrence Greve, and Blacklog Investments, Inc., an affiliate of The Hillman Company, negotiated this private buyout, arranged the financing and participated as principal investors.

Effective: December 1, 1982

This announcement appears as a matter of record only.

WALLNER & CO.
Private Investors

Wallner & Co., La Jolla, California

Buyout Publications, Inc.

a company organized by Wallner & Co.

has acquired certain assets and liabilities of

Buyout Publications

a partnership

Nicholas Wallner, Ph.D., J. Terrence Greve, and Frederick J. Oshay negotiated this private buyout and participated as principal investors.

Effective: December 1, 1982

This announcement appears as a matter of record only.

WALLNER & CO.
Private Investors

Wallner & Co., La Jolla, California

HEH Associates, Inc.

a company organized by Wallner & Co.

has acquired certain assets and liabilities of

H.E. Harris & Co., Inc.

a subsidiary of General Mills, Inc.

Nicholas Wallner, Ph.D. and Peter S. Redfield negotiated this private buyout, arranged the financing and participated as principal investors along with the management.

Effective: August 27, 1982

This announcement appears as a matter of record only.

WALLNER & CO.
Private Investors

Wallner & Co., La Jolla, California

S.S.W. Associates, Inc.

a company organized by Wallner & Co.

has acquired certain assets and liabilities of

S.S. White Retail

a division of Pennwalt Corporation

Nicholas Wallner, Ph.D. and Peter S. Redfield negotiated this private buyout, arranged the financing and participated as principal investors along with the management.

Effective: January 31, 1982

This announcement appears as a matter of record only.

Wallner & Co., La Jolla, California

ASI Associates, Inc.

a company organized by Wallner & Co.

has acquired certain assets and liabilities of

Aloha State Sales Co., Inc.

Nicholas Wallner, Ph.D. and Peter S. Redfield negotiated this private buyout, arranged the financing and participated as principal investors along with the management.

Effective: August 14, 1981

This announcement appears as a matter of record only.

WALLNER & CO.
Private Investors

Wallner & Co., La Jolla, California

L-D Associates, Inc.

a company organized by Wallner & Co.

has acquired the outstanding shares of

LaSalle-Deitch Company, Inc.

a subsidiary of The Magnavox Company,
a subsidiary of North American Philips Corporation

Nicholas Wallner, Ph.D. and Peter S. Redfield negotiated this private buyout, arranged the financing and participated as principal investors along with the management.

Effective: December 31, 1980

This announcement appears as a matter of record only.

WALLNER & CO.
Private Investors

Wallner & Co., La Jolla, California

Sparta Instrument Corporation

a company organized by Wallner & Co.

has acquired certain assets of

Sparta Instruments

a division of Cooper Medical Devices, Inc.,
a subsidiary of Cooper Laboratories, Inc.

Nicholas Wallner, Ph.D. and Peter S. Redfield negotiated this private buyout, arranged the financing and participated as principal investors along with the management.

Effective: November 7, 1980

This announcement appears as a matter of record only.

APPENDIX C

LETTER OF INTENT

Wallner & Co.

LETTER OF INTENT

WALLNER & CO.
La Jolla, California

C-1

October 31, 1980

The Magnovox Company
Fort Wayne, Indiana

LETTER OF INTENT

Gentlemen:

This letter confirms that we have reached a general understanding with you ("Seller"), a Delaware corporation, as to the essential features of a proposed purchase from you by a California corporation ("Buyer") controlled by Nicholas Wallner, Peter S. Redfield and Joseph N. Ellis of all of the outstanding capital stock (the "Shares") of LaSalle-Deitch Co., Inc. (the "Company"), a Delaware corporation. Subject to the preparation, execution and performance of a definitive written agreement (the "Sale Agreement") containing the mutual convenants and agreements of both parties and such other terms, conditions, covenants, representations and warranties as either party in good faith may require, we have agreed in principle to the following general terms:

1. On a date to be agreed upon (the "Closing Date"), which we will attempt to have occur before December 31, 1980, Buyer will purchase the Shares from Seller, and Seller will sell and transfer the Shares to Buyer. The purchase price ("Purchase Price") of the Shares has been tentatively established as $28.2 million (assuming the Company has $1.8 million in cash on the Closing Date) subject to adjustment as provided in paragraph 3 below.

2. On the Closing Date, Buyer will deliver to Seller, as the tentative Purchase Price, cash and promissory notes ("Notes") aggregating $28.2 million as follows:

The Magnovox Company
October 31, 1980
Page Two

(a) A cashier's check in the amount of $10.0 million.

(b) A promissory note ("Note I") in the principal amount of $7.0 million, secured by a first lien on the Company's real property, bearing interest at 11% per annum, with principal and interest payable and other terms as provided in paragraph 4.1;

(c) A promissory note ("Note II") in the principal amount of $5.2 million secured by a lien on the Company's assets other than real property subordinate only to the rights of "Senior Indebtedness" as defined in paragraph 5, bearing interest at 9% per annum for four years following the Closing Date, at 11% per annum for the next three years and at 13% per annum for the next three years, with principal and interest payable and other terms as provided in paragraph 4.2; and

(d) A promissory note ("Note III") in the principal amount of $6.0 million secured by a lien on the assets of the Company's "Instamatic Division" subordinate only to the rights of "Senior Indebtedness" as defined in paragraph 5, bearing interest at 7% per annum, with principal and interest payable and other terms as provided in paragraph 4.3.

3. Following the Closing Date, Seller will deliver to Buyer audited financial statements of the Company as of and for the year ended December 31, 1980, including a balance sheet as of December 31, 1980. Thereafter, in accordance with such applicable procedures, if any, as may be contained in the Sale Agreement, the Purchase Price shall be increased or decreased retroactive to the Closing Date to equal the net worth of the Company as of December 31, 1980, and the principal amount of Note II shall be adjusted retroactive to the Closing Date to reflect the increase or decrease of the Purchase Price from $28.2 million.

The Magnovox Company
October 31, 1980
Page Three

4. Additional terms of the Notes are set forth below:

4.1 <u>Note I</u>: No payment of principal or interest on Note I shall be due or payable for three years following the Closing Date. On the third anniversary of the Closing Date a principal payment of $5.0 million shall be due and payable; interest accrued during the first three years and tenth anniversary of the Closing Date, both inclusive. Buyer intends to fund the $5.0 million principal payment due on the third anniversary of the Closing Date by borrowing from institutional lenders and using the Company's real property as collateral; Seller will subordinate its lien on said real property to a new first lien in favor of said institutional lenders. From and after said payment until Note I is paid in full, the lien in favor of Seller on the Company's real property will be subordinate to the lien in favor of said institutional lenders.

4.2 <u>Note II</u>: Interest on the unpaid balance of Note II, at the rates set forth therein, shall be paid annually on the anniversary of the Closing Date. Principal shall be paid in four equal annual installments commencing on the seventh anniversary of the Closing Date and continuing until the tenth anniversary of the Closing Date, both inclusive.

4.3 <u>Note III</u>: No payment of principal or interest on Note III shall be due or payable for five (5) years following the Closing Date, except in the event of the sale of the Company's Instamatic Division. Interest of $2.1 million accrued during the first five (5) years following the Closing Date shall be added to principal, and the sum of principal and accrued interest shall be paid in ten equal annual installments commencing on the sixth anniversary of the Closing Date and continuing until the fifteenth anniversary of the Closing Date, both inclusive. Along with each such installment Buyer shall pay to Seller interest at the prime rate in effect from time to time (adjusted quarterly) at the main office of the Seller's principal commercial bank lender. Following the Closing Date Buyer shall endeavor to sell the Instamatic Division at a price equal to or greater than the principal amount of Note III. If any such sale is effected, Buyer will pay the proceeds of the sale (up to the amount of principal and accrued interest of Note III) to Seller in retirement of Note III. Alternatively, in connection with any such sale, Buyer shall have the right to delegate its duties under Note III to a financially responsible purchaser of the Instamatic Division acceptable to Seller, and the purchaser shall assume such obligations. Immediately upon such assumption, the obligation of Buyer under Note III shall be automatically extinguished.

4.4 Upon any sale of any substantial portion of the assets of the Company (other than the Instmatic Division) outside of the ordinary course of business at a price in excess of the book value of such assets, the amount by which the sale proceeds exceeds such book value shall be applied to prepay the Notes in the following order: first Note II, then Note III and finally Note I. Each such payment shall reduce the payments next coming due under the applicable note.

5. On the Closing Date Buyer, the Company and Seller will execute and deliver a Collateral Security Agreement ("Security Agreement") under which Seller will be granted a security interest in all of the assets of the Company other than its real property as collateral for Note II and a security interest in the assets of the Instamatic Division as collateral for Note III. The Security Agreement will contain such affirmative and negative covenants and agreements and such other terms and conditions as either party in good faith may require. Under the Security Agreement the security interest in favor of Seller shall be subject and subordinate to the rights of, including security interests existing or granted to, the holders of "Senior Indebtedness," which term, as will be more specifically set forth in the Security Agreement, will

include (a) the Company's debts existing at the Closing Date, (b) purchase money indebtedness in an amount not in excess of the cost of the property acquired therewith, (c) indebtedness to the lender referred to in paragraph 6(d), and (d) indebtedness incurred by the Company to provide funds required in its business, on terms and within limits to be set forth in the Security Agreement.

6. The Sale Agreement will contain representations and warranties of Seller based on the financial statements of the Company as of and for the nine months ended September 30, 1980. Consummation of the purchase of the Shares under the Sale Agreement will be subject, among other things, to the following conditions, unless waived:

(a) The trust and accuracy of the representations and warranties contained in the Sale Agreement and the absence of any material adverse change in the affairs of the Company;

(b) Execution and delivery by the Company and key employees designated by Buyer of employment agreements satisfactory to such persons and to Buyer;

(c) Execution and delivery by Seller to Buyer of a covenant not to compete in form to be agreed to by Buyer and Seller;

(d) Buyer's obtaining a loan of not less than $10.0 million from a secured lender, and the execution by Seller and said lender of an intercreditor agreement with respect to the relative priority of their respective security interests in the assets of the Company, in form and substance satisfactory to Seller and said lender; and

(e) the absence of any pending or threatened litigation which, in the opinion of counsel to either Buyer or Seller, has or could have any material adverse

The Magnovox Company
October 31, 1980
Page Five

effect on the consummation of the sale and purchase of the Shares and/or the enjoyment of the benefits thereof.

7. So long as Buyer is indebted to Seller under any of the Notes, Seller shall be entitled to designate one director of the Company, and Buyer will provide Seller unaudited monthly financial statements and annual audited financial statements of the Company.

As long as Buyer and Seller continue to negotiate in good faith with a view to preparing the executing the Sale Agreement, Seller will refrain from all negotiations and transactions consummation of which would be inconsistent with the sale of the Shares to Buyer. Either party may abandon the proposed sale and purchase without liability by written notice to the other at any time if it shall reasonably determine in good faith that the sale and purchase of the Shares cannot be consummated within four (4) months from the date of this letter for any bona fide reason.

If the foregoing correctly expresses our understanding, please so indicate by signing and dating the enclosed copy of this letter at the bottom and returning it to the undersigned.

Very truly yours,

Nicholas Wallner

THE FOREGOING CORRECTLY
EXPRESSED OUR UNDERSTANDING

The Magnovox Company

By ______________________________
Dated: November ____, 1980

APPENDIX D

DUE DILIGENCE CHECKLIST

(Short Form)

DUE DILIGENCE CHECKLIST

(Short Form)

Income Statement - last 5 years
Balance Sheet - last 5 years
Balance Sheet - latest interim period
Budget for current year
Sales of ten largest customers - last 3 years
Accounts Receivable aging - latest month
Bad Debt Expenses - last 5 years
Inventory List and Method of Accounting
Equipment List (serial no., purchase date, depreciation)
Equipment Appraisals (if available)
Real Estate List
Real Estate Appraisals (if available)
Life Insurance Policy Information
Trade Payable Aging - latest month
List of Other Liabilities
Loan Documents (if financing to be assumed)
Leases
Pending Lawsuits
Major Contracts (supplier, customer, union, etc.)
Pension, Profit Sharing or ESOP plan
Employee Schedule (title, salary and years with firm)
Shareholder List

APPENDIX E

ACQUISITION CHECKLIST

Wallner & Co.

ACQUISITION CHECKLIST
by
Wallner & Co.

This comprehensive business checklist includes all information required by the seller before an analysis can be made by the buyer. The businessman's review is a further audit of the books and records of the company.

I. THE COMPANY
   A. Present legal name.
   B. Address and phone number of main office.
   C. Type of business.
   D. Description of business activity.
   E. Changes in business activity.
   F. Date company originated.
   G. State of incorporation.
   H. States where company is allowed to do business.
   I. List of subsidiaries - divisions.
   J. Addresses of all facilities.
   K. List of shareholders if privately held.
   L. Number of shares owned by principals.
   M. List of types of securities.
   N. Number of shares outstanding.
   O. Number of shares in float if publicly held.
   P. Price range of stock if publicly held.
   Q. Stock sales volume if publicly held.
   R. Number of shares authorized.
   S. Number of shares of treasury stock.
   T. List of other operating investments and amounts.
   U. List of any unusual situations or circumstances.
   V. Name, address, phone number of company's bank.
   W. Name, address, phone number of company's auditor.
   X. Name, address, phone number of company's attorney.
   Y. Name, address, phone number of other company advisors.

II. HISTORICAL SUMMARY

- A. How company was originally formed.
- B. Reason for founding.
- C. Names of founders and successors.
- D. Brief review of sales progress.
- E. Brief review of profit progress.
- F. Brief review of product line history.

III. MANAGEMENT, PERSONNEL AND POLICIES

- A. Number of employees by department.
- B. Organizational chart.
- C. List of officers.
- D. Is there an operations manual?
  - 1. List of all duties?
  - 2. Is it up to date?
  - 3. Are all work rules and regulations defined?
- E. Information on principals and key employees.
- F. List and summarize employment contracts.
- G. Are there new management requirements?
- H. Is secondary management strong?
- I. Will management stay if there is a change of ownership?
- J. What are rates of compensation for management?
  - 1. List salaries of key executives.
  - 2. Is there an incentive program?
- K. Are outside consultants used?
- L. Are office accommodations appropriate?
- M. How is morale?
- N. List fringe benefits to management.
- O. Production labor (if manufacturing).
  - 1. Average hourly rate.
  - 2. Names of unions.
  - 3. Past labor relations.
  - 4. Present or future labor problems.
  - 5. List of hourly rates and job classifications.
  - 6. Payroll procedures.
  - 7. Productivity experience.
  - 8. General employee morale.
  - 9. Procedures for hiring and firing.
  - 10. Union contract expiration dates.
  - 11. Number of hours in work week.
  - 12. Advancement and promotion procedures.
- P. Employee benefits.
  - 1. Incentive plans.

2. Pension plans.
3. Vacation plans.
4. Number of paid holidays.
5. Medical, life insurance, dental.
6. Stock options.
7. Bonuses.
8. Profit sharings.
9. Recreation facilities.
10. Employee discounts.
11. Employee social functions.

IV. THE FACILITIES

A. Land and buildings.

1. Location and zoning.
2. Legal description and ownership.
3. Mortgages (amount, terms and conditions).
4. Description of lease(s).
5. Appraisals (if owned).
6. Plans and drawings.
7. Insurance.
    a. Sprinklers.
    b. Fire protection.
    c. Police protection.
8. Condition.
9. Repairs needed.
10. Improvements.
11. Amount of square feet in buildings.
12. Amount of square feet of land.
13. Amount of rent.
14. Amount of property taxes.
15. Amount of office space in building.
16. Amount of warehouse space.
17. Number of shipping docks.
18. Type of electrical power.
19. Compliance with OSHA.
20. Compliance with Environmental Protection Agency.
21. Space for expansion.
22. Location of public storage facilities.
23. How long will existing facilities be appropriate?
24. Where would you move if you had to?
25. What are comparable property costs?
26. Are security systems adequate?
27. Housekeeping.

28. Is location desirable?
    a. Labor.
    b. Marketing.
    c. Shipping.
    d. Materials.
    e. Transportation
29. What is production and sales capacity of facilities?
30. What percent of present facilities are being used?
31. If retail facilities --
    a. Approximate size of trade areas.
    b. Demographics of trade areas.
32. Location of nearest:
    a. Post office.
    b. Airport.
    c. Railroad.
    d. Port.
33. Is area serviced by common carriers and United Parcel?

B. Equipment.
1. List of equipment: age, date purchased, cost, stock number, condition.
2. List of tooling, dies, jigs, fixtures.

V. PRODUCTION (IF MANUFACTURING)

A. Production costs.
1. Labor cost as percent of sales.
2. Material cost as percent of sales.
3. Manufacturing overhead as percent of sales.
4. Possible improvements and economics.
5. Future cost prospects of labor, material and manufacturing overhead.
6. Production costs and profits by product.

B. Production procedures.
1. Are production schedules established and kept current?
2. Flexibility.
    a. Is there flexibility to increase and decrease production?
    b. Can profit margins be maintained?
3. What is minimum production required for breakeven?
4. Are assembly procedures efficient?
5. What percent of product is bought out?
6. Quality control and inspection.

7. How is salvage handled?
8. Are material handling procedures efficient?
9. Are all safety precautions being followed?
10. Are preventive maintenance procedures followed?
11. Is there a continuing program to improve procedures?
12. List the production obstacles.
13. What is maximum production capacity with existing equipment?
14. Type of cost controls.
15. How is inventory controlled?
16. How often is physical inventory taken?
17. Are there time studies?
18. Lead time.
    a. How long?
    b. Can it be reduced?
19. What other types of controls are there?
20. Is there proper coordination between sales and production?

C. Engineering, research and development
1. R&D cost as a percent of sales.
2. Number of employees.
3. Explain market research program.
4. Furnish list of patents, copyrights, trademark and all new applications.
5. What is patent agreement with employees?
6. Is there patent licensing arrangement?
7. Is current R&D budget sufficient to maintain the company's competitive position?

VI. MARKETING AND PRODUCTS

A. Product lines.
1. List of principal products.
2. If retail or distribution:
    a. Identify suppliers.
    b. Exclusive arrangements/contracts.
    c. Nature of trade practices.
    d. Price comparisons.
    e. Packaging comparisons.
    f. Utility comparisons.
    g. Value comparisons.
    h. Type of cooperation.
3. Uses and application.

4. Brochures and price lists.
5. Competitors.
    a. List with estimated sales and profits.
    b. Competitors' brochures and price lists.
    c. Nature of trade practices.
    d. Price comparisons.
    e. Packaging comparisons.
    f. Utility comparisons.
    g. Value comparisons.
    h. Type of cooperation.
6. Seasonability.
    a. Are there seasonal characteristics?
    b. Other available products to round out season.
7. Pricing.
    a. What effect would an increase have?
    b. Are prices stable?
    c. Future pricing considerations.
    d. Are there fair trade laws?
    e. How many different price lists?
    f. What are bidding conditions?
    g. Should prices be increased on some products?
    h. Should prices be decreased on some products?
8. How complete is product line?
9. What effect do general economic conditions have on product line?

B. Sales.
1. Breakdown by product last 5 years.
2. Breakdown by product next 5 years.
3. Methods of distribution.
    a. Should a change be considered?
    b. Are all markets being covered?
    c. Should some markets be eliminated?
    d. Should the company go direct?
    e. Can methods of obtaining distributors or dealers be improved?
    f. Identify specific areas covered.
    g. Are customers considered faithful to company?
        1. Is there a big turnover of customers?

   2. What is the nature of reorders?

h. Is there use of private brand?

i. Are other methods of distribution being considered?

j. Can sales to original equipment manufacturers be profitable?

k. Do customers have a good attitude toward the company?
   1. How can it be improved?

l. What effect does franchising have?

m. If retail:
   1. Should more stores be opened?
   2. Should some existing stores be closed?
   3. What areas or stores?
   4. Credit policies.
   5. Sales department.

n. Number of employees and organizational chart.

o. What are sales methods?

p. Percent of sales to top 5 customers.

q. List top 20 customers and sales volume.

r. How are salesman paid?

s. Types of sales incentive programs.

t. Nature of sales expenses.
   1. Should they be increased or decreased?
   2. Can existing profit margins afford changes?

u. New business.
   1. What is being done to get it?
   2. What percent are new customers each year?

v. How can existing customer sales be increased?

w. How can average order be increased?

x. Are there special promotions?
   1. Should they be increased or decreased?

y. What is policy on service and returns?

z. Sales forecasts
   1. Are sales forecasts and budgets kept current

2. How accurate have they been?

aa. Does the company know where it wants to be in 5 years?

bb. How can it reach that goal with existing program?

cc. How does the company develop new products?

dd. Is proper use made of telephone?

ee. Are sales people making best use of time?

ff. Government business.

1. Is company getting its share of government business?
2. How can present program be improved?

C. Advertising and sales promotion.

1. Name and address of advertising agency.
2. To what extent does it do its own advertising?
3. Is present agency doing a good job?
4. Is advertising budget on target?
5. List of advertising media.
6. What is dollar amount of advertising budget?
   a. As percent of sales.
   b. Breakdown of budget for magazines, newspapers, trade directories, mail order, phone directories, radio, TV, trade shows, special promotions, premiums.
7. Is a steady public relations program maintained?
8. Does the company make use of testimonials?
9. How often does a publicity release go out?
10. Is company image and logo right?
11. How many trade shows are attended?
12. Is advertising program ready for a new theme?
13. Are mailings made at lowest rate?
14. Are customers and potential customers being followed up as part of each campaign?
15. Are results of advertising being measured?

VI. FINANCIAL
- A. Current financial statement.
- B. Financial statements past 5 years.
- C. Summary for past 10 years.
- D. Average profit for past 3 years - dollars and percent of sales.
- E. Projection for next 5 years.
  1. Sales and profits.
  2. Cash flow.
- F. Dividend policy and record for past 5 years.

VII. LEGAL CONSIDERATIONS.
- A. State and local laws.
  1. States in which incorporated.
  2. States in which qualified to do business.
  3. Local restrictions.
  4. Shareholders.
     - a. Number of voting shares required to merge.
     - b. Dissenter's rights.
     - c. Notice requirements.
     - d. Pre-emptive rights.
  5. Board of Directors - actions required in corporate sale, purchase or merger.
  6. Mergers.
     - a. Restrictions with respect to foreign corporations - domestic corporations.
  7. Negotiating permit requirements.
  8. Requirements and exemptions for registration.
  9. Requirements and exemptions to give proper notice.
  10. Bulk sales laws.
      - a. Compliance requirements and exemptions.
      - b. Penalties.
  11. Consumer laws and considerations.
  12. "Fair trade" considerations.
  13. "Right-to-work" labor laws.
  14. Zoning laws and restrictions.
- B. Federal laws.
  1. Anti-trust laws.
     - a. Sherman Act.
     - b. Robinson-Patman Act.
     - c. Clayton Act.

- d. Federal Trade Commission rulings.
- e. Department of Justice rulings.
- f. Court rulings.
- g. Company's past and present anti-trust history.

2. Anti-pollution laws.
3. Labor laws.
4. Other regulatory agencies.
5. Tariffs and quotas.
6. Securities & Exchange Commission requirements.
7. Government contracts.

C. Outstanding contracts.

1. With suppliers.
2. With subcontractors.
3. With customers.
4. With unions.
5. With distributors/franchisees.
6. With government.
7. Contingent or implied contracts.

D. Corporate by-laws.

1. Charter and amendments.
2. Shareholder's rights.
3. Capital structure.
   - a. Classes of stock.
   - b. Classes of debt securities.
   - c. Warrants, covertibles and other securities.
4. Rules for issuing and selling stock and other securities.

E. Corporate records.

1. Number of outstanding shares.
2. Number of shares authorized.
3. Names, addresses and number of shares of principal shareholders.
4. Amount of treasury stock.
5. Status of stock options.
6. Is minute book up to date?
7. Restrictions on transfer of shares.
8. Are all outstanding shares validly issued?
9. Are all employee plans documented?
   - a. Profit sharing.
   - b. Retirement.
   - c. Pension.
   - d. Insurance.
   - e. Bonus.
   - f. Options and warrants.

F. Labor considerations.
   1. Union rights.
   2. Pensions.
   3. Safety and working conditions.
   4. Minimum wage.
   5. Maximum hours.
   6. Overtime.
   7. Child labor.
   8. Discrimination -- racial and sexual.

G. Patents.
   1. License agreements.
   2. Trade secrets.
   3. Trademarks.
   4. Copyrights.
   5. List of patents with numbers.
   6. List of patents pending.

APPENDIX F

BUSINESSMAN'S REVIEW OUTLINE

Deloitte Haskins & Sells

BUSINESSMAN'S REVIEW OUTLINE

by

DELOITTE HASKINS & SELLS

This businessman's review has been excerpted in part from the Deloitte Haskins & Sells businessman's review, which the author deems to be the most comprehensive guideline available. This analysis relates primarily to financial statements, facts and information supplied by the seller and discovered during a field audit of the company's books and records.

I. ACCOUNTING POLICIES

A. Analyze any changes in accounting principles or accounting estimates in the last five years and most recent interim period that had the effect of increasing or decreasing earnings.

B. Review any items of income and expense that are included in operating results for the last five years and most recent interim period that more properly could have been included in previous periods if all the facts had been known at earlier dates.

C. Obtain a listing of year-end non-recurring adjustments made as of the end of the latest fiscal year.

D. Review goodwill carried in the balance sheet for possible diminution in value and for acceleration of amortization where this seems prudent.

E. Review any proposed FASB pronouncements or SEC regulations that are expected to materially affect the company's reporting of financial position or operating results in the near future.

F. Review the method used by the company to determine cost of sales in interim financial statements; also analyze procedures used in interim financial statements to charge operations for major expense items (such as advertising) and for income taxes.

G. Are there any generally accepted accounting practices followed by a majority of the other companies in the industry that are not being followed by the company? Some examples are:

1. Additions to inventory for carrying costs (interest, warehousing, handling).

2. Methods of depreciation and valuations of inventory.

3. Classification in current assets of certain items which may not be sold or realized within one year.

4. Basis of valuing long-term investments.

II. ANALYSIS OF EARNINGS

A. Read the company's financial statements for the last five years (including internal financial statements, annual reports, etc.) and for the most recent interim period (and) corresponding period of the preceding (years). Note any unusual matters. Read the independent public accountants' report on the financial statements and note any qualifications, exceptions or disclaimers.

B. Read the summary of earnings (to the extent possible before allocations) by major product lines (or by plant and subsidiary) for the last five years and for the most recent interim period (and corresponding period of the preceding year) and investigate any significant fluctuations.

C. Analyze sales (by quantity and unit selling price), cost of sales and direct selling and administrative expenses for each individual major product (or product line) by quarter (for the last two years), and by month (for the most recent interim period and corresponding period of the preceding year). Obtain explanations for any significant fluctuations in sales, gross profit or selling and administrative expense ratios. Also, obtain and read the similar analysis of sales, etc. for such periods, by major customers. If the company is particularly dependent upon several principal customers, obtain pertinent financial information with respect to such companies in order to evaluate their operating performance, growth trends, financial condition, etc. Also note any seasonal trends of the business.

D. Analyze the cost of sales by major product line, by cost component (material, labor and overhead) by quarter (for the last two years) and by month (for the most interim period and corresponding period of the preceding year). Note any significant fluctuations in such cost components.

E. Analyze sales by major product, by month for the last year and the most recent interim period. Inquire as to whether there has been any unusual sales activity (such as during the last month of a quarter or of the year).

F. Read the summary of sales to affiliated, controlled or associated persons, and to competitors for the last five years and the most recent interim period. Inquire as to whether the selling prices are comparable to those posted on sales to other customers.

G. Analyze sales returns and sales allowances separately by quarter for the last year and by month for the most recent interim period. Obtain explanations for any unusual amounts of returns or allowances.

H. Analyze warranty reserves, by quarter for the last year and by month for the most recent period. Obtain explanations for unusual fluctuations. Discuss the warranty program from the standpoint of its uniqueness in the industry.

I. Analyze the summary of firm order backlog by product line as of the most current date, the comparable date in the preceding year and several immediate preceding dates. Investigate any unusual fluctuations. Inquire as to whether the company produces principally against firm orders or for inventory.

J. Analyze the summary of major general, selling, administrative and interest expenses by quarter for the last two years and most recent interim period. Note any unusual fluctuations or any "discretionary" reductions of certain expenses (advertising, research, etc.) which could affect future earnings. Compute the effect on future earnings, from the reduction of interest expense due to early extinguishment of debt or more favorable rates as a result of the acquisition. Also, compute the impact that certain assumed increases in prime interest rates or scheduled increases in specified rates would have on future earnings.

K. Review comparison of originally forecasted earnings to actual earnings by product line (or plant and subsidiaty) by quarter for the last two years and the most recent interim period. Obtain explanations for significant differences between forecasted and actual results.

L. Analyze the composition of all extraordinary charges and credits, "catch-up" adjustments, prior period adjustments and other nonrecurring or unusual charges and credits for the last five years and the most recent interim period. Inquire as to whether any operating charges may have been inadvertently included therein. Also, inquire as to the basis upon which any such items have been computed.

M. Is a material part of the enterprise dependent upon a single customer or a few major customers, and would the loss of any one or more have a materially adverse effect on the operations of the company? Inquire as whether any foreign customers constitute a significant portion of the company's business (determine names, countries and amounts) and if recent changes in international exchange rates, import quotas or other restrictions will have any material impact on such business.

N. Evaluate explanations of significant items of "miscellaneous income" and miscellaneous expense" for the last two years and most recent interim period and any other similar type of income or expense that has been applied to cost of goods sold or other accounts.

O. Does the company have any contingency plans whereby overhead and corporate expenses could be reduced if there were a general recession in the industry or a particularly recessive condition prevailed with respect to the company? Inquire as to what severance payments would be required under union and other agreements if lay-offs were required.

III. ANALYSIS OF CURRENT ASSETS

A. Analyze the summary of cash balance by major depositories, divisions or other appropriate categories as of the last year-end and the current date.

B. Investigate banking arrangements, including withdrawal restrictions and requirements to maintain compensating balances, and consider the depth and reliability of such arrangements.

C. Analyze a summary of trade receivables by major product line, division, customer, geographical area, as of the last year-end and the current date.

D. Inquire about normal and special credit terms (including rebates) and credit policies in effect as of the current date and any change during the last two years and the most interim period.

E. Review pledged receivables, accounts sold with recourse, factoring arrangements, etc., as of the current date.

F. Analyze an aged summary of trade receivables as of the last year-end and the current date. Obtain management's explanation as to the collectibility of large overdue balances or old balances due from major customers, etc., and read credit files relating to these accounts.

G. Obtain a summary of bad debt experience for the last five years and the most recent interim period and consider the adequacy of the allowance for doubtful accounts.

H. Compute accounts receivable turnover ratios by appropriate categories for the:
   1. Last two years
   2. Most recent interim period.

I. Inquire about collateral held by the company and the basis for determining market value, etc., as of the current date.

J. Review any miscellaneous receivables by major categories (officers, directors, stockholders, employees, subsidiaries, affiliates, etc.) as of the last year-end and the current date and investigate the nature of such receivables.

K. Review an aged summary of miscellaneous receivables as of the last year-end and the current date and obtain management's opinion as to the collectibility.

L. Inquire about collateral held by the company and the basis for determining market value, etc., as of the current date.

M. Analyze summary of inventories by major product lines, divisions, cost centers, or other appropriate categories as of the last two year-ends and the current date.

N. Compute inventory turnover ratios by appropriate categories for the:
   1. Last two years.
   2. Most recent interim period.

O. Review an aged inventory summary as of the current date. Inquire about obsolete, slow-moving, bill and hold, close-outs, seconds, irregulars, markdowns, and expires sale contract inventories on hand as of the current date. Analyze the procedures followed in determining whether any such inventory should be written off.

P. Ascertain amount of obsolete inventories written off during the last two years and the reason (s) therefor.

Q. Analyze procedures used to determine that inventories are stated at the lower of cost or market and consider the propriety of inventory valuation methods.

R. Review inventory adjustments as of the last two year-ends and the most recent interim period and as to the transactions in any inventory reserves for the last two years and the most recent interim period. Inquire about the nature of any recorded reserves and adjustments (book versus physical, pricing errors, over or underabosorbed costs).

S. Does a cost system exist? If a standard cost system is used, inquire as to the frequency of updating standard costs and the procedures for accumulating and reviewing standard cost procedures.

T. Inquire about the existence and nature of perpetual inventory records and the reliance placed thereon for interim financial statement purposes.

U. Has the company made any unusual commitments regarding the purchase or bulk sale of inventories?

V. Review any pledged inventories as of the last year-end and the current date.

W. Are any inventories held on consignment or consigned to others as of the last year-end and the current date?

X. Investigate long-term contracts in process as of the current date, including consideration of:

a. Method of accounting for long-term contracts (completed contract or percentage of completion).

b. Basis of computing the percentage of completion.

c. Management's opinion as to the adequacy of the provision for losses on uncompleted contracts.

d. The company's actual experience in realizing profits or losses on long-term contracts for the last two years.

IV. PROPERTY AND OTHER ASSETS

A. Analyze significant acquisitions and disposals of property for the last two years and the most recent interim period.

B. Review carrying value of property and indicate any portion not carried at cost.

C. Inquire as to whether all obsolete plant and equipment has been written off and whether depreciation has been accelerated on plant equipment where it would appear that technological changes will require replacement earlier than originally anticipated. Inquire as to the reasons for any underutilization of property and equipment, particularly in those industries where high volume is necessary to absorb fixed costs. Also inquire as to the degree of manual, semi-automated and fully-automated operations and as to an estimate of the cost of fully-automating the facilities.

D. Review the reasonableness of the estimated useful lives being used for book depreciation purposes. Compare the age of major facilities to such lives and inquire whether any significant expenditures will be necessary in the near future.

E. Inquire about recent property appraisals, tax assessment valuations, etc. and relate these to original costs (particularly in purchase transactions).

F. Analyze accounting policies for capitalization of property items.

G. Analyze pledged property as of the current date.

H. Visit the principal operating locations. Observe the flow of materials through the production process and note the general layouts of the plant. Inquire as to compliance with environmental and safety requirements, source of utilities (gas, electricity and steam), warehouse facilities and plant security. Be alert for obsolete or idle equipment or facilities.

I. Review a summary of prepaid expenses, deferred charges and other assets by major categories (insurance, taxes, interest, etc.) as of the last year-end and the current date and investigate the nature of such assets.

J. Analyze a summary of insurance coverage as of the current date and inquire about its adequacy. Compare coverage with available information such a appraisal value, replacement cost, book value, etc.

K. Review amortization methods and rates for the last two years and the most recent interim period.

V. ANALYSIS OF CURRENT LIABILITIES

A. Analyze trade payables by major categories (divisions, suppliers, age, etc.) as of the last year-end and the current date.

B. Review special credit terms (including rebates) with suppliers as of the current date.

C. Summarize cash discounts taken or lost for the last two years and the most recent interim period.

D. Review accrued liabilities (other than taxes) by major categories (payroll, interest, etc.) as of the last year-end and the current date.

E. Are there any other significant accrued liabilities?

F. Are appropriate accruals made for such items a advertising, retroactive wage adjustments, pensions, litigation, warranties under contracts, sales allowances and credits, provisions for enviromental problems and foreign currency losses?

G. Are there any material contingent liabilities (including pending claims, litigation, etc.) as of the last year-end and the most recent date? Discuss the effect of pending claims and litigation on the financial position of the company with the company's counsel.

H. Read copies of federal and state income tax returns for the last three years. Inquire about any unusual items noted therein.

I. Obtain a summary of federal and state taxes payable as of the last year-end and the current date, showing separately, amounts applicable to prior years.

J. Analyze available carry-overs (net operating loss, investment credit, foreign tax credit, contributions, etc.) and related expiration dates as of the current dates.

VI. DEBT

A. Analyze short-term and long-term debt by major categories (notes, bonds, etc.) showing principal holders, stated and effective interest rates, maturities, etc., as of the last year-end and the current date.

B. Review copies of loan agreements for short-term and long-term debt.

C. Investigate principal features of loan agreements, including consideration of:
1. Convertibility.
2. Collateral.
3. Restrictions on company activity such as working capital requirements, other permitted debt and dividend, consolidation or merger limitations.
4. Events of default.
5. Prepayment premiums.
6. Sinking fund requirements.

D. Are there any definitional problems raised with respect to convenants in loan agreements and is the company's counsel satisfied that all convenants are being met?

VII. EQUITY

A. Review a summary of equity accounts as of the last year-end and the current date, showing changes in the last five years and the most recent interim period. Summary should indicate the voting rights, conversion rights dividend and liquidation preferences for each class of equity securities.

B. Read copies of documents relating to stock options and purchase plans and warrant arrangements.

C. Review a summary of stock options and warrants as of the last year-end and the current date.

APPENDIX G

COMPUTER FORECASTING MODEL

BUYOUT CANDIDATE CORPORATION
PROJECTED BALANCE SHEET
(in thousands)

	PRO FORMA Feb-87	1 Feb-88	2 Feb-89	3 Feb-90
CURRENT ASSETS:				
CASH	350	252	253	322
ACCTS. REC.	3,000	3,500	3,675	3,859
INVENTORY	3,000	3,033	3,185	3,344
PREPAID EXPENSES	150	150	160	170
OTHER	0	0	0	0
TOTAL CURRENT	6,500	6,935	7,273	7,695
FIXED ASSETS:				
MACHINERY & EQUIP.	2,000	2,150	2,300	2,450
BUILDINGS	1,750	1,800	1,850	1,900
LAND	0	0	0	0
LESS: ACCUM. DEP.	(250)	(458)	(679)	(913)
TOTAL FIXED	3,500	3,492	3,471	3,437
OTHER ASSETS				
INTANGIBLES	0	0	0	0
TOTAL OTHER	0	0	0	0
TOTAL ASSETS	10,000	10,427	10,744	11,132
CURRENT LIABILITIES:				
Short Term Debt:				
REV LOAN #1	2,400	2,975	3,124	3,280
REV LOAN #2	1,250	1,213	1,274	1,338
Total S.T. Debt	3,650	4,188	4,398	4,618
ACCTS. PAYABLE	1,800	1,706	1,792	1,881
ACCRUALS	200	210	220	231
OTHER	0	0	0	0
TOTAL CURRENT	5,650	6,104	6,410	6,730
LONG TERM DEBT:				
TERM DEBT #1	1,000	800	600	400
TERM DEBT #2	2,450	2,352	2,254	2,156
SUB. DEBT #1	0	0	0	0
SUB. DEBT #2	0	0	0	0
TOTAL LONG TERM	3,450	3,152	2,854	2,556
EQUITY:				
PREFERRED STOCK	0	0	0	0
COMMON STOCK	900	900	900	900
RETAINED EARNINGS	0	271	580	946
TOTAL EQUITY	900	1,171	1,480	1,846
TOTAL LIAB. & EQUITY	10,000	10,427	10,744	11,132

4 Feb-91	5 Feb-92	6 Feb-93	7 Feb-94	8 Feb-95	9 Feb-96	10 Feb-97
462	688	1,174	1,730	2,363	3,077	3,876
4,052	4,254	4,467	4,690	4,925	5,171	5,430
3,511	3,687	3,871	4,065	4,268	4,481	4,705
180	193	206	220	233	248	264
0	0	0	0	0	0	0
8,205	8,822	9,718	10,705	11,789	12,977	14,274
2,600	2,750	2,900	3,050	3,200	3,350	3,500
1,950	2,000	2,050	2,100	2,150	2,200	2,250
0	0	0	0	0	0	
(1,160)	(1,420)	(1,693)	(1,979)	(2,278)	(2,590)	(2,915)
3,390	3,330	3,257	3,171	3,072	2,960	2,835
0	0	0	0	0	0	0
0	0	0	0	0	0	0
11,595	12,152	12,975	13,876	14,861	15,937	17,109
3,444	3,616	3,797	3,987	4,186	4,395	4,615
1,404	1,475	1,548	1,626	1,707	1,792	1,882
4,848	5,091	5,345	5,613	5,893	6,188	6,497
1,975	2,074	2,178	2,287	2,401	2,521	2,647
243	255	268	281	295	310	325
0	0	0	0	0	0	0
7,066	7,420	7,791	8,181	8,589	9,019	9,469
200	0	0	0	0	0	0
2,058	1,960	1,862	1,764	1,666	1,568	1,470
0	0	0	0	0	0	0
0	0	0	0	0	0	0
2,258	1,960	1,862	1,764	1,666	1,568	1,470
0	0	0	0	0	0	0
900	900	900	900	900	900	900
1,371	1,872	2,422	3,031	3,706	4,450	5,270
2,271	2,772	3,322	3,931	4,606	5,350	6,170
11,595	12,152	12,975	13,876	14,861	15,937	17,109

PROJECTED INCOME STATEMENT
(in thousands)

	PRO FORMA Feb-87	1 Feb-88	2 Feb-89	3 Feb-90
REVENUES				
SOURCE 1	10,000	10,500	11,025	11,576
SOURCE 2	8,000	8,400	8,820	9,261
SOURCE 3	2,000	2,100	2,205	2,315
TOTAL REVENUES	20,000	21,000	22,050	23,152
LESS: COST OF SALES				
MATERIALS	10,304	10,817	11,358	11,926
LABOR	1,500	1,575	1,654	1,736
OVERHEAD	1,000	1,050	1,103	1,158
TOTAL COGS	12,804	13,442	14,115	14,820
GROSS PROFIT	7,196	7,558	7,935	8,332
LESS: OP. EXP.				
DEPRECIATION EXP.	196	208	221	234
GENERAL & ADMIN.	4,000	4,200	4,410	4,631
SELLING	1,000	1,050	1,103	1,158
OTHER	500	525	551	579
TOTAL OP. EXP.	5,696	5,983	6,285	6,602
OPERATING INCOME	1,500	1,575	1,650	1,730
LESS: INT. EXPENSE				
REV LOAN #1	408	442	488	512
REV LOAN #2	213	214	220	231
TERM DEBT #1	170	153	119	85
TERM DEBT #2	343	336	322	309
SUB. DEBT #1	0	0	0	0
SUB. DEBT #2	0	0	0	0
TOTAL INT. EXP.	1,134	1,145	1,149	1,137
TOTAL OPERATING INC.	366	430	501	593
NON-OPERATING INC.	21	21	15	15
NON-OPERATING EXP.	0	0	0	0
LESS: NOL CARRYFWD	0	0	0	0
PRE-TAX INCOME	387	451	516	608
LESS: INCOME TAXES	155	180	206	243
NET INCOME	232	271	310	365

4	5	6	7	8	9	10
Feb-91	Feb-92	Feb-93	Feb-94	Feb-95	Feb-96	Feb-97
12,155	12,763	13,401	14,071	14,775	15,513	16,289
9,724	10,210	10,721	11,257	11,820	12,411	13,031
2,431	2,553	2,680	2,814	2,955	3,103	3,258
24,310	25,526	26,802	28,142	29,550	31,027	32,578
12,522	13,148	13,806	14,496	15,221	15,982	16,781
1,823	1,914	2,010	2,111	2,216	2,327	2,443
1,216	1,276	1,340	1,407	1,477	1,551	1,629
15,561	16,338	17,156	18,014	18,914	19,860	20,853
8,749	9,188	9,646	10,128	10,636	11,167	11,725
247	260	273	286	299	312	325
4,862	5,105	5,360	5,628	5,910	6,205	6,516
1,216	1,276	1,340	1,407	1,477	1,551	1,629
608	638	670	704	739	776	814
6,933	7,279	7,643	8,025	8,425	8,844	9,284
1,816	1,909	2,003	2,103	2,211	2,323	2,441
538	565	593	623	654	687	721
243	255	268	281	295	310	325
51	0	0	0	0	0	0
295	281	268	254	240	226	213
0	0	0	0	0	0	0
0	0	0	0	0	0	0
1,127	1,101	1,129	1,158	1,189	1,223	1,259
689	808	874	945	1,022	1,100	1,182
19	28	41	70	104	142	185
0	0	0	0	0	0	0
0	0	0	0	0	0	0
708	836	915	1,015	1,126	1,242	1,367
283	334	366	406	450	497	547
425	502	549	609	676	745	820

BUYOUT CANDIDATE CORPORATION

PROJECTED CASH FLOW
(in thousands)

	PRO FORMA Feb-87	1 Feb-88	2 Feb-89	3 Feb-90
FROM OPERATIONS:				
NET INCOME	232	271	310	365
DEPRECIATION	250	208	221	234
DEFERRED INTEREST	0	0	0	0
TOTAL	482	479	531	599
WORKING CAPITAL				
ACCTS. RECEIVABLE	0	(500)	(175)	(184)
INVENTORY	0	(33)	(152)	(159)
PREPAID EXPENSES	0	0	(10)	(10)
OTHER CURR. ASSETS	0	0	0	0
ACCTS. PAYABLE	0	(94)	85	90
ACCRUALS	0	10	10	11
OTHER CURR. LIAB.	0	0	0	0
TOTAL	0	(617)	(242)	(252)
FIXED ASSETS				
PURCHASES	0	(200)	(200)	(200)
DISPOSITIONS	0	0	0	0
TOTAL	0	(200)	(200)	(200)
CHANGES IN DEBT:				
REV LOAN #1	0	575	149	156
REV LOAN #2	0	(37)	61	64
TERM DEBT #1	0	(200)	(200)	(200)
TERM DEBT #2	0	(98)	(98)	(98)
SUB. DEBT #1	0	0	0	0
SUB. DEBT #2	0	0	0	0
TOTAL DEBT CHANGE	0	240	(88)	(78)
PREFERRED STOCK	0	0	0	0
DIVIDENDS	0	0	0	0
REDEMPTIONS	0	0	0	0
NET CASH FLOW	250	(98)	1	69
BEG. CASH BALANCE	350	350	252	253
END. CASH BALANCE	600	252	253	322

4 Feb-91	5 Feb-92	6 Feb-93	7 Feb-94	8 Feb-95	9 Feb-96	10 Feb-97
425	502	549	609	676	745	820
247	260	273	286	299	312	325
0	0	0	0	0	0	0
672	762	822	895	975	1,057	1,145
(193)	(203)	(213)	(223)	(235)	(246)	(259)
(167)	(176)	(184)	(194)	(203)	(213)	(224)
(11)	(12)	(13)	(13)	(14)	(15)	(16)
0	0	0	0	0	0	0
94	99	104	109	114	120	126
12	12	13	13	14	15	15
0	0	0	0	0	0	0
(265)	(280)	(293)	(308)	(324)	(339)	(358)
(200)	(200)	(200)	(200)	(200)	(200)	(200)
0	0	0	0	0	0	0
(200)	(200)	(200)	(200)	(200)	(200)	(200)
164	172	181	190	199	209	220
67	70	74	77	81	85	90
(200)	(200)	0	0	0	0	0
(98)	(98)	(98)	(98)	(98)	(98)	(98)
0	0	0	0	0	0	0
0	0	0	0	0	0	0
(67)	(56)	157	169	182	196	212
0	0	0	0	0	0	0
0	0	0	0	0	0	0
0	0	0	0	0	0	0
140	226	486	556	633	714	799
322	462	688	1,174	1,730	2,363	3,077
462	688	1,174	1,730	2,363	3,077	3,876

APPENDIX H

LBO FINANCING PACKAGE OUTLINE

SUGGESTED OUTLINE OF A TYPICAL LEVERAGED BUYOUT FINANCING PACKAGE

The leveraged buyer, whether it is an incumbent manager or outside entrepreneur, must always be cognizant that the financing package is first and foremost a communications tool. It must communicate the salient facts about the proposed deal to lenders and/or investors. In doing so, it must strike a balance between brevity and thoroughness.

There is no "ideal" length of an LBO financing package. The ultimate size will depend upon many factors, including complexity of the deal, buyers experience and familiarity with financing sources, and time constraints. If it doesn't clearly reveal pertinent facts, the package is too brief. However, if it puts the reader asleep with irrelevant minutia, it's too long. In putting the financing package together, the buyer must constantly ask himself: "Am I communicating important information, the absence of which would leave the lender or investor with an incomplete picture of the deal"?

The following is a suggested outline for a typical LBO financing package. A brief description of the topics to cover in each section are included to guide the reader through the preparation process.

I. EXECUTIVE SUMMARY

Because most lenders and investors in LBO'S are busy people, it is helpful to summarize the key points of the deal in two or three pages. It should be briefly describe the target company, proposed transaction, requested financing and buyer credibility.

II. HISTORY AND BACKGROUND

This section should include a more detailed description of the target company, its business and future prospects. More importantly, it should discuss the buyers relationship with the seller and current status of the negotiations.

III. PRODUCTS AND MARKETS

It is important to convey to financing sources the characteristics of the marketplace and where the company's products and services fit in. This should include an analysis of the competition, relative market shares, and what unique attributes the company has that will enable it to maintain or improve its position.

IV. FACILITIES AND CAPITAL EQUIPMENT

Some capital intensive companies require a more detailed description of the productive facilities. It should emphasize their condition and estimated timetables to refurbish or replace on order to maintain the company's competitive position. This discussion should tie into capital budgeting assumptions in the projected financial statements (see below).

V. OPERATING PLAN

The integrity of the proposed operating plan after the closing is a key factor in persuading financing sources to to participate. Therefore the buyer must state the key operating assumptions which form the basis of financial projections. This includes revenue assumptions, cost reduction programs, capital equipment purchase, etc. It must convey thorough understanding of the dynamics of the business.

VI. FINANCIAL STATEMENTS AND PROJECTIONS

Obviously, the package should include historical financial statements, preferably for the past 5 years. In addition, there should be projections of income, cash flow and financial position for a period of at least 5 years, and preferably 10 years. These projections should reflect the assumptions described in the operating plan, as well as the proposed financial structure of the transaction. It is also helpful to include one set of contingency projections that reflect the consequences of a "worst case" scenario.

VII. PERSONNEL

Biographies of key managers should be included along with a current (and proposal) organization chart. If applicable, any labor contracts should also be discussed in this section.

APPENDIX I

CLOSING DOCUMENT CHECKLIST

H.E. Harris & Co., Inc.

SALE OF ASSETS
OF
H.E. HARRIS & CO., INC.

INDEX OF CLOSING DOCUMENTS

1. Sale Agreement

Exhibit A	"Buyer's Note" $3,980,000 (Section 2.1)
Exhibit B	Balance Sheet and other (Section 3.1)
Exhibit C	Material Contracts (Section 4.5)
Exhibit D	Title to Property (Section 4.6)
Exhibit E	Patents, Trademark (Section 4.10)
Exhibit F	Litigation (Section 4.11)

2. Opinion of Seller's Counsel (Section 8.1)

3. Opinion of Buyer's Counsel (Section 8.2)

4. Promissory Note to be executed ($3,980,000)

5. Collateral Security Agreement

6. Form UCC-1 -- Massachusetts
   New Hampshire

7. Stock Powers

8. Plate Sale Agreement
   Exhibit A - Description
   Exhibit B - Note $100,000
   Exhibit C - Bill of Sale

9. Bill of Sale - Plates

10. Promissory Note to be executed ($100,000)

11. Real Estate Agreement
    Exhibit A - Description of Property
    Exhibit B - Note for $20,000

12. Warranty Deed

13. Promissory Note to be executed ($20,000)

14. Purchase Money Mortgage

15. Guaranty of General Mills, Inc. in favor of Maryland National Industrial Corporation

16. Opinion of Counsel of General Mills, Inc. relating to guaranty

17. Subordination Agreement

18. Certified copies of resolution of the Board of Directors of General Mills, Inc. relating to sale of assets of H.E. Harris & Co., Inc.

19. Certified copies of resolutions of Board of Directors and shareholders of H.E. Harris & Co., Inc.

20. General Bill of Sale

21. Assumption of Liabilities Agreement

22. Certified copy of resolution of Board of Directors of H.E.H. Associates, Inc.

23. Vehicle Agreement

24. Funding Instructions

25. Letter to H.E.H. Associates, Inc.

APPENDIX J

ACQUISITION TIMETABLE

Wallner & Co.

WALLNER & CO.

PRELIMINARY TIMETABLE

1. Table of Contents

2. Parties

3. Pre-Closing Documentation
   - 3.1 Sale Contracts & Exhibits
   - 3.2 "Transfer Asset" Review
   - 3.3 "Transfer Asset" Liabilities (Leases in 3.2)
   - 3.4 "Purchase Asset" Review
   - 3.5 Title & Title Insurance
   - 3.6 "Purchase Asset" Liabilities (Leases in 3.4)
   - 3.7 Buyer Financing
   - 3.8 Licenses, Permits and Government Approvals
   - 3.9 Assignments and Third Party Consents
   - 3.10 Labor Matters
   - 3.11 Patents, Trademarks and Other Matters
   - 3.12 ERISA
   - 3.13 Legal Review (Except Litigation)
   - 3.14 Litigation Review (Except Insured)
   - 3.15 Accounting Review
   - 3.16 Insurance, Risk Management, Insured Litigation
   - 3.17 Taxes

4. Closing Documentation
   - 4.1 Sale Contracts Amendments, Waivers, Consents (3.1.4)
   - 4.2 Further Actions (Bd. Dirs. Etc.) of FM, FWDR Assoc., FD Partners
   - 4.3 Bills of Sale; Deeds; any UCC Releases
   - 4.4 Asset Assignments, Third Party Consents and Estoppel Certificates (3.9)
   - 4.5 Vehicle Registration Transfers
   - 4.6 Legal Opinions
   - 4.7 Audit and Cold Comfort Letter
   - 4.8 Licenses and Permits (3.8)
   - 4.9 Labor Union Contract Assumptions (3.10)
   - 4.10 Patent, TM, etc. and Licensing Assignments (3.11)
   - 4.11 ERISA Matters (3.12) if any
   - 4.12 Fictitious Name Abandonments and Buyer Filings
   - 4.13 Officers Certificates
   - 4.14 Payment and Receipts
   - 4.15 UCC Financing Statements (3.7.5)
   - 4.16 Post-Closing Leases, etc.
   - 4.17 Title Insurance
   - 4.18 Post-Closing Transmittals
   - 4.19 Sales and Realty Tax Payments and Returns
   - 4.20 ERISA Filings: IRS, PBGC, Dept. Labor Notices to participants

5. Business Review
   - 5.1 Re Management
   - 5.2 Antitrust and Pricing
   - 5.3 Books and Records
   - 5.4 Benefits
   - 5.5 Security and Appraisals
   - 5.6 Accounting
   - 5.7 Legal
   - 5.8 Foreign
   - 5.9 Personnel

6. Transition
   - 6.1 Pre-Closing Consents, etc.
   - 6.2 "Service Agreement" Matters
   - 6.3 Data Processing
   - 6.4 Financial
   - 6.5 Post-Closing
   - 6.6 Miscellaneous

2. PARTIES

Party	Role	Abbreviation
	Sell	FM
	The assets	FD
Wallner Associates	--	
FWDR Associates, Inc.	Buyer-personality	FWDR
FD Partners	Buyer-realty	FD PTNRS.
Nicholas Wallner		WALLNER
Peter O. Redfield		REDFIELD
Walter Heller	Financing	HELLER
	FM outside counsel	
Ervin, Cohen & Jessup	Buyer counsel	ECJ
Levy & Norminton	HEL counsel	LEVY
Deloitte, Haskins & Sells	FM CPA	DH&S
Arthur Andersen & Co.	WALLNER CPA	AA

3. PRE-CLOSING DOCUMENTATION

This section includes all documents except actual closing documents.

Item	Document	Schedule
3.1	Sale Contracts and Exhibits	
3.1.1	Asset Sale Agreement "asa"	Revise 8-23
3.1.1.1	asa Schedules "asa scheds"	Review 8-25
3.1.2	Purchase Agreement "pa"	Complete 8-27; Review 8-30
3.1.2.1	pa Schedules "pa scheds"	Negotiate 8-20 Sign 9-1
3.1.3	Press Releases "press"	Complete 8-27; Review 8-30 Issue 9-1 Again re Closing
3.1.4	Amendments, Waivers, Consents	--
3.1.5	FM Corporate Action	Bd. Mtg. 9-1
3.1.6	FDWR Corporate Action	Sign 8-31
3.1.7	Service Contract "servcon" open items, process drafts, vehicle maintenance	Discuss 8-20 Draft 9-1 Sign 9-15

3.1.8	Organize FWDR; FD Partners	Now
3.1.9	Qualify FWDR and FD Partners in states	By 9-30
3.1.10	Issue Stock and Partnership Interests (Blue Sky?) (Tax?)	By 8-30

<u>See also</u> subject matter §§, e.g. 3.12 for any agreements for the handling of ERISA trust funds or welfare plans.

3.2 Transfer Asset Review

3.2.1	Guidelines for schedules of owned assets, leased assets, misc. assets, assets used but now owned or leased; consent requirements; purchase options.	Discuss 8-20
3.2.2	Transfer Asset Schedule "ta schedules	Complete 8-27 Review 8-30
3.2.3	Reconciliation of ta scheds to Balance Sheet	By 9-15
3.2.4	List FM retained assets used in connection with FD, e.g., computer system description, parent co. offices, personnel. Prepared Excluded Asset Schedule	Complete 8-27 Review 8-30
3.2.5	Review of Documents	From 8-17
3.2.6	Collect Vehicle registration	Sept.

3.3 "Transfer Asset" Liabilities

3.3.1	Guidelines for Assumed Liabilities Schedule	Discuss 8-20
3.3.2	Schedule of Assumed Liabilities	Complete 8-27 Review 8-30
3.3.3	UCC Searches, Chattel Mortgages	By 9-15
3.3.4	CPA Worksheets re absence of liens, etc.	By 9-15

3.4 "Purchase Asset" Review

3.4.1	Guidelines for schedules of owned assets, leased assets, misc.	Discuss 8-20

		assets, assets used but not owned or leased; consent requirements; purchase options	
	3.4.2	Decide which entity acquires cattle	Wallner 8-18
	3.4.3	"Purchase Assets" Schedules "pa scheds"	Complete 8-27 Review 8-30
	3.4.4	Reconciliation of pa scheds to Balance Sheet	By 9-15
	3.4.5	Does FM retain any realty assets used in connection with FD?	8-27
	3.4.6	Smithway Lease Assignment (sensitive, Yellon controls)	By 9-15
	3.4.7	Review of Documents	From 8-17

See also 3.5 Title and Title Insurance.

3.5	Title and Title Insurance		
	3.5.1	Guidelines for reviewing title (e.g., value, purchase date, prior title insurance or opinion)	Discuss 8-20
	3.5.2	Opinions (in states not having insurance)	Check 8-20
	3.5.3	PTRs	Order Now Get By 9-10
3.6	"Purchase Asset" Liabilities		
	3.6.1	Guidelines for Schedule	Discuss 8-20
	3.6.2	Schedule of Assumed Liabilities	Complete 8-27
	3.6.3	UCC Searches, Chattle Mortages - See 3.3.3	Review 8-30
	3.6.4	CPA Worksheets re absense of liens, etc. - See 3.3.4	
3.7	Buyer Financing		
	3.7.1	Commitment Letter from Heller	By 8-27
	3.7.2	Agreement with Heller "hel agmt"	By ?
	3.7.3	Schedules "hel scheds"	By ?
	3.7.4	Bank Syndication Agreement "synd"	By 9-15
	3.7.5	Financing Statements for closing "hel fs"	By 9-22

3.8	**Licenses, Permits and Government Approvals**	
3.8.1	Schedule of Dairy and Other Licenses and Transfer Procedure	ASAP
3.8.2	Memo on any FDA requirement (Existing approvals, pending matters, compliance requirements)	By 9-15
3.8.3	Hart-Scott-Rodino (30 day waiting period)	Complete 8-27 File 9-1
3.9	**Assignments and Third Party Consents**	
3.9.1	FM Lenders	Request 9-3
3.9.2	Landlords	Request 9-3
3.9.3	Equipment Leases	Request 9-3

List from 3.2 and 3.4 leased asset schedules; see also 3.8 licenses and permits.

3.10	**Labor Matters**	
3.10.1	Schedule of Labor Contracts Union Organizing Activities	By 9-8
3.10.2	Buyer Agreements to Succeed to Labor Contracts	By 9-24
3.10.3	Schedule of any Known or Alleged Contract or Labor Law Noncompliances Grievances, Requests for Arbitration	By 9-15
3.10.4	Notice of Requests: Will FD be bound; restrictions, e.g., on relocating any facilities	?
3.11	**Patents, Trademarks and Other Matters**	
3.11.1	Intangible Rights and Ownership	Schedule 8-24 Review 8-25 Assign Docs 9-17
3.11.2	License Rights Owned	Schedule 8-24 Review 8-25 Assign Docs 9-17
3.11.3	License Rights Granted	Schedule 8-24 Review 8-25 Assign Docs 9-17

Item	Description	Timing
3.11.4	Fictitious Names by State	Schedule 9-10 New Docs 9-17
3.11.5	What Name Will FM Use?	Discuss 8-20

3.12 ERISA (Plans Involving FD Employees)

Item	Description	Timing
3.12.1	Schedule of "Pension" and "Welfare" Plans (as broadly defined in ERISA)	Complete 9-8 Review 9-10
3.12.2	Copy of Each Plan, Trust, IRS Determination Letter, Summary Plan Description, Annual Reports Last 3 Years (11-K's?), Any Insurance Policies Which Fund Trusts	By 9-10
3.12.3	Any Multi-Employer Plans? (For MEPPA liability analysis)	By 8-24

For the above purposes, "pension plans" include qualified pension, profit sharing and stock bonus plans, and variations thereof, as well as non-qualified deferred compensation arrangements with any employees. For the above purposes, "welfare benefit plans" include any plan, fund or program maintained by the employer or an employee organization for the purpose of providing employees or their beneficiaries, through insurance or otherwise, medical, surgical, hospital care or benefits, sickness, accident, disability, death or employment benefits, vacation benefits, day care centers, scholarship funds or prepaid legal services.

3.13 Legal Review (Except Litigation)

Item	Description	Timing
3.13.1	List of all states having FD operations, activities or offices, with further detail where FWDR and/or FD PTNRS may or may not have to qualify to do business.	By 9-10
3.13.2	Copy of FM minutes 4 years shareholders, directors, committees).	By 9-10 Review 9-17
3.13.3	Schedule and copies of all partnerships and joint ventures	By 9-10
3.13.4	Copy of FM articles, by-laws (re no shareholder vote)	By 9-15 Review 9-22

3.13.5	Political/lobbying policies and compliance	By 9-15
3.13.6	Any consent decrees or injunctions?	9-8
3.13.7	Compliance: FTC, FDA, EPS, OSHA, EEOC, Questionable Payments	Memo 9-10

3.14 Litigation Review (Except Insured)

3.14.1	Schedule of all litigation not fully insured, pending and threatened	By 9-8

3.15 Accounting Review

3.15.1	Unaudited FD 5 years + interim financial statements + by business unit	ASAP
3.15.2	Access to auditors, work papers, adjusting and trial balances of FD and relevant FM	Continuing
3.15.3	3 years auditor inquiry responses	By 8-25
3.15.4	3 years auditor letters to management (FD items). Are there any corrective response memos?	By 8-25

3.16 Insurance, Risk Management, Insured Litigation

3.16.1	Schedules	By 9-8
3.16.2	FD management analysis?	By 9-8
3.16.3	Workers' compensation analysis	Discuss 8-20 By 9-8

3.17 Taxes

3.17.1	Determine sales taxes, realty transfer taxes; plan minimization	By 9-15

4. CLOSING DOCUMENTATION

4.1 Sale Contracts Amendments, Waivers, Consents (3.1.4)

4.2 Further Actions (BD, DIRS., etc.) of FM, FWDR Assoc. FD Partners

4.3 Bills of Sale; Deeds; any UCC Releases

4.4 Asset Assignments, Third Party Consents and Estoppel Certificates (3.9)
4.5 Vehicle Registration Transfers
4.6 Legal Opinions
4.7 Audit and Cold Comfort Letter
4.8 Licenses and Permits (3.8)
4.9 Labor Union Contract Assumptions (3.10)
4.10 Patent, TM, etc. and Licensing Assignments (3.11)
4.11 ERISA Matters if any (3.12)
4.12 Fictitious Name Abandonments and Buyer Filings by State
4.13 Officers Certificates
4.14 Payment and Receipts
4.15 UCC Financing Statements (3.7.4)
4.16 Post-Closing Leases, etc.
4.17 Title Insurance
4.18 Post-Closing Transmittals
4.19 Sales and Realty Tax Payments and Returns
4.20 ERISA Filings: IRS, PBGC, Department of Labor Notices to Participants

5. BUSINESS REVIEW

See preceding §§ re documents and certain reviews, e.g., accounting, legal, labor, ERISA.

5.1 Management
- 5.1.1 FD (FM if same) management policies (any manual?)
- 5.1.2 Tables of organization (operations and personnel)
- 5.1.3 (25?) most highly compensated officers and employees, their employment contracts and secrecy agreements (if any).
- 5.1.4 Schedule of FM stock options, SAR's, etc. of FD employees. Option plan and sample option.
- 5.1.5 R&D (it is FM corporate level)
- 5.1.6 Obtain history of labor negotiations past 5 years.
- 5.1.7 Obtain projections and plans. What is planning process?
- 5.1.8 Trade association and other memberships.
- 5.1.9 Lobbying

5.2 Antitrust and Pricing
- 5.2.1 FD (or FM re FD) antitrust policies, reviews
- 5.2.2 FD (or FM re FD) pricing policies, studies

5.3 Books and Records
- 5.3.1 Schedule of FM (not FD) personnel, books and records pertinent to FD, e.g., internal audit, FM legal and tax records. Proposed to stay with FM or go to FD Assoc.?
- 5.3.2 Access to books, records, tax data and returns, personnel, etc. needed after closing?
- 5.3.3 Copies of tax returns, backup, audit and revenue agent reports, settlement documents, waivers of limitations relevant to FD (federal, state, local) all open years and last closed year.

5.4 Benefits
- 5.4.1 If any pension plans transferring: actuarial review and reports; calculations using PBGC assumptions.
- 5.4.2 Fringe benefit and perquisites review
- 5.4.3 Fringe benefits, perquisities, vacation, sick pay accruals
- 5.4.4 Do plans own FM stock?

5.5 Security and Appraisals
- 5.5.1 Appraisals (primarily rolling stock) (Norman Dalton) 8-20
- 5.5.2 Heller review of A/R, other security. A/P 8/20

5.6 Accounting and Data Processing
- 5.6.1 Plan creation of data processing function and transfer of software. Computer hardware is FM's; software goes with FD
- 5.6.2 Need lock boxes and bank accounts
- 5.6.3 Create treasurer and internal audit functions.
- 5.6.4 Analyze books and records systems to establish new books
- 5.6.5 Would any short term leases save ITC?

5.7 Legal
- 5.7.1 Foods group uses 2 FM attorneys part time. State regulation, etc.

5.8 Foreign
- 5.8.1 No foreign assets except license to dairy in British Columbia

5.9 Personnel
- 5.9.1 Are all personnel records and functions at FD level? If not, transfer to FD?

6. TRANSITION AND POST-CLOSING

6.1 Pre-Closing Consents, etc.

6.2 "Service Agreement" Matters
- 6.2.1 Negotiate any open items. By 9-8 Refer to 3.2.4 list of FM retained assets related to FD FD (computer, offices, personnel)
- 6.2.2 Space in FM building

6.3 Data Processing

6.4 Financial
- 6.4.1 Will agreement with Heller cover all post-closing financing? If not, plan rest.
- 6.4.2 Set up banking and draft accounts, lock boxes, new books, etc.

6.5 Post-Closing
- 6.5.1 Review of purchase order, invoice, etc. forms
- 6.5.2 Any Commerce Department forms?
- 6.5.3 Bound volumes

6.6 Miscellaneous
- 6.6.1 Security (anti-theft) precautions during transition?
- 6.6.2 Adopt table of organization, appoint officers

Appendix K

The Directory of Financing Sources for Buyouts and Acquisitions

The fastest route to your financing sources

Will you ever find yourself in *any* of the following situations?

- A manager seeking to structure and finance a management buyout.
- A financial executive with the responsibility of raising capital for your company.
- An investment banker whose deals often hinge on available financing.
- A lawyer, CPA, or consultant who advises clients on acquisition financing.

If the answer is "yes," you need the *Directory of Financing Sources for Buyouts & Acquisitions*. This one-of-a-kind reference source will:

- Help you close your deal by putting you in direct contact with the *right* financing sources.
- Make it easier to obtain the capital you need to finance your company's growth.
- Save you time and effort by screening out those sources that don't make sense for your deals.

Detailed profiles of relevant information

The Directory of Financing Sources provides detailed profiles on over 400 firms which are classified into one of the following groups:

- **Senior Lenders** — The most active banks and asset-based lenders involved in LBO's today.
- **Mezzanine Lenders and Equity Investors** — Venture capital funds, insurance companies, LBO pools and private investment groups.

This organization makes it easy for you to quickly identify the lender or investor that is most appropriate for your needs. It will save you time and lead you directly to the best sources.

The Directory of Financing Sources provides information on buyout and acquisition financing that is available nowhere else. Here's just a small sample of what you'll get:

- Level of lending/investment activity.
- Investment size criteria.
- Industry preferences and exclusions.
- Collateral advance rates.
- Debt coverage requirements.
- Buyer equity requirements.
- Role in the dealmaking process.
- Role after closing.
- Information required to evaluate proposal.
- Turnaround time.
- Lender/investor fees.

Newly updated and expanded

The *new 5th edition* has just been updated and expanded for 1989. It contains more than 400 profiles of the most active lenders and investors in buyouts and acquisitions. At least 30% are new listings—firms whose profiles were not published in prior editions.

New insights into the LBO financing process

The new *Directory of Financing Sources* doesn't stop at telling you **where** to go to get the financing you need. It also tells you **how** to do it with several in-depth articles on the LBO financing process. For example:

- How to write an LBO business plan.
- Characteristics of a successful LBO management team.
- How to structure an LBO
- High yield bonds and the LBO market.
- Exit strategies for leveraged acquisitions.

BPI-565 400+ pages, hardbound $125.00

To order call 1-619-549-7200

Appendix L

The Directory of Intermediaries

for mergers, buyouts and acquisitions

Finding a company to buy—or selling one you already own—can be a difficult and time-consuming process. It often takes months, even years, to identify viable acquisition candidates without outside help. And if you're a seller, finding a truly qualified buyer can be extremely frustrating.

What the experienced dealmakers do

Smart buyers and sellers avoid this fruitless expenditure of time and effort. They know that the bringing together of committed sellers and qualified buyers is best handled by a select group of merger and acquisition intermediaries. Since these skilled professionals interface with buyers and sellers on a regular basis, they can help you locate "the other half of the deal" in the shortest possible time.

The selection process simplified

Once you've decided to use an intermediary, how do you select the one that can assist you the most? *The Directory of Intermediaries* is compiled specifically for this purpose. it takes the "legwork" out of the intermediary selection process. It has carefully screened the most effective intermediary firms based upon their prior experience in the merger, acquisition and buyout field.

In-depth intermediary profiles

Detailed information — the kind you can use to further narrow down the field — is provided on over 400 firms. These firms act either as M&A intermediaries (between buyer and seller), financial intermediaries (between borrower and lender) or both. Each profile includes:

- The experience of the firm's principals in the acquisition field.
- Number of professionals on staff.
- Major focus of services.
- Who (most often) pays his fee.
- Geographic limitations, if any.
- Preferred transaction price range.
- Deals closed during the past year.
- Broker cooperation policy.
- Involvement in turnaround situations.
- Other services provided (such as: strategic planning, consulting and fairness opinions).

Newly revised and expanded

The *Directory of Intermediaries* has just been updated and expanded for 1989. Over 400 M&A firms—many of them brand-new profiles of leading professionals—are included in the latest issue. In addition, all previous profiles have been completely updated for changes in personnel, phone numbers and new services.

Now it's more than a directory!

But the *new 5th edition* is now more than a directory of key contacts. For the first time, it contains a wealth of practical articles on how to succeed in the M&A field. Here's just a sample of the more than *ten articles* that are included in the latest edition:

- Recent trends in mergers, buyouts and acquisitions.
- How to choose an intermediary
- The 10 most common mistakes in buying or selling a business.
- How to qualify and analyze a target company.
- The legal process of executing a leveraged acquisition.

BPI-567 400+ pages, hardbound $125.00

To order call 1-619-549-7200

Appendix M

The Acquisition Mart

The newsletter of corporate acquisition opportunities

The most important — and difficult — step in buying a company

The most important step in a successful acquisition is the first one: finding the **right** company to buy. Unless you have access to acquisition candidates which fit your criteria, nothing else happens.

But finding the **right** company to buy is no easy task. Even the most experienced buyers claim their biggest challenge is to generate "deal flow" — a steady flow of potential acquisition prospects. It can be a very time-consuming and frustrating process unless you have help. Now you can get the help you need with the *Acquisition Mart*, the marketplace of corporate acquisition opportunities.

End the frustration

With the *Mart*, you can end the frustration — and save yourself hours of wasted time! Published **monthly**, it puts you in direct contact with the key people you need to know to have access to the right opportunities. Each issue contains:

- Fresh, new profiles on over 40 companies **ripe for acquisition**. Each profile contains descriptive and financial information which enables you to pinpoint the companies that fit your acquisition criteria.
- Detailed descriptions of **active acquirers**, which include their specific acquisition criteria as well as prior track record. One (or more) could be just the buyer you're looking for.

No other publication puts you in touch with as many key M&A players on such a timely basis.

Something for everyone!

Whether you are a buyer, seller or an intermediary who represents them, the *Acquisition Mart* has something for you:

- **Buyers** — a steady flow of new corporate acquisition opportunities of "middle market" companies.
- **Sellers** — leads on corporate and private acquirers who are most active in today's market.
- **Intermediaries** — access to new sellers and buyers who just might be the "other half" of the deal you are working on.
- **Lawyers and CPA's** — key contacts with buyers and sellers for your clients who are actively playing the acquisition game.
- **Appraisers** — the information contained in the *Mart* keeps you on top of the marketplace and what sellers are asking for companies.

Best tool available

The *Mart* is the most effective and efficient tool available to expand your dealmaking network — quickly!

- **Easy to use**. Most sources of deals (and all buyer contacts) are listed in the Mart so you can contact them directly regarding your particular interest.
- **Fresh, new deals**. Because it is **published monthly**, the inventory of acquisition candidates contains the latest new prospects.

> *"We have found Acquisition Mart to be an excellent source of deals. It's updated frequently, provides ready access to listing intermediaries, and has put us in touch with serious sellers throughout the country."*
>
> Steven Graham
> RAF Industries
> Elkins Park, PA

BPI-604 12-month subscription (12 issues) $195.00

To order your subscription call 1-619-549-7200

Appendix N

DealBase™

The new electronic acquisition search tool

DealBase™ is the revolutionary new tool that will make your search for the *right* acquisition candidates faster and easier. It will:

- Help you locate acquisition candidates that *meet your specific criteria.*
- *Save you time* by identifying only those companies that fit your needs.

This powerful software system works with any IBM compatible PC, XT or AT. It is extremely simple and easy to use. In fact, a secretary with no prior computer experience can easily perform routine searches based upon your specified criteria.

What is included with DealBase?

- A growing database of over 600 corporate acquisition opportunities on a 5 1/4" floppy disk. You will receive an updated disk with new deals every 30 days.
- A proprietary software system that enables you to selectively search the database for candidates that meet your specific criteria.
- An operating manual that gives you clear instructions on using the system.

Selective search capability

What makes *DealBase*™ a truly valuable tool is its unique, easy-to-use software which enables you to selectively search the database to identify **only** those companies that make sense for you to acquire. These search parameters include:

- Company size (sales and/or purchase price).
- Geographic location.
- Type of business.
- Industry or type of products.
- Management preference (stay, leave, consult).
- LBO status (is company an LBO candidate?)
- Payment method (cash, stock, notes).

Example of searches

With *DealBase*™, you can use an unlimited combination of these parameters to identify prospective acquisitions. For example, you can search for:

- "All companies engaged in plastics manufacturing located in the northeastern U.S. with sales in excess of $10 million and profits of at least $1 million where management is willing to stay."
- "All LBO candidates in the western U.S. with a purchase price of at least $10 million."

Descriptions of the companies meeting your criteria and contacts for additional information "pop up" right on the screen in front of you. Or you can easily print them out for future reference.

NOW UPDATED WITH NEW DEALS EVERY MONTH

What DealBase™ can do for you

If you are a BUYER . . .

- Dramatically ***increase your deal flow*** from reputable sources.
- ***Save you time*** by conducting searches that would ordinarily take hours — in less than a minute. And with very little effort!
- Help you identify acquisition targets that ***meet your specific criteria.***
- ***Expand the scope of your dealmaking network***—intermediaries who understand your needs and requirements.

If you are a M&A INTERMEDIARY . . .

- Help you ***close more deals*** by putting you in touch with the most highly-qualified and active buyers in the marketplace.
- Quickly identify those deals where listing M&A intermediaries are willing to cooperate.
- Allow you to list the companies you have for sale in the database FREE OF CHARGE.
- You will receive a regular "update report" which allows you to delete companies no longer for sale, or modify price, terms, etc.

BPI-710	One year subscription (12 monthly diskettes)	$395.00

To order your subscription call 1-619-549-7200

Appendix O

LBO PLAN II

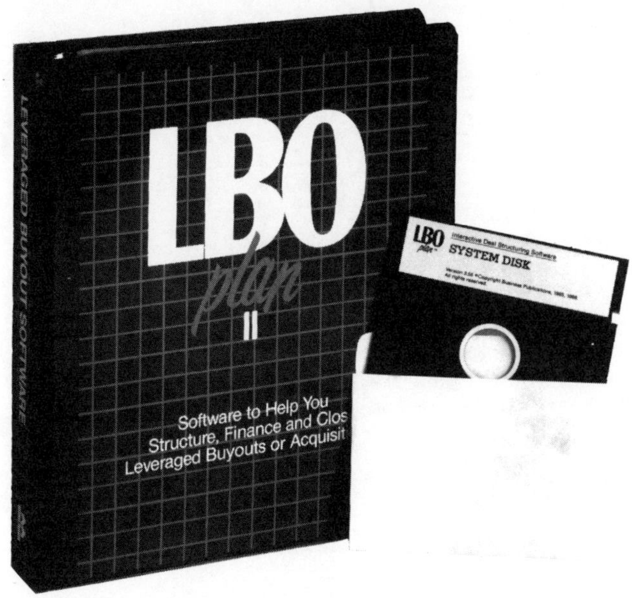

The Easy-to-Use Deal Structuring Software Tool

Creating the best financial structure for leveraged buyouts used to be a difficult, time-consuming task. Now, with *LBO Plan II* and your personal computer, you can quickly perform critical financial analyses with ease.

LBO Plan II is a menu- driven Lotus 1-2-3** template that will:

- **Save you time** by quickly performing thousands of "what-if" analyses that would otherwise take hours, even days, to complete!
- **Help you negotiate** with sellers, lenders, investors or managers by testing the impact of alternative financial structures.
- **Reveal potential problems** before they become real problems!

More Than A Tool For LBO's

Although *LBO Plan II* was designed to evaluate leveraged buyouts, you can put its powerful features to work in any business. It is an excellent corporate financial planning tool for companies that need capital to:

- Finance future growth.
- Cash out other stockholders.
- Finance acquisitions.

LBO Plan II performs the **mundane** functions and countless repetitive computations. It allows you to focus your time and energy on the **creative** aspects of deal structuring and financing.

How It Works

This easy-to-use, menu-driven system walks you step-by-step through the entire process of financing an acquisition or an existing business, including:

- **Data Input** of historical financials that are the basis of projecting future results.
- **Key assumptions** on future operations.
- **Purchase price and terms.**
- **Structure the financing** using any combination of 14 layers of senior debt, subordinated debt and preferred stock.

Within 30 seconds of inputting your data and assumptions, *LBO Plan II* projects financial results for the next 10 years or 12 months. These include:

- **Proforma Balance Sheet** which clearly displays how quickly any new debt is paid off.
- **Proforma Income Statement** that reflects the impact of operating and financing assumptions.
- **Proforma Cash Flow** that reveals if the proposed deal is feasible.

"What If" Analysis

The real value of *LBO Plan II* comes into play in "testing" alternative financial structures or changes in operating assumptions. Within seconds, you can have answers to such key questions as:

- **"What if"** interest rates increase in 3 years and a recession occurs in the following year?
- **"What if"** certain assets are sold next year?
- **"What if"** the deal is structured with less debt and more equity?

Enhanced With Powerful New Features

LBO Plan II has been recently enhanced and updated to make it the most powerful and easy- to-use tool of its kind.

- Fixed asset depreciation schedules that reflect changes in the 1986 Tax Reform Act.
- The financial impact of fixed asset sales.
- The ability to structure buyouts as either "stock purchases" or "asset purchases".
- A new easy-to-follow operating manual with a simulated buyout.

System Requirements

All you need to put *LBO Plan II* to work is an IBM* PC, XT, AT, PS/2 or compatible computer with at least 640K RAM and Lotus 1-2-3** (Version 1A or 2.01)

**IBM PC is a trademark of International Business Machines*
***Lotus 1-2-3 is a trademark of Lotus Development Corp.*

PBI-721 LBO Plan II $495.00

To order call 1-619-549-7200